INTERNATIONAL BIBLE LESSON COMMENTARY

The New Standard In
Biblical Exposition Based
On The International
Sunday School
Lessons (ISSL)

Building the New Generation of Believers

An Imprint of Cook Communications Ministries • Colorado Springs, CO

NexGen® is an imprint of
Cook Communications Ministries, Colorado Springs, CO 80918
Cook Communications, Paris, Ontario
Kingsway Communications, Eastbourne, England

THE NIV INTERNATIONAL BIBLE LESSON COMMENTARY

© 2005 Cook Communications Ministries

First printing, 2005
Printed in U.S.A.
1 2 3 4 5 6 7 8 9 10 Printing/Year 10 09 08 07 06

Editor: Daniel Lioy, Ph.D
Product Development Manager: Karen Pickering
Cover Design: Ray Moore/Two Moore Design
Cover Photo: ©2000-2005 PhotoSpin, Inc.

ISBN: 078144182X

You Will Be My Witnesses

God's Commitment—Our Response

Living in and as God's Creation

Called to Be a Christian Community

Use The NIV International Bible Lesson Commentary with Materials from These Publishers

Sunday school materials from the following denominations and publishers follow International Sunday School Lesson outlines (sometimes known as Uniform Series). Because *The NIV International Bible Lesson Commentary* (formerly *Peloubet's*) follows the same outlines, you can use *The NIV International Bible Lesson Commentary* as an excellent teacher resource to supplement the materials from these publishing houses.

NONDENOMINATIONAL:

Standard Publishing: *Adult*

Urban Ministries

Echoes Teacher's Commentary (Cook Communications Ministries) *: Adult*

DENOMINATIONAL:

Advent Christian General Conference: *Adult*

American Baptist *(Judson Press): Adult*

United Holy Church of America: *Adult*

Church of God in Christ *(Church of God in Christ Publishing House): Adult*

Church of Christ Holiness: *Adult*

Church of God *(Warner Press): Adult*

Church of God by Faith: *Adult*

National Baptist Convention of America *(Boyd): All ages*

National Primitive Baptist Convention: *Adult*

Progressive National Baptist Convention: *Adult*

Presbyterian Church *(U.S.A.) (Bible Discovery Series—Presbyterian Publishing House or P.R.E.M.): Adult*

Union Gospel Press: *All ages*

United Holy Church of America: *Adult*

United Methodist *(Cokesbury): All ages*

You Will Be My Witnesses

The Coming of the Spirit

DEVOTIONAL READING

Psalm 16

DAILY BIBLE READINGS

Monday August 29
*Joel 2:23-29 God's Spirit
Will Be Poured Out*

Tuesday August 30
*Psalm 16:5-11 God Is
Always with Us*

Wednesday August 31
*Acts 2:1-13 The Holy Spirit
Comes*

Thursday September 1
*Acts 2:14-21 Peter Speaks to
the Crowd*

Friday September 2
*Acts 2:22-28 Peter Speaks
about the Crucified Jesus*

Saturday September 3
*Acts 2:29-36 Peter Speaks
about the Risen Christ*

Sunday September 4
*Acts 2:37-42 Three
Thousand Are Baptized*

Scripture

Background Scripture: *Acts 2:1-42*
Scripture Lesson: *Acts 2:1-8, 38-42*
Key Verse: *"Repent and be baptized, every one of you, in the
name of Jesus Christ for the forgiveness of your sins. And you
will receive the gift of the Holy Spirit."* Acts 2:38.
Scripture Lesson for Children: *Acts 2:1-8, 38-39, 41-42*
Key Verses for Children: *When the day of Pentecost came,
they were all together in one place. . . . All of them were filled
with the Holy Spirit.* Acts 2:1, 4a.

Lesson Aim

To encourage boldness in witnessing based on faith in
God's provision of the Holy Spirit.

Lesson Setting

Time: *A.D. 30*
Place: *Jerusalem*

Lesson Outline

The Coming of the Spirit
  I. The Arrival of the Spirit: Acts 2:1-4
    A. *The Meeting of Jesus' Followers: vs. 1*
    B. *The Appearance of the Tongues of Fire: vss. 2-4*
  II. The Manifestation of the Spirit: Acts 2:5-8
    A. *The Presence of Devout Jews: vs. 5*
    B. *The Crowd's Confusion: vss. 6-8*
  III. The Exhortation of Peter: Acts 2:38-42
    A. *The Summons to Repent: vss. 38-39*
    B. *The Favorable Response: vss. 40-41*
    C. *The Fellowship of the Believers: vs. 42*

Introduction for Adults

Topic: *Encountering the Spirit*

People are usually skeptical if they cannot see evidence of a claim. The motto of the state of Missouri (the "Show Me State") reflects the attitude of most adults. If we claim that God's Spirit is dwelling in us, then we need to give evidence of His presence. One way to show we have had a genuine and lasting encounter with the Spirit is by shunning sin and trusting in the Savior.

This was the central thrust of Peter's message on the day of Pentecost. Adults need to know that Peter's promise of forgiveness and the Holy Spirit extended beyond his current audience to future generations and to those living in other lands. Although Peter may not have realized it, his words included the Gentiles as well.

Introduction for Youth

Topic: *Power for My Life*

Some of the most interesting conversion stories I have heard involve people studying to be ministers. The standard assumption is that these people are already saved. Occasionally, this isn't the case.

There are many reasons why individuals want to train for church leadership. Even teens are known to wrestle with this issue. Often, though, the desire—whether it is to help others, exercise abilities in teaching and counseling, enjoy a position of respect and influence, and so on—is void of God's presence and power.

An individual claiming to be a Christian, regardless of his or her age, is spiritually powerless when not connected with the Savior and operating in the Spirit. What a dynamic change occurs when a young person stops trying to live for God in his or her own strength and starts serving Him with the limitless resources of the Spirit!

Concepts for Children

Topic: *God's People Get the Power*

1. The Holy Spirit was sent in fulfillment of a promise made by Jesus.
2. God gave the Holy Spirit as a special gift to believers.
3. The coming of the Holy Spirit on a day called Pentecost was a unique experience.
4. The Holy Spirit's presence was shown by tongues, as a fire, on each believer.
5. The Holy Spirit gives us the strength to share the Good News with other people.

Lesson Commentary

I. THE ARRIVAL OF THE SPIRIT: ACTS 2:1-4

A. The Meeting of Jesus' Followers: vs. 1

When the day of Pentecost came, they were all together in one place.

The Book of Acts picks up where the Gospels leave off by telling about the early days of the Christian church. Moreover, Acts bridges the gap between the Gospel accounts and the letters of instruction that compose most of the rest of the New Testament.

In Acts we learn that, after Jesus returned to heaven, the church experienced significant growth. We also discover that Jesus did not leave His followers unprepared for the task at hand. He gave them the gift of the Holy Spirit, who filled them with supernatural power to do God's work. Some of the events narrated in Acts will motivate and encourage us. Others may disturb or even alarm us. Either way, the book is guaranteed not to bore us.

Luke began his historical account of the Christian church with a description of Jesus' ascension into heaven. Christ's last words to His disciples were His promise to send the Holy Spirit, who would enable them to be Jesus' witnesses (1:1-11).

The disciples were obedient to the Lord's command. They returned to Jerusalem to wait until the Holy Spirit came as promised. About 120 followers of Christ spent 10 days together, praying and encouraging each other. During that time, Matthias was selected to replace Judas Iscariot, who had committed suicide after betraying Jesus (vss. 12-26).

The events of this week's lesson took place on the "day of Pentecost" (2:1). The name *Pentecost* comes from a Greek word meaning "fiftieth," because the festival fell on the fiftieth day after the Passover Sabbath. Along with the festivals of unleavened bread and tabernacles, Pentecost was one of the three great Jewish religious holy days. The population of Jerusalem swelled during each of these festivals as pilgrims streamed into the city from all over.

In response to Jesus' command (see Luke 24:49; Acts 1:4), His disciples had gathered together "in one place" (Acts 2:1). Two truths are evident from this statement. First, the disciples were assembled in a single location. Second, they were in agreement in their thinking and purpose.

B. The Appearance of the Tongues of Fire: vss. 2-4

Suddenly a sound like the blowing of a violent wind came from heaven and filled the whole house where they were sitting. They saw what seemed to be tongues of fire that separated and came to rest on each of them. All of them were filled with the Holy Spirit and began to speak in other tongues as the Spirit enabled them.

All at once and unexpectedly the disciples heard a sound from heaven that was similar to that of a turbulent "wind" (Acts 2:2). The noise filled the entire house where they were meeting. Some think Christ's followers were at that moment in one of the courts of the Jerusalem temple (Luke 24:52-53), while others maintain the disciples were in the upper room of a house (Acts 1:13).

In the context of this incident, the wind was a physical indication of the presence of the Spirit (2:2). In Scripture wind and breath are common symbols of God's Spirit (Ezek. 37:9, 14; John 3:8).

The sight of "tongues of fire" (Acts 2:3) was even more unusual than the sound of the wind. These tongue-shaped flames appeared to stand over each disciple's head. This incident was significant, for it indicated that God's presence was among Jesus' followers.

The disciples could sense the Spirit's coming audibly (through wind) and visibly (through fire). Moreover, they were filled with the Holy Spirit (vs. 4). As evidence of His presence, the Spirit enabled them to speak in other tongues. Apparently these were actual languages or dialects being voiced by the disciples to the visitors from many countries in Jerusalem. The Spirit had come to empower Jesus' followers to reach out to the lost with the saving message of the Gospel.

II. THE MANIFESTATION OF THE SPIRIT: ACTS 2:5-8

A. The Presence of Devout Jews: vs. 5

Now there were staying in Jerusalem God-fearing Jews from every nation under heaven.

The disciples, being enthusiastic in their baptism of power, spilled out into the streets of Jerusalem. As was noted earlier, the population of Jerusalem swelled with pilgrims attending the feast of Pentecost (Acts 2:5). This event proved to be a strategic time for God to send the Holy Spirit. Visitors who heard God miraculously praised in their own languages—and perhaps were among that day's 3,000 converts—could take the good news of salvation in Christ back with them to their homelands.

B. The Crowd's Confusion: vss. 6-8

When they heard this sound, a crowd came together in bewilderment, because each one heard them speaking in his own language. Utterly amazed, they asked: "Are not all these men who are speaking Galileans? Then how is it that each of us hears them in his own native language?"

When the foreign Jews heard the sound of tongues-speaking, they were amazed that locals could fluently speak languages from around the Roman Empire. Their curiosity aroused, crowds of people quickly gathered together to discuss what could be behind all the commotion. Some joked, making fun of the disciples for being drunk, but others were unsure (Acts 2:6-13).

People are often bewildered or confused when they encounter God at work in an unusual or phenomenal manner. Human limitations restrict our ability to understand God and His ways. Try as we would like, we cannot put God in a box of our own definitions or experiences.

How easy it is for God to surprise us, and how difficult it is for us to move out of our personal comfort zone and into new territory with God. When we have been content for some time, satisfied with God's work in our lives, it becomes much more challenging to be open to something new that He may desire to do in us.

Peter, being led by the Spirit, explained the meaning of the Christians' speaking in tongues. This phenomenon was evidence that God was fulfilling His promise to pour out His Spirit upon people (vss. 14-21).

As we read through Peter's sermon, we cannot miss the studied contrast between the nation of Israel's estimate and God's estimate of Jesus (vss. 22-35). The Jewish people had despised and crucified the Messiah; but the Father had exalted the Son as Lord and Christ (vs. 36). This placed them in a dreadful position: they were at enmity with God Himself.

III. The Exhortation of Peter: Acts 2:38-42

A. The Summons to Repent: vss. 38-39

Peter replied, "Repent and be baptized, every one of you, in the name of Jesus Christ for the forgiveness of your sins. And you will receive the gift of the Holy Spirit. The promise is for you and your children and for all who are far off—for all whom the Lord our God will call."

The central topic of Peter's sermon was Jesus' resurrection (Acts 2:32-36). In its abbreviated form, the message has just one verse covering the life and ministry of Christ (vs. 22) and another verse covering God's plan accomplished through the cross (vs. 23); but it has 13 verses telling of Jesus' resurrection and its implications (vss. 24-36).

As we study Acts, we will see this theme turning up again and again in the life and message of the early church. It became the loom that held the fabric of the Gospel together. Without the Resurrection, there would have been nothing to say.

Jesus' resurrection must remain central to our faith. We cannot reserve it for a seasonal emphasis at Easter and still have the vibrancy of faith that the apostles had. Christ's resurrection should be the foundation for everything we build as a church.

Upon hearing Peter's words, the crowd became remorseful (vs. 37). The Greek verb translated "cut to the heart" is found only here in the New Testament. It means that the people's consciences had been smitten violently. The sense of guilt was overwhelming.

The listeners, genuinely grieving over their rejection of the Messiah, asked what was necessary for them to get right with God. The audience responded this way to Peter because he had communicated the Gospel with power and courage. More importantly, the apostle's message convicted his hearers of sin and then spoke of God's mercy and love.

Peter told his audience to repent and be baptized in the name of Jesus Christ (vs. 38). "Repent" implies a complete change of mind. The people needed to alter their thinking about Jesus. Instead of rejecting Him, they needed to trust in Him.

Some have noted that the baptismal formula in this verse is shorter than the one appearing in Matthew 28:19. Based on this difference, it is suggested that at least two different versions were used in the early church. Others think the shorter version complemented the fuller one. According to this view, the shorter formula was used to underscore the new relationship between Christ and believers, while the longer formula emphasized their intimate union with all three Persons of the Godhead.

Baptism would publicly announce the audience's new relationship as believers in Jesus. In Bible times, religious rites involving water were commonplace. For example, baptism was a requirement for Gentile proselytes to Judaism. This was their way of openly identifying themselves with the God of Israel, His laws, and His people.

Some think "for the forgiveness of your sins" (Acts 2:38) means that baptism is indispensable to salvation; but the New Testament never makes baptism a condition for divine pardoning. Forgiveness is based on repentance, which includes faith and is closely connected with the rite of baptism. Thus, the latter is the symbol of the inward transformation effected by faith.

By trusting in Jesus the Messiah for salvation, the people would be forgiven of all their transgressions and experience God's mercy. Peter assured his listeners they would also receive the gift of the Holy Spirit. God's promise of the Spirit was not meant just for those listening to Peter. It was also intended for their descendants and people in distant places who would receive Christ (vs. 39).

B. The Favorable Response: vss. 40-41

With many other words he warned them; and he pleaded with them, "Save yourselves from this corrupt generation." Those who accepted his message were baptized, and about three thousand were added to their number that day.

Luke gave an abbreviated version of all that Peter said, for the apostle preached for quite a while. As he did so, he strongly exhorted his listeners to save themselves from their "corrupt generation" (Acts 2:40). Faith in Jesus was the way for this to happen. That day 3,000 people believed in Christ for salvation (vs. 41). They in turn gave evidence to the reality of their faith by being baptized. Here we see that God worked powerfully among Jesus' followers to bring many more converts to the faith.

C. The Fellowship of the Believers: vs. 42

They devoted themselves to the apostles' teaching and to the fellowship, to the breaking of bread and to prayer.

The Holy Spirit gave profound unity and joy to the early believers. The large group listened to the apostles' teaching. They gave themselves to fellowshipping with one another. They remembered Christ's death through the celebration of a common meal. They also spent hours in prayer, praising God and interceding for one another (Acts 2:42).

Praying is talking to God. The act of praying does not change what God has purposed to do; rather, it is the means by which He accomplishes His will. Talking to God is not a method of creating a positive mental attitude in ourselves so that we are able to do what we want to be done. Instead, prayer creates within us a right attitude with respect to the will of God. Prayer is not so much getting God to do our will as it is demonstrating that we are as concerned as He is that His will be done (Matt. 6:10).

Discussion Questions

1. How did the Spirit reveal His presence to the crowds?
2. What did Peter emphasize in his sermon to the crowds?
3. How many were converted on the day of Pentecost?
4. To what things did the Jerusalem saints devote themselves?
5. How does the preaching of Peter support the necessity of proclaiming the Gospel?

Contemporary Application

Luke's description of life in the early church appears to be so idyllic that we might think it's impossible to reproduce today. Would not it be wonderful, we say, if thousands were saved every day? Would not it be great if we shared our possessions, prayed together, and worshiped and witnessed in unity?

Of course, our immediate response would be *yes*, but then we confess that such things just do not happen that way in our churches. We admit defeat without really looking at the reasons for what happened on Pentecost. It is true that some aspects of that time period were unique; nevertheless, the principles evident from the way in which God worked have not changed.

For instance, the Holy Spirit dwells in God's people and enables them to tell others about Christ's death and resurrection. The Lord calls believers to unity, generosity, prayer, and worship. When they confess their need for spiritual power, God answers.

Perhaps our problem is that we do not desire these things as much as we say we do. Perhaps we have higher priorities and goals for ourselves and our churches. It is only when we put Jesus and His people first in our lives that we will see the Lord adding to our congregations those who are being saved.

Life among the Followers

DEVOTIONAL READING

Romans 8:9-17

DAILY BIBLE READINGS

Monday September 5
*Deuteronomy 15:4-8 Share
with Those in Need*

Tuesday September 6
*Isaiah 55:1-7 Come to an
Abundant Life*

Wednesday September 7
*Luke 12:13-21 The Parable
of the Rich Fool*

Thursday September 8
*Luke 12:22-34 Do Not
Worry about Possessions*

Friday September 9
*Acts 2:43-47 The Believers
Grow in Faith Together*

Saturday September 10
*Acts 4:32-37 The Believers
Share Their Possessions*

Sunday September 11
*Acts 5:12-16 Many Sick
People Are Cured*

Scripture

Background Scripture: *Acts 2:43-47; 4:32-35*
Scripture Lesson: *Acts 2:43-47; 4:32-35*
Key Verse: *All the believers were together and had everything
in common.* Acts 2:44.
Scripture Lesson for Children: *Acts 2:44-47; 4:32-35*
Key Verse for Children: *All the believers were together and
had everything in common.* Acts 2:44.

Lesson Aim

To emphasize that the Spirit indwells believers and
helps them to care for others in need.

Lesson Setting

Time: A.D. *30*
Place: *Jerusalem*

Lesson Outline

Life among the Followers

   I. The Believers Meet Together: Acts 2:43-47
      A. *Apostolic Miracles: vs. 43*
      B. *Mutual Generosity: vss. 44-45*
      C. *Joyous Worship: vss. 46-47*
  II. The Believers Share Their Possessions:
      Acts 4:32-35
      A. *United in Mind and Heart: vs. 32*
      B. *Powerful Witness in Word and Deed: vss. 33-35*

Introduction for Adults

Topic: *Sharing Community*

> Urban ministry can be pictured as a pot of steaming stew. If it is made of healthy, compatible ingredients, the supper served will be nutritious and palatable. If not, it can leave a bitter aftertaste—or worse, its foul smell can turn away the hungry.
>
> The large city I live near has a program in which churches cooperate with one another to meet needs in the community. Some run soup kitchens. Others arrange housing for those who cannot find or afford it. Some concentrate their efforts on job training. Others offer child care programs. Some have ministries that target alcoholics, drug users, and prostitutes. The list runs on because the needs run on. With a concerted effort, help is consistently offered in the name of Christ.

Introduction for Youth

Topic: *We Belong Together*

> Saved young people are in a time of their lives when it can be difficult for them to think beyond themselves. And their self-focused concerns can distract them from noticing the concerns and needs of their fellow Christians. Believing teens also might not realize at times that they and other members of the church belong together in one united fellowship.
>
> Imagine adolescents within a congregation working together with other church members to help people in need. But in order for this to happen, saved teens must say *no* to some of their own desires. By saying *yes* to the Spirit of God, young people have a wonderful opportunity to glorify the Lord and be a powerful witness to the lost.

Concepts for Children

Topic: *God's People Share*

1. In the early days of the church, believers met together and shared everything they had.
2. The followers of Jesus also got together for prayer and singing.
3. God continued to bring more and more people to faith in Jesus.
4. God also did powerful things through those who led the believers in the early church.
5. God is pleased when we share what we have with others.

Lesson Commentary

I. THE BELIEVERS MEET TOGETHER: ACTS 2:43-47

A. Apostolic Miracles: vs. 43

Everyone was filled with awe, and many wonders and miraculous signs were done by the apostles.

In last week's lesson, we learned how the earliest Christians manifested their new-found spiritual unity by devoting themselves to several things (Acts 2:42). The first of these was the teaching of the apostles. This represented the core truths about Christ that undergirded the faith of the early church.

The second thing to which the church devoted itself was fellowship. This is a reference to all that the believers have in common as a distinct group. As proclaimers of the risen Christ, they now had their own identity, and they shared love and loyalty. The third element was "breaking of bread." This refers either to the Lord's Supper (see Luke 22:19; 1 Cor. 11:20-26) or to ordinary meals (see Acts 20:11). In either case, it was an occasion for joy and praise.

The fourth element was prayers (2:42). These may have included both spontaneous and more formal public prayers. The Old Testament psalms, as well as familiar Jewish prayers, may have served as bases for their supplication and praise.

As a result of Peter's sermon, scores of people were added to the church (vss. 40-41). Even people who did not respond to Peter's message were filled with amazement at what they heard and saw (vs. 43). The implication is that the early believers enjoyed the favor of many of the unbelieving Jews in Jerusalem. Truly, the presence and power of God were evident among His people.

The Spirit gave further vindication of the Pentecost events by empowering the apostles to perform signs and wonders. They did not regard these miracles as an end in themselves. Rather, the works of power were done in the name of Christ and for His glory. The signs and wonders were intended to point people to Jesus and the truth of God's saving power through faith in Him.

B. Mutual Generosity: vss. 44-45

All the believers were together and had everything in common. Selling their possessions and goods, they gave to anyone as he had need.

All those who had trusted in Christ not only stayed together but also shared their belongings with one another. In fact, God's people were willing to sell their possessions and goods. The mutual generosity of the believers ensured that those who were in need of essentials had those needs fully met.

The fact that the early believers "had everything in common" (Acts 2:44) does not mean that they engaged in communal living. The early believers still resided in their own homes and had their own household possessions. The sharing of possessions demonstrated the unity and oneness of the infant church, and the Lord was glorified in the process.

Jesus' followers recognized that one of their responsibilities was to help people in whatever way possible. By doing this, they gave evidence of the Spirit's presence in their lives and showed that He had transformed them from selfish individuals into members of a caring community.

A key test of our commitment to Christ is our love for other believers (John 13:34). Such compassion is not a dry doctrine we affirm or a vague intellectual abstraction. Rather, God calls us to show love in concrete, relevant ways (1 John 3:16-18). It is not just our words that express our concern for others, but our attitudes and actions as well. Jesus did not say that others would know we are His disciples by what we say, how we dress, or what we know. Rather, it would be through our unselfish, unconditional love (John 13:35).

C. Joyous Worship: vss. 46-47

Every day they continued to meet together in the temple courts. They broke bread in their homes and ate together with glad and sincere hearts, praising God and enjoying the favor of all the people. And the Lord added to their number daily those who were being saved.

The new converts to the faith had no formal meeting place of their own, so they gathered every day in the "temple courts" (Acts 2:46). They also met in their homes to share meals and especially observe the Lord's Supper. Their days were marked by genuine joy and sincerity. They encouraged one another, witnessed to the unsaved about Jesus, and worshiped the Lord.

Verse 47 says that the disciples gave praise to God and enjoyed the favor of all the people. The English word "praise" comes from a Latin verb that means "to value" or "to price." (Note its kinship with "appraise.") The idea is that to give praise to God is to proclaim His merit or worth.

Praise is an act of worship in which we acknowledge the virtues and deeds of someone else. Often one human praising another, while sometimes commendable (1 Cor. 11:2), can become a snare (Prov. 27:21). In contrast, the praise we give to God honors Him and uplifts our soul (1 Chron. 29:13).

Acts 2:47 suggests that no opposition to the new faith had yet arisen. The inhabitants of Jerusalem were initially impressed by what they saw in the Spirit-filled believers. As a result, new converts were made daily. It is significant that the Lord took care of the increase in numbers as His people continued to manifest Christ to others.

II. THE BELIEVERS SHARE THEIR POSSESSIONS: ACTS 4:32-35

A. United in Mind and Heart: vs. 32

All the believers were one in heart and mind. No one claimed that any of his possessions was his own, but they shared everything they had.

After Pentecost, God continued to work miracles among the Christians. For instance, at the gate of the temple in Jerusalem, Peter and John encountered a man who was lame from birth. In Jesus' name, Peter healed the man, who then leaped about and praised God (Acts 3:1-10).

After the people at the temple found out about the healing, they were full of amazement. Peter told a crowd that it was by faith in Jesus, whom they had disowned but whom God had raised from the dead, that the man had been healed (vss. 11-16). The apostle also related that, since the Messiah had come in fulfillment of prophecy, they should repent of their sins (vss. 17-26).

In reaction to the apostle's public preaching, temple officials arrested Peter and John. During the trial, Peter again boldly witnessed about Jesus' resurrection and the salvation He offers. The judges released Peter and John with a warning not to preach in Jesus' name anymore. When Peter and John were reunited with their fellow believers, the group asked God to give them boldness in preaching. All present received a powerful new filling of the Holy Spirit (4:1-31).

Perhaps if it had been any other group, the repeated trials being experienced would have resulted in bickering and division; but this was not the case with the early church. All those who trusted in Christ for salvation were one in heart and soul. This means they were united in their attitudes and focused on the same goals (vs. 32).

In particular, Jesus' followers desired to glorify the Lord by proclaiming the Gospel and encouraging one another in the faith. To that end, nobody claimed that their possessions were their own. Instead, the disciples shared everything they had with each other.

God's people realized that He had showered them with His love when He sent His Son to die on the cross. Perhaps out of gratitude for being saved, the believers in the early church wanted to help their fellow Christians in need. Another possible reason is that the early church wanted to show the unsaved how much believers cared for one another.

This practice of Jesus' early followers was not dictated by the apostles; it was purely voluntarily. No doubt the saints' unusual circumstances in Jerusalem, where they remained together with many not earning a daily income, made this a natural expression of love.

We are not called to seek all the experiences and imitate all the practices of the Jerusalem church; but if we submit ourselves to the control of the Holy Spirit and the teaching of God's Word, we too will experience the joy and blessing of the sovereign God.

B. Powerful Witness in Word and Deed: vss. 33-35

With great power the apostles continued to testify to the resurrection of the Lord Jesus, and much grace was upon them all. There were no needy persons among them. For from time to time those who owned lands or houses sold them, brought the money from the sales and put it at the apostles' feet, and it was distributed to anyone as he had need.

Earlier the disciples had prayed for boldness in witnessing (Acts 4:29), and we see this petition being answered in verse 33. Luke noted that the Spirit gave the apostles great power to continue testifying to Jesus' resurrection from the dead. Because He is the Lord of life, not even the persecution of earthly authorities could halt the witness of the early church.

It is no wonder that the grace of God was powerfully at work among the believers in Jerusalem. This was evident, for example, in the fact that no one went in need of anything (vs. 34). The reason is that those who owned property—whether land or houses—would sell it and bring the money to the apostles. The leaders would then distribute the proceeds to those who needed it (vs. 35).

Joseph was especially known for his generosity. He was a Levite from Cyprus, a large island in the eastern Mediterranean Sea (vs. 36). The apostles called him Barnabas, which means "son of encouragement." He was commended for selling a field he owned and giving the money from the sale to the apostles (vs. 37). He served as a good example of a Christian who freely gave to the needs of others.

Although the Word of God does not say, it is possible that Barnabas was the first to sell land and give it to the apostles. Another possibility is that he gave an unusually large amount. In either case, the believers were under no obligation to donate all of the proceeds, as long as they were honest about their giving (see 5:1-10).

Discussion Questions

1. What sorts of activities were the apostles doing in the early church?
2. What characterized the church life of Jesus' followers?
3. What attitude did God's people have toward their possessions?
4. In what way was God's grace evident among His people?
5. What did the apostles do with the money from the sales that they received?

Contemporary Application

The presence of the Spirit in the lives of the early Christians was demonstrated as they preached the Gospel to the lost and shared their wealth with the needy. When we are saved, the Spirit also abides in us and helps us to live for the Lord Jesus Christ.

This truth is important to remember, for we face a daily struggle with sinful habits and ungodly temptations. When we yield control of our lives to the Spirit, He helps us overcome our selfish impulses. He also enables us to consider the needs of other people above our wants and desires.

In order to meet the needs of others, we must say no to some of our desires. This is often difficult to do in a materialistic, self-centered culture. If we succumb to the temptation to try to be powerful, wealthy, or famous, we will think more of ourselves than we do of others, and we will miss the many opportunities that exist in our lives to minister to others in the Spirit's power.

Each of us as believers has received at least one special ability, which the Spirit has graciously given us so that we can serve one another (see 1 Pet. 4:10). We should never forget that what the Spirit gives us, He intends for us to use. In fact, the Spirit displays His power in us when we minister our God-given gifts to one another.

There are countless ways the Spirit enables us to help others. For example, if someone needs a word of encouragement, the Spirit will give us the wisdom to know how to say it. If people are in financial difficulty, the Spirit will give us the desire to help them in whatever way we can.

As members of God's family, we have a responsibility to meet the needs of others. We may be tempted to think only of ourselves, but we must look beyond our own lives to the circumstances of others. When the Spirit is powerfully at work in our lives, we will be able to do far more for others than we ever imagined possible.

Peter and John Heal a Lame Man

DEVOTIONAL READING

Luke 7:18-23

DAILY BIBLE READINGS

Monday September 12
Luke 7:18-23 Jesus Tells of His Healing Power

Tuesday September 13
Luke 9:1-6 The Twelve Receive Power to Heal

Wednesday September 14
Luke 4:31-37 Jesus Rebukes a Demon

Thursday September 15
Acts 3:1-5 A Beggar Asks for Alms

Friday September 16
Acts 3:6-10 A Man Is Healed

Saturday September 17
Acts 3:11-16 Peter Speaks to the People

Sunday September 18
Acts 3:17-26 Peter Tells the People to Repent

Scripture

Background Scripture: *Acts 3:1-26*

Scripture Lesson: *Acts 3:1-16*

Key Verse: *Then Peter said, "Silver or gold I do not have, but what I have I give you. In the name of Jesus Christ of Nazareth, walk."* Acts 3:6.

Scripture Lesson for Children: *Acts 3:1-10*

Key Verse for Children: *Taking [the lame man] by the right hand, [Peter] helped him up, and instantly the man's feet and ankles became strong.* Acts 3:7.

Lesson Aim

To encourage students to rejoice in the life-changing power of Jesus Christ.

Lesson Setting

Time: *A.D. 30*

Place: *Jerusalem*

Lesson Outline

Peter and John Heal a Lame Man

   I. The Healing of a Lame Man: Acts 3:1-8
      A. *The Trip to the Temple: vs. 1*
      B. *The Request of the Lame Man: vss. 2-3*
      C. *The Offer of Jesus: vss. 4-6*
      D. *The Removal of Lameness: vss. 7-8*
  II. The Explanation Offered by Peter: Acts 3:9-16
      A. *The Formation of a Crowd: vss. 9-11*
      B. *The Apostle's Disclaimer: vs. 12*
      C. *The Emphasis on Jesus' Resurrection: vss. 13-15*
      D. *The Mention of Jesus' Name: vs. 16*

Introduction for Adults

Topic: *The Gift of Healing*

What if Peter and John had not believed that God wanted to heal the crippled man? What if the crippled man had refused to take Peter's hand? What if Peter and John had decided that they were too ordinary to proclaim the truth before a crowd of onlookers? Nothing extraordinary would ever have happened in any of these circumstances.

Faith links God's desires for our participation in His extraordinary plan with our actually being a part of it. God wants to work in our ordinary lives in extraordinary ways; and, of course, we want Him to do His amazing work of healing in and through us. The starting point is for us to trust Him to do so for His glory.

Introduction for Youth

Topic: *Healing the Whole Person*

Peter and John were ordinary people. However, when empowered by the Holy Spirit and full of faith in Jesus' promises, they stepped out of their ordinariness into the amazing lives to which the Lord had called them.

Jesus is also calling saved teens to be willing and ready to serve Him. The Savior wants them to minister to every aspect of other people's needs. And Jesus is able to do through adolescents all that He has planned. Saved teens are qualified to be a part of His plan, not because of who or what they are, but because of who Jesus is and what He has made them by His saving and transforming power.

Concepts for Children

Topic: *God's People Heal*

1. One afternoon during a time of prayer two believers named Peter and John went to a place of worship called the temple.
2. As Peter and John came near the temple, they met a man who could not walk and who was begging for money.
3. God used Peter to heal the man.
4. The healed man not only put his faith in Jesus, but also praised God for this miracle.
5. We can praise and thank God for the wonderful ways He works in our lives.

Lesson Commentary

I. THE HEALING OF A LAME MAN: ACTS 3:1-8

A. The Trip to the Temple: vs. 1

One day Peter and John were going up to the temple at the time of prayer—at three in the afternoon.

Signs and wonders were among the activities performed by the early church (see Acts 2:43). Now in chapter 3, Luke singled out one significant work of power, undoubtedly because of the great impact it had on the witness of Jesus' disciples.

The miracle occurred when Peter and John entered the Jerusalem temple at "the time of prayer—at three in the afternoon" (vs. 1). The early Jewish believers did not at first abandon their religious customs. For a while they still worshiped at the temple. They also still prayed daily at the three traditional times: the time of the morning sacrifice (about 9:00 A.M.), the time of the evening sacrifice (about 3:00 P.M.), and sunset. Undoubtedly, they prayed at other times as well. The ninth hour would have been the 3 P.M. observance.

B. The Request of the Lame Man: vss. 2-3

Now a man crippled from birth was being carried to the temple gate called Beautiful, where he was put every day to beg from those going into the temple courts. When he saw Peter and John about to enter, he asked them for money.

As Peter and John approached the temple, they saw a beggar sitting by the temple's Beautiful Gate (Acts 3:2); and when he saw the two about to enter, he asked them for some money (vs. 3). This entrance to the sanctuary was renowned for its splendor. Although some uncertainty exists regarding the exact identification of the gate, it is most likely what was called the Nicanor Gate, which led from the court of the Gentiles into the women's court.

This gate would be a particularly good place for alms gathering because of the heavy traffic through it. At 50 feet in height, this gate was larger than all the other temple entrances. Along with the gold and silver that covered the other gates, the Nicanor Gate was also overlaid in Corinthian brass and was referred to as the Corinthian Gate by Josephus, the first-century A.D. Jewish historian.

The contrast between the richly ornamented, brass-covered gate and the beggar in rags must have been a striking one. Every day he asked people entering the temple for donations. Now past the age of 40 (see 4:22), he had been crippled from birth and was dependent on others.

In societies with no governmental welfare programs or social security, the unemployed and disabled sometimes must resort to begging. The frequent mention of beggars in the New Testament suggests that they were a common sight on city streets in Palestine. Many Jews gave money to beggars because they thought it would gain them merit with God. The beggar mentioned in 3:2 positioned himself near the temple, probably hoping to profit from the religious mood of passersby.

It is hard to imagine how the lame man could have missed Jesus during the

Lord's frequent visits to the temple. Since the beggar sat at one of the more heavily used entrances, he must have seen Jesus pass by on more than one occasion. Perhaps with the crowds and confusion that often accompanied Jesus, the man had not been able to get to Jesus for healing.

We cannot dismiss another possible explanation: that God may have reserved this miracle of healing until after Jesus had ascended. Done later, the miracle certified the ministry of the disciples and provided a major help for the young church. In a sense, if this explanation is correct, the man had to wait for a miracle because there was more at stake than just his healing.

C. The Offer of Jesus: vss. 4-6

Peter looked straight at him, as did John. Then Peter said, "Look at us!" So the man gave them his attention, expecting to get something from them. Then Peter said, "Silver or gold I do not have, but what I have I give you. In the name of Jesus Christ of Nazareth, walk."

By 3:00 P.M., when Peter and John arrived at the temple, the beggar may already have been at his post by the gate for most of the day. Perhaps upon seeing the two men, the cripple gave out his usual call for alms. The man took no special notice of Peter and John. Most people passed by without giving anything; the beggar probably thought these two men would do the same.

The situation would be different that day, however. Both Peter and John directed their gaze straight at the cripple; and as the apostles looked intently at the beggar, Peter invited him to give his full attention in return. The man complied, eagerly expecting to receive some sort of handout from the two (Acts 3:5).

The beggar got something from the apostles, but it was not what he expected. He was anticipating them to toss a coin at him; but instead, Peter announced that he did not have any money, such as precious silver or gold coins. Rather, the apostle offered the man the good news of salvation. Peter accordingly declared, "In the name of Jesus Christ of Nazareth, walk" (vs. 6).

Peter spoke with authority in Jesus' name, for it unleashed the miraculous power for healing. The disciples were not interested in gaining attention or a following for themselves. They had only one priority—to accomplish the work Jesus had given them to do. They wanted to proclaim the good news about Jesus everywhere they could to everyone they could.

Here we see that the apostles looked beyond the beggar's surface need for money to his deeper need for healing. There will always be opportunities for us to help others if we can look beneath the surface. When we limit ourselves only to the obvious, we will not always have the necessary resources to help; but when we peel back the surface, we can find deep personal and spiritual needs that we can address in God's wisdom.

D. The Removal of Lameness: vss. 7-8

Taking him by the right hand, he helped him up, and instantly the man's feet and ankles became strong. He jumped to his feet and began to walk. Then he went with them into the temple courts, walking and jumping, and praising God.

Having commanded the healing, Peter reached out and pulled the beggar up onto his feet. Instantly, strength surged through the man's feet and ankles, and he stood. Imagine the look of amazement on his face. He was actually standing!

Perhaps the beggar had heard about Jesus before, and had been thinking about Him. At any rate, when Peter ordered him in Jesus' name to walk, he dared to believe. With faith of one degree or another, he responded to Peter's words (Acts 3:7). This fact suggests that the greatest healing the man experienced on that day was not the restoration of his legs but the healing of his sin-sick soul. The church got a new member that day.

As realization of his healing sank in, the beggar's joy grew. First, he tried walking. Then, entering the inner courts of the temple with Peter and John, he began to jump and shout praises to God (vs. 8). Lest we think this was an overreaction, we should remember that this was the first time the former cripple had ever walked. He did not have to learn to crawl first and then take baby steps. God took care of all the learning at once.

II. THE EXPLANATION OFFERED BY PETER: ACTS 3:9-16

A. The Formation of a Crowd: vss. 9-11

When all the people saw him walking and praising God, they recognized him as the same man who used to sit begging at the temple gate called Beautiful, and they were filled with wonder and amazement at what had happened to him. While the beggar held on to Peter and John, all the people were astonished and came running to them in the place called Solomon's Colonnade.

God worked the miracle performed by Peter amid a crowd that could see the transformation and hear the praise; but this was not a throng of strangers. They recognized the man as the same person who used to sit begging at the Beautiful Gate. As the crowd reflected on the unfolding chain of events, they were astounded at what had happened to the former cripple (Acts 3:9-10).

The response of the throng was exactly what God wanted. The miracle gave His spokesperson, Peter, an ideal opportunity to address the crowd and focus their attention on the risen Christ.

After giving thanks to God with Peter and John in the inner temple courts, the beggar tightly held on to them, not wanting to let them go. Together, the three moved out to the larger Court of Gentiles, and took up a position in a covered porch with one side open to the court. There at Solomon's Colonnade a crowd quickly gathered to see if the fast-spreading rumor of a miracle was true (vs. 11).

B. The Apostle's Disclaimer: vs. 12

When Peter saw this, he said to them: "Men of Israel, why does this surprise you? Why do you stare at us as if by our own power or godliness we had made this man walk?"

An opportunity to preach to a crowd was just what Peter wanted. He began by answering the questions on everyone's lips with queries of his own. He asked why the throng was surprised and why they stared at himself and John as if they, by their own power or holiness, had enabled the cripple to walk (Acts 3:12).

The disciples knew their own human weakness; they knew that they could do nothing of themselves. On the other hand, they also knew something of God's limitless power available through Christ. Their hope was to be vessels through whom God's power could flow, bringing people to faith in Jesus.

C. The Emphasis on Jesus' Resurrection: vss. 13-15

"The God of Abraham, Isaac and Jacob, the God of our fathers, has glorified his servant Jesus. You handed him over to be killed, and you disowned him before Pilate, though he had decided to let him go. You disowned the Holy and Righteous One and asked that a murderer be released to you. You killed the author of life, but God raised him from the dead. We are witnesses of this."

Peter made it clear that he was not representing some new deity. The miracle had come from the God of Abraham, Isaac, and Jacob—the God all Jews professed to serve; but this God had healed the man through faith in Jesus. This meant Jesus is divine. Peter's hearers had borne some of the responsibility for crucifying Jesus, but God proved Jesus is the Messiah by raising Him from the dead.

Like waves pounding the shore, Peter's accusations beat on the hearts of his listeners. In Acts 3:13-15, the apostle noted that his fellow Jews had handed Jesus over to the Romans to be crucified. They disowned the Holy and Righteous One (even though the governor had decided to release Him) and demanded that a murderer instead be let go. Although the nation of Israel was guilty of executing the Author of life, God raised Him from the dead. Both Peter and John bore witness to this truth.

Some people wonder why the Father would allow His Son to die on the cross. The answer is that Jesus tasted death so that the sinful human race might live. He was the Author of physical life; and by giving His life, He showed Himself to be the Author of spiritual life.

As we saw in the first lesson, the Resurrection was of highest importance for the early church. To glorify someone meant to honor, raise up, and exalt that person. Thus to glorify Jesus, the Father first had to raise Him up from the grave. The Father subsequently honored His Son through the healing of the crippled beggar.

D. The Mention of Jesus' Name: vs. 16

"By faith in the name of Jesus, this man whom you see and know was made strong. It is Jesus' name and the faith that comes through him that has given this complete healing to him, as you can all see."

We can imagine the dismay that swept through the crowd as Peter spoke. The listeners were being told that they had killed God's Servant. Some no doubt scoffed at this; but others with softer hearts must have begun to wonder, if all this was true, how they could make things right with God. Peter would have something to say about that, too. The apostle declared that it was by faith in the name of Jesus the well-known crippled beggar had been healed (Acts 3:16).

In Jewish thought a name did not just identify a person. More than that, a name expressed the person's nature and character. For example, a foreign ambassador, by speaking in the name of the ruler who had sent him, brought that ruler's authority to bear on a situation. By invoking the name of Jesus, Peter released Jesus' power to heal the crippled beggar (vs. 6); and by faith in that name, the beggar received the power (vs. 16). From this we see that the man's response of faith made that power effective in his life.

Discussion Questions

1. When and why did Peter and John go to the temple?
2. Why did the crippled man beg the apostles for money?
3. How did Peter and John focus the attention of the beggar and the crowds on Jesus?
4. What was Peter's point in discussing the resurrection of Jesus?
5. What does it mean to have faith in Jesus' name?

Contemporary Application

One of the clearest evidences of the Spirit's work was the change in the disciples after the resurrection of Jesus. Consider Peter. Because of his denial of Jesus before His crucifixion, we would hardly expect Peter to witness boldly in Jerusalem for the Savior; yet when challenged by the authorities, Peter unflinchingly stood tall for Christ.

In addition to being courageous, the apostles resisted the temptation to take credit for the miraculous healing of the crippled man. Instead, Peter and John focused the people's attention on Christ and His power through the Spirit to bring about healing and wholeness to people.

The Spirit's power still changes lives. At times the power is evident in health situations where medical science has no explanation for the apparent healing. The Spirit's power also brings changes in behavior, turning around those who once lived selfishly, so that their lives now focus on others.

Although many worldly forces are intent on removing Christ from people's lives, they are feeble when they encounter the Savior's power. Thus we can rejoice, not only because His power is far greater than any earthly power, but also because His power has changed us.

The Time for Boldness

DEVOTIONAL READING

Ephesians 6:10-20

DAILY BIBLE READINGS

Monday September 19
*Ephesians 6:10-20 Be
Strong in the Lord*

Tuesday September 20
*1 Thessalonians 2:1-8 Paul
Preaches the Gospel
Courageously*

Wednesday September 21
*Acts 4:1-7 Peter and John
Are Arrested*

Thursday September 22
*Acts 4:8-12 Peter Speaks
about Jesus Christ*

Friday September 23
*Acts 4:13-17 Peter and John
Are Warned*

Saturday September 24
*Acts 4:18-22 Peter and John
Refuse to Stop*

Sunday September 25
*Acts 4:23-31 The Believers
Pray for Boldness*

Scripture

Background Scripture: *Acts 4:1-31*
Scripture Lesson: *Acts 4:1-4, 23-31*
Key Verse: *"Lord, . . . enable your servants to speak your
word with great boldness."* Acts 4:29.
Scripture Lesson for Children: *Acts 4:1-5, 18-21, 23, 31*
Key Verse for Children: *They were all filled with the Holy
Spirit and spoke the word of God boldly.* Acts 4:31.

Lesson Aim

To explore what obedience to God means when one's
faith in Christ is challenged.

Lesson Setting

Time: A.D. 30
Place: Jerusalem

Lesson Outline

The Time for Boldness

  I. The Apostles before the Sanhedrin: Acts 4:1-4
    A. The Agitation of the Religious Leaders: vss. 1-2
    B. The Arrest of Peter and John: vss. 3-4
 II. The Prayer Request of the Believers: Acts 4:23-31
    A. The Report Made by Peter and John: vs. 23
    *B. The Fulfillment of Old Testament Prophecy
       concerning the Messiah: vss. 24-26*
    *C. The Sovereign Plan of the Father concerning His
       Son: vss. 27-28*
    D. The Petition for Boldness and Power: vss. 29-30
    E. The Divine Response: vs. 31

Introduction for Adults

Topic: *Power to Be Bold*

At an International Congress on World Evangelization held in Lausanne, Switzerland, an evangelistic rally took place in a local stadium. Speakers from around the world told how Jesus Christ had changed their lives.

An Indian neurosurgeon of Hindu background told how the Lord had freed him from depression and guilt and given him joy in serving others. A Japanese evangelist, raised a Buddhist, described the brokenness of his boyhood home and the emptiness of his life until as a student in high school he met a missionary who led him to Christ. An African bishop, born into a home where tribal gods were worshiped, told how the forgiveness of Jesus had liberated him from the disease of hatred.

These are just a few examples of how Christians were bold in their witness and how the Lord used the sharing of the truth to powerfully change lives.

Introduction for Youth

Topic: *Courage to Speak Out*

It is not easy for many saved teens to tell their peers about the Lord. Believing adolescents run the risk of being rejected, shunned, or ostracized. These dire prospects can easily squelch the enthusiasm youth have for the things of Christ.

Praying with the teens in your class is one way to address this problem. Another way is to invite them to share their perspective on the challenges they face in witnessing for Christ. Finally, you can remind your students of the presence and power of the Spirit to work through them to impact their peers for the Savior.

Concepts for Children

Topic: *God's People Speak Boldly*

1. A group of religious leaders were upset with what Peter and John had done.
2. The religious leaders put the two believers in jail for telling others about Jesus.
3. The religious leaders told Peter and John to stop speaking about Jesus.
4. The two decided that God wanted them to tell others about Jesus.
5. When we tell others about the Savior, they learn how to put their faith in Him.

Lesson Commentary

I. THE APOSTLES BEFORE THE SANHEDRIN: ACTS 4:1-4

A. The Agitation of the Religious Leaders: vss. 1-2

The priests and the captain of the temple guard and the Sadducees came up to Peter and John while they were speaking to the people. They were greatly disturbed because the apostles were teaching the people and proclaiming in Jesus the resurrection of the dead.

Over the course of Jesus' earthly ministry, the religious leaders grew increasingly opposed to Him. They envied His popularity, resented His challenges to their traditions, and hated His exposure of their hypocrisy. Undoubtedly, the religious elite wondered whether Jesus had political aspirations and worried about how His increasing influence would affect their control over the people. In short, the Pharisees and scribes allowed their petty concerns to blind them to the truth that Jesus was their Messiah.

It should come as no surprise that the religious leaders responded similarly to Jesus' disciples. For example, Peter's teaching about Jesus disturbed the religious establishment. In fact, the commotion caused by the healing and preaching of Peter caught the attention of the temple authorities, who intervened in the middle of the apostle's message (Acts 4:1).

The priests were probably the usual temple priests who served in their appointed rotation. The captain of the temple guard commanded the sanctuary police force. In rank, he was only below the high priest. The captain was responsible for maintaining order in the temple courts and may have been worried about a riot with all the commotion surrounding the healing and preaching of Peter. The temple captain led 24 guard posts stationed throughout the sanctuary complex as well as 21 groups of Levites who were placed primarily at the gates. The one in this position kept a close watch on all temple activity.

The Sadducees were a prominent Jewish religious sect. They were primarily from the wealthy class, and they dominated the high priesthood. The entire high priestly family belonged to this group. While the Sadducees accepted the law, they rejected the oral traditions of the rabbis.

The Sadducees also rejected the supernatural, including the doctrines of the resurrection of the dead (see Luke 20:27), the existence of angels, and the notion of a personal Messiah who would rescue Israel. Moreover, the Sadducees accepted and supported the Roman rule over their land in exchange for Rome's protection of their power and prestige.

This information helps to explain why the religious leaders were agitated with the apostles' teaching the people, especially the proclamation that Jesus had risen from the dead (Acts 4:2). Peter and John were seen as uncredentialed preachers who had no authority to provide religious instruction (see vs. 13). In addition, the two were viewed as a threat the religious leaders' political power.

B. The Arrest of Peter and John: vss. 3-4

They seized Peter and John, and because it was evening, they put them in jail until the next day. But many who heard the message believed, and the number of men grew to about five thousand.

Even though the Sadducees had no case against Peter and John, they had the two seized, removed from the crowd, and imprisoned (Acts 4:3). The mention of it being evening is important for several reasons. The temple gates closed at four in the afternoon, and judgments involving life and death had to begin and conclude on the same day. Since it was already too close to evening, their case could not be adequately heard before nightfall. The Sanhedrin, the supreme Jewish court, would hear their case on the following day.

Despite the official opposition, the message of the crucified and risen Messiah, supported by the compelling evidence of a healing miracle, had a far-reaching effect. There were more conversions; in fact, the total of those who believed grew to about 5,000 men (vs. 4). Because this figure only included men, the total number of believers in Jerusalem was actually much higher than that by now. When women and children are included, the number may have been closer to 20,000.

II. THE PRAYER REQUEST OF THE BELIEVERS: ACTS 4:23-31

A. The Report Made by Peter and John: vs. 23

On their release, Peter and John went back to their own people and reported all that the chief priests and elders had said to them.

When the Sanhedrin met the next day, they questioned Peter and John about the source of power for the miracle that had been performed. By this time everyone knew about the miracle; and the members of the council could not deny it, for the healed man was standing there before the council. Peter, empowered by the Holy Spirit to speak, pointed to Jesus—the one the religious elite had crucified and God had raised—as the healer of the crippled man (Acts 4:5-12, 14, 16).

The council members took note that the apostles had been with Jesus (vs. 13). Perhaps they were remembering that even though Jesus did not receive any formal religious training, He also could not be matched in His handling of the Old Testament (see John 7:14-15).

The Sanhedrin concluded that the only thing they could do in this situation was warn Peter and John not to speak or teach anymore in the name of Jesus, an order that the disciples refused to obey (Acts 4:18-20). The widespread knowledge and rejoicing over the healing of the lame man kept the Sanhedrin from punishing the apostles (vss. 21-22).

Once Peter and John were released, they rejoined their fellow believers. Undoubtedly, the disciples were overjoyed to see the two apostles. At some point, Peter and John reported everything that the high priests and elders had said to them (vs. 23). The ensuing response of Jesus' followers was characterized by praise, song, and prayer.

B. The Fulfillment of Old Testament Prophecy concerning the Messiah: vss. 24-26

When they heard this, they raised their voices together in prayer to God. "Sovereign Lord," they said, "you made the heaven and the earth and the sea, and everything in them. You spoke by the Holy Spirit through the mouth of your servant, our father David: 'Why do the nations rage and the peoples plot in vain? The kings of the earth take their stand and the rulers gather together against the Lord and against his Anointed One.'"

The believers were united in mind and heart as they lifted up their voices in prayer (Acts 4:24). They acknowledged God as being the sovereign Lord and Creator of the universe and everything in it. Jesus' disciples also saw God as being in control of time and eternity. That is why, by means of the Holy Spirit, the Lord declared long ago through King David, the ancestor of the Jews, truths having messianic importance.

The quote in verses 25-26 is from Psalm 2. Christ's followers made it a part of their prayer to God. They voiced the truth that the opposition they experienced from the religious establishment mirrored what they found in this psalm and anticipated its full and final fulfillment in the end times.

David declared that the Gentile nations raged in opposition against the Lord and His Anointed One, the Messiah. Furthermore, the unsaved people of the earth wasted their time concocting futile plans. The most vain of all would be their brazen attempt in the last days to assemble together in battle against the Father and His Son.

C. The Sovereign Plan of the Father concerning His Son: vss. 27-28

"Indeed Herod and Pontius Pilate met together with the Gentiles and the people of Israel in this city to conspire against your holy servant Jesus, whom you anointed. They did what your power and will had decided beforehand should happen."

The early church recognized that the opposition they and their Savior experienced from the religious leaders of their day was a harbinger of more sinister times to come at the end of the age. In particular, Christ's followers noted how, in Jerusalem, Herod Antipas, Pontius Pilate, and the people of Israel united together against Jesus, God's holy Servant, whom He had anointed (Acts 4:27).

From a legal perspective the crucifixion of the Messiah was a travesty of justice; yet all the dastardly things the Roman and Jewish rulers did to Jesus were in accordance with the eternal will and plan of God (vs. 28). In a sense, the Lord had sovereignly determined beforehand that Christ would die on a cross and be raised from the dead.

D. The Petition for Boldness and Power: vss. 29-30

"Now, Lord, consider their threats and enable your servants to speak your word with great boldness. Stretch out your hand to heal and perform miraculous signs and wonders through the name of your holy servant Jesus."

Because the disciples recognized God's control over the unfolding chain of events, they shunned the temptation to seek relief from their trials or revenge on their antagonists. Instead, Jesus' followers asked the Lord to take notice of the threats of their enemies and give His servants the courage to proclaim His good news of redemption with boldness (Acts 4:29).

The early church petitioned God to complement their verbal witness with works of power. In particular, Jesus' followers asked the Lord to extend His hand to heal as well as to bring about miraculous signs and wonders. These were to be done in the name of Jesus, God's holy servant (vs. 30).

This last point indicates that the miracles were not to be done as an end in itself. Also, they were not to draw attention to the believers. Instead, the miracles were to spotlight the Messiah and the good news of His power to save the lost. In short, the early church asked God to use episodes of persecution to bring glory to Himself.

E. The Divine Response: vs. 31

After they prayed, the place where they were meeting was shaken. And they were all filled with the Holy Spirit and spoke the word of God boldly.

The petition of Jesus' followers met with God's approval. This is evident from the divine response. The building where the disciples had gathered was shaken. This phenomenon was a clear sign that the Lord was in the midst of His people (see Exod. 19:18; Ps. 114:7; Isa. 6:4; Acts 16:26).

In addition to this, Acts 4:31 says the believers were all filled with the Holy Spirit. This means He empowered them for effective service, and they in turn yielded fully to His control. For instance, they began to herald the divine message of salvation with boldness and courage. From this we see that the prayer uttered by the early church was answered immediately.

Discussion Questions

1. What happened to Peter and John as they were speaking to the people?
2. What upset the religious leaders concerning the apostles' activities?
3. How did Jesus' followers respond to the news Peter and John shared about their experience with the religious authorities?
4. What role did the sovereign Lord have in the series of events involving Peter and John?
5. What did the early church pray for in response to the persecution being encountered?

Contemporary Application

The disciples of our Lord recognized that the council's order to quit teaching about Jesus directly challenged their Christian commitment. Believers living in the complexities of our modern society will likely find their commitment to Jesus challenged as well.

We should not be surprised by this. As the world around us becomes increasingly secular, our loyalty to Christ will come under more frequent attack. Our culture entices us to seek material prosperity, achieve personal pleasure, and fulfill our every desire for a life of ease.

Because these nonreligious values and attitudes bombard us from the media and have nearly universal acceptance, we may be as unconscious of them as we are of the invisible ocean of air in which we live and breathe. This makes living in the culture all the more dangerous.

Sometimes these challenges against our commitment to Jesus are open and obvious. Militant opponents may try to restrict religious expression or caricature believers as old-fashioned and bigoted.

In such an environment, we need to be clear about the nature of our relationship to Christ. We no longer belong to ourselves, since our precious Savior has purchased us by His death on the cross (1 Pet. 1:18-19). It follows that we are to love Him with all our heart and to follow Him with all our energy.

Furthermore, we are not to feel at home in this world of sin and selfishness, because our citizenship is in heaven, where Christ lives to intercede for us. We need to remind ourselves of the truths that were important to us when we first placed our faith in Christ.

Moreover, believers need to revisit what God has told us in Scripture about who He is, what our responsibility is to Him, and what our duty is toward a world of unsaved human beings. Only by keeping this Christian view of the world in mind can we recognize the true nature of the numerous challenges that arise around us.

How did the early church withstand the challenges to their commitment? Their victory flowed from genuine discipleship. The disciples personally believed in Jesus and had committed themselves to His service. Our ability to overcome begins at the same point—with a personal trust in Christ that expresses itself in determination to serve Him. Moreover, our commitment to serve our Lord has to draw upon the strength that only the Holy Spirit provides to those who are united with Christ.

Stephen

DEVOTIONAL READING

Isaiah 6:1-8

DAILY BIBLE READINGS

Monday September 26
Acts 6:8-15 Stephen Is Arrested

Tuesday September 27
Acts 7:1-8 Stephen Speaks to the Council

Wednesday September 28
Acts 7:9-16 Stephen Tells the Joseph Story

Thursday September 29
Acts 7:17-29 Stephen Tells Moses' Early Story

Friday September 30
Acts 7:30-43 Stephen Tells of Moses, the Liberator

Saturday October 1
Acts 7:44-53 Stephen Challenges His Hearers

Sunday October 2
Acts 7:54-60 Stephen Is Stoned to Death

Scripture

Background Scripture: *Acts 6:8—7:60*
Scripture Lesson: *Acts 6:8-15; 7:53-60*
Key Verse: *Stephen, a man full of God's grace and power, did great wonders and miraculous signs among the people.* Acts 6:8.
Scripture Lesson for Children: *Acts 6:1-12, 15*
Key Verse for Children: *"Choose seven men from among you who are known to be full of the Spirit and wisdom."* Acts 6:3.

Lesson Aim

To evaluate the importance of being both bold and gracious in one's witness for Christ.

Lesson Setting

Time: *A.D. 32*
Place: *Jerusalem*

Lesson Outline

Stephen

I. The Arrest of Stephen: Acts 6:8-15
    A. *The Performance of Miracles: vs. 8*
    B. *The Debate with Antagonists: vss. 9-10*
    C. *The Presentation of False Accusations: vss. 11-14*
    D. *The Countenance of Stephen: vs. 15*
II. The Stoning of Stephen: Acts 7:53-60
    A. *The Indignation of the Religious Leaders: vss. 53-54*
    B. *The Vision Experienced by Stephen: vss. 55-56*
    C. *The Abusive Treatment of the Mob: vss. 57-58*
    D. *The Martyrdom of Stephen: vss. 59-60*

Introduction for Adults

Topic: *Faithful Servant*

Organizations in the West can be very competitive. This is evident from the sports teams that dominate athletics and the fierce rivalry that exists among businesses. Even the entertainment industry is marked by ruthless self-interest.

Individuals are also competitive. Students try to outdo their peers in terms of grades. Employees do whatever they can to climb to the top of their professions. Many people want to drive a better car and own a nicer home than their neighbors.

Being a faithful servant is a revolutionary concept to adults who are highly competitive. When you put the interests of others first, you're not thinking of eliminating them to get to the top. Instead, you're cultivating relationships and showing love. Isn't this what being a Christian is really all about?

Introduction for Youth

Topic: *Me, a Leader?*

There are many ideas of what constitutes effective leadership. And some of the more unsavory notions encourage using deceit and manipulation to get ahead. It should come as no surprise to the teens that the biblical view of leadership is entirely different.

Consider Stephen. He did not court trouble, and yet he encountered opposition because many people did not understand or accept his zeal for Christ. Unlike many, however, he did not become either overly aggressive or timid in his witness. He exercised true leadership by maintaining a balance between boldness and graciousness. And through this class session, you can encourage your students to do so as well.

Concepts for Children

Topic: *God's Special Helpers*

1. As more and more people became believers, the needs of some of Jesus' followers were being overlooked.
2. The problem grew worse and worse until important leaders in the early church decided what to do.
3. Seven believers were chosen to solve the problem.
4. One of these believers, a person named Stephen, was arrested by the authorities for speaking out boldly in the name of Jesus.
5. God wants us to be His special helpers at home and in school.

Lesson Commentary

I. THE ARREST OF STEPHEN: ACTS 6:8-15

A. The Performance of Miracles: vs. 8

Now Stephen, a man full of God's grace and power, did great wonders and miraculous signs among the people.

We learn from the Book of Acts that after Christ ascended, the church experienced explosive growth. People were entering God's kingdom by the thousands, far more than the 12 apostles could possibly minister to. Soon conflict arose between the Christians of two backgrounds over caring for the poor. Seven wise, Spirit-filled men were chosen to take care of these problems so that the apostles could devote themselves to praying and preaching the Word of God (Acts 6:1-7).

A believer named Stephen was one of the seven chosen. He was full of faith, wisdom, power, and grace (vs. 8). These qualities indicate that he was totally committed to Christ, and thus a vessel through whom the power of God could flow. For instance, Stephen performed "great wonders and miraculous signs among the people." This is a case where Stephen had been faithful in the modest task of food distribution. Thus God now entrusted him with a wider ministry. The Lord was enabling Stephen to perform works like those of the apostles and of Jesus Himself.

B. The Debate with Antagonists: vss. 9-10

Opposition arose, however, from members of the Synagogue of the Freedmen (as it was called)—Jews of Cyrene and Alexandria as well as the provinces of Cilicia and Asia. These men began to argue with Stephen, but they could not stand up against his wisdom or the Spirit by whom he spoke.

In addition to performing miracles, Stephen also proclaimed the Gospel, which disturbed the Jews who had come from different parts of the Roman Empire. One group was the "Synagogue of the Freedmen" (Acts 6:9). No one knows much about this party. The founders might have been released Roman slaves who had converted to Judaism.

It is also possible the freedmen were Jews whom the Romans had enslaved and later released in Rome. Their homes may have been in Rome, but they built a synagogue in Jerusalem, which they often visited. A third possibility is that the freedmen were Jews who lived in the African city of Liberatum and had come to Jerusalem to worship in the temple.

The synagogue was attended by Jews from Cyrene, Alexandria, Cilicia, and Asia. Both the Cyrenians and the Alexandrians had come from major cities in North Africa. Cilicia was located in the southeast corner of Asia Minor, and "Asia" (in today's Turkey) was a Roman province in the western part of Asia Minor.

The Hellenist Jews were constantly battling an image of being "second class" to their Hebrew brothers and sisters. Even the Talmud said these people were not to be trusted. Since they wanted to be fully accepted as Jews, they no doubt squelched any behavior that challenged Jewish traditions.

Perhaps just when the Hellenist Jews seemed to be making some headway, a young Greek-speaking Jew turned Christian came on the scene, preaching repentance and belief in Jesus as the Messiah. Though the Hellenist Jews were incensed with Stephen, they were not able to refute his message by debating with him (vs. 10).

C. The Presentation of False Accusations: vss. 11-14

Then they secretly persuaded some men to say, "We have heard Stephen speak words of blasphemy against Moses and against God." So they stirred up the people and the elders and the teachers of the law. They seized Stephen and brought him before the Sanhedrin. They produced false witnesses, who testified, "This fellow never stops speaking against this holy place and against the law. For we have heard him say that this Jesus of Nazareth will destroy this place and change the customs Moses handed down to us."

Stephen's opponents secretly persuaded others to testify that he had blasphemed against Moses and God. Naturally, what the false witnesses claimed alarmed the Jewish people and their rulers in Jerusalem. This led to Stephen's arrest and appearance before the Sanhedrin (Acts 6:11-12).

A group of false witnesses claimed that Stephen spoke against the cherished institutions and customs of Judaism (vs. 13). In particular, he was accused of claiming that Jesus would destroy the temple and change Mosaic customs—charges similar to those that had been brought against Jesus at His trial (vs. 14). Some think the indictment represents a garbled version of the episode recorded in John 2:19-22.

D. The Countenance of Stephen: vs. 15

All who were sitting in the Sanhedrin looked intently at Stephen, and they saw that his face was like the face of an angel.

As Stephen stood before the high council, all those who were sitting looked at him intently. The reason for their fixed gaze is that the face of Stephen beamed as bright as that of an angel (Acts 6:15). In the speech that he offered in his defense, he also manifested divinely given wisdom and courage.

II. THE STONING OF STEPHEN: ACTS 7:53-60

A. The Indignation of the Religious Leaders: vss. 53-54

"You who have received the law that was put into effect through angels but have not obeyed it." When they heard this, they were furious and gnashed their teeth at him.

Stephen's defense to the Sanhedrin (Acts 7:2-53) is the longest recorded speech in Acts. Bible scholars have discussed why it so enraged the religious leaders (vs. 54) and why Luke may have given it so much attention. The intensity of their fury is captured in the phrase "they were furious and gnashed their teeth at him."

Some have noted that the speech is a refutation of the three things a first century A.D. Jew most revered: the land, the law, and the temple. The Jews venerated the promised land; but Stephen argued that, while the land of promise was important,

God's activities in Israel's history often took place outside that area. Stephen also noted that wherever God is, is holy ground (vss. 2-36).

The Jews also revered the law and, in turn, the person who gave them the law—Moses; but Stephen reminded his listeners that Moses clearly pointed to a coming Prophet who was greater than he. Regrettably, the people even rejected Moses and embraced idol worship, just as they rejected Jesus (vss. 37-43).

Finally, the Jews looked on the temple as the symbol of God's past workings with the nation of Israel. Sadly, many also seemed to confine God's work to the temple alone, so that they could not see Him living among them as Jesus, nor could they recognize the work of the Holy Spirit. Instead, they killed the Messiah, as they had all of God's messengers, rather than listening to His truth (vss. 44-53).

In summary, Stephen had knocked down the three so-called pillars of the Jewish faith, and proclaimed that Jesus is the Messiah, the long-awaited "Righteous One" (vs. 52). The natural reaction of the religious leaders was to brand Stephen as a blasphemer and take him out to be stoned (vs. 54).

B. The Vision Experienced by Stephen: vss. 55-56

But Stephen, full of the Holy Spirit, looked up to heaven and saw the glory of God, and Jesus standing at the right hand of God. "Look," he said, "I see heaven open and the Son of Man standing at the right hand of God."

Stephen remained undaunted by the angry reaction of the Sanhedrin. This Spirit-filled disciple described a heavenly vision in which he saw the glory of God, and the Messiah sanding at the place of honor at the Father's right hand (Acts 7:55-56).

In essence, Stephen was echoing the very words Jesus Himself had spoken in His earlier trial before the same men (see Mark 14:62). While Jesus is customarily pictured as seated at the Father's right hand, Stephen saw the Messiah standing. Some have suggested that Christ had risen on this occasion to welcome the first martyr of the church.

C. The Abusive Treatment of the Mob: vss. 57-58

At this they covered their ears and, yelling at the top of their voices, they all rushed at him, dragged him out of the city and began to stone him. Meanwhile, the witnesses laid their clothes at the feet of a young man named Saul.

Stephen's words were so blasphemous to the religious leaders that they put their hands over their ears and drowned out his voice with their shouts. Perhaps with the fury of an uncontrollable mob, the council rushed at Stephen, dragged him out of the city, and began to stone him (Acts 7:57-58).

In ancient Israel, stoning was the most commonly prescribed form of execution for capital offenses. These offenses usually involved the breaking of particular Mosaic laws. Included among the crimes that carried the death penalty were child sacrifice (Lev. 20:2), involvement with the occult (20:27), working on the Sabbath (Num. 15:32-36), worshiping false gods (Deut. 13:10), rebellion against parents

(21:18-21), adultery (22:21-24; Ezek. 16:38-40), and blasphemy (Lev. 24:14-16; John 10:31-33).

The men of the community normally carried out the sentence of stoning (Deut. 21:21). In cases involving capital crimes, the testimony of at least two witnesses was required, and those witnesses were obligated to cast the first stones (Deut. 17:5-7; John 8:7; Acts 7:58). Execution normally occurred somewhere outside city or camp boundaries.

The members of the Sanhedrin, not Stephen, were guilty of rebelling against God. Though he faced imminent death, Stephen demonstrated before his antagonists what it truly meant to honor the Lord. Stephen's desire was not to perpetuate a dead institution and its lifeless traditions; rather, he sought to please God, regardless of the circumstances or the cost to himself.

While these things were taking place, the official witnesses took off their outer garments and laid them at the feet of a young man named Saul. (He is later called Paul in Acts 13:9.) He was a Pharisee and associated with the Sanhedrin (Phil. 3:5). Possibly Saul was an instigator of Stephen's trial (Acts 8:3; 9:1-2).

D. The Martyrdom of Stephen: vss. 59-60

While they were stoning him, Stephen prayed, "Lord Jesus, receive my spirit." Then he fell on his knees and cried out, "Lord, do not hold this sin against them." When he had said this, he fell asleep.

As he was being murdered, Stephen neither begged for mercy nor renounced Christ. Rather, Stephen committed himself to the Lord Jesus and asked Him to forgive the religious leaders (Acts 7:59-60). His words were similar to those spoken by Jesus at His crucifixion (Luke 23:34). Thus, despite the terrifying prospect of death, Stephen remained calm and hopeful. Unlike his detractors, he had the assurance that God the Son—his Savior and Lord—would receive him into His glorious presence.

Stephen was the church's first recorded martyr, though not its last. The early believers were glad to suffer as Jesus had suffered, for it meant they were counted worthy (Acts 5:41). Perhaps like Stephen, these unnamed martyrs also had a forgiving heart toward their foes. Such a response comes only from the Spirit.

Discussion Questions

1. What qualities characterized Stephen?
2. Why was Stephen able to stand up against his antagonists?
3. What charges were brought against Stephen?
4. Why were the Jewish leaders infuriated with Stephen?
5. How did Stephen respond to those who stoned him to death?

Contemporary Application

In the earliest days of the church (Acts 1—5), the apostles remained in Jerusalem, proclaiming the Gospel only to the Jews; however, it was God's intention that the Good News be taken to all people throughout the whole world (Matt. 28:19-20; Acts 1:8). Beginning in Acts 6, Luke recounted how God accomplished His plan for church expansion and the spread of the Gospel through the persecution that followed Stephen's death.

First, Luke explained how Stephen rose to a leadership position within the church. In the process, Luke revealed that the most important qualification for Christian service is being controlled by the Holy Spirit. Stephen was a man who possessed this quality in a remarkable way. Through God's grace and power, this wise servant (6:3) became a great miracle worker (vs. 8), evangelist (vs. 10), and the first to give his life for the cause of Christ.

For many of us, the thought of telling others about our faith brings on sweaty palms and a suddenly vacant mind. We fear embarrassment, ridicule, and rejection. We also fear violating the rules of etiquette that religion should never be discussed in polite society. Perhaps ultimately we are afraid of failing—the possibility of losing face as well as a soul for the kingdom of God.

Stephen's testimony before the people and leaders of the Jews provides us with an excellent example of how to boldly witness to God's grace. Stephen spoke his mind straightforwardly and authoritatively, even when he encountered opposition.

Maintaining a bold witness does not mean we are disrespectful, obnoxious, or overly aggressive. We are not trying to pick a fight with others or alienate them from Christ and His Gospel. Our desire is to be persistent and make the truth known in a way that is biblically accurate and relevant.

Doing this is not always easy, and without God's help, we will fail. That is why we should continue to trust Him to give us the wisdom we need to remain focused and godly as we maintain a bold witness.

We should also look to God for inner strength and clarity of mind to say the right words at the right time. God can and does empower His people to boldly present the truth of His grace in ways they never imagined. The key, of course, is to completely rely on Him.

The Samaritans and Philip

DEVOTIONAL READING

Acts 19:1-10

DAILY BIBLE READINGS

Monday October 3
*Matthew 19:1-12 Jesus
Teaches in Judea*

Tuesday October 4
*Matthew 20:29-34 Healing
in Jericho*

Wednesday October 5
*Luke 19:1-10 A Visit in
Jericho*

Thursday October 6
*John 4:1-10 Jesus Meets a
Samaritan Woman*

Friday October 7
*John 4:11–26 Water
Gushing Up to Eternal Life*

Saturday October 8
*Acts 8:4-13 Philip Preaches
in Samaria*

Sunday October 9
*Acts 8:14-25 Peter and John
Preach in Samaria*

Scripture

Background Scripture: *Acts 8:4-25*
Scripture Lesson: *Acts 8:4-17*
Key Verse: *When the apostles in Jerusalem heard that
Samaria had accepted the word of God, they sent Peter and
John to them.* Acts 8:14.
Scripture Lesson for Children: *Acts 8:4-6, 8-17*
Key Verse for Children: *Philip went down to a city in
Samaria and proclaimed the Christ there.* Acts 8:5.

Lesson Aim

To emphasize that God provides many opportunities
for us to share the Gospel.

Lesson Setting

Time: *Around A.D. 34*
Place: *Samaria*

Lesson Outline

The Samaritans and Philip

I. The Ministry of Philip in Samaria: Acts 8:4-8
  A. *The Spread of the Gospel: vs. 4*
  B. *The Evangelistic Outreach of Philip: vss. 5-8*
II. The Encounter with Simon the Sorcerer:
  Acts 8:9-17
  A. *The Sorcery of Simon: vss. 9-10*
  B. *The Decision of Simon to Believe: vss. 11-13*
  C. *The Dispatching of Peter and John: vss. 14-17*

Introduction for Adults

Topic: *Christians without Borders*

In his book *Cultural Anthropology,* Paul G. Hiebert defines a social culture as an "integrated system of learned patterns of behavior, ideas and products, characteristic of a society." The social setting that we come from usually defines who we are as a person. Most people are comfortable living and working around those with whom they are most familiar and with whom they share a social culture.

When Christ comes into our lives, He begins to replace our fear of other people with a love for them. Instead of fearing how they might harm or reject us, we are more able to think of their need for Christ and, therefore, we will want them to experience God's forgiveness and love.

Introduction for Youth

Topic: *Old Enemies—New Friends*

The formation of cliques remains a prevalent phenomenon among teens. And with the existence of such groups can come the notion that people in one clique are unwelcome in another clique.

This adversarial mentality runs counter to the gospel of Christ. He wants saved teens to share the Good News even with those they might feel are their enemies. To be sure, this can be difficult to do. But it's amazing how the power of Christ can break down such barriers between people.

The mission field of believing young people may begin with their families, then extend into their neighborhood, and finally into the larger society. Regardless of whom the Lord brings into the lives of your students, they should be alert to the opportunities to tell others how much Jesus means to them.

Concepts for Children

Topic: *God's People Tell Good News*

1. A believer named Philip went to a place called Samaria to tell people about Jesus.
2. While Philip was there, he did many works of power.
3. God used Philip to encourage a well-known person named Simon to believe in Jesus.
4. Church leaders in a city called Jerusalem sent two believers named Peter and John to encourage the Christians in Samaria.
5. God wants us to share our faith with people who may not belong to any church.

Lesson Commentary

I. THE MINISTRY OF PHILIP IN SAMARIA: ACTS 8:4-8

A. The Spread of the Gospel: vs. 4

Those who had been scattered preached the word wherever they went.

Stephen's death unleashed a firestorm of hatred against the followers of Christ. The church, being no more than a few years old at the beginning of Acts 8, faced its first real persecution. While it lasted but a few months, the maltreatment spearheaded by a young Jew named Saul was nevertheless severe.

Saul was a Pharisee and perhaps a member of the Sanhedrin. He was bent on stamping out this new religious movement (9:1). He sought to have the followers of Jesus imprisoned (8:3), beaten (22:19), whipped, and even executed (26:10-11). Unwittingly, those who persecuted the church played an important part in causing its teaching to spread. In fact, God used the adversity to provide believers with opportunities to share the Gospel with those outside the Jewish community.

We learn in 8:4 that the believers who had fled Jerusalem went wherever they could to spread the good news of salvation. The unsaved learned that Jesus is the promised Messiah of the Old Testament and that, despite His death on the cross, He rose from the dead. Furthermore, the message being heralded included an emphasis on repentance and faith.

This outcome underscores that good can result from dire situations. Also, short-term hardships can produce long-term benefits. Whoever trusts in God can look beyond temporary hardships, anticipating fruit that will last for eternity.

B. The Evangelistic Outreach of Philip: vss. 5-8

Philip went down to a city in Samaria and proclaimed the Christ there. When the crowds heard Philip and saw the miraculous signs he did, they all paid close attention to what he said. With shrieks, evil spirits came out of many, and many paralytics and cripples were healed. So there was great joy in that city.

Among the believers scattered by the persecution was Philip (Acts 8:5). He was one of the persons previously selected along with Stephen to look after the Greek-speaking widows (see 6:5). Philip, like Stephen, illustrates how a person faithful in one ministry was given a wider sphere of service. His works in this chapter were only the beginning of a long, fruitful span of service (see 21:8).

Philip traveled "down" (8:5; or downhill) from Jerusalem to a "city in Samaria." Samaria was a region in central Palestine first occupied by the tribe of Ephraim and part of the tribe of Manasseh. One of the region's most prominent centers, the ancient town of Shechem (near Mount Gerizim, Samaria's highest peak), became the capital of the northern kingdom of Israel under Jeroboam (931–910 B.C.; 1 Kings 12:25). Later, a city named Samaria (begun by Omri around 880 B.C.) became the capital of the northern kingdom, and remained so through several kings until it fell to the Assyrians in 722 B.C.

When the northern kingdom fell, most of its prominent citizens were deported to Assyria, Aram (Syria), and Babylon. The depleted Israelite population was then replaced with foreigners from Babylon and elsewhere (2 Kings 17:24). Through the intermarriage between the newcomers and the Israelites left in the land, the resulting people later known as Samaritans were formed.

Because of their mixed Jewish-Gentile blood, early pagan worship (vs. 29), and later religious ceremonies that centered on Mount Gerizim rather than the temple in Jerusalem (John 4:20-22), the Samaritans were generally despised by the Jews throughout their history. This certainly remained true in New Testament times. In fact, the Jews of Philip's day were unrelenting in their view that the Samaritans were racially impure.

The Jews also saw Samaritans as religious half-breeds since Samaritans rejected much of the Scriptures, accepting only the first five books. Moreover, despite their common ancestry, their equal regard for the law, and their shared hope for a Messiah, Jews and Samaritans usually refused to have anything to do with each other (Luke 9:51-56; John 4:9).

There is some doubt about the exact identity of the city where Philip took up temporary residence (Acts 8:5). Some conjecture it was the region's capital, also called Samaria. Regardless of which particular city it was, there Philip proclaimed the truth about Christ to the residents.

It is somewhat surprising that the Samaritans listened to Philip, a Jew (vs. 6). It may have helped that he was a Hellenistic Jew (6:1), that is, a Jew who spoke Greek and was influenced by Greek culture. It also may have helped that he had recently endured Jewish persecution. Perhaps the Samaritans had heard about and approved of disputes about the temple that Christians such as Stephen had carried on with Jews (vss. 13-14).

At any rate, when the Samaritans heard Philip's message and saw the miracles he performed, they listened intently to what he proclaimed (8:6). They knew something unusual was happening among them. They watched wide-eyed as those with evil spirits were set free and as paralytics and cripples walked (vs. 7).

The record of the miracles Philip performed reads like a listing of the very signs Jesus Himself had earlier done. God was giving evidence of His presence and truth to a previously despised, neglected people. It is no wonder "there was great joy in that city" (vs. 8).

II. THE ENCOUNTER WITH SIMON THE SORCERER: ACTS 8:9-17

A. The Sorcery of Simon: vss. 9-10

Now for some time a man named Simon had practiced sorcery in the city and amazed all the people of Samaria. He boasted that he was someone great, and all the people, both high and low, gave him their attention and exclaimed, "This man is the divine power known as the Great Power."

Supernatural power was impressive to the Samaritans. For instance, many Samaritans followed Simon, a sorcerer (Acts 8:9). In the ancient world, the kind of magic he practiced flourished. Luke recorded three incidents related to magic: the account of Simon (vss. 9-24), the account of Elymas (13:4-12), and the account of seven Jewish exorcists (19:13-20).

Details about the magic practiced by those magicians are mostly lacking; but more generally, we know that Greco-Roman magic combined ideas from a number of sources. Assyrian and Babylonian magic contributed knowledge of astrology. Egyptian magic contributed a belief in the power of secret names. Persian magic contributed ways of using spirits for good and evil ends. Israelite magic contributed a body of divine and angelic names thought effective in incantations (magic spells). Greco-Roman magic tended to be practical. On behalf of their clients, ma-gicians tried to prevent or avert harm, to hurt enemies with curses, to inspire love or sub-mission in others, and to gain revelations from the spirit world.

Simon's own involvement with magic extended back a number of years. He beguiled people with his antics and boasted that he was someone important (8:9). He was able to convince the Samaritans—from the least to the most prominent— that he was the great power of the divine (vs. 10). The idea probably is that Simon either claimed to be God or alleged to be God's chief representative.

B. The Decision of Simon to Believe: vss. 11-13

They followed him because he had amazed them for a long time with his magic. But when they believed Philip as he preached the good news of the kingdom of God and the name of Jesus Christ, they were bap-tized, both men and women. Simon himself believed and was baptized. And he followed Philip every-where, astonished by the great signs and miracles he saw.

It was because of the magic Simon performed that he held such sway over the peo-ple of Samaria; but the arrival of Philip changed all that. Philip's miracles were so superior to Simon's that the people turned away from the sorcerer. They now believed Philip's message concerning the kingdom of God (Acts 8:11-12).

We learn in Scripture that the divine kingdom embraces all who walk in fellow-ship with the Lord and do His will. The kingdom is governed by God's laws, which are summed up in our duty to love the Lord supremely and love others as our-selves. Moreover, this kingdom, which was announced by the prophets and intro-duced by Jesus, will one day displace all the kingdoms of this world, following the return of Jesus Christ.

As a result of Philip's evangelistic activities, many men and women put their trust in the Messiah. They also gave evidence of their decision to believe by being bap-tized. Simon himself, astonished by what he saw, likewise believed and was baptized (vs. 13).

It was the grace of God that enabled the Samaritans and Simon to give up their sinful attitudes and believe in Jesus. Similarly, when we come to Christ, we must sur-render our old life so that we can receive a new life. Our old ways of thinking, our old attitudes and prejudices, and our old habits and lifestyles must all be given up so that God can do His work in us.

As Simon followed Philip wherever he went, the former sorcerer was astounded by the great miracles and signs the evangelist performed. Philip's intent, however, was not to make a name for himself. His goal was to confirm the truth he proclaimed, especially Jesus' ability to rescue people from their life of sin.

There is a lingering question as to whether Simon was a genuine believer. While verse 13 seems to indicate that he was, verses 20-23 seem to indicate that he was not. There are several possible answers to this question. Some say Simon had only appeared to believe when he saw Philip's power. Others say Peter used exaggerated terms, meaning only that Simon had sinned badly, not that he was an unbeliever. A third group maintains that Simon abandoned his faith when he tried to buy divine power.

C. The Dispatching of Peter and John: vss. 14-17

When the apostles in Jerusalem heard that Samaria had accepted the word of God, they sent Peter and John to them. When they arrived, they prayed for them that they might receive the Holy Spirit, because the Holy Spirit had not yet come upon any of them; they had simply been baptized into the name of the Lord Jesus. Then Peter and John placed their hands on them, and they received the Holy Spirit.

In the persecution following Stephen's stoning, the apostles bravely maintained the church's presence at its original center, Jerusalem. There news of Philip's successes in Samaria reached them. Peter and John, as representatives of the apostles, went to see for themselves what was happening in Samaria (Acts 8:14).

Peter and John arrived at a city that had been transformed by the power of God. They were able to build on the foundation laid by Philip. The apostles wanted to strengthen and develop the faith of the new believers. Thus, the first thing Peter and John did was pray that the new converts might receive the Holy Spirit (vs. 15).

Luke explained that the Spirit had not yet come upon any of the converts (vs. 16). The reason is that the Samaritan believers had only been baptized into the name of the Lord Jesus. This statement raises an intriguing question. How was it possible for the Spirit not to be received by those who had believed the truth about "the kingdom of God and the name of Jesus Christ" (vs. 12)?

Bible scholars differ in their answers to this question. Problematic is the notion that Peter's and John's ministry conveyed a second work of grace—a work of the Spirit beyond His initial indwelling. Some view the apostles' work as a sort of confirmation with the goal of bringing intellectual faith up to a higher level. The most likely explanation is that this was a unique occurrence in which God used Peter and John to communicate the Spirit in such a way that the Jerusalem believers would accept the Samaritans.

Peter and John clearly expected something more to happen in the Samaritans' lives. Thus, the apostles laid their hands on the new converts and prayed that the Holy Spirit might come to them (vs. 17). The laying on of hands was a common practice among Jews for blessing people or putting them into a ministry or service.

Luke did not tell what followed the praying and laying on of hands, other than to say that the Samaritan believers received the Holy Spirit. Luke had earlier described in greater detail signs that accompanied fillings by the Holy Spirit (2:2-4; 4:31). Though we are not told exactly what happened when the Spirit came upon the Samaritans, we know some demonstration of God's power appeared. This was recognized as a supernatural event by those who looked on.

Discussion Questions

1. What did Philip do once he reached the city of Samaria?
2. How did the people respond to Philip's evangelistic ministry?
3. What did Simon observe as he followed Philip wherever he went?
4. What job were Peter and John given to do in Samaria by the Jerusalem church?
5. What happened when the apostles laid their hands on the Samaritan converts?

Contemporary Application

Despite Jesus' command to witness to the ends of the earth, the church might have stayed comfortably in Jerusalem if the early Christians had not been persecuted (Acts 8:1-3). Thankfully, under God's direction, Philip was willing to be used in the proclamation of the Gospel to the Samaritans. The evangelist was not put off, either, by their despised status in the Jewish society of the day.

We function better within our comfort zone, where people are familiar and circumstances are easy. Often, though, God sends us into unfamiliar or scary places because He has work for us there.

A sign in a church which people see as they leave says, "You are now going out into the mission field." Where might God be sending you to share the Gospel? You may say, "I do not speak very well." Instead, you can smile and say "God loves you" to a very tired store clerk; or you could tell a peer at work or school that you are a Christian; or you could help a person carry heavy packages as a prelude to sharing your faith.

God may place you in an unusual situation. If so, submit to Him in the power of His Spirit. The Lord might want you to talk to a handicapped person. You could feed a child who comes to the local soup kitchen or join with others in your church to resettle a refugee family. Any of these contacts might open a door to share the Gospel.

You should prepare yourself to witness through Bible study and prayer. You will want to be friendly and show interest in the person before you launch into a spiritual discussion. If you sense the Spirit's nudging to talk with someone, be sure to pray first. Ask God for His words, not yours. If you obediently share as God provides opportunity, He will bless you for your faithfulness, not your eloquence.

The Ethiopian Official

Scripture

Background Scripture: *Acts 8:26-40*
Scripture Lesson: *Acts 8:26-38*
Key Verse: *Then Philip began with that very passage of Scripture and told [the Ethiopian] the good news about Jesus.* Acts 8:35.
Scripture Lesson for Children: *Acts 8:26-38*
Key Verse for Children: *Then Philip began with that very passage of Scripture and told [the Ethiopian] the good news about Jesus.* Acts 8:35.

Lesson Aim

To consider how to overcome social barriers in order to share the Gospel with others.

Lesson Setting

Time: *Around A.D. 34*
Place: *The desert road going from Jerusalem to Gaza*

Lesson Outline

The Ethiopian Official

I. The Details of the Situation: Acts 8:26-28
   A. *The Divine Command: vs. 26*
   B. *The Sighting of the Ethiopian Official: vss. 27-28*
II. The Conversion of the Ethiopian Official: Acts 8:29-38
   A. *The Invitation Given to Philip: vss. 29-31*
   B. *The Old Testament Passage Being Read: vss. 32-33*
   C. *The Explanation Offered by Philip: vss. 34-35*
   D. *The baptizing of the Ethiopian official: vss. 36-38*

Introduction for Adults

Topic: *Interpreting the Word*

      While returning from a conference in Los Angeles, a very tired pastor from Boston wanted nothing more than a long nap on the plane ride home. But as he sat down, he noticed a young Indian man sitting beside him who seemed terrified. The minister, accustomed to following the leading of the Lord, realized that God had identified a need.

      It turns out the Indian was a Hindu going to Harvard University as an exchange student. This young person also had no faith to ease his fear of flying. The pastor took the opportunity to open his Bible and share meaningful truths from it. He explained to the student that God loved him and that Christ had died for his sins. Before they reached Boston, the young man had accepted the Lord!

Introduction for Youth

Topic: *Commitment to Study*

      In this week's lesson we learn how Philip listened to God's command and left his thriving first ministry to go to the desert. Because of Philip's prior commitment to study God's Word, he was able to explain the meaning of a Scripture passage to a troubled Ethiopian. The official not only turned to Christ in faith, but also went home to share the Gospel with others.

      Being faithful to God's Word means saved teens take the time to study it as well as apply it to their lives. It also means they feel sufficiently comfortable with the information in the Bible that they are ready and willing to share the truth with others. Each time believing adolescents follow God's will in sharing their faith, the Holy Spirit can work through them with amazing results.

Concepts for Children

Topic: *God's People Tell about Jesus*

1. An important official from a place called Ethiopia had gone to a city named Jerusalem to worship the Lord.
2. While this person was returning home, the Holy Spirit had a believer named Philip go to the official and tell him about Jesus.
3. In order to help the official understand the Good News, Philip had to explain to him a passage from the Book of Isaiah.
4. The Lord used Philip to lead the official to faith in Jesus.
5. We can use the Bible in a powerful way to encourage others to trust in Jesus.

Lesson Commentary

I. THE DETAILS OF THE SITUATION: ACTS 8:26-28

A. The Divine Command: vs. 26

Now an angel of the Lord said to Philip, "Go south to the road—the desert road—that goes down from Jerusalem to Gaza."

In this week's lesson, we learn about the conversion of a man from Ethiopia. In ancient times Ethiopia was located in the region of Nubia, just south of Egypt, where the first waterfall of the Nile goes into the Sudan. The modern nation of Ethiopia is located further to the southeast.

Many Bible scholars equate Ethiopia with the land of Cush (Gen. 2:13; Isa. 11:11). Cush was an enemy of Egypt for centuries, gaining and losing independence, depending on the pharaoh. After the Assyrians conquered the Egyptians in 671 B.C., Ethiopia maintained a strong center of trade. Job saw Cush as a rich source of topaz and other minerals (Job 28:19). The most influential Ethiopian leader, Tirhakah, aided Hezekiah when Sennacherib invaded Judah in 701 B.C. (2 Kings 19:9; Isa. 37:9).

The capital, Napata, was abandoned around 300 B.C. The capital of Ethiopia then moved south to Meroe, where the kingdom continued on for another 600 years. Archaeological digs in Napata and Meroe have disclosed a number of pyramid tombs, as well as temples to the Egyptian god Amun.

During the New Testament era, several queens of Ethiopia bore the name Candace, which was probably a title, not a proper name. Modern Ethiopian Christians consider the eunuch of this week's text their country's first evangelist. In fact, many regard his conversion as the beginning of the fulfillment of Psalm 68:31.

The narrative begins with Philip, who must have enjoyed the evangelistic fruit borne in Samaria. Great miracles were happening, many were responding to his preaching, and many were turning to Christ. If he was like a lot of people, he would have wanted to stay and enjoy the results of his ministry; but God had something quite different prepared for him.

An angel of the Lord told Philip to leave the city and go south to the road that led from Jerusalem to Gaza (Acts 8:26). In ancient times Gaza was a town located about 50 miles from Jerusalem. The original city was destroyed in the first century B.C. and a new city was built near the coast.

Not knowing what he would find on the desert road, Philip obeyed. Leaving behind the excitement and action among the new Samaritan converts, he traveled into the desert. God's opportunities may not always excite us. We may think we see greater potential elsewhere. Obedience like Philip's, however, opens the door for God to do things we could never have imagined.

B. The Sighting of the Ethiopian Official: vss. 27-28

So he started out, and on his way he met an Ethiopian eunuch, an important official in charge of all the treasury of Candace, queen of the Ethiopians. This man had gone to Jerusalem to worship, and on his way home was sitting in his chariot reading the book of Isaiah the prophet.

Running through the desert south of Jerusalem was a well-traveled road, a main route toward Egypt. On the road was a eunuch returning from Jerusalem to his native Ethiopia. By the man's chariot and servants, Philip could see he was an important governmental official. In fact, he was a sort of secretary of the treasury for "Candace, queen of the Ethiopians" (Acts 8:27).

Officials in the courts of ancient rulers were often eunuchs, that is, castrated men. Not being subject to the drives of other men, eunuchs could even be trusted to oversee the king's harem (see Esth. 2:15). In some cases, however, the word *eunuch* seems to have been purely a governmental title, not necessarily applied to a castrated man.

Some commentators believe the Ethiopian "eunuch" (Acts 8:27) was of this type. They say this, for one thing, because the eunuch had been in Jerusalem for worship. Jewish law prohibited the participation of eunuchs in the Jewish assembly (Deut. 23:1; but see Isa. 56:4-5). Also, the Ethiopian was in charge of finances, not a harem.

As he rode along in his chariot, the Ethiopian read aloud to himself (Acts 8:28). This was a common practice in those days for those who had reading materials; but scrolls and other reading materials, transcribed by hand, were not readily available to the average person. Only the wealthy and influential could afford literature. Even more rare was a non-Jew possessing Hebrew Scripture, as this man did.

Because the Ethiopian had managed to obtain a copy of Isaiah, and since he had traveled to worship at the temple in Jerusalem, we may conclude that he was a convert to the Jewish faith. If not, he must surely have been a "God-fearer"—a label given to Gentiles who believed in the one true God of Israel but who had not been circumcised. The Ethiopian worshiped the true God.

II. THE CONVERSION OF THE ETHIOPIAN OFFICIAL: ACTS 8:29-38

A. The Invitation Given to Philip: vss. 29-31

The Spirit told Philip, "Go to that chariot and stay near it." Then Philip ran up to the chariot and heard the man reading Isaiah the prophet. "Do you understand what you are reading?" Philip asked. "How can I," he said, "unless someone explains it to me?" So he invited Philip to come up and sit with him.

Philip sensed the Holy Spirit urging him closer to the chariot (Acts 8:29). A simple but profound lesson for us here is that in order to receive this *specific* divine guidance Philip first had to obey God's *general* command (see vs. 26). Had the evangelist refused to go southward to this desert area, he would not have been available to receive this command. Likewise, we need to make ourselves available to God by following the clear and basic principles of His Word.

Philip obeyed by running up to the Ethiopian (vs. 30). Since the official was reading aloud, Philip knew the Scripture verses the eunuch was contemplating. Knowing that this passage referred to the suffering Servant, Philip asked the Ethiopian if he understood what he was reading.

The official did not try to hide his ignorance. As one who wanted to comprehend God's Word, he admitted that he needed someone to explain the prophet's words. Perceiving that Philip was such a person, the Ethiopian invited Philip to sit next to him in his chariot (vs. 31).

While it is true that the meaning of many portions of Scripture is self-evident, some passages are difficult to understand. For this reason, God has provided gifted believers who through study and the illumination of the Spirit can expound His Word.

B. The Old Testament Passage Being Read: vss. 32-33

The eunuch was reading this passage of Scripture: "He was led like a sheep to the slaughter, and as a lamb before the shearer is silent, so he did not open his mouth. In his humiliation he was deprived of justice. Who can speak of his descendants? For his life was taken from the earth."

The Ethiopian had been mulling over Isaiah 53:7-8. This passage describes a person who submitted to affliction and death without objection. He would do so to atone for humankind's sin. He was willing to die for others because He loved sinners and wanted to remove their transgressions.

By oppression and unjust judgment, this person would be taken away to His death. Isaiah asked who could speak of this person's descendants. The Jews believed that to die without children was a tragedy (2 Sam. 18:18). The suffering Servant would have no physical descendants, for His life would be "taken from the earth" (Acts 8:33). Indeed, He would be stricken for the sins of humanity.

Luke quoted from the Septuagint (or ancient Greek) translation of the Old Testament, the most common version used in New Testament times. This explains why the wording of Acts 8:32-33 is slightly different from what is printed in Isaiah 53:7-8 of our English Bibles.

C. The Explanation Offered by Philip: vss. 34-35

The eunuch asked Philip, "Tell me, please, who is the prophet talking about, himself or someone else?" Then Philip began with that very passage of Scripture and told him the good news about Jesus.

The eunuch asked Philip whether Isaiah was talking about himself or referring to someone else (Acts 8:34). What an opportunity this was to tell the good news about Christ! Philip explained how Jesus fulfilled the prophecy, namely, how He had been condemned and crucified as the Lamb of God, and how He rose from the dead (vs. 35).

This information is not the answer the Ethiopian would have received from non-Christian, first century A.D. Jews. Most saw the passage as referring to Isaiah himself, or to the nation of Israel, not to a suffering Messiah, since that did not fit in with their idea of a conquering Savior who would deliver them from the Romans. Actually, Luke 22:37 indicates that Jesus first applied Isaiah 53 to Himself before His crucifixion, when He quoted verse 12 to the apostles.

D. The baptizing of the Ethiopian official: vss. 36-38

As they traveled along the road, they came to some water and the eunuch said, "Look, here is water. Why shouldn't I be baptized?" Philip said, "If you believe with all your heart, you may." The eunuch answered, "I believe that Jesus Christ is the Son of God." And he gave orders to stop the chariot. Then both Philip and the eunuch went down into the water and Philip baptized him.

We do not have the details of the conversation between Philip and the Ethiopian, but we may assume that the evangelist covered all the basics, including baptism. It was the Ethiopian himself, not Philip, who noticed water along the way and proposed that he should be baptized (Acts 8:36). Philip's statement and the official's response show that the Ethiopian believed Jesus was indeed the fulfillment of Isaiah's prophecy. (Note that some late Greek manuscripts add all or most of verse 37.)

Since the Ethiopian now trusted in Jesus, he ordered his driver to stop his chariot. The vehicle referred to in verse 38 was probably an ox-drawn wagon. Most likely the Ethiopian was part of a caravan journeying in the same direction and moving slowly down the road.

Once the chariot had stopped, the official stepped into some nearby water and allowed Philip to baptize him. The baptism could have taken place at any number of locations. Tradition identifies the spot as near the town of Bethsura. The baptism, however, may have taken place nearer Gaza.

Verse 39 says that once the two came out of the water, the Spirit of the Lord "took Philip away." Some see in this description a miracle in which the evangelist was transported from the site of the baptism to Azotus. Others, however, interpret this as merely Philip's abrupt departure under the compulsion of the Spirit. The biblical text leaves no doubt that Philip carried his preaching mission farther to the north (vs. 40).

The Ethiopian eunuch was not disturbed by Philip's sudden departure. He continued his journey, rejoicing in his new faith. Irenaeus, an early church leader who lived between A.D. 130–202, wrote that the official returned to Ethiopia and became a missionary to his own people.

The religious authorities had persecuted the church in order to halt the spread of the Gospel. Ironically, in causing Jesus' followers to scatter, the leaders in Jerusalem also caused the Gospel to spread far and wide. Now it had gone beyond the borders of Judea and Samaria.

Sometimes we have to become uncomfortable before we will move. We may not want to experience it, but discomfort may be the best thing for us because God may be working through our hurts. In the midst of painful circumstances, we may want to stop and ask whether God might be preparing us for a special task.

Discussion Questions

1. How did Philip respond to the command he received from the angel of the Lord?
2. What had the Ethiopian official been doing in Jerusalem?

3. What did Philip do to engage the official in conversation?
4. What explanation did Philip offer to the Ethiopian's question regarding Isaiah 53:7-8?
5. How do you think the conversion of the official helped the spread of the Gospel?

Contemporary Application

It is usually difficult to be one of the first to do something new. Philip was a groundbreaker. He went beyond the barriers of race and social class to tell the good news of Jesus to an Ethiopian official. Philip was obedient to God and overcame social barriers in the process.

Often Christians allow social differences to hinder their relationships with others; however, the command to spread the Gospel demands that we see all people as individuals of sacred worth and value, created in the image of God.

Venturing into new and unfamiliar social situations can be frightening. Feelings of inadequacy and fear of rejection can make us feel powerless in sharing our faith in Christ; nevertheless, we must never lose sight of the truth that God will be with us when we encounter social barriers. Through Christ we can overcome these barriers and share the good news of Jesus with those who are different from us.

This requires us to be open to telling unbelievers about Christ wherever they may be. Indeed, it is often outside the church building that people are converted to Christ. Jesus preached in the synagogues (Luke 4:44), taught a multitude by the seashore (5:3), privately ministered to Nicodemus at night (John 3:1-2), and on a mountain explained principles of God's kingdom (Matt. 5:1-2). Christ ventured into different contexts to share God's love. Can we do less?

Our mission field may begin with our families, then extend into our neighborhood, and finally into larger society. Regardless of the individual or situation, we need to be alert to the opportunities to tell people how much Jesus means to us.

Cornelius and the Gentiles

DEVOTIONAL READING

Acts 13:44-49

DAILY BIBLE READINGS

Monday October 17
Acts 10:1-8 Cornelius Has a Vision

Tuesday October 18
Acts 10:9-16 Peter Has a Vision

Wednesday October 19
Acts 10:17-22 Cornelius's Men Call on Peter

Thursday October 20
Acts 10:23-33 Peter Visits Cornelius

Friday October 21
Acts 10:34-43 Peter Shares the Good News

Saturday October 22
Acts 10:44-48 Gentiles Receive the Holy Spirit

Sunday October 23
Acts 11:1-15 Peter Explains How Gentiles Also Believed

Scripture

Background Scripture: *Acts 10:1-48*
Scripture Lesson: *Acts 10:1-20*
Key Verses: *While Peter was still thinking about the vision, the Spirit said to him, "Simon, three men are looking for you. So get up and go downstairs. Do not hesitate to go with them, for I have sent them."* Acts 10:19-20.
Scripture Lesson for Children: *Acts 10:1-3, 5-8, 21-24, 34-36, 44-48*
Key Verse for Children: *[Peter] ordered that [the Gentiles] be baptized in the name of Jesus Christ.* Acts 10:48.

Lesson Aim

To consider how God can help the students overcome prejudices they may have toward others.

Lesson Setting

Time: *About A.D. 40*
Place: *Caesarea*

Lesson Outline

Cornelius and the Gentiles
  I. The Summons for Peter: Acts 10:1-8
      A. *The Religious Devotion of Cornelius: vss. 1-2*
      B. *The Directive concerning Peter: vss. 3-6*
      C. *The Compliance of Cornelius: vss. 7-8*
  II. The Vision Experienced by Peter: Acts 10:9-20
      A. *The Decision to Pray: vss. 9-10*
      B. *The Heavenly Command: vss. 11-16*
      C. *The Directive from the Spirit: vss. 17-20*

Introduction for Adults

Topic: *Breaking the Gospel Barriers*

Many of the personal prejudices of adults have been ingrained in them since childhood. On their own they don't have the determination and strength to overcome their deep-seated prejudices. Only God can remove those biases, which are also barriers to the spread of the Gospel.

If there is any doubt about prejudice in the church, ask yourself why the statement "Sunday morning remains the most segregated time of the week" still rings true. Possibly members of your class are extremely alike. Can it be that personal prejudices have made it uncomfortable for other kinds of people to feel welcomed?

This week's lesson encourages your students to seek God's help in overcoming whatever prejudices they may have toward others. This will also help to break down Gospel barriers so that they can present a truly Christian witness to others.

Introduction for Youth

Topic: *God's Favorite: Everyone*

Most teens struggle with some form of prejudice in their lives. Such intolerance among Christians is like a disease that threatens to harm and destroy the church. Taking a close look at our attitudes toward others is the first step in eliminating prejudice. It means we are willing to admit that when it comes to salvation, everyone is God's favorite.

In this regard, saved teens can take some pointers from the first Christians, who were Jews. Regrettably, they had been taught to hate and fear Gentiles. This week's lesson will help your students to examine Peter's visit to Cornelius and how the Holy Spirit helped the apostle triumph over his prejudice.

Concepts for Children

Topic: *God's People Baptize*

1. There was a devout Roman army officer named Cornelius who lived in a town called Caesarea.
2. An angel appeared to Cornelius and told him to send for an important believer named Peter.
3. Peter left where he was, traveled to Caesarea, and shared the Good News with Cornelius and his family and friends.
4. This group of people accepted what Peter said and were baptized in the name of Jesus Christ.
5. God wants us to do all we can to help others understand the truth of the Gospel.

Lesson Commentary

I. THE SUMMONS FOR PETER: ACTS 10:1-8

A. The Religious Devotion of Cornelius: vss. 1-2

At Caesarea there was a man named Cornelius, a centurion in what was known as the Italian Regiment. He and all his family were devout and God-fearing; he gave generously to those in need and prayed to God regularly.

After the conversion of Saul (Paul), another important event took place: the first Gentiles became believers. Luke set the stage for this event by describing some of Peter's travels. The apostle went to Lydda, where he healed a paralytic. Then he went to Joppa, where he raised a dead woman. Many in those cities and in nearby Sharon turned to the Lord (Acts 9:32-43). While Peter was staying at Joppa (now Jaffa, Israel), God did something unusual in a city 30 miles to the north.

In 10:1, we learn about a Gentile named Cornelius. As a Roman centurion, Cornelius commanded at least 100 soldiers. He was stationed at Caesarea, a city on the coast of Palestine south of Mount Carmel (not Caesarea Philippi). It was known as "Caesarea by the sea." Largely Gentile, it was a center of Roman administration and the location of many of Herod the Great's building projects.

Centurions were the equivalent of today's U.S. army sergeant major. *Centurion* was the highest rank that an ordinary enlisted soldier could attain. Promotion to this position was dependent upon battle experience and military savvy. Since centurions were given a great deal of autonomy on the battlefield, they had to think well on their feet.

The position of centurions was prestigious, and they were generally paid quite well. If his superiors thought well of him, a centurion could serve throughout the Roman Empire; and if a soldier reached the level of centurion, he generally stayed in that position for life.

Knowing these facts, we might expect Cornelius to have been a hardened military man, committed to might and duty above all; but that seems not to have been the case. He and all his family were known for their piety and generosity. He gave to the poor and prayed regularly to God (vs. 2).

What had made the difference? Cornelius, apparently an Italian, had adopted the religion of his new land. Like a number of other Gentiles, he had converted to Judaism. He had turned away from the pagan polytheism of his culture so that he could worship the one true God.

Attracted by Judaism's higher ethical standards and disillusioned with the parade of pagan gods, many Gentiles seriously considered converting. More women than men actually converted to Judaism, however, because they needed to fulfill only two of the three requirements: (1) to be circumcised, (2) be baptized, and (3) offer a sacrifice. Those who had not met all the requirements but were close were called "God-fearers." They could worship in the synagogues. Cornelius the centurion was a God-fearer.

B. The Directive concerning Peter: vss. 3-6

One day at about three in the afternoon he had a vision. He distinctly saw an angel of God, who came to him and said, "Cornelius!" Cornelius stared at him in fear. "What is it, Lord?" he asked. The angel answered, "Your prayers and gifts to the poor have come up as a memorial offering before God. Now send men to Joppa to bring back a man named Simon who is called Peter. He is staying with Simon the tanner, whose house is by the sea."

Acts 10:3 more literally reads, "the ninth hour of the day." This would have been the customary time for prayer in first-century Judea. By our reckoning, it would have been three o'clock in the afternoon when Cornelius had a vision. It began with an angel of God appearing and calling the centurion's name. Staring at the angel in fear, Cornelius somehow managed to reply, "What is it, Lord?" (vs. 4). The soldier naturally wondered why the angel had come to him.

The heavenly visitor explained that he had come because God had chosen Cornelius to be an instrument of His grace. Cornelius's good works (and the true piety behind them) had not gone unnoticed in heaven. The angel compared the centurion's prayers and charitable gifts to a memorial offering to God. This was a portion of the grain offering burned on the altar (Lev. 2:2). It was pleasing to God.

Sometimes we may wonder whether God actually hears our prayers and sees our good works. Does He appreciate our sacrifices for Him? We may never receive God's confirmation through a vision, as Cornelius did; but in the life to come, all true followers of Christ will hear God's words of approval for acts of faithfulness. In the meantime, we can be confident that He sees our good works.

Having assured Cornelius of God's approval, the angel gave Cornelius his instructions. The centurion was to send for a man named Simon Peter. He could be found staying at the home of a tanner, also named Simon, who lived near the sea in Joppa (Acts 10:5).

A tanner made his living by turning the hides of animals into leather goods. Peter's host, the tanner Simon, may have made his home by the sea for convenience. Sea salt was sometimes used for curing leather before tanning.

Handling carcasses was distasteful for Jews because it left a person ritually unclean (Lev. 11:8, 39-40). For a tanner such as Simon, purification would have been quite difficult. His daily contact with dead animals left him almost perpetually unclean. Peter showed his openness toward unclean people, which included Gentiles, by staying at the home of a tanner.

C. The Compliance of Cornelius: vss. 7-8

When the angel who spoke to him had gone, Cornelius called two of his servants and a devout soldier who was one of his attendants. He told them everything that had happened and sent them to Joppa.

As a soldier, Cornelius was familiar with obeying orders as well as giving them. Thus, while he must have been overwhelmed by the vision, he nevertheless hastened to do as he had been commanded. He told two of his servants and a devout soldier (who was one of his personal attendants) what had happened and then sent them on to bring back Peter from Joppa (Acts 10:7-8).

We should note that Cornelius obeyed even though he did not know fully why the angel wanted him to send for Peter. Cornelius just obeyed. We are in a similar position. God, in His Word, presents us with guidelines for living and expects us to follow them; yet we do not know exactly where following those guidelines will get us in this life. The future is like unexposed film to us, though God sees the developed picture clearly. We must act in faith, obeying and believing that God will work everything out for our good.

II. THE VISION EXPERIENCED BY PETER: ACTS 10:9-20

A. The Decision to Pray: vss. 9-10

About noon the following day as they were on their journey and approaching the city, Peter went up on the roof to pray. He became hungry and wanted something to eat, and while the meal was being prepared, he fell into a trance.

As Cornelius's servants neared Joppa, God had to prepare Peter to receive them and their message. They were, after all, uncircumcised Gentiles, people whom strict Jews avoided. Furthermore, Jewish practice declared that it would be wrong for a Jew, such as Peter, to enter the home of a non-Jew, such as Cornelius.

Thus, in advance, God overcame Peter's hesitation by showing him a vision. In Acts 9, Luke narrated how God drew Saul and Ananias together by giving each a vision. God worked in the same way in bringing Peter and Cornelius together. The Lord was about to work through them to teach the revolutionary truth that Gentiles can become a part of the church.

Peter's vision took place on the flat roof of Simon's house (10:9). Roofs in that era were used something like suburban decks are used today. Peter had gone to the roof at about noon for prayer. It must have been a pleasant place to pray, with the Mediterranean sparkling in the distance and the call of seabirds in the air.

Eventually Peter became hungry and asked for lunch. While waiting to eat, Peter fell into a trance and saw a vision. Like dreams, visions were experiences through which supernatural insight or awareness was bestowed by divine revelation. While dreams occurred only during sleep, visions could happen while a person was awake (see Dan. 10:7). In Peter's case, he was filled with a heightened awareness of God's will regarding Cornelius.

B. The Heavenly Command: vss. 11-16

He saw heaven opened and something like a large sheet being let down to earth by its four corners. It contained all kinds of four-footed animals, as well as reptiles of the earth and birds of the air. Then a voice told him, "Get up, Peter. Kill and eat." "Surely not, Lord!" Peter replied. "I have never eaten anything impure or unclean." The voice spoke to him a second time, "Do not call anything impure that God has made clean." This happened three times, and immediately the sheet was taken back to heaven.

In Peter's vision, a kind of sheet was lowered from heaven by its corners. The sheet contained many kinds of mammals, reptiles, and birds. As a Jew, Peter immediately recognized that the sheet contained both clean and unclean creatures. Among the clean animals may have been cows, sheep, and fish. Among the unclean animals may have been pigs, lizards, and vultures. Since the animals were all mixed together, by Jewish thinking even the clean animals were now unclean (Acts 10:11-12).

Old Testament law made a distinction between clean and unclean animals (Lev. 11). Jews were permitted to eat clean animals, but not unclean ones. The distinction between and unclean creatures did not necessarily have anything to do with the actual dirtiness of the animals. The differentiation itself was what was important. It symbolized the distinction between God's covenant people—the Jews—and all others.

Under the new covenant established by Christ, Jews and Gentiles are equals within the church. Thus the distinction symbolized by uncleanness no longer exists. This was a key emphasis in Peter's vision (see Acts 10:34-35; 11:17).

The incredible sight unfolding before Peter was accompanied by a voice commanding the apostle to kill and eat the creatures on the large sheet (10:13). Though he was hungry, Peter protested that he had never eaten anything unclean (vs. 14). Jesus had already taught that the food laws were obsolete (Matt. 15:11); but apparently Peter had not yet learned the lesson. He thought God could not seriously want him to eat unclean meat.

For each of us, learning what God expects is a lifelong process. God forgives us when we repent; but He wants us to move along in our understanding of His wishes and our obedience to them as fast as we are able.

As Peter's vision continued, the voice sounded again, this time forbidding Peter (and all Christians) from calling anything common or unclean (and thus unacceptable) that God had called clean (and thus acceptable; Acts 10:15). By telling Peter to eat the animals on the sheet, God had declared the animals clean.

Symbolically, the Lord had done away with the distinction between clean and unclean animals; but, as noted earlier, the vision was not mainly about food. God reinforced the impact of the vision by showing it to Peter three times. Then the vision ended (vs. 16).

C. The Directive from the Spirit: vss. 17-20

While Peter was wondering about the meaning of the vision, the men sent by Cornelius found out where Simon's house was and stopped at the gate. They called out, asking if Simon who was known as Peter was staying there. While Peter was still thinking about the vision, the Spirit said to him, "Simon, three men are looking for you. So get up and go downstairs. Do not hesitate to go with them, for I have sent them."

While Peter was contemplating the meaning of the vision, the men Cornelius had dispatched discovered the location of Simon the tanner's house. The men approached the gate and asked whether this was the place where Peter was lodging.

Meanwhile, as the apostle puzzled over the vision, the Spirit disclosed that three men were looking for him. He was to get up, go downstairs, and accompany them without hesitation. The apostle could travel with these Gentiles without any misgivings, for the Lord ultimately was responsible for sending them (Acts 10:17-20).

Discussion Questions

1. Who was Cornelius?
2. How did Cornelius respond to the angel's command?
3. What was the nature of the vision Peter experienced?
4. What was the point of Peter's vision?
5. Why did Peter initially struggle to understand and obey the command of God conveyed in the vision?

Contemporary Application

God's great mission of peace originally had been given to the Israelites. Through the truth of the Gospel, they learned about Jesus their Messiah and the new life they could have with Him. With the resurrection and ascension of Christ, Gentiles as well as Jews were included in His mission of peace. This meant He accepted all people who trusted in Him for salvation regardless of their nationality, cultural background, or economic status.

Peter's audience knew that at one time he would not have associated with Gentiles. The fact that he was now meeting with Cornelius and his household was undeniable proof that God could change someone from being prejudiced to being equitable and loving. Peter's personal testimony powerfully influenced other believers to reach out to all people with the Gospel.

At first we may not be in the mood to change the way we think about others. In these situations we should choose to obey God regardless of how we feel. This is an act of faith on our part. We are trusting the Lord to help us overcome our prejudices. We know that He will not let us down. In time we will change our feelings to match the way we are acting.

It is humbling to learn that we may have prejudiced views about others. When the Spirit shines His truth into our lives, we should not retreat into the darkness. We also should not rationalize that everybody else feels the same way. Instead, we should ask God to help us overcome our prejudices and send us to a specific person outside our group who needs Christ. Then we need to reach out in the name of the Lord Jesus.

Like Peter, we may continue to struggle with prejudices that tend to prevent or weaken our outreach to certain people (see Gal. 2:11-14). We can overcome our irrational attitudes by *including* all types of people, rather than *excluding* certain ones, as we tell them the good news about Christ.

Peter in Prison

DEVOTIONAL READING

Psalm 46

DAILY BIBLE READINGS

October 24 Monday
  *Acts 9:32-42 Peter Heals
  One and Revives Another*

October 25 Tuesday
  *Luke 4:1-13 Jesus Is
  Tempted*

October 26 Wednesday
  *Matthew 26:36-46 Jesus
  Prays in Gethsemane*

October 27 Thursday
  *Mark 15:33-37 Jesus Dies
  on the Cross*

October 28 Friday
  *Acts 12:1-5 James Is Killed
  and Peter Imprisoned*

October 29 Saturday
  *Acts 12:6-11 An Angel Frees
  Peter from Prison*

October 30 Sunday
  *Acts 12:12-17 Peter Tells the
  Others What Happened*

Scripture

Background Scripture: *Acts 12:1-17*
Scripture Lesson: *Acts 12:1-16*
Key Verse: *Suddenly an angel of the Lord appeared and a light shone in the cell. He struck Peter on the side and woke him up. "Quick, get up!" he said, and the chains fell off Peter's wrists.* Acts 12:7.
Scripture Lesson for Children: *Acts 12:1-16*
Key Verse for Children: *Peter . . . described how the Lord had brought him out of prison.* Acts 12:17.

Lesson Aim

To stress the importance of going to the Lord in prayer in a consistent, fervent manner.

Lesson Setting

Time: *About A.D. 43*
Place: *Jerusalem*

Lesson Outline

Peter in Prison
  I. The Detaining of Peter: Acts 12:1-5
      A. *The Execution of James: vss. 1-2*
      B. *The Arrest and Imprisonment of Peter: vss. 3-4*
      C. *The Response of the Church: vs. 5*
  II. The Freeing of Peter: Acts 12:6-11
      A. *The Guarding of Peter: vs. 6*
      B. *The Appearance of an Angel: vss. 7-10*
      C. *The Realization of Peter: vs. 11*
  III. The Reunion with the Disciples: Acts 12:12-16
      A. *The Encounter with Rhoda: vss. 12-15*
      B. *The Astonishment of the Believers: vs. 16*

Introduction for Adults

Topic: *Never Alone*

"I have no idea why I'm telling you this, but . . ." Sitting before me was the daughter of overseas missionaries. Not ready to leave the security of her parents, she had been afraid and lonely on her own. She searched for and found a replacement for her love, but she also got something she hadn't bargained for: a truckload of guilt. She knew she had been heading down the wrong path, but she couldn't stop herself.

In the conversation that followed, the young woman learned about God's ability to bring forgiveness, healing, and restoration into her life. She also discovered the truth that through faith in Christ she had the abiding presence of the Holy Spirit. This young woman found out that the One in whom she now trusted would never abandon her.

Introduction for Youth

Topic: *An Unbelievable Rescue*

At times even saved adolescents can feel trapped by their circumstances. It might be peer pressure, the lack of social outlet, sagging self-confidence, or family problems (among other things) that can create such an impression. Who can believing teens turn to for help?

Young people need to know there isn't a problem that can arise that the Lord doesn't care about. And there isn't a problem that can arise that His grace—His unmerited favor—won't see them through. The Lord was concerned enough about Peter to rescue him from prison. And the Savior's involvement in lives of your students assures their eternal success.

Concepts for Children

Topic: *God's People Are Rescued*

1. There was a ruler named King Herod who tried to harm the followers of Jesus.
2. King Herod had one church leader named James killed.
3. King Herod then had Peter imprisoned so he also could be killed.
4. The Lord, however, answered the prayers of His people by sending an angel to set Peter free from prison.
5. When God meets our needs or answers our prayers, it sometimes surprises us.

Lesson Commentary

I. THE DETAINING OF PETER: ACTS 12:1-5

A. The Execution of James: vss. 1-2

It was about this time that King Herod arrested some who belonged to the church, intending to perse-cute them. He had James, the brother of John, put to death with the sword.

The Jewish believers in Jerusalem could not fathom the extraordinary work of God among the Gentiles. They criticized Peter, who was forced to defend his actions and show that the gift of the Spirit to Gentile believers was God's decision. Finally convinced, the church praised God (Acts 11:1-18). More Gentiles were converted at Antioch, and Barnabas and Saul began a ministry there (vss. 19-26). Meanwhile, another wave of persecution came against the church to test the faith and resolve of Jesus' followers.

The disciples in the Antiochian congregation had been collecting relief funds for their fellow believers in Jerusalem and sent Barnabas and Paul to deliver the monetary gift (11:27-30). It was around that time when King Herod Agrippa I began a second episode of persecution against Jesus' followers (12:1).

Agrippa was the son of Aristabulus and the grandson of Herod the Great. Agrippa thus was an Edomite, not a Jew. Agrippa spent his youth in Rome, where he made friends with Gaius (also known as Caligula), who later became emperor. As a result, Gaius favored Agrippa.

In A.D. 37, Gaius gave Agrippa the tetarchies of Philip, the brother of Antipas. These territories included districts north and east of Galilee, as well as Lysanias, which was in southern Syria (see Luke 3:1). In A.D. 39, Galilee and Perea were added to Agrippa's realm. Then in A.D. 41, he was made King of Judea, ruling over an area approximately the same in extent as his grandfather, Herod the Great, had once controlled.

Agrippa made it plain that he would do all in his power to be agreeable to the Jewish people, who responded by according him widespread popularity. Because of his position as king, Agrippa felt able to do what no Roman procurator in previous years would have dared to do, attack the church.

Acts 12:1 suggests that there were a number of individuals whom Agrippa mal-treated; but Luke names only two, both of whom were apostles. The first victim was James, the brother of John and a son of Zebedee. James, along with his brother and father, was originally a fisherman on the Sea of Galilee.

Sometime between A.D. 42–44, Agrippa had James arrested and put to death by the sword (vs. 2), which probably means he was beheaded. James was the first of the apostles to be executed and the only one whose martyrdom is mentioned in the New Testament.

B. The Arrest and Imprisonment of Peter: vss. 3-4

When he saw that this pleased the Jews, he proceeded to seize Peter also. This happened during the Feast of Unleavened Bread. After arresting him, he put him in prison, handing him over to be guarded by four squads of four soldiers each. Herod intended to bring him out for public trial after the Passover.

Agrippa's direct action against the church met with great approval among the Jewish leaders. It showed how little Judaism had become reconciled to the existence of Christian beliefs in Judea. Like Stephen, the apostle James was martyred for his faith. Though we may not understand why, it was God's sovereign will to allow James to be executed.

Agrippa next targeted Peter, having him arrested during the Feast of Unleavened Bread (Acts 12:3). This weeklong festival was also known as Passover (see Luke 22:1), which should not be confused with the meal by the same name that was eaten at twilight on the fourteenth of Nisan. The Feast of Unleavened Bread involved eating bread made without yeast, holding several assemblies, and making designated offerings. It was designed to commemorate how the Lord rescued the Israelites out of Egypt with rapid speed.

Because there were so many zealous Jews in Jerusalem to observe the feast, it was an opportune time for Agrippa to execute another prominent Christian leader. After Peter was found and seized, he was thrown in prison and placed under the guard of four squads (Acts 12:4). Each squad had a detachment of four soldiers, who worked three-hour shifts.

Both of the apostle's wrists were chained, and he had a soldier on each side. Also, two more soldiers stood guard outside Peter's cell. The tighter security was to ensure the apostle would not escape a second time (see 5:19). Some think Peter was jailed at the Fortress of Antonia, which was in the northwest corner of the temple area. In that day, a battalion of Roman soldiers was stationed there.

After the Passover celebration, Agrippa planned to bring the apostle out for public trial, with condemnation and death being the assured outcome. While Jesus had foretold the martyrdom of James (see Mark 10:39), the Savior explicitly stated that Peter would lose his life only when he was old (John 21:18-19). Thus, in the wave of persecution over the church instigated by Agrippa, the time for Peter to die had not yet come.

C. The Response of the Church: vs. 5

So Peter was kept in prison, but the church was earnestly praying to God for him.

The news of Peter's imprisonment undoubtedly shocked and troubled the Jerusalem church; but rather than be paralyzed by fear, Jesus' followers went to the Lord in prayer. The disciples did not just do this once or twice. The biblical text indicates they did so constantly and earnestly (Acts 12:5). Luke portrays what follows as an answer to prayer.

II. THE FREEING OF PETER: ACTS 12:6-11

A. The Guarding of Peter: vs. 6

The night before Herod was to bring him to trial, Peter was sleeping between two soldiers, bound with two chains, and sentries stood guard at the entrance.

The narrative next spotlights the very night before Agrippa was going to bring Peter to trial. The ruler wanted to ensure that the apostle was present for the proceeding. Agrippa thus had Peter chained between two soldiers. Meanwhile, sentries in front of the entrance stood guard over the prison complex (Acts 12:6). The series of events that were about to unfold show that Peter's release was a miracle from God.

B. The Appearance of an Angel: vss. 7-10

Suddenly an angel of the Lord appeared and a light shone in the cell. He struck Peter on the side and woke him up. "Quick, get up!" he said, and the chains fell off Peter's wrists. Then the angel said to him, "Put on your clothes and sandals." And Peter did so. "Wrap your cloak around you and follow me," the angel told him. Peter followed him out of the prison, but he had no idea that what the angel was doing was really happening; he thought he was seeing a vision. They passed the first and second guards and came to the iron gate leading to the city. It opened for them by itself, and they went through it. When they had walked the length of one street, suddenly the angel left him.

While Peter was sleeping between two soldiers, perhaps resigned to the inevitability of being executed within a short period of time, an angel of the Lord suddenly appeared. His presence was also accompanied by a bright light in the apostle's prison cell. The celestial being "struck" (Acts 12:7) the apostle on his side. The term refers to a push or a light tap that was sufficiently forceful to awaken Peter.

The angel next directed the apostle to get up quickly, perhaps even helping him to his feet, while the chains on his wrists fell off. The heavenly visitor then told Peter to get dressed, which involved donning his cloak, fastening his belt or sash, and putting on his sandals (vs. 8). The apostle, though possibly groggy and confused, did as the angel directed. Peter then followed the celestial being out of the prison. All the while, the apostle thought he was seeing a vision. At first, he did not realize the episode was actually happening (vs. 9).

The angel led Peter past the first and second guard posts and then to an iron gate that led into the city (vs. 10). The presence of an iron gate shows how important security was here. This entry point, which was more secure than one made of wood (the more common material), opened all by itself. The two then exited the prison and started walking down a narrow street or alley when the angel suddenly departed.

C. The Realization of Peter: vs. 11

Then Peter came to himself and said, "Now I know without a doubt that the Lord sent his angel and rescued me from Herod's clutches and from everything the Jewish people were anticipating."

The apostle soon realized that what had transpired was not a vision. It actually occurred. The Lord had sent an angel to rescue Peter from the clutches of Agrippa and from what the Jewish leaders (along with the people they represented) were hoping would be done to the apostle (Acts 12:11).

Scripture reveals a great deal about angels. They are spirit beings (Heb. 1:14) who do not marry or reproduce (Matt. 22:30). Because they are not subject to death

(Luke 20:36), they will live forever and remain constant in number.

Angels exist as a hierarchy (Col. 1:16), abide in heaven (Matt. 22:30), and are sent to earth as messengers by God. They are mighty (Ps. 103:20) and powerful (2 Thess. 1:7) and possess great wisdom (2 Sam. 14:20). Ordinarily they are invisible to us (2 Kings 6:17), though they have appeared as men (Luke 24:4).

Among their duties, angels serve God by serving us (Heb. 1:14), provide us with protection (Dan. 6:22), guard us (Ps. 91:11), guide us (Acts 8:26), and help us (Dan. 10:13). In addition to the elect angels, who worship God and serve His purposes (1 Tim. 5:21; Heb. 1:6), there are also fallen angels, who serve the purposes of Satan (Rev. 12:7-9).

III. THE REUNION WITH THE DISCIPLES: ACTS 12:12-16

A. The Encounter with Rhoda: vss. 12-15

When this had dawned on him, he went to the house of Mary the mother of John, also called Mark, where many people had gathered and were praying. Peter knocked at the outer entrance, and a servant girl named Rhoda came to answer the door. When she recognized Peter's voice, she was so overjoyed she ran back without opening it and exclaimed, "Peter is at the door!" "You're out of your mind," they told her. When she kept insisting that it was so, they said, "It must be his angel."

Once Peter had collected his thoughts, he decided to go the home of a believer named Mary, who was also the mother of John Mark. The latter was the cousin of Barnabas, an occasional traveling companion of Peter and Paul, and most likely the author of the second Synoptic Gospel. Mary evidently was an influential woman of Jerusalem, for she owned a sizeable house with servants.

It was at Mary's home that a group of Jesus' followers had gathered to pray for Peter (Acts 12:12). When he knocked at the door of the outer gate, a servant girl named Rhoda came to open it (vs. 13). When she recognized the voice of the apostle, Rhoda became so filled with joy that, instead of opening the gate to let Peter in, she rushed back inside the house to announce to everyone that the apostle was standing at the gate (vs. 14).

The irony is that this group of believers, who had fervently prayed for Peter's release, failed to recognize that God had literally and immediately answered their petition. Instead of taking Rhoda at her word, the disciples maintained she had lost her mind. Even when the servant girl insisted otherwise, the believers decided she must have seen an angel the Lord had assigned to attend to Peter (vs. 15; see Gen. 48:16; Matt. 18:10).

B. The Astonishment of the Believers: vs. 16

But Peter kept on knocking, and when they opened the door and saw him, they were astonished.

Despite being ignored for an unspecified period of time, Peter thankfully continued to knock at the door of the gate. This in turn got the attention of the disciples. Though Rhoda had insisted that she had seen Peter, and though the believers had been praying for his release, they were amazed to see him when they finally went outside and opened the gate (Acts 12:16).

Evidently the astonishment was accompanied by a considerable amount of commotion. The apostle, sensing this would draw the unwanted attention of nearby soldiers, signaled with his hand for the disciples to be quiet. Then Peter recounted how the Lord had brought him out of the prison. Before departing, the apostle directed that the leaders of the Jerusalem church be informed of what had happened (vs. 17).

God continued to watch over Peter. Despite the great commotion that resulted from his escape from the jail and the subsequent search for him, the authorities were not able to find the apostle (vss. 18-19). Throughout the rest of his life, Peter remained a faithful servant of the Lord. He was a pioneer among the apostles and the early church, breaking ground that other believers would later follow.

Discussion Questions

1. What did King Herod plan to do to Peter after arresting him?
2. What command did the angel give to Peter?
3. What convinced Peter that the Lord had rescued him?
4. How did Rhoda initially respond to Peter's presence?
5. How did the praying believers initially respond to Rhoda's statement concerning the arrival of Peter?

Contemporary Application

The episode involving the arrest and miraculous release of Peter represents the Lord's answer to the prayers of His people on behalf of the apostle. While the account of Peter's release is stirring and inspiring, we should not conclude that God always works in this way or that there is some mysterious procedure we must follow to see similar results from the Lord.

Simply put, praying is talking to God. The act of praying does not change what God has purposed to do; rather, it is the means by which He accomplishes His will. Talking to God is not a method of creating a positive mental attitude in ourselves so that we are able to do what we have asked to be done; instead, prayer creates within us a right attitude with respect to the will of God. Prayer is not so much getting God to do our will as it is demonstrating that we are as concerned as He is that His will be done (Matt. 6:10).

Perhaps the most unpopular concept regarding the practice of prayer is persistence. Whatever our misgivings about coming before the all-knowing, all-powerful God with the same specific petitions over and over, persistence is scriptural (Luke 18:1-8).

God does not become more willing to answer because of perseverance; rather, the petitioner may become more capable of receiving God's answer to his or her request. Also, perseverance can clarify in our minds deep-seated desire from fleeting whim. Moreover, talking to God about the deepest desires of our heart can prepare our soul to more fully appreciate the answer He gives to our request.

Thanksgiving is to be a regular part of our daily prayer life (1 Thess. 5:18). Thanksgiving is an aspect of praise in which we express gratitude to God. It should spring from an appreciative heart, though it is required of all believers, regardless of their initial attitude.

We can thank God for His work of salvation and sanctification, for answering our prayers, and for leading us in the path of righteousness (Phil. 1:3-5; Col. 1:3-5). We can also express gratitude to God for His goodness and unending mercy, and for leading us to spiritual victory in Christ (Ps. 107:1; 1 Cor. 15:57).

Paul Becomes a Follower

DEVOTIONAL READING

Acts 9:23-31

DAILY BIBLE READINGS

Monday October 31
  *Luke 5:4-11 Jesus Calls
  Disciples and Changes Lives*

Tuesday November 1
  *Acts 11:1-10 Peter Responds
  to Criticism from Believers*

Wednesday November 2
  *Acts 11:11-18 The Believers
  in Jerusalem Praise God*

Thursday November 3
  *Acts 9:1-9 Saul Sees a
  Vision of Jesus*

Friday November 4
  *Acts 9:10-16 Ananias
  Receives Instructions in a
  Vision*

Saturday November 5
  *Acts 9:17-22 Saul Begins to
  Proclaim Jesus*

Sunday November 6
  *Acts 9:23-31 Saul and the
  Disciples Proclaim Jesus*

Scripture

Background Scripture: *Acts 9:1-31*

Scripture Lesson: *Acts 9:3-18*

Key Verse: *Immediately, something like scales fell from Saul's eyes, and he could see again. He got up and was baptized.* Acts 9:18.

Scripture Lesson for Children: *Acts 9:3-12, 17-20*

Key Verse for Children: *"[Paul] is my chosen instrument to carry my name before the Gentiles and their kings and before the people of Israel."* Acts 9:15.

Lesson Aim

To urge students to commit their lives fully to Christ.

Lesson Setting

Time: A.D. *35*

Place: *Damascus*

Lesson Outline

Paul Becomes a Follower

  I. The Conversion of Saul: Acts 9:3-9
      A. *The Encounter with the Risen Christ: vss. 3-7*
      B. *The Journey to Damascus: vss. 8-9*
  II. The Commission of Saul: Acts 9:10-18
      A. *The Lord's Directive to Ananias: vss. 10-12*
      B. *The Misgivings of Ananias: vss. 13-14*
      C. *The Insistence of the Lord: vss. 15-16*
      D. *The Compliance of Ananias: vss. 17-18*

Introduction for Adults

Topic: *Encountering Truth*

At our first meeting, Bobby sat uncomfortably on a very comfortable couch. Like so many before him—those with broken lives seeking counsel—he had come to me searching for the life preserver as he felt himself going down for the last time.

Bobby had been a professional soccer player with a promising career, but drugs, alcohol, and a steady stream of lies and deceit had finally brought him down. After losing his dream, a wife, and a young daughter, Bobby was now in danger of losing his freedom. At that moment, only the judge knew for sure.

As I shared with Bobby the truth of the Gospel and the power of the risen Christ, the young man immediately took hold of this life preserver from heaven. Bobby experienced a glorious conversion that day—plucked out of the kingdom of darkness and transplanted into the kingdom of God's Son.

Introduction for Youth

Topic: *From Persecutor to Believer*

The account of Saul's conversion is one of the most pivotal moments in early church history. At one point this influential religious leader was poised to bring a crippling blow on the fledgling group of Jesus' followers living in Damascus. But then Saul encountered the risen Christ and his life was forever changed.

Teens need to know that Christ still transforms lives. We come to Him first for our salvation, an act dependent on His power and grace alone. Then, as the Holy Spirit works through our obedience and submission, day by day, the risen Christ is changing us into His image (Rom. 12:1-2).

Concepts for Children

Topic: *Paul's Life Changes*

1. A person named Saul (or Paul) was heading to a city named Damascus so that he could find and arrest followers of Jesus.
2. While Saul was on his way, the Lord Jesus made His presence known through a bright light, which left him blind, and a voice from heaven.
3. Saul learned that the harm he wanted to bring on Jesus' followers was like hurting Jesus, too.
4. Once Saul arrived in Damascus, the Savior had a follower named Ananias go to Saul, restore his sight, and encourage him as a believer in Jesus.
5. When we put our faith in Jesus, He can help us to change.

Lesson Commentary

I. THE CONVERSION OF SAUL: ACTS 9:3-9

A. The Encounter with the Risen Christ: vss. 3-7

As he neared Damascus on his journey, suddenly a light from heaven flashed around him. He fell to the ground and heard a voice say to him, "Saul, Saul, why do you persecute me?" "Who are you, Lord?" Saul asked. "I am Jesus, whom you are persecuting," he replied. "Now get up and go into the city, and you will be told what you must do." The men traveling with Saul stood there speechless; they heard the sound but did not see anyone.

Acts 9 records one of the great turning points in human history. Saul of Tarsus, an accomplice in the stoning of Stephen and the driving force behind the first great persecution of the church, met the living Christ on the road to Damascus. Next to the Lord Himself, the apostle Paul was perhaps the most influential man who has ever lived. As the first great missionary of the church, Paul began to proclaim the Gospel to the Gentile world and was responsible for the starting of congregations in the most important centers of the world of his day.

The account of Saul's conversion from Christian-hater to devout disciple is described in three places in Acts (9:1-19; 22:2-21; 26:9-18). The basic narrative is the same in each case, but there are slight differences in the details in each telling of the account.

After persecuting the believers in Jerusalem, Saul decided to go after those Christians who had fled the city, to bring them back to face trial before the Sanhedrin and possible execution (9:1-2; 22:4-5; 26:9-11). On the road near Damascus (9:3), about noon one day (22:6), a light far brighter than the sun (26:13) blazed around Saul and his companions, who all fell to the ground (vs. 14).

Saul heard the voice of Jesus repeat his name and ask why he was persecuting the Savior (9:4). Saul's traveling companions were witnesses that something had happened; but though they could hear the sound of Jesus' voice and see the light of His presence, they did not comprehend what was happening (vs. 7; see 22:9).

Since the message was not directed to these men, it makes sense why only Saul understood the words. He recognized this voice as coming from God; yet as far as Saul knew, he had never persecuted God. Saul, thinking he was maltreating God's enemies, asked, "Who are you, Lord?" (9:5).

The reply came back that it was Jesus, whom Saul had been persecuting. Saul must have been dumfounded to learn that Jesus was not a dead blasphemer but the living Lord. This would require a complete change of Saul's beliefs—and indeed, of his life. Saul must have been in shock, with a dawning sense of horror at what he had done; but perhaps hope dawned too, for Jesus told Saul to arise and go into Damascus, where he would receive instructions (vs. 6).

Because of its location, Damascus was a major trade center during the first century A.D. As the capital of Syria, the city had close economic ties with Israel. Two major highways ran through Damascus: the Via Maris, which ran from Mesopotamia to the Mediterranean coast; and the King's Highway, which ran south all the way to Arabia. The city was considered an oasis in the middle of the desert because of its abundant water supplies from the Abana and Pharpar rivers.

A long list of conquerors ruled Damascus: the Assyrians, Babylonians, Persians, Greeks, Ptolemies, Seleucids, and finally the Romans. The city grew even larger in area and importance after Pompey, a Roman general, made Syria into a province of the Roman Empire in A.D. 64. Once the Romans occupied the city, many Jews migrated there and established synagogues. Damascus eventually became an important city in the history of the Christian church.

Jesus' instructions to Saul implied that the Savior, in His mercy, would forgive even His persecutor. The account of Saul's conversion can restore our hope for people whose conversion seems impossible. If God can turn a violent enemy like Saul into a friend, then God's grace can transform anyone (see 1 Tim. 1:16).

B. The Journey to Damascus: vss. 8-9

Saul got up from the ground, but when he opened his eyes he could see nothing. So they led him by the hand into Damascus. For three days he was blind, and did not eat or drink anything.

Apparently, during the short conversation, Saul kept his eyes shut against the bright light. When he opened them afterward, he could not see; and so the proud Pharisee had to be led by the hand like a child into Damascus (Acts 9:8). It must have felt quite humiliating. For three days Saul touched no food or water; the blind man just looked inward (vs. 9).

No one can honestly meet God and remain proud or independent. God wants us to humble ourselves, admit our need, and receive His work in our lives. Humbled, Saul quit doing his own thing and started doing God's will. Is this not what a Christian is—someone who is willing to trade in his or her own agenda for the will of God?

II. THE COMMISSION OF SAUL: ACTS 9:10-18

A. The Lord's Directive to Ananias: vss. 10-12

In Damascus there was a disciple named Ananias. The Lord called to him in a vision, "Ananias!" "Yes, Lord," he answered. The Lord told him, "Go to the house of Judas on Straight Street and ask for a man from Tarsus named Saul, for he is praying. In a vision he has seen a man named Ananias come and place his hands on him to restore his sight."

Ananias is one of those unsung heroes of faith—men and women who do what they have to do, without recognition or reward. We know practically nothing about Ananias; yet God used this faithful disciple to lead Saul into the Kingdom. From out of the shadows of one of the least-known stepped one of the best-known figures in the Bible.

When the Lord called to Ananias in a vision, he responded as a true disciple of the Savior (Acts 9:10). The Lord in turn directed Ananias to go to the house of a man named Judas, whose home was located on the street called "Straight" (vs. 11). This was a mile-long boulevard from one end of Damascus to the other. It still exists today and is about as wide as an alley.

Ananias was told to inquire about a man from Tarsus named Saul. God revealed to Ananias that Saul had had a vision. The blind Pharisee had seen Ananias restoring his eyesight through the laying on of hands. This is the reason Saul was immersed in prayer (vs. 12).

In the first century A.D., Damascus had a large Jewish minority. According to one contemporary estimate, more than 10,000 Jews lived there. Some of these Jews were Christians; most were not. Ananias was a believer, but we do not know whether the Judas with whom Saul was staying was a Christian.

We also do not know why the Lord chose Ananias, instead of some other Christian, to be Saul's helper. Perhaps it was because of Ananias's character or obedience. At any rate, the Lord brought the two men together by communicating to each in a vision.

B. The Misgivings of Ananias: vss. 13-14

"Lord," Ananias answered, "I have heard many reports about this man and all the harm he has done to your saints in Jerusalem. And he has come here with authority from the chief priests to arrest all who call on your name."

Ananias hesitated; he was not sure helping Saul was a good idea. Ananias told the Lord that he had heard many reports from others about the Pharisee. In particular, Ananias was aware of how much harm Saul had done to the saints of the Lord living in Jerusalem (Acts 9:13).

Saul's tirade against Jesus' followers did not stop there. Ananias knew the Pharisee's mission was to terrorize the believers in Damascus. The chief priests had authorized him to imprison everyone who called on Christ's name in saving faith (vs. 14). If Saul's purpose in coming to the city was ever meant to be a secret, the secret was out, for word had preceded him.

C. The Insistence of the Lord: vss. 15-16

But the Lord said to Ananias, "Go! This man is my chosen instrument to carry my name before the Gentiles and their kings and before the people of Israel. I will show him how much he must suffer for my name."

The Lord did not let the protests of Ananias continue any further. He was to obey the Savior without hesitation. The Lord revealed that Saul would be His chosen instrument (or tool) to herald His name to Gentile kings and their subjects as well as to the people of Israel (Acts 9:15).

Here we discover that this once proud Pharisee would minister to all nations, including Israel (see Rom 1:16-17). Before his encounter with the risen Christ, Saul had vigorously persecuted the church. Now, as a follower of Jesus, Saul would learn from personal experience what it meant to suffer for the sake of the Savior's name

(Acts 9:16). Despite such a prospect we should note that toward the end of the apostle's life, he affirmed the following: "I have fought the good fight, I have finished the race, I have kept the faith" (2 Tim. 4:7).

The Lord's reply to Ananias recorded in Acts 9:16 foretold a dramatic and complete turnaround for Saul. Jesus' former enemy was to become a chief ally—not just a neutral observer in the spiritual war. The defender of the law and the Jewish nation would take the message of grace to all sorts of people. Instead of having influence with the authorities, he would suffer at their hands for the name of the Lord.

Persuaded by the Lord, Ananias was willing to adapt. He went to Saul. From this we see that God is full of surprises. Just as we are getting used to the old, He springs the new on us. A couple think they will go through life childless, and then the pregnancy test comes out positive. A church member thinks he will be most effective in the visitation program, and then through prayer he realizes that God wants him teaching in Sunday school.

Growing and changing require us to be flexible. We must be willing to adapt ourselves to keep following where the Lord leads. Looked at in faith, change is not threatening but exciting. Who knows what might happen next?

D. The Compliance of Ananias: vss. 17-18

Then Ananias went to the house and entered it. Placing his hands on Saul, he said, "Brother Saul, the Lord—Jesus, who appeared to you on the road as you were coming here—has sent me so that you may see again and be filled with the Holy Spirit." Immediately, something like scales fell from Saul's eyes, and he could see again. He got up and was baptized.

Ananias departed, went to the house of Judas, and placed his hands on Saul. Ananias then gave this remarkable greeting: "Brother Saul" (Acts 9:17). Ananias accepted Saul for what he had become, not rejected him for what he had been. Ananias did not condemn Saul for his former life; Ananias set aside the past and turned his attention instead to the present. Saul, now his Christian brother, needed to be healed and filled with the Spirit.

Saul and Ananias were brothers because both had come to know the Messiah in a convincing way. Ananias made sure Saul knew that Jesus had sent him, implying that it was Jesus who would bring about the miracle Ananias was about to perform.

By mentioning Saul's encounter with Jesus on the Damascus road, Ananias may have been letting Saul know that he had supernatural knowledge of the event. This, too, would have validated Ananias's divine commission. Of course, rumors of Saul's conversion may have reached Ananias, just as rumors of Saul's persecution mission had reached him.

In any case, several actions followed in swift succession. A crusty covering like scales peeled away from Saul's eyes and he could see again. Moreover, he received the Holy Spirit, he got up from where he had been resting and praying, he was baptized, and he had something to eat (vss. 18-19). Now a new believer stood in the midst of a local church that was not quite sure it was ready for him.

Discussion Questions

1. Why do you think Saul (Paul) was so determined to stamp out Christianity?
2. Why do you think Saul was so shocked at the sight of the risen Lord?
3. What did Saul do for three days following his encounter with Jesus?
4. Why did Ananias initially hesitate when the Lord directed him to go to Saul?
5. In what way had Jesus completely changed Saul?

Contemporary Application

"Who is Jesus?" is the question of the ages. It is the question Saul asked when the Lord stopped him on the road to Damascus and spoke to him. Some say that Jesus was a great ethical teacher, but certainly not God. Others say Jesus is a god, but one among many. In fact, according to them, there are greater gods than He. Still others say Jesus had faults like everyone else. All these beliefs diminish Christ's true glory.

People can be saved only by one who possesses the credentials of a bona fide Savior. The apostles proclaimed Jesus as the only way to the Father (John 14:6; Acts 4:12); and Paul risked his life to tell Jews that Jesus is the Son of God (Acts 9:20-25). In fact, Scripture consistently teaches that Jesus is the God-man. One of the church's greatest hymn writers, Isaac Watts, indicated correctly that the ball bearing (metaphorically speaking) of everything we hold dear turns upon how we view the identity of Christ.

In *Evidence That Demands a Verdict,* Josh McDowell lists a number of conversion testimonies of people from a wide variety of backgrounds. One is Christa Nitzschke, who had read a number of pagan philosophers. Through a girlfriend's help, however, Christa trusted in Jesus. "I committed my life to Him," Christa declared.

Charlie Abero was a radical Marxist in India. Through a Christian speaker, Charlie heard a presentation that made much more sense to him than communism. "I became a Christian," he testified. "I have found purpose and meaning for my life."

These testimonies, along with that of Saul of Tarsus, indicate that it is not enough to assent to the messiahship of Jesus. Even demons believe that there is one God and fear Him (Jas. 2:19), but they do not worship and obey Him. Correct information is insufficient. Belief entails an unswerving faith in Christ. Have you committed yourself to Jesus in this way, trusting Him for eternal life?

Lydia: A Committed Woman

DEVOTIONAL READING

Acts 16:25-34

DAILY BIBLE READINGS

Monday November 7
Hebrews 13:1-6 Show Hospitality to Strangers

Tuesday November 8
Luke 10:38-42 Mary and Martha Welcome Jesus

Wednesday November 9
1 Peter 4:7-11 Serve One Another Using Your Gifts

Thursday November 10
Acts 16:11-15 Lydia Becomes a Faithful Follower

Friday November 11
Acts 16:16-24 Paul and Silas Are Imprisoned

Saturday November 12
Acts 16:25-34 Converted, the Jailer Shows Hospitality

Sunday November 13
Acts 16:35-40 Paul and Silas Are Freed

Scripture

Background Scripture: *Acts 16*
Scripture Lesson: *Acts 16:6-15*
Key Verse: *"If you consider me a believer in the Lord,"* [Lydia said,] *"come and stay at my house."* Acts 16:15.
Scripture Lesson for Children: *Acts 16:9-15*
Key Verse for Children: *"If you consider me a believer in the Lord,"* [Lydia said,] *"come and stay at my house."* Acts 16:15.

Lesson Aim

To emphasize the importance of being undeterred in our evangelistic efforts.

Lesson Setting

Time: A.D. *50*
Places: *Phrygia, Galatia, Mysia, Troas, Samothrace, Neapolis, Macedonia, Philippi, Gangites River*

Lesson Outline

Lydia: A Committed Woman

I. The Vision of the Macedonian Man: Acts 16:6-10
   A. *Prevented by the Spirit: vss. 6-7*
   B. *Permitted by the Spirit: vss. 8-10*

II. The Conversion of Lydia: Acts 16:11-15
   A. *Arriving at Philippi: vss. 11-12*
   B. *Bearing Spiritual Fruit: vss. 13-15*

Introduction for Adults

Topic: *Offering of Oneself*

In China alone it is estimated that 28,000 people are giving their lives to Christ every day. That's revival! And the "wall" continues to come down in Eastern Europe, opening up countries previously closed to the Gospel. Missionary opportunities are springing up in many new places. How can adults in your class offer themselves in support and participate in your church's missionary efforts?

Three ways in which adults can participate in missions is through giving financially, going on short-term missionary trips, and joining the missions committee or the group of individuals that establishes the missions strategy in your church. Stepping out into missions will stretch their faith in Christ, and that is a great blessing.

Introduction for Youth

Topic: *A Gracious Convert*

Jesus encouraged His followers to store up "treasures in heaven" (Matt. 6:20). What better way for teens to do that—and thereby become more gracious converts—than to prayerfully support those taking the Gospel to people who otherwise would not hear it?

Believing young people can participate in missions by encouraging their parents to offer food and lodging for ministers and their families on furlough. Saved teens can attend missions conferences and work to enhance the quality of their church's missionary efforts. Finally, your students can befriend missionaries and offer them encouragement and advice at critical times.

Concepts for Children

Topic: *Lydia Welcomes New Friends*

1. One night while a church leader named Paul was traveling with some believers, the Lord made it clear to Paul that he should go to a place called Macedonia to spread the Gospel.
2. Paul and his friends decided to leave at once for Macedonia.
3. The group eventually made their way to a city named Philippi, where they met a group of women.
4. One of these women was named Lydia, and she believed the Good News about Jesus.
5. Hearing the Gospel with an open heart can lead to belief in Jesus.

Lesson Commentary

I. THE VISION OF THE MACEDONIAN MAN: ACTS 16:6-10

A. Prevented by the Spirit: vss. 6-7

Paul and his companions traveled throughout the region of Phrygia and Galatia, having been kept by the Holy Spirit from preaching the word in the province of Asia. When they came to the border of Mysia, they tried to enter Bithynia, but the Spirit of Jesus would not allow them to.

Acts 16 describes how Paul, Silas, and Timothy traveled through many regions of Asia Minor, delivering the decisions reached by the Jerusalem Council (vss. 3-4). If Acts pictures the church in its infancy, then the debates recorded in Acts over what constituted salvation are the colicky moments of the infant church.

The events of chapter 15 helped to soothe the doctrinal colic brought on by the erroneous teaching of "some of the believers who belonged to the party of the Pharisees" (vs. 5), that Gentile converts to Christianity needed to be circumcised and obey the law of Moses to be saved. These Jews (vss. 1-2, 5) are sometimes called "Judaizers." The group of apostles and elders who assembled to confront this legalism became what is commonly called the "Jerusalem Council."

The Council did not meet to decide what the Gospel was; to them that was never in doubt. They met to counteract the serious ethnic tensions between Jews and Gentiles that were tearing at the delicate unity of the early church. Part of the solution was to officially declare what the Gospel given them by Jesus was: that all people—Jew and Gentile alike—are saved in the same way, namely, "by faith . . . through the grace of our Lord Jesus" (vss. 9, 11).

The prohibitions outlined in the Jerusalem Council's letter to Gentile believers abroad (vss. 20, 23-29) have parallels with Old Testament law stipulations. Israel was commanded not to eat meat with blood in it, and sexual immorality was expressly forbidden as well (Lev. 17:10-14; 18). The letter itself communicated more than just these prohibitions (Acts 15:24-27), and conveyed to Gentiles that the Jerusalem church recognized their inclusion by faith in God's family. That's why the Gentiles received the letter favorably (15:31; 16:4-5).

The letter has to be understood in the context of the ethnic conflicts that prompted the events of chapter 15. Though there were to be no *distinctions* between Jew and Gentile, since both were saved the same way, there were *differences* in how each lived; but these did not have to cause divisions in the Church. While the stipulations the letter set forth had parallels with Jewish ceremonial law, it was not an attempt to get Gentiles to keep the law. The real thrust of the letter was to appeal to Gentiles to respect the consciences of their fellow Jewish believers (Rom. 14:14-21; 1 Cor. 8:4-13). The Gentiles' abstinence would be good for them and good for their relationships with Jewish believers.

As we turn our attention to Paul's travels in Acts 16, it is clarifying to note that these are part of the second of his three missionary journeys recorded in Acts. The Gospel was spreading throughout the Gentile world despite ethnic tensions between Jews and Gentiles. The Council's decision had a strengthening effect on a number of growing, vibrant churches (vs. 5); but they were existing in such hostile environments that they might have withered under the relentless pressure unless they received help. Paul and his companions were that help. They encouraged the churches in their suffering and instructed them in sound doctrine.

The missionary party traveled throughout the region of Phrygia and Galatia. Phrygia was a district in central Asia Minor west of Pisidia. "Galatia" (vs. 6) refers to either (1) the region of the old kingdom of Galatia in the central part of Asia Minor (North Galatia), or (2) the Roman province of Galatia, whose principal cities in the first century were Ancyra and Pisidian Antioch (South Galatia). The exact extent and meaning of this area has been a subject of considerable controversy in modern New Testament studies.

The biblical text does not state why the Holy Spirit prevented the missionary team from proclaiming the Good News in the Roman province of Asia, which made up of about one-third of the west and southwest end of modern Asia Minor. Asia lay to the west of Phrygia and Galatia.

The group next came to the borders of Mysia, which was a province in northwest Asia Minor. They then attempted to go into Bithynia, which was a province in northern Asia Minor northeast of Mysia; but as before, the Spirit would not allow them to go in this direction (vs. 7).

It is not clear how the Spirit made His will known in either of these instances. Because Silas was a prophet (see 15:32), the Lord possibly used him in some way. While we may not be able to figure out what exactly occurred, it is clear that Paul and his companions faithfully followed the Spirit's guidance.

B. Permitted by the Spirit: vss. 8-10

So they passed by Mysia and went down to Troas. During the night Paul had a vision of a man of Macedonia standing and begging him, "Come over to Macedonia and help us." After Paul had seen the vision, we got ready at once to leave for Macedonia, concluding that God had called us to preach the gospel to them.

The missionary team decided to pass by Mysia and went down to Troas, which was a port city on the northwest coast of Asia Minor, near ancient Troy (Acts 16:8). The group was now heading in a westward direction toward the continent of Europe. We can only imagine the struggles Paul and his companions must have experienced as they tried to discern and follow the will of God each step of the way in their travels.

Verse 9 states that during the night, Paul had a vision. The apostle saw a man from the Roman province of Macedonia in northern Greece standing and urging the missionary team (which evidently now included Luke) to come and help. When Paul related the vision to the group, they concluded that God had summoned them to proclaim the Good News in Macedonia (vs. 10).

II. THE CONVERSION OF LYDIA: ACTS 16:11-15

A. Arriving at Philippi: vss. 11-12

From Troas we put out to sea and sailed straight for Samothrace, and the next day on to Neapolis. From there we traveled to Philippi, a Roman colony and the leading city of that district of Macedonia. And we stayed there several days.

From the port city of Troas the evangelists put out to sea and sailed a straight course to Samothrace, which was a small island in the northern part of the Aegean Sea. The next day, the group went on to Neapolis, which was a seaport on the southern coast of Macedonia about 10 miles from Philippi (Acts 16:11). The latter is the city where Paul and his companions remained for several days (vs. 12). Luke may have been a resident of Philippi, for he apparently stayed there when Paul left and did not rejoin the group again until the apostle revisited the city on his third missionary journey (20:5-15).

Philippi was founded in 356 B.C. by Philip II of Macedonia, the father of Alexander the Great, and named for him. The city became a Roman possession in the second century B.C. In the time of Paul, Philippi was a Roman colony and a leading city in the eastern portion of Macedonia. This meant Philippi was responsible directly to the government in Rome, not the administration of the province. The city's people, though living away from Rome, had all the rights of Roman citizenship.

B. Bearing Spiritual Fruit: vss. 13-15

On the Sabbath we went outside the city gate to the river, where we expected to find a place of prayer. We sat down and began to speak to the women who had gathered there. One of those listening was a woman named Lydia, a dealer in purple cloth from the city of Thyatira, who was a worshiper of God. The Lord opened her heart to respond to Paul's message. When she and the members of her household were baptized, she invited us to her home. "If you consider me a believer in the Lord," she said, "come and stay at my house." And she persuaded us.

There evidently were not enough Jews in Philippi to formally establish a synagogue. (Ten men would have been required to have one.) Thus on the Sabbath, the Jewish residents merely met for prayer outside the city gates by the banks of the Gangites River. Paul and his companions joined the ones who had gathered to pray (apparently all women) and began to share the Gospel with them (Acts 16:13).

Although a man in a vision had summoned Paul into Europe, the first recorded person to receive the Gospel in Europe was a woman. Her name was Lydia, and she was a businesswoman who sold purple cloth (vs. 14). These fabrics were in great demand because purple was used for the official togas in Rome and its colonies.

Most likely Lydia was single or widowed and wealthy. She had settled in Philippi to carry on her trade. Her native home was some 600 miles away in Thyatira. This city was located in the district of Lydia, a region in western Asia Minor. The city had long been a center for the production of expensive purple dyes.

Lydia was also a worshiper of God. This means she was a Gentile who venerated the Lord of Israel and heeded the moral teachings of the law; however, she had not become a full proselyte to Judaism.

As Paul made clear elsewhere, gender is no barrier to the spread of the Gospel (Gal. 3:28). While Lydia listened, the Lord enabled her to understand and believe what the apostle had been saying. Later Lydia and her household were baptized (Acts 16:15).

The Bible presents people as sinners who do not naturally seek God (Rom. 3:11); yet all people are invited to believe in Christ (John 3:16-18). For a person to do that, God must take the initiative to save him or her (1 John 4:19). Even today the Spirit works in every person who receives Christ, inclining the individual to believe what is read or heard about Him.

Lydia's faith in and devotion to the Lord quickly blossomed. It must have outshined her success in sales. That Lydia was successful is evident by her sizable house in Philippi, which could accommodate not only her household (probably relatives, servants, and dependents) but also several traveling missionaries.

Lydia's newfound faith expressed itself in generous hospitality toward Paul and his group, a hospitality that extended beyond this first visit (Acts 16:15, 40). Perhaps Lydia also wanted to give the missionaries a base of operations from which they could rest and plan what they wanted to do next.

Discussion Questions

1. What prevented the missionaries from proclaiming the Gospel in the Roman province of Asia?
2. In what ways do you think the Spirit directed the steps of Jesus' evangelists?
3. What was the reason for Paul and his traveling companions spending time in the city of Philippi?
4. What was Lydia's response to the proclamation of the Gospel?
5. Why do you think Lydia wanted to be so hospitable to the missionaries?

Contemporary Application

C.T. Studd was a missionary in China. After he spoke about Jesus on one occasion, a Chinese man responded, "I am a murderer, an adulterer, and a confirmed opium smoker. He cannot possibly save me." The words of this man did not deter Studd from pressing home the truth. As a result, the Chinese man repented and was saved.

The Chinese convert returned to his hometown and shared what had happened to him. Instead of rejoicing, the local council ordered him whipped several times with bamboo. After he recovered from his critical condition, he returned and preached in the same place. The council put him in jail, but the gaps in the walls afforded space for groups to gather and hear him. He would not be deterred from sharing the Good News.

Since the council decided the man would cause less commotion by being released from prison, he was discharged. The Chinese convert kept telling what Jesus had done for him.

We all encounter situations that could frustrate our efforts to spread the Gospel. Like the Chinese convert, we should not let the problems we face derail us from the supreme goal of telling others about Jesus. God can enable us to triumph over our times of difficulty and to remain undeterred in our efforts to share the Good News with the lost.

What situations could test our resolve to be undeterred? We might encounter rejection from our peers, harassment from local authorities, and even public protests. We could face ridicule from those who consider the Gospel to be a myth or fable. We might encounter jealousy, antipathy, or power struggles within our faith community.

We might face racial, social, and economic challenges when presenting the Gospel in our society. Perhaps one of the toughest issues to deal with is the tendency to stereotype nonbelievers, particularly when we encounter people who come from another geographic location or a different set of circumstances. Thankfully, none of these situations are too big for God to handle.

Priscilla and Aquila: Team Ministry

Scripture
Background Scripture: *Acts 18:1—19:10*
Scripture Lesson: *Acts 18:1-4, 18-21, 24-28*
Key Verse: *Because [Paul] was a tentmaker as [Aquila and
Priscilla] were, he stayed and worked with them.* Acts 18:3.
Scripture Lesson for Children: *Acts 18:1-3, 18-21, 24-26*
Key Verse for Children: *Because [Paul] was a tentmaker as
[Aquila and Priscilla] were, he stayed and worked with them.*
Acts 18:3.

Lesson Aim
To encourage students to evaluate the ministries they
are or could participate in.

Lesson Setting
Time: A.D. *51–53*
Places: *Athens, Corinth, Cenchrea, Ephesus, Jerusalem,
Caesarea, Syrian Antioch, Galatia, Phrygia, and Achaia*

Lesson Outline
Priscilla and Aquila: Team Ministry
   I. Joint Ministry in Corinth: Acts 18:1-4
       A. *From Athens to Corinth: vs. 1*
       B. *Tentmaking with Priscilla and Aquila: vss. 2-3*
       C. *Reasoning in the Synagogues: vs. 4*
   II. Joint Ministry in Ephesus: Acts 18:18-21
       A. *Arriving at Ephesus: vss. 18-19*
       B. *Returning to Jerusalem: vss. 20-21*
   III. Team Ministry to Apollos: Acts 18:24-28
       A. *The Limited Understanding of Apollos: vss. 24-25*
       B. *The Teaching Ministry of Priscilla and Aquila:
          vs. 26*
       C. *The Ongoing Ministry of Apollos: vss. 27-28*

Introduction for Adults

Topic: *Working Together in Ministry*

One of the tragedies in the paradigm of the Christian church over the centuries has been (and continues to be) its overemphasis on the distinctions between laity and clergy. In Martin Luther's day it had gotten so far out of hand that the common people felt incapable of approaching God, except through the offerings of the priest, who would mediate for them.

Today, there seems to be a fresh rekindling of the passions of all Christians to do the work of the Lord. Believers everywhere—like the students in your class— are realizing that the work of the ministry is not just done behind pulpits or in church buildings. The saints are rejoicing that—as Jesus often proclaimed—the world is the field and they are the laborers.

Introduction for Youth

Topic: *Team Players*

In the Book of Acts, Luke did not give all the details of how the followers of Jesus were team players in ministry. But it is probably safe to assume that the church members prayed zealously for their fellow believers who traveled about heralding the Good News of Christ.

By being involved in missionary work, your students are able to stay in touch with the missionary heart of God. The class members are also able to demonstrate that they are committed to the spiritual redemption of the lost. By participating in efforts to take the Gospel to unsaved people in various parts of the world, your students remain balanced in their focus. They recognize the dual importance of reaching the lost and of spiritually strengthening one another.

Concepts for Children

Topic: *T.E.A.M. (Together Everyone Accomplishes More)*

1. A church leader named Paul left the city of Athens and traveled to another city named Corinth.
2. While in Corinth, Paul met a married couple named Priscilla and Aquila, both of whom were followers of Jesus.
3. After some time had passed, Paul left Corinth and returned to the city of Antioch in a place called Syria.
4. Meanwhile, Priscilla and Aquila had gone to the city of Ephesus, where they met a believer named Apollos and whom they helped to understand more clearly the truth about Jesus.
5. Those who know the Word of God are obligated to share it with others.

Lesson Commentary

I. JOINT MINISTRY IN CORINTH: ACTS 18:1-4

A. From Athens to Corinth: vs. 1

After this, Paul left Athens and went to Corinth.

After Paul's ministry in Philippi, he and his companions went on to Thessalonica and Berea (Acts 17:1-15). The apostle then journeyed alone to Athens, where he first preached at the local marketplace; and it was there that Paul gained an invitation to present his views to the Areopagus, Athen's chief council (vss. 16-21).

Before this dignified gathering, the apostle proclaimed the true God, who far exceeded the bounds of the Greeks' prevailing religious views; however, when Paul mentioned the Resurrection, his listeners began to dispute. Only a few Athenians were converted (vss. 22-34). Thankfully, Paul did not quit. In the face of possible discouragement, he went on to the next place, where greater things awaited him.

It was the middle of the first century A.D. when Paul traveled from Athens to Corinth—about a 50-mile trek (Acts 18:1). If Athens was the center of Greek culture, Corinth was the locus of Greek commerce. It was many times larger than Athens, probably exceeding 600,000 inhabitants.

The Romans destroyed Corinth in 146 B.C., and the city remained in ruins for the next century. In 46 B.C., Julius Caesar rebuilt the city at a location more accessible to the sea. Because Corinth was situated on a narrow strip of land between the Aegean Sea and the Adriatic Sea, it became a major port. Furthermore, all land trade in Greece from north to south passed through Corinth. The city was also famous for its rampant immorality. For instance, the temple of Aphrodite at one time had 1,000 prostitutes.

B. Tentmaking with Priscilla and Aquila: vss. 2-3

There he met a Jew named Aquila, a native of Pontus, who had recently come from Italy with his wife Priscilla, because Claudius had ordered all the Jews to leave Rome. Paul went to see them, and because he was a tentmaker as they were, he stayed and worked with them.

Paul came to Corinth to preach the Gospel; and it was there that the apostle met Aquila, a Jewish man originally from Pontus (a Roman province south of the Black Sea in Asia Minor). Aquila and his wife, Priscilla, had traveled to Corinth from Italy because Emperor Claudius had ordered the Jewish people to leave Rome (Acts 18:2). The emperor had issued this edict about A.D. 50 to maintain public order. Evidently the proclamation of the Gospel had caused an uproar among the Jewish residents of Rome.

The apostle Paul may have met Priscilla and Aquila in the local synagogue at Corinth. The couple soon became friends with the evangelist, no doubt because of their common vocation as tentmakers and their Jewish heritage, which dovetailed into their Christian faith. The devout couple were people of generosity and wealth. They not only agreed to let this Jewish missionary work with them in their business, but also invited him to stay in their home (vs. 3).

Since people in Bible times widely used tents, there was a great demand for tentmakers. Nomadic and seminomadic peoples such as Abraham's clan used large, heavy tents as their primary dwelling; and many travelers used less bulky tents on their journeys.

In New Testament times, Jewish fathers would teach their sons a trade. While Joseph taught Jesus the carpentry profession, Paul's father evidently taught him tentmaking skills. Presumably Paul learned how to tan animal hides for making leather tents. He may have also learned how to prepare rough goat's hair for use as tent material. As he assembled tents, he would have sewn together the proper lengths of cloth and attached loops and ropes.

C. Reasoning in the Synagogues: vs. 4

Every Sabbath he reasoned in the synagogue, trying to persuade Jews and Greeks.

Because Paul ministered in cities where there were no churches to pay him a salary, he had to support himself while preaching the Gospel. He evidently worked during the week to earn his living. Then on the Sabbath at the synagogue he spoke and debated with Jews and Greeks in an effort to persuade them about Christ (Acts 18:4).

A synagogue was a place for Jewish prayer and worship, with recognized leadership (see Luke 8:41). Though the origin of the synagogue is not entirely clear, it seems to have arisen in the post-exilic community during the intertestamental period. A town could establish a synagogue if there were at least 10 men. In normative Judaism of the New Testament period, the Hebrew sacred writings were read and discussed in the synagogue by the men who were present.

After a time, Silas and Timothy rejoined Paul. They apparently had been with him for a while in Athens, and then had been sent away again by the apostle (1 Thess. 3:1); but now they rejoined him. With the assistance they provided, Paul was able to quit his tentmaking and devote himself full-time to preaching (Acts 18:5).

Paul's ministry in Corinth took on the typical pattern, and it was not long before Jewish opposition became abusive. Despite this, many Corinthians became believers. Most of these converts, no doubt, were Gentiles; but the ruler of the synagogue, Crispus, and his household also joined the church (see 1 Cor. 1:14).

II. JOINT MINISTRY IN EPHESUS: ACTS 18:18-21

A. Arriving at Ephesus: vss. 18-19

Paul stayed on in Corinth for some time. Then he left the brothers and sailed for Syria, accompanied by Priscilla and Aquila. Before he sailed, he had his hair cut off at Cenchrea because of a vow he had taken. They arrived at Ephesus, where Paul left Priscilla and Aquila. He himself went into the synagogue and reasoned with the Jews.

After having success with Jews and Gentiles, Paul saw a vision telling him that he should not fear. This encouraged him to weather an incident in which some opponents brought a lawsuit against the apostle; thankfully, the case was thrown out (Acts 18:9-17).

For a year and a half Paul taught God's message to the people (vss. 5, 11). When the apostle's ministry in Corinth came to an end, he left the followers of the Lord in the city and sailed for Syria with Priscilla and Aquila (vs. 18). Since Luke often listed Priscilla before her husband, Bible scholars think she either came from a higher social class or played a more prominent role than Aquila in their joint ministry in the Gospel.

Before Paul set sail, he had his head shaved at Cenchrea (the eastern port of Corinth) because he had made a Nazarite vow. It is not exactly clear why the apostle made this pledge to God. Having his hair cut indicated the conclusion of the vow and perhaps represented an expression of gratitude to God (Num. 6:18; Acts 21:24). Since the vow had to be fulfilled in Jerusalem, Paul would travel there to present his hair to the Lord and offer sacrifices in the temple.

When the three of them arrived in Ephesus (the leading city of Asia Minor), Paul left Priscilla and Aquila there. Before sailing on to Caesarea, however, the apostle spent some time reasoning with the Jews in the synagogue (Acts 18:19).

B. Returning to Jerusalem: vss. 20-21

When they asked him to spend more time with them, he declined. But as he left, he promised, "I will come back if it is God's will." Then he set sail from Ephesus.

Those attending the synagogue at Ephesus invited Paul to stay longer, but he declined the offer (Acts 18:20). He wanted to reach Jerusalem for the festival season before the seas became impassable during the winter. Before leaving, though, the apostle pledged that he would return to Ephesus, if the Lord permitted (vs. 21).

Paul's second missionary journey ended with him reaching his home church in Syrian Antioch, which was due north of Jerusalem (vs. 22). After spending some time there, the apostle left for the region of Galatia and Phrygia to begin his third evangelistic tour (vs. 23). His intent was to strengthen "all the disciples."

III. TEAM MINISTRY TO APOLLOS: ACTS 18:24-28

A. The Limited Understanding of Apollos: vss. 24-25

Meanwhile a Jew named Apollos, a native of Alexandria, came to Ephesus. He was a learned man, with a thorough knowledge of the Scriptures. He had been instructed in the way of the Lord, and he spoke with great fervor and taught about Jesus accurately, though he knew only the baptism of John.

During this time, a Jewish man named Apollos came to Ephesus (Acts 18:24). He had been in Alexandria, Egypt, a major city of the Roman Empire. Alexandria was a literary and scientific center for Greek culture. Its university atmosphere included an extensive library and many scholars.

A Greek style of learning influenced the large Jewish community in Alexandria. Alexandrian Jews translated the Old Testament into Greek and developed allegorical methods of studying Scripture, looking for deeper interpretations beneath its history, poetry, and law. Apollos may have used allegorical methods in his interpretation of the Bible.

Apollos was well educated, thoroughly familiar with the Hebrew Scriptures, and eloquent in speech. He had a basic knowledge of the Christian faith and was filled with zeal and conviction as he taught. Although the truths Apollos proclaimed about Jesus were correct, they were only partial, for all he knew was John's message about baptism (vs. 25). Apollos evidently understood the importance of repentance and that the Messiah was coming; however, he may not have known about the finished work of Christ on the cross. Probably Apollos had not heard about a number of other important Christian truths as well.

B. The Teaching Ministry of Priscilla and Aquila: vs. 26

He began to speak boldly in the synagogue. When Priscilla and Aquila heard him, they invited him to their home and explained to him the way of God more adequately.

Apollos started speaking bravely in the local synagogue at Ephesus. That is where Priscilla and Aquila met him. Perhaps recognizing the significant potential Apollos had for ministry, this couple invited him into their home and helped him understand the Christian faith better (Acts 18:26). Their timely instruction helped Apollos become more effective in his proclamation of the Gospel.

God's purposes are often accompanied by the coordinated efforts of many willing disciples. Apollos taught what he knew; and Priscilla and Aquila contributed their part to strengthen his ministry. We all have a role to play. Even without public speaking abilities, we can still do something valuable and important.

C. The Ongoing Ministry of Apollos: vss. 27-28

When Apollos wanted to go to Achaia, the brothers encouraged him and wrote to the disciples there to welcome him. On arriving, he was a great help to those who by grace had believed. For he vigorously refuted the Jews in public debate, proving from the Scriptures that Jesus was the Christ.

Apollos desired to cross over to Achaia. This region was organized by the Romans as a separate province in 27 B.C. and was located across the Aegean Sea from Ephesus. The city of Corinth was in Achaia.

The believers in Ephesus encouraged Apollos in his plans. They even wrote a letter of commendation to the Christians in Achaia in which the latter were asked to welcome Apollos. Upon his arrival in Achaia, Apollos proved himself to be a great asset (Acts 18:27). In public debate, he used convincing arguments to refute his Jewish opponents. Apollos demonstrated from the Old Testament that Jesus is the Messiah (vs. 28).

Discussion Questions

1. Why did Aquila and Priscilla leave Rome and travel to Corinth?
2. In what way did Paul and Aquila and Priscilla work together?
3. Why did Paul cut his hair at Cenchrea?
4. How much understanding did Apollos initially have about Christianity?
5. How did Aquila and Priscilla remedy the lack of awareness that Apollos had regarding the faith?

Contemporary Application

Because most of us lead busy, hectic lives, it is hard for us to find the time to participate in one or more Christian ministries. No doubt Priscilla and Aquila were busy people too. They had a thriving tentmaking business and they evidently did a fair amount of traveling.

Despite their busy schedule, this godly couple made themselves available for ministry. We do not know whether they were incredibly talented or gifted; but we do know they took their God-given abilities and used them for Christ's glory.

By making ourselves available for ministry, we can significantly impact the lives of others. Such a commitment might mean saying no to some other things in our lives. Admittedly, it can be a difficult process deciding what ministries we should commit ourselves to and whether we have assumed too little or too much responsibility. With the Lord's help and the wise counsel of others, we will be able to figure out what He wants us to do.

Furthermore, regardless of the sacrifices and adjustments we have to make, they are worth it in order to minister to others. Through our willing spirit, God can accomplish much of eternal value. It is impossible to imagine how much good even our smallest efforts can make for the kingdom of God.

Paul's Farewell

DEVOTIONAL READING

Acts 20:31-35

DAILY BIBLE READINGS

Monday November 21
*Ruth 1:6-14 Naomi and
Ruth Part with Orpah*

Tuesday November 22
*1 Samuel 20:32-42 David
and Jonathan Part*

Wednesday November 23
*Acts 20:1-6 Paul Stops in
Greece and Macedonia*

Thursday November 24
*Acts 20:7-12 Paul's Farewell
Visit to Troas*

Friday November 25
*Acts 20:17-24 Paul Speaks
to the Ephesian Elders*

Saturday November 26
*Acts 20:25-31 Paul Warns
the Elders to Be Alert*

Sunday November 27
*Acts 20:32-38 Paul and the
Elders Say Goodbye*

Scripture

Background Scripture: *Acts 20:17-38*
Scripture Lesson: *Acts 20:17-28, 36-38*
Key Verse: "*Keep watch over yourselves and all the flock of
which the Holy Spirit has made you overseers.*" Acts 20:28.
Scripture Lesson for Children: *Acts 20:18-24, 35-38*
Key Verses for Children: *They all wept as they embraced
[Paul] and kissed him. What grieved them most was his state-
ment that they would never see his face again.* Acts 20:37-38.

Lesson Aim

To encourage the students to serve God with faith and
confidence even in the midst of difficulties.

Lesson Setting

Time: A.D. *57–58*
Places: *Miletus and Ephesus*

Lesson Outline

Paul's Farewell

    I. The Faithfulness of Paul: Acts 20:17-21
        A. *The Request for the Ephesian Elders: vs. 17*
        B. *The Endurance of Many Trials: vss. 18-19*
        C. *The Bold Declaration of the Truth: vss. 20-21*
   II. The Determination of Paul: Acts 20:22-28
        A. *The Certainty of Imprisonment and Hardship:
           vss. 22-24*
        B. *The Assurance of a Clear Conscience: vss. 25-27*
        C. *The Exhortation to Vigilance: vs. 28*
  III. The Farewell of Paul: Acts 20:36-38
        A. *A Time of Mutual Prayer: vs. 36*
        B. *An Emotional Send-off: vss. 37-38*

Introduction for Adults

Topic: *Saying Goodbye*

As adults get older, they increasingly experience a number of goodbyes. These might take the form of older relatives passing away, of children growing up and leaving the home, or of friends relocating to other distant places. With so many goodbyes having to be said, where can the adults in your class turn for stability?

The answer, of course, is the Lord Jesus. He is like a spiritual anchor who can keep a troubled soul firmly grounded in times of change. He is an ever-present source of reassurance when personal losses seem too overwhelming to handle. If any of your students are struggling with having to say goodbye, for whatever reason, encourage them to lean on the Lord Jesus, who is with them no matter where they are.

Introduction for Youth

Topic: *Sad Goodbyes*

Morris ("Morrie") Schwartz was born in Chicago of Russian Jewish immigrant parents and raised in New York. When Morrie was only eight years old, his mother died. Having to say goodbye to his mom was very emotionally difficult for Morrie.

Eventually Morrie's father remarried. Morrie's stepmother was nurturing and kind, so Morrie learned early about loss and vulnerability as well as kindness and mercy. These are themes of lifelong interest to him and he has written about them in a book titled *Morrie: In His Own Words*.

In 1995, Morrie passed away from the effects of Lou Gehrig's disease. But his reflections on calmness and compassion are helpful reminders for saved teens concerning how to handle personal losses in their lives. And Jesus can empower them to do so through the ministry of the Spirit and the Word.

Concepts for Children

Topic: *It's So Hard to Say Goodbye*

1. A church leader named Paul stopped for a brief while in a port city named Miletus so that he could meet with some other church leaders from a nearby town called Ephesus.
2. Paul told these church leaders that he never failed to do the Lord's work.
3. Paul also said that he was heading to a city named Jerusalem and that he did not know what would happen to him for telling people about Jesus.
4. As Paul made plans to leave, it was very hard for him and the other church leaders to say goodbye.
5. Even when we say goodbye to others, God never says goodbye to us, for He is always with us.

Lesson Commentary

I. THE FAITHFULNESS OF PAUL: ACTS 20:17-21

A. The Request for the Ephesian Elders: vs. 17

From Miletus, Paul sent to Ephesus for the elders of the church.

Throughout his missionary travels, Paul made many friends and enemies. The enemies were worth forgetting, but the friends were worth all the afflictions he suffered (see Acts 20:23). The apostle endeared himself quickly to the people he served; and in chapter 20 he conveyed his care and concern to one particular group, the Ephesian elders. The events of this week's lesson take place during Paul's third evangelistic tour (Acts 18:23—21:14) as he hurried himself to Jerusalem (21:15).

After his first visit to Philippi, Paul stopped there again on his third missionary journey (20:6), which had taken him back to the churches he had started in Asia Minor and Greece. Throughout Greece, he collected an offering for the suffering church in Jerusalem (1 Cor. 16:1-4). Now he was on his way to Jerusalem to deliver that offering.

Consequently, Paul was in a hurry to reach the holy city before Pentecost with the offering (Acts 20:16); and the apostle did not want to be slowed down by changing ships for a stop in Ephesus. Instead, he asked the elders from the Ephesian church to come to meet him in Miletus (vs. 17). This was a seaport on the western coast of Asia Minor (about 40 miles south of Ephesus) where boats would dock to load and unload cargo.

The Greek term rendered "elders" is borrowed from the Jewish synagogue. It referred to those who were held in respect as the leaders of a particular fellowship. In verse 28, the elders are called "overseers," which underscores their pastoral role of spiritually feeding and leading God's people.

B. The Endurance of Many Trials: vss. 18-19

When they arrived, he said to them: "You know how I lived the whole time I was with you, from the first day I came into the province of Asia. I served the Lord with great humility and with tears, although I was severely tested by the plots of the Jews."

Once the elders from Ephesus had arrived, Paul began his farewell message to them (Acts 20:18). He first targeted how he had lived with them from the first day he had set foot in the Roman province of Asia. During his third missionary journey, Paul spent most of his time in Ephesus, preaching and teaching there for over two years (19:8, 10; 20:31).

The apostle's ministry effectiveness caused a riot, started by the silversmiths of the town, who saw their business decline as people stopped buying silver images to take to the famous temple of the goddess Artemis (Diana) in the city (19:23-41). Christianity had become so widely accepted that it was damaging the local economy, which thrived on the worship of the image of the great temple.

Despite repeated trials and testings (especially due to the diabolical plots of

Jewish antagonists), Paul served the Lord with humility and tears (20:19). From this we see that the apostle was not some kind of missionary robot. Any perception of him as a staid scholar hunched over his letters needs to be dispelled.

Though Paul was singularly focused on his task (vs. 24), he had great feeling for the Lord (vs. 19) and for the people to whom he had been sent (vss. 36-38). Paul may have set his face like a flint on the mission constantly before him, but his heart was soft. He often conveyed to people his affection (see Phil. 1:3-7; 1 Thess. 2:11, 19; 3:9; 1 Tim. 1:2; Titus 1:4; Philem. 10-12), but he also furrowed his brow and tightened his gaze on occasion.

Paul conveyed his frustration with people when they departed in faith or practice from what they had been taught (1 Cor. 5:1-2; 2 Cor. 10; Gal. 1:6; 3:1; 4:12-16). He made his feelings known with regard to those who opposed him or caused trouble in the churches (Acts 18:6; Gal. 5:12; Phil. 3:2; 1 Tim. 4:2; 2 Tim. 4:14; Titus 1:10-16). Paul was not driven by his feelings (Phil. 1:15-18), but neither were his feelings absent from his purpose.

C. The Bold Declaration of the Truth: vss. 20-21

"You know that I have not hesitated to preach anything that would be helpful to you but have taught you publicly and from house to house. I have declared to both Jews and Greeks that they must turn to God in repentance and have faith in our Lord Jesus."

Paul declared that he did not hold back from proclaiming to the Ephesian elders anything that would be beneficial or helpful (Acts 20:20). This was crucial, for the city was rife with false teaching and ungodly practices, including those of exorcists (19:13-16), sorcerers (vss. 18-20), and devotees of Artemis (vss. 23-28).

The apostle was willing to teach publicly (or openly) and from house to house (which was more private). Regardless of the mode or method of instruction, Paul's singular goal was to testify to both Jews and Greeks about the necessity of them repenting from sin and turning to God. The apostle coupled such an emphasis with the need for all people to trust in Christ for salvation (20:21).

II. THE DETERMINATION OF PAUL: ACTS 20:22-28

A. The Certainty of Imprisonment and Hardship: vss. 22-24

"And now, compelled by the Spirit, I am going to Jerusalem, not knowing what will happen to me there. I only know that in every city the Holy Spirit warns me that prison and hardships are facing me. However, I consider my life worth nothing to me, if only I may finish the race and complete the task the Lord Jesus has given me—the task of testifying to the gospel of God's grace."

Paul related that he was bound by the Spirit to go to Jerusalem, even though the apostle was unclear about all that would happen to him there (Acts 20:22). This journey suggests a parallel between Paul and Jesus, since the Jerusalem journey motif figures so prominently in Luke's Gospel (9:51—19:44).

The apostle's inner compulsion was joined with an awareness from the Spirit that imprisonment and suffering awaited him (Acts 20:23). The Spirit had repeatedly made this clear to Paul (possibly through Christian prophets) as he journeyed from one city to the next. This sentiment also corresponds with the statement of the Lord Jesus recorded in 9:16. He intended to show the apostle how much he had to suffer for the Messiah.

Paul was undeterred by these dire prospects, for he did not consider his life worth anything apart from testifying to the good news of God's grace (20:24). The apostle was fully committed to this task, which the Lord Jesus had assigned to him. Like a champion athlete who ran a race, Paul likened his efforts to straining to reach the finish line so that he might receive his eternal reward for faithful service to Christ (Phil. 3:13).

Although Paul carried out his task undeterred, he still felt enormous pressures. His travels through the Roman province of Asia had been particularly trying; and yet, for Paul, the proclamation of the Gospel was all-consuming. He wanted to finish his assignment, no matter what happened to him.

B. The Assurance of a Clear Conscience: vss. 25-27

"Now I know that none of you among whom I have gone about preaching the kingdom will ever see me again. Therefore, I declare to you today that I am innocent of the blood of all men. For I have not hesitated to proclaim to you the whole will of God."

Paul was convinced that the Ephesian elders, who were the recipients of his preaching about the kingdom, would never see him again (Acts 20:25). Paul's usage of the expression "preaching the kingdom" is associated and intertwined with his testifying to the good news of God's grace. From this we see that, for Paul, the two concepts were interrelated.

The apostle's Jewish opponents had been unrelenting in their attack on the Gospel he proclaimed. They maintained that full acceptance with God required adherence to the Jewish law and rituals. Paul declared to the Ephesian elders that he had been faithful in renouncing this heretical teaching, especially as he affirmed the gospel of God's grace.

Moreover, the apostle maintained that he was innocent of "the blood of all men" (vs. 26). This idiomatic expression might be paraphrased, "if any of you should be lost, I am not responsible." Paul had a clear conscience, because he had faithfully carried out his responsibility of announcing to the Ephesians the whole purpose or plan of God (vs. 27).

C. The Exhortation to Vigilance: vs. 28

"Keep watch over yourselves and all the flock of which the Holy Spirit has made you overseers. Be shepherds of the church of God, which he bought with his own blood."

Paul completed his responsibility by warning the Ephesians to be on guard for themselves and for the flock of believers the Spirit had assigned to their care. The elders were to oversee and shepherd their local congregation. This group was part of God's church, which His Son obtained or acquired with His own blood (Acts 20:28). This is one of only two explicit statements in Luke-Acts highlighting the substitutionary nature of Christ's death. The other is in Luke 22:19.

Scripture depicts elders as under-shepherds of Christ, the Chief Shepherd (John 10:11, 14; 1 Pet. 5:4). While the apostles and prophets laid the doctrinal foundation upon which the church is built, with Christ being the foundation's cornerstone (Eph. 2:19-22), the task of teaching and preserving that doctrine was entrusted to elders. Thus, in a sense, a congregation's overseers are its doctrinal guides and guardians.

Paul's exhortation was made against the backdrop of spiritual predators infiltrating the Ephesian congregation (Acts 20:29). Even some from within the church would use distortions of the truth to mislead believers (vs. 30). Paul's life and ministry in Ephesus was to serve as an example of the importance of remaining vigilant as a church leader (vs. 31).

III. THE FAREWELL OF PAUL: ACTS 20:36-38

A. A Time of Mutual Prayer: vs. 36

When he had said this, he knelt down with all of them and prayed.

After entrusting the Ephesian elders and congregation to God and His gospel of grace (Acts 20:32), Paul knelt down and prayed with the church leaders (vs. 36). He was confident that during his time of ministry, he had conducted himself among his peers with humility and generosity (vss. 33-35).

B. An Emotional Send-off: vss. 37-38

They all wept as they embraced him and kissed him. What grieved them most was his statement that they would never see his face again. Then they accompanied him to the ship.

As the elders embraced and kissed Paul, they all wept loudly (Acts 20:37). Their actions were a sign of affection. The entire scene shows how much interrelationship Paul had in his two-plus years of ministry and how much he and the Ephesians meant to each other.

Especially distressing to the elders was the possibility of never seeing Paul again (vs. 38). An examination of 2 Timothy 4:9-13 suggests that Paul was able to return to Ephesus at a later date. In any case, the elders accompanied the apostle (and his traveling companions) down to the ship that would take him from Miletus to Jerusalem.

Discussion Questions

1. What characterized Paul's service among the Ephesian believers?
2. What was the heart of the message Paul proclaimed in Ephesus?
3. Why did Paul suspect he might not ever see the Ephesian believers again?
4. What threats faced the believers in the Ephesian church?

5. How can God's grace enable you to remain faithful to Him despite trials you might face?

Contemporary Application

This week's lesson stresses that a clear and guarded Gospel is vital to the health of the church. The Gospel must remain an undiluted message of salvation by grace through faith and must be guarded from convolutions.

The task of clearly "testifying to the gospel of God's grace" (Acts 20:24) belonged first to the apostles like Paul and then was passed on to the church's elders. Just as in a relay race a baton is passed from one runner to another, so too the apostles passed the shepherding task of believers on to the elders, the "shepherds of the church" (vs. 28). They were charged to guard the church, to "keep watch" over it. Congregational leaders share the same mandate today and seek to remain as faithful to it as Paul was in his day.

There are two additional facts about the apostle that rise to surface in this week's lesson; and they apply to all of us as believers, regardless of whether we shoulder church leadership responsibilities. First, Paul always saw himself as a servant of the church, not its boss. Second, he resolutely taught the necessity of turning from sin and turning to God in faith. In the apostle's mind, experiencing God's grace was the only way for Christians to survive and grow spiritually.

Paul's warning to the Ephesian elders is a sobering reminder that the church faces attacks from those inside and outside the fellowship. This should not shock us. After all, spiritual wolves love sin, hate God, and reject Christ. They will do anything to destroy the work of God among His people. God alone has the power to rescue us from dire circumstances, uphold us in our darkest moments, strengthen us to live in a godly manner, and enable us to be fruitful in our ministries.

God's Commitment—Our Response

Justice for All

Scripture

Background Scripture: *Isaiah 41—42*
Scripture Lesson: *Isaiah 42:1-8*
Key Verse: *"I, the LORD, have called you in righteousness; I
will take hold of your hand. I will keep you and will make you
to be a covenant for the people and a light for the Gentiles."*
Isaiah 42:6.
Scripture Lesson for Children: *Isaiah 40:3; Luke 1:13-24*
Key Verse for Children: *"Zechariah . . . your wife Elizabeth
will bear you a son, and you are to give him the name John."*
Luke 1:13.

Lesson Aim

To encourage the students to be gentle and fair as they
minister to others.

Lesson Setting

Time: *740–700 B.C.*
Place: *Judah*

Lesson Outline

Justice for All

  I. The Servant's Mission: Isaiah 42:1-4
      A. *To Bring Justice: vs. 1*
      B. *To Bring Peace and Healing: vss. 2-3*
      C. *To Establish Truth and Righteousness: vs. 4*
  II. The Servant's Call: Isaiah 42:5-8
      A. *God the Creator: vs. 5*
      B. *God's Care of His Servant: vs. 6*
      C. *God's Intention for His Servant: vs. 7*
      D. *God's Integrity: vs. 8*

Introduction for Adults

Topic: *Serving Others*

Adults often feel that what they do or can do to serve the Lord and others is unimportant. Since they aren't leaders or doing something that radically impacts the culture in which we live, they reason that their ministry or possible ministry isn't significant.

Bill Bennett, however, writes that in our effort to impact our culture and society, what really matters is "what we do in our daily lives—not the big statements that we broadcast to the world at large, but the small messages we send through our families and our neighborhoods and our communities." This week's lesson assures us that God seeks to sustain us in the ministry to which He has called us. God will never call us where His grace will not sustain us.

Introduction for Youth

Topic: *God's Servant Messiah*

One day a man was hauled into court because he had stolen a loaf of bread. When the judge investigated the matter, he discovered that the man was unemployed and could not find work. In desperation to feed his family, the man had decided to steal a loaf of bread.

During the court proceedings, the judge said to the man, "I'm sorry I have to punish you. I have to assess a fine of 10 dollars. But I want to pay the money myself." He reached into his pocket, pulled out a 10-dollar bill, and handed it to the man. As soon as the man took the money, the judge said, "Now I also want to remit the fine." This meant the man could keep the money. "Furthermore, I instruct the bailiff to pass around a hat to everyone in this courtroom, and I fine all who are assembled here 50 cents for living in a city where a man has to steal in order to have bread to eat." After the money was collected, the judge gave it to the man.

Like the judge, God's Servant, who is our Messiah, diligently pursued His mission with unparalleled mercy.

Concepts for Children

Topic: *An Angel Visits Zechariah*

1. An angel named Gabriel told an elderly couple named Zechariah and Elizabeth that the wife would give birth to a son.
2. The son's name would be John and he would show his devotion to God by telling others about the coming of the Messiah.
3. Because Zechariah doubted the angel's promise, Zechariah lost the ability to speak until his son was born.
4. Everything that the angel had promised came to pass.
5. God gives us opportunities to prove our faithfulness and obedience.

Lesson Commentary

I. THE SERVANT'S MISSION: ISAIAH 42:1-4

A. To Bring Justice: vs. 1

"Here is my servant, whom I uphold, my chosen one in whom I delight; I will put my Spirit on him and he will bring justice to the nations."

Throughout his long ministry, Isaiah preached about God's righteousness, warned about judgment for sin, and proclaimed the Lord's love and forgiveness. Isaiah also prophesied the glory that awaits those who remain faithful to God. Beyond that, the Book of Isaiah contains more prophecies about the Messiah, Jesus, than any other portion of the Old Testament. In fact, Isaiah saw Jesus' "glory and spoke about him" (John 12:41). We can appreciate why, among Christians, the Book of Isaiah is one of the best-loved portions of the Old Testament.

In terms of orienting ourselves to this week's Scripture portion, it's helpful to note the connection between Isaiah 42:1-8 and chapters 40 and 41. These portions of Isaiah are filled with majestic themes and memorable verses rich with prophecy. It all could have seemed overwhelming to God's people. Chapters 40 and 41 reassured them that, regardless of the turbulent political atmosphere and the terrible afflictions to come, their nation was firmly in God's hands.

The hardships the Israelites experienced were due in part to their worship of idols, a sordid matter that plagued them for many years. In chapter 41, we find that God had summoned idolaters to His court, where He made His case against them (vss. 1-7). God emphasized to them that He alone is in control of human history. Indeed, He would be the one to raise up a ruler named Cyrus, who would liberate the Jews from Babylon.

Then, in verses 8-20, God's people were encouraged by promises for the future. These promises include protection, deliverance from enemies, and blessing upon the land. In verses 21-29, we find God summoning the idols themselves and demanding that they interpret, predict, or act in history. Of course, they could do none of these things, but God was raising up a deliverer and had predicted this beforehand by Isaiah.

In 42:1, the Lord directed His people to focus their attention on His true Servant. Some think this is a reference to the nation of Israel. It is best to see God speaking partly about His servant Israel, but mainly about Jesus Christ. Israel, as the servant of the Lord, was supposed to bring a knowledge of God to the world (Deut. 4:6); but where the nation failed, the Messiah as the ideal Israel would succeed (Isa. 49:6). The nation was supposed to be a kingdom of priests (Exod. 19:6); but Jesus would be the High Priest who offered Himself as a sacrifice to redeem humanity from sin (Isa. 53:4-12; Heb. 8:1; 9:28).

The Messiah is the standard toward which every one of God's servants is to strive. God chose His Servant and upheld Him in all He would do. God was pleased with His Servant and empowered Him to take His Word to a world of unbelievers. God, through His Spirit, would also enable the Messiah to establish a righteous system of government among the nations.

B. To Bring Peace and Healing: vss. 2-3

"He will not shout or cry out, or raise his voice in the streets. A bruised reed he will not break, and a smoldering wick he will not snuff out. In faithfulness he will bring forth justice."

Isaiah contrasted the characteristics of God's Servant with the common expectations of servants and saviors alike. The prophet did so by describing how the Messiah would fulfill His call to ministry. First, He would not yell or talk loudly in public; that is, He would not call attention to Himself with a loud voice or flashy rhetoric; instead, He would humbly point people to God (Isa. 49:2).

Second, God's Servant would neither snap off a damaged reed nor snuff out a smoldering flax wick in a lamp; in other words, He would not harm people who were hurting or discouraged. Unlike the corrupt and selfish leaders of Israel, He would tenderly and mercifully heal broken lives.

Third, God's Servant would remain loyal and undeterred in establishing justice on the earth (vs. 3). Mere mortals can easily falter, get discouraged, and give up pursuing their goals. But regardless of how difficult the Messiah's task might be, He would never falter or be crushed in His noble endeavor. He would continue to work until His task was successfully completed.

Many of us, at one time or another, feel as though our lives are in need of mending. Sometimes circumstances become too burdensome and they break us. How wonderful that we can bring all our needs to Christ, the divine Servant, who heals all our wounds and carries all our burdens!

Some scholars believe Isaiah 42:3 is an example of antenantiosis. This term refers to a figure of speech in which negative expressions are used to make a positive point. For example, when someone says of a person "he or she is no fool," the intended meaning is "he or she is very wise." Similarly, consider the first two portions of Isaiah 42:3, "A bruised reed he will not break, and a smoldering wick he will not snuff out." As an antenantiosis, this verse communicates the idea that the Servant would strengthen the bruised reed and rekindle the smoldering wick.

C. To Establish Truth and Righteousness: vs. 4

"He will not falter or be discouraged till he establishes justice on earth. In his law the islands will put their hope."

A fourth thing the Servant of God would do to fulfill His ministry involved bringing the law (or teaching) of the Lord to the Gentile nations, or "islands" (Isa. 42:4). ("Islands" was a word often used for any distant nation.) In a future day they would eagerly desire to learn the truth promulgated by the Servant. The ultimate mission of the Servant of God would not be completed until they had received the law of God.

II. THE SERVANT'S CALL: ISAIAH 42:5-8

A. God the Creator: vs. 5

"This is what God the LORD says—he who created the heavens and stretched them out, who spread out the earth and all that comes out of it, who gives breath to its people, and life to those who walk on it."

In Isaiah 42:5-7, God is no longer presenting His Servant; rather, He is speaking directly to His Servant, telling what He would enable the Servant to do. Verse 5, in particular, contains Isaiah's identification of the One who would be speaking to the Servant. (This identification lent weight to what God would say.) The speaker is the supreme Lord of Israel and the world. He created and sustains the heavens, the earth, and all the plant life on the globe. He gave breath and a living spirit to all the people of the earth.

B. God's Care of His Servant: vs. 6

"I, the LORD, have called you in righteousness; I will take hold of your hand. I will keep you and will make you to be a covenant for the people and a light for the Gentiles."

It was the Lord who chose and commissioned His Servant to fulfill a righteous mission; and God was absolutely just in picking this course of action (Isa. 42:6). The Lord pledged to sustain and protect His Servant in all phases of His ministry. For instance, the Messiah would be "a covenant for the people." This means the Servant would fulfill the Davidic covenant as King (9:6), and He would institute a new covenant by His death (Jer. 31:31-34).

The Savior would also be a "light for the Gentiles" (Isa. 42:6). Israel had originally been commissioned to be a light to the nations, but had failed in that mission. What Israel failed to accomplish, the divine Servant would achieve. The Messiah would be a source of truth and deliverance to Gentile believers. Thus through the Messiah the scope of God's revelation would widen from the Jews to the Gentiles.

C. God's Intention for His Servant: vs. 7

"To open eyes that are blind, to free captives from prison and to release from the dungeon those who sit in darkness."

God's Servant would give sight to the Jews and Gentiles who were spiritually blind. God's Servant would also liberate those who were in bondage to sin (Isa. 42:7). In ancient times prisons were known for their dampness and darkness. God's Servant would free those living in the dark prison of superstition, unbelief, and rebellion.

"To open eyes that are blind" and "to free captives from prison" refer to the salvation and healing that God would give to believing Jews and Gentiles alike. While these acts might not involve literally healing the blind or opening wide the doors of prisons, they would result in spiritual healing and liberation for all who would believe.

D. God's Integrity: vs. 8

"I am the LORD; that is my name! I will not give my glory to another or my praise to idols."

In Isaiah 42:8, God declared that His name is *Yahweh* (in Hebrew). The Lord did this to remind His people that He was eternal in His existence and dynamically involved in their lives. In effect, God was assuring the listeners of Isaiah's message that the Lord would be true to His promise of delivering them out of darkness.

God's own name, which reflected His character, would guarantee that He would remain utterly faithful to His word. As Yahweh, God is eternal, choosing His people and performing for them the act of redemption.

Throughout Israel's history, almighty God used people like King Cyrus of Persia to deliver them from bondage; nevertheless, the Lord pledged that He would never share His glory (or splendor) with anyone else. Likewise, He would not allow idols to take the praise that was rightfully His. There was no entity, whether real or imagined, that could steal His honor and power. Only He had the authority to relinquish it, which He refused to do.

The all-powerful and sovereign Lord remained intensely zealous for the devotion of His people. He would not permit anything to draw them away from Him. This same powerful God would succeed in delivering His people through the ministry of His Servant, the Messiah.

Discussion Questions

1. What was the mission of God's Servant?
2. How would the Messiah go about fulfilling this mission?
3. What type of character traits would the Redeemer of Israel need to fulfill such a mission?
4. In what way would the Servant be a covenant—or a contract—between God and His people?
5. Do you think Jesus fulfills this mission? In what way?

Contemporary Application

Michael and Janet are a husband and wife who are both fighting cancer. Michael is a seminary student studying for the ministry. He has bone cancer that has twice been in remission, only to come back stronger each time. Janet is a college instructor and girls' volleyball coach who suddenly discovered after two years of watching her husband battle his disease that she herself had a serious form of leukemia. They have shared a hospital room and chemotherapy sessions. I cannot imagine a worse situation.

Despite the tragedy, however, Michael and Janet are praising God for their lives together and for the work they feel God is even now calling them to do. Michael continues to devote as much time as possible to his ministerial studies; and Janet makes every effort to coach the girls' volleyball team. Although both have lost all of their hair and much of their energy, they have not lost their devotion to God's call on their lives.

Michael and Janet are not unique in their hardships. Many of us face crises that threaten to derail us from our ministries, perhaps that threaten our very lives. If the crisis is not an accident or disease, it could be the loss of income or the death of a loved one. Our afflictions remind us of our mortality and our need to completely depend on Jesus.

Just as the Savior has sustained Michael and Janet in the midst of their pain and uncertainty, so He is sufficient to help all of us diligently pursue our ministries here on earth. The great and awesome Servant, who created the universe and sustains everything in it, is able to uphold and empower us to do His will.

Strength for the Weary

Scripture

Background Scripture: *Isaiah 49—50*

Scripture Lesson: *Isaiah 49:5-6; 50:4-9*

Key Verse: *Because the Sovereign LORD helps me, I will not be disgraced. Therefore have I set my face like flint, and I know I will not be put to shame.* Isaiah 50:7.

Scripture Lesson for Children: *Isaiah 49:8; Luke 1:26-33*

Key Verse for Children: *The angel said to her, "Do not be afraid, Mary, you have found favor with God."* Luke 1:30.

Lesson Aim

To underscore the importance of seeking the Lord's help in times of trial.

Lesson Setting

Time: *740–700 B.C.*

Place: *Judah*

Lesson Outline

Strength for the Weary

    I. The Servant's Twofold Mission: Isaiah 49:5-6

        A. To the Tribes of Jacob: vs. 5

        B. To the Gentiles: vs. 6

    II. The Servant's Teachable Spirit: Isaiah 50:4-5

        A. An Instructed Tongue: vs. 4

        B. A Yielded Disposition: vs. 5

   III. The Servant's Trial of Shame: Isaiah 50:6-9

        A. A Willingness to Suffer: vs. 6

        B. An Assurance of Help: vss. 7-9

Introduction for Adults

Topic: *Strength from God*

What prevents some adults from having more perseverance and resolve? Children are usually much poorer at sticking with something than adults. They get bored easily and often leave things half done. They will quit when the going gets ugly. Sadly, some adults never grow out of that mindset.

The way for adults to remedy this problem is by refocusing their attention on God. As Isaiah 50:7 indicates, the all-powerful Lord is the source of the believer's strength. He is also our source of justice (vs. 8). And He is always on our side to uphold and vindicate us (vs. 9). Because our hope is in Him, we need never falter in our walk with Christ.

Introduction for Youth

Topic: *Power Aid*

Even saved teens can wane in their ability to serve the Lord with diligence. This is especially true in the midst of pain and uncertainty. But even when tragedy strikes, they need not despair. The great and awesome God, who created the universe and sustains everything in it, is able to uphold and empower believing adolescents to do His will.

God's constant presence gives your students the strength they need to live out His will for them despite their circumstances. And because of His strength, saved teens need not become overwhelmed by frustration, anger, or fear. Since they have God's power working through them, they need only surrender to His gentle, just Spirit.

Concepts for Children

Topic: *An Angel Visits Mary*

1. Six months after Elizabeth became pregnant, the Lord sent the angel Gabriel to a young woman named Mary.
2. Mary was living in a village called Nazareth in a region named Galilee, and she was engaged to a man named Joseph.
3. Mary was surprised when she learned from Gabriel that she would become pregnant and have a son, whom she would name Jesus.
4. Gabriel explained that the Holy Spirit would enable Mary to become pregnant and give birth to Jesus, the Savior of the world.
5. God always keeps His promises to us.

Lesson Commentary

I. THE SERVANT'S TWOFOLD MISSION: ISAIAH 49:5-6

A. To the Tribes of Jacob: vs. 5

And now the LORD says—he who formed me in the womb to be his servant to bring Jacob back to him and gather Israel to himself, for I am honored in the eyes of the LORD and my God has been my strength.

When Isaiah began his ministry in 740 B.C., the northern kingdom of Israel was near collapse due to political, spiritual, and military deterioration. Things were going from bad to worse. In 723 B.C., the weakened northern kingdom finally fell to the Assyrian Empire, which had been expanding steadily for the past century and a half.

The southern kingdom, Judah, was heading for a similar disastrous end. Under the leadership of wicked King Ahaz, Judah was ripe for a fall. The nation had become corrupt socially, politically, and religiously. It was during this time that Isaiah delivered his messages to the people of Judah.

Isaiah called Judah to repent of idolatry and moral degeneracy. But then, failing to turn the nation Godward, Isaiah informed the people of Judah that their rebellion would lead to captivity at the hands of the Babylonians. Isaiah also predicted that, following the captivity, God would restore His people. God's foretelling all this in advance (through Isaiah) was intended to highlight His sovereignty in contrast to the powerlessness of false gods.

An example of these grand themes can be found in Isaiah 42:10—48:22, which contains prophecies on various subjects. Condemnation of the people's sin is one issue; and the promise of liberation from exile is another; but perhaps the most common subject in these chapters is the contrast between the powerless idols of Babylon and the all-powerful God of Israel. This part of the book ends with a call to leave Babylon.

In chapter 49, the spotlight shifts to the commissioning of the Servant. This chapter has much in common with 40:1-11. The time of servitude has ended (40:2) and the time of favor has come (49:8). In each passage there is a leveling of desert barriers (40:3-5; 49:10-12), a note of consolation (40:1; 49:13), and the care of the shepherd (40:11; 49:9).

Because of God's blessing on the Servant (49:1-4), the latter was assured of unqualified success in His mission. Moreover, the Servant's effective ministry ensured that the salvation of Gentiles and the restoration of the Jewish nation were on the horizon. Isaiah therefore encouraged the downtrodden with the news of redemption.

Isaiah 49:5-6 reveals the twofold mission that God assigned to His Servant, whom He formed for that role before His earthly birth. First, the Servant was to reunite Israel with God. Like a shepherd rounding up a dispersed flock, the Servant was to call back these exiles, not merely from Babylon, but from sin and rebellion. While sin divides and disperses, God's Servant unites. Whatever Israel's outcome, the Messiah would be honored in God's sight and would be empowered by the Lord.

B. To the Gentiles: vs. 6

He says: "It is too small a thing for you to be my servant to restore the tribes of Jacob and bring back those of Israel I have kept. I will also make you a light for the Gentiles, that you may bring my salvation to the ends of the earth."

Restoring the Israelites was an important task; and yet so great was the Servant that it was too small a thing for Him (Isa. 49:6). The Servant's second—and even greater—mission was to become a light for the Gentiles and to proclaim salvation to all the nations. In this verse, "light" refers to the truth of God's salvation, which people could not appreciate because of the darkness of their sins (2 Cor. 4:3-4). Both God's light and salvation dispel evil (John 3:19-21).

All along, God's aim was to bless one nation (Israel—the descendants of Abraham, Isaac, and Jacob) so that He could bless all nations through them. That was both God's desire and the Servant's supreme duty: to declare God's glory to all the peoples of the earth so that they might be saved.

Jesus, of course, is the Servant who brings salvation to the nations, "a light for revelation to the Gentiles" (Luke 2:32). He declared God's glory and called all peoples to receive salvation. Because the Lord's Servant humbled Himself and was obedient even to the point of death, God exalted Him (Phil. 2:8-11).

New Testament teaching confirms other vital truths about Christ that are worth mentioning. Jesus not only saves us from our sins, but also delivers us from spiritual darkness. He breaks Satan's power over us. And His light shines in our hearts to enable us to know the glory of God (2 Cor. 4:6).

II. THE SERVANT'S TEACHABLE SPIRIT: ISAIAH 50:4-5

A. An Instructed Tongue: vs. 4

The Sovereign LORD has given me an instructed tongue, to know the word that sustains the weary. He wakens me morning by morning, wakens my ear to listen like one being taught.

In Isaiah 50, the prophet contrasted God's rebellious servant, Israel, with His obedient Servant, the Messiah. In verses 1-3 the argument is dominated by the metaphors of divorce and indebtedness. On the one hand, God was waiting for faithless Israel to return to Him. On the other hand, because of their sins, the people were responsible for their years of captivity and for their troubled relationship with the Lord. Unlike the nation, the Servant would be completely obedient to almighty God.

In verse 4, an individual began to speak in the first person singular. This indicates that a new entity was communicating—not the faithless servant Israel, but God's blameless Servant, the Messiah. The Lord's sovereignty was the basis for the Servant's confidence. Knowing that God is in control, that the Servant's accusers could do nothing apart from the Lord's permission, gave the Servant the courage to face the opposition and indignity He did not deserve.

Four times the Servant referred to the Creator as "the Sovereign LORD" (vss. 4-5, 7, 9). This repeated designation not only stresses the majesty of God but also validates the Servant's ministry because the Lord had ordained it and equipped Him to carry it out.

The sovereign Lord had given His Servant "an instructed tongue" (vs. 4). This is a reference to words of wisdom and it enabled the Servant to operate as the Lord's true spokesperson. The Servant not only had the ability to teach, but also to counsel and comfort the weak. The Messiah's instructed tongue would be able to pass along God's truth to those who would accept it. In fact, those who received the Word of God through His Servant would find rest for their souls.

B. A Yielded Disposition: vs. 5

The Sovereign LORD has opened my ears, and I have not been rebellious; I have not drawn back.

In Isaiah 50:5 we learn about the Servant's "opened . . . ears," a statement assuring that He would understand fully what God required of Him. We know from the Gospel accounts that Jesus gave His Father His undivided attention, which resulted in unconditional obedience. In fact, as Isaiah 50:4 reveals, the Servant was attentive to the sovereign Lord during the morning watch.

Not only did the Servant have the ability to teach and comfort, but He also had an ear to "listen like one being taught." The idea is that, unlike Israel, God's faithful Servant had a teachable spirit. This truth is reinforced in verse 5, which indicates that the Messiah was attentive to what the Lord wanted Him to learn. The reason is that He knew the knowledge of God to be a source of great happiness and joy, even during times of turmoil.

III. THE SERVANT'S TRIAL OF SHAME: ISAIAH 50:6-9

A. A Willingness to Suffer: vs. 6

I offered my back to those who beat me, my cheeks to those who pulled out my beard; I did not hide my face from mocking and spitting.

The Suffering Servant of Isaiah 50 is said to endure punishment that He does not deserve. In the ancient Near East, such included being stoned, beaten with rods or switches, and whipped with leather strips having pieces of metal or bone tied to the ends. Moreover, fallen kings were often paraded through the streets of their victorious opponents, pulled by a nose ring attached to a chain.

The severity of some forms of punishment depended upon the degree of humiliation that could be inflicted upon the recipient. One of the worst forms of disgrace a Jewish male could endure was to have his beard plucked from his face. Not only was this painful and bloody, but it also disfigured his physical appearance. To spit in a man's face was a second form of humiliation. The shame associated with these acts was often an effective deterrent against future offenses being committed. The Servant's dependence upon God was so strong that He could face these kinds of insults without attaching the assumed shame and disgrace (vs. 6).

B. An Assurance of Help: vss. 7-9

Because the Sovereign LORD helps me, I will not be disgraced. Therefore have I set my face like flint, and I know I will not be put to shame. He who vindicates me is near. Who then will bring charges against me? Let us face each other! Who is my accuser? Let him confront me! It is the Sovereign LORD who helps me. Who is he that will condemn me? They will all wear out like a garment; the moths will eat them up.

Isaiah 50:7 reveals that God—who had opened the ear of the Servant (see vs. 4)—helped Him. And unlike Israel, this Servant did not turn away from the Lord's instruction. His heart was obedient, not rebellious. Despite the anguish that was before Him, the faithful Servant of God did not turn and run.

A person who is being justly punished for a crime knows why he or she is suffering. The person who is innocent or being overpunished often becomes confused about why such suffering is being required of him or her. The Servant, however, knew that God would help Him and that He was suffering unjustly. He was confident that one day His innocence would be evident to all.

In the midst of His suffering, the Servant was resolute. Though He offered Himself to tormentors, He had set His face "like flint" (vs. 7). Flint is a dark, hard-grained silica rock that was often used for blades or tools during Old Testament times. Because of its hardness, flint could take a beating and remain relatively undamaged. The injury happening to the Servant on the outside did not alter the disposition of His heart. Though His experience was difficult and painful, the Lord would sustain His spirit during this ordeal.

In verse 8 the Servant declared that the Lord, His source of justice, was near. Thus, who would dare accuse the Servant of injustice or dispute His innocence? The Servant was so confident of His blamelessness that He challenged His detractors.

Though the Servant knew He might not receive earthly justice, He firmly believed the sovereign Lord would vindicate Him in front of His enemies on the day of judgment. All who dared to condemn the Servant would wear out like a garment, and a moth would eat away at them (vs. 9); in other words, when the perjury of the Servant's accusers was discovered, they would be destroyed.

Discussion Questions

1. What had the Lord commissioned His Servant to do?
2. What would the Servant be to the Gentiles?
3. What characterized the Servant's speech?
4. How did the Servant respond to the Lord's will for Him?
5. How could the Servant remain resolute in His God-given task?

Contemporary Application

The faithful Servant of this week's lesson is Jesus Christ. As Isaiah described in the Scripture text, Jesus is the one who remains attentive to God and ready to obey His Father in an instant. Jesus is also the one who comforts us with His words.

Many Christians find themselves in the middle of an intense trial and cannot understand why these anguishing times are happening to them. They forget that when believers faithfully do what God desires, they inevitably face opposition (see 1 John 3:13). If Jesus experienced intense opposition during His life, then those who follow Him must expect these kinds of trials as well.

Today many Christians are criticized and in some cases persecuted because of what they believe, but that is seldom the reason given. People with hard hearts find it difficult to be in the presence of believers because of what the latter stand for. If a Christian offers them a helping hand, these people often feel resentful. No matter how gracious, kind, or approachable believers might be, they may become the target of malicious insults and slander, and are excluded.

In the midst of His trial, the Servant was confident that the sovereign Lord would come to His rescue. Likewise, in the middle of a trial, believers can rest in the same confidence. They have the assurance of knowing that Lord unfailingly loves and watches over them.

Hope for Those Who Suffer

DEVOTIONAL READING

Romans 12:9-16

DAILY BIBLE READINGS

Monday December 12
Isaiah 52:13—53:3
Despised, Rejected, a Man of
Suffering

Tuesday December 13
Isaiah 53:4-12 He Bore the
Sins of Many

Wednesday December 14
Luke 1:5-17 John the
Baptist's Birth Foretold

Thursday December 15
Luke 1:26-38 The Birth of
Jesus Foretold

Friday December 16
Luke 1:39-45 Mary Visits
Elizabeth

Saturday December 17
Luke 1:46-55 Mary's Song
of Praise

Sunday December 18
Romans 5:1-11 Hope Comes
through Suffering

Scripture

Background Scripture: *Isaiah 53; Luke 1*
Scripture Lesson: *Isaiah 53:1-3; Luke 1:47-55*
Key Verse: "*His mercy extends to those who fear him, from*
generation to generation." Luke 1:50.
Scripture Lesson for Children: *Isaiah 52:7; Luke 1:46-55*
Key Verse for Children: *Mary said: "My soul glorifies the*
Lord." Luke 1:46.

Lesson Aim

To emphasize the value of glorifying the Lord and
rejoicing in Him.

Lesson Setting

Time: *740–700 B.C.; about 6–5 B.C.*
Place: *Judah and the hill country of Judea*

Lesson Outline

Hope for Those Who Suffer
   I. The Sorrow of the Lord's Servant: Isaiah 53:1-3
      A. *The Good News about Salvation: vs. 1*
      B. *The Humble Circumstances of the Messiah: vss. 2-3*
  II. The Mercy and Might of the Lord: Luke 1:47-50
      A. *The Response of Joy: vs. 47*
      B. *The Reason for Joy: vss. 48-50*
 III. The Faithfulness and Justice of the Lord:
      Luke 1:51-55
      A. *The Reversal for Fortunes: vss. 51-53*
      B. *The Divine Pledge to Be Merciful: vss. 54-55*

Introduction for Adults

Topic: *Hope for Those Who Suffer*

Every believer encounters challenges, frustrations, and opposition. These parts of maturing in Christ are like foothills that sometimes block the view of the lofty snowcapped peaks. But because the peaks are there, Christians, like a mountain hiker, can push onward and upward.

What is the highest peak of biblical hope? It is the return of Jesus and eternal life in His presence. That hope should lighten every step and quicken the heart of every believer. Because the Lord is the "God of hope" (Rom. 15:13), He is able to "fill you with all joy and peace as you trust in him, so that you may overflow with hope by the power of the Holy Spirit."

Introduction for Youth

Topic: *God Keeps Promises*

When Mary visited Elizabeth, she was met with words of praise for being chosen to be the mother of the Lord. In response, Mary proclaimed her own privileged role, then declared how her son Jesus would humble the proud and mighty while bringing mercy to God's people.

None of us can know exactly how Mary felt, but all of us can express a similar attitude toward God for faithfully keeping His promises. Put differently, as followers of Jesus Christ, we can gladly exalt the Father in our hearts and before others because He fulfills what He has pledged to do through His Son.

Concepts for Children

Topic: *Mary Sings Praise to God*

1. The news that Mary had received from the angel Gabriel as well as Mary's later visit to a relative named Elizabeth filled Mary with joy.
2. Mary especially rejoiced in the goodness that her God and Savior had shown to her.
3. Mary noted that the Lord had shown His favor on her, a poor young girl.
4. Mary praised God for remaining faithful to His promises to His people.
5. We can respond with joy and praise to God for all He has done for us.

Lesson Commentary

I. THE SORROW OF THE LORD'S SERVANT: ISAIAH 53:1-3

A. The Good News about Salvation: vs. 1

Who has believed our message and to whom has the arm of the LORD been revealed?

The Jews in the Exile, one and a half centuries after Isaiah, were hoping for a deliverer who would free them from bondage. They got one in Cyrus the Persian; but Isaiah looked further ahead to another Deliverer, the Messiah, who would free repentant sinners from judgment.

Three times previously Isaiah had spoken about the Servant of the Lord (Isa. 42:1-4; 49:1-7; 50:4-9). In 52:13—53:12, the prophet for a final time spoke explicitly about the Servant. In Isaiah's descriptions we find seemingly contradictory pictures. The Servant is both humiliated and glorious, both a sufferer and a conqueror. Who can combine the two roles?

Jesus Christ combines the roles. In His first coming, He died to redeem people from sin; but in His second coming, He will appear as King to establish justice forever. In 52:13, we are first told that the Servant would "act wisely," which is a sign of His obedience to the will of God. Also, the Servant would "be raised and lifted up and highly exalted." These are the very words Isaiah used to describe God in the temple vision of Isaiah 6. The Servant's exaltation would reach to the level of God Himself.

The keys to understanding 52:14-15 are the opening words of each verse: "Just as . . . so will." Just as one thing is true, so another thing will be true. The point of the comparison in these verses is this: Just as the Servant's suffering and humiliation would be appalling (vs. 14), so His glory and exaltation would be astonishing (vs. 15).

Moreover, Isaiah declared in verse 15 that the Servant of the Lord would sprinkle many nations as a symbol of their purification from sin (see Lev. 4:6). As a result of witnessing the Servant and His work, monarchs would be speechless with astonishment at how one who would suffer such humiliation would be so highly exalted. (Note that while Isaiah used the past tense in describing the Servant, the latter had not appeared in the prophet's time.)

In Isaiah 53:1, the speaker shifted from God to an unidentified group. The content of the speech suggests that the prophet spoke as a representative of the sinful nation Israel. Isaiah asked who among God's people had believed the message (or good news of salvation). The prophet also wondered to whom had the Lord's arm, or saving power, been revealed? Tragically, such things had gone largely unnoticed by the Jewish nation.

B. The Humble Circumstances of the Messiah: vss. 2-3

He grew up before him like a tender shoot, and like a root out of dry ground. He had no beauty or majesty to attract us to him, nothing in his appearance that we should desire him. He was despised and rejected by men, a man of sorrows, and familiar with suffering. Like one from whom men hide their faces he was despised, and we esteemed him not.

Isaiah next provided details of his message. He first described the Servant as One who would grow up before God as a "tender shoot" (Isa. 53:2) and a "root out of dry ground" (see 11:1). Despite the aridness and sterility of the soil, one tender green shoot (the Messiah) would sprout and thrive. These descriptions suggest that the Servant's origins would be both humble and miraculous.

Moreover, the Servant would not have the majesty and earthly grandeur one would normally expect of a king. He would appear ordinary or lowly. In fact, He would have no stately majesty or form to catch one's attention; also, there would be nothing special about His appearance to draw any followers. In the New Testament, Paul exhorted believers to imitate Christ's humility (see Phil. 2:1-4).

People, not recognizing the Servant's exalted nature, would despise and reject Him (Isa. 53:3). The Hebrew word rendered "despised" carries the idea of "treat with contempt." Tragically, the Servant would be disdained by the very people whom He came to save.

The Servant would be known for His sorrows, especially physical pain and emotional anguish. Despite His glorious heavenly status, people would reject Him and refuse to have anything to do with Him; and even though He was the Lord of humankind, they would scorn Him and treat Him as being insignificant. The Servant is comparable to a seriously ill person who is shunned by others because of his or her horrible disease.

Such suffering was commonly viewed as a sign of God's displeasure. It is thus understandable that people would assume that the Servant's woes were due to personal sin; but they would be mistaken. The Servant would suffer for the sins of others (vss. 4-6), not for His own, for He would have none (see 2 Cor. 5:21; Heb. 4:15; 7:26).

II. THE MERCY AND MIGHT OF THE LORD: LUKE 1:47-50

A. The Response of Joy: vs. 47

"And my spirit rejoices in God my Savior."

Long before Luke recorded the events of Jesus' birth, the Old Testament anticipated what the angel would tell Mary. The prophets pinpointed the place of the Messiah's birth (Mic. 5:2), and some commentators say even the time (Dan. 9:25) and the who—not Mary by name, but that the Redeemer would be born to a virgin (Isa. 7:14). Thus, Luke was careful in his Gospel to underscore Mary's virginity even before he introduced her by name (Luke 1:27). The Virgin Birth (or conception) is essential to Jesus' deity.

The Virgin Birth was likely even foreshadowed in the Garden of Eden, when the serpent was told that the *woman's* seed would "crush your head" (Gen. 3:15), previewing Christ's ultimate victory over sin, Satan, and death. Descendants were usually traced through fathers, but the unique designation of the woman's seed implies that the Messiah would have no natural father. In Luke 3:23, the writer was careful to qualify that Jesus was only "thought" to be Joseph's son. Also, the angel Gabriel emphasized Jesus' identity as God's Son and David's Son (see 2 Sam. 7:16; Pss. 2; 89:3-4, 20-37).

In harmony with the Old Testament messianic prophecies, Luke 1:26-38 foretells the birth of Jesus. Mary was a virgin, engaged to a man named Joseph, who was a descendant of David. Mary was probably a teenager at this time. When Elizabeth was six months into her pregnancy, Gabriel appeared to Mary and gave her an unforgettable greeting. Gabriel then declared that Mary would bear a son who would be named Jesus. He was God's Son and would rule eternally on David's throne.

Gabriel also revealed that the Holy Spirit would initiate the life within Mary's womb, so that the child would be called the Son of God. Jesus would be fully divine and fully human. Moreover, Gabriel told Mary about her relative Elizabeth, who was six months pregnant, even in her old age. In response, Mary offered herself as a humble servant of the Lord.

Mary then hurried to visit Elizabeth at her home in the hill country of Judea (vss. 39-45). In the song Mary uttered (traditionally known as the Magnificat) while there, she rejoiced in her privilege of serving God's purposes. Mary began by exalting or praising the Lord (vs. 46). His greatness was evident in providing salvation for all who put their trust in His Son (vs. 47), the suffering Servant of Isaiah 53. God's glory was also seen in choosing a humble young woman named Mary to give birth to the Christ child.

B. The Reason for Joy: vss. 48-50

"For he has been mindful of the humble state of his servant. From now on all generations will call me blessed, for the Mighty One has done great things for me—holy is his name. His mercy extends to those who fear him, from generation to generation."

The Greek noun rendered "servant" (Luke 1:48) comes from a verb that means "to serve as a slave." The underlying idea is to be subject to the will of another. Such a concept would have been objectionable in Greek thought. It was commonly taught that achieving one's potential for excellence was the foremost duty of every person. Such a self-centered mindset is far removed from Mary's attitude. She saw herself as the Lord's humble servant.

Despite Mary's status in Jewish society as a lowly servant girl, generations to come would call her "blessed," for God had manifested His grace on her. Mary referred to the Lord as being mighty and holy (vs. 49). He alone is the sovereign Ruler of the universe and absolutely set apart from sin; yet, despite God's exalted status, He willingly had done and would do great things for Mary (especially through her Son).

In particular, the Messiah would make the mercy of the Lord available to all who repent and believe. Mary alluded to this truth when she declared that God showers His mercy from one generation to the next on those who fear Him (vs. 50). This refers to those who show God a reverential respect for His sovereignty.

There are strong literary and thematic parallels between Mary's song and Hannah's ode of praise, which is recorded in 1 Samuel 2:1-10. For instance, Mary, like Hannah, extolled God's greatness; and both women are called God's handmaidens, or maidservants, which underscores their availability to do the Lord's will.

Mary's situation was much different than Hannah's. While Hannah sang for joy after her stigma of barrenness was gone, Mary sang for joy in the face of possible (though undeserved) alienation and shame. Mary chose not to focus on what others might think of her, but on what God thought of her and what she knew of Him.

III. THE FAITHFULNESS AND JUSTICE OF THE LORD: LUKE 1:51-55

A. The Reversal for Fortunes: vss. 51-53

"He has performed mighty deeds with his arm; he has scattered those who are proud in their inmost thoughts. He has brought down rulers from their thrones but has lifted up the humble. He has filled the hungry with good things but has sent the rich away empty."

Mary represents people of faith throughout history who have looked to the Lord as their ultimate source of deliverance. Such hope is not in vain, for God has manifested power with His mighty arm; by way of example, the Lord is known for dispersing the proud because of the haughty imaginations they entertain in their heart (Luke 1:51).

Mary was rebuking the sheer arrogance of the proud, who thought that power was their sovereign right. The Lord had toppled such authoritative rulers from their thrones and exalted those of lowly or humble position (vs. 52). The contrast between the mighty and the lowly dominates the literary landscape of Luke's Gospel. The broader truth is that God cares for those that the powerful ignore.

Verse 53 continues this emphasis by declaring that God has satisfied the hungry with good things; meanwhile, He has sent the rich away with empty hands. "Good things" refers not merely to material abundance, but to blessings that come from knowing God.

B. The Divine Pledge to Be Merciful: vss. 54-55

"He has helped his servant Israel, remembering to be merciful to Abraham and his descendants forever, even as he said to our fathers."

The Lord's mercy extended even to the nation and people of Israel. They were the recipients of His help and the objects of His unfailing love (Luke 1:54). Mary's song underscores that Israel had a special role in serving the Lord and making Him known to the world.

This truth is reinforced in verse 55, where Mary reiterated God's promise to Abraham and his descendants (see Gen. 22:16-18). The Lord would remain forever true to His pledge to bless His covenant people. Now, through the covenant with Abraham, God's promises and mercy would extend to all peoples in all generations, especially through faith in the Messiah.

Discussion Questions

1. Under what circumstances did the Servant grow up in the Lord's presence?
2. What was it about the Servant's life that made it characterized by sorrow and grief?
3. Why did Mary rejoice in God her Savior?
4. What great thing had the Lord done for Mary?
5. What reversal of situations is noted in Mary's hymn of praise?

Contemporary Application

My wife and I were 36 when we learned that we would be parents. After a time of extended waiting to finally have a child of our own, the confirmation that a baby was coming was probably the most wonderful news either of us had ever received. We certainly felt that God had exceedingly blessed us.

This marvelous good news was not the only occasion for celebration. When my wife's dear friend passed away a few years ago, it could have been a time of great sorrow. She was certainly one of the sweetest persons I have known. As a practicing physician, she had brought healing to many lives; yet, her loving and warm spirit had enriched the lives of far more.

Though this woman died in her early forties, her family and friends celebrated her farewell into the presence of Christ because she had been so close to Him. We all could rejoice because, as James 1:2 says, we should consider it nothing but joy when we fall into various trials. The reason is that God is making us complete in Him (see vss. 3-4). That is also why we can glorify the Lord and rejoice in Him regardless of the situations we are facing.

Good News for the World

Scripture

Background Scripture: *Isaiah 61:1-3; Luke 2:8-20*
Scripture Lesson: *Isaiah 61:1-2; Luke 2:8-20*
Key Verse: "*Today in the town of David a Savior has been born to you; he is Christ the Lord.*" Luke 2:11.
Scripture Lesson for Children: *Isaiah 61:1-2; Luke 2:8-20*
Key Verse for Children: "*Today in the town of David a Savior has been born to you; he is Christ the Lord.*" Luke 2:11.

Lesson Aim

To stress that the Savior's birth is for all people.

Lesson Setting

Time: *740–700 B.C.; about 6–5 B.C.*
Place: *Judah; Nazareth and Bethlehem*

Lesson Outline

Good News for the World
  I. The Ministry of Restoration: Isaiah 61:1-2
  II. The Announcement of the Angel: Luke 2:8-14
      A. *The Angel of the Lord: vss. 8-12*
      B. *The Heavenly Host: vss. 13-14*
  III. The Visit of the Shepherds: Luke 2:15-20
      A. *To Bethlehem: vss. 15-16*
      B. *To Spread the Word: vss. 17-18*
      C. *The Response of Mary: vs. 19*
      D. *To Praise God: vs. 20*

Introduction for Adults

Topic: *Be Joyful*

Frances Smith was born in Uvalde, Texas, on October 31, 1912. She became a pop singer and starred in Western movies in the 1940s and 1950s. In fact, she and her husband became the king and queen of the West. We know her better by the name Dale Evans.

But Dale Evans (who passed away in 2001) was much more than a film and television celebrity. She was a Christian who served the Lord with joy through her speaking and books. Indeed, Dale touched the lives of millions of people in a positive, uplifting way by sharing how Jesus carried her through times of grief and struggle. It's no wonder He remained the true source of rejoicing in Dale's life.

Introduction for Youth

Topic: *The Messiah Is Born*

The two women showed up at my door while I was making Christmas cookies. Our conversation meandered a bit until I asked them whether they believed in Jesus Christ. "Why, yes. We just don't celebrate Christmas. We celebrate other holidays instead," the younger woman offered.

I shared, "In our home, we celebrate the birth of Jesus Christ because He is our Savior." "We believe Jesus was a good man—a fine moral teacher, too," the elder woman cut in. "Kind of like Gandhi?" I asked? "Yes," the two responded in unison.

Without the birth of the Messiah and all that it stands for—His crucifixion for our sins, resurrection, and ascension to heaven—there is no reason to celebrate Christmas. If we take away the real meaning of Jesus' birth, we simply have a cozy wintertime drama around which we can build comfortable but ultimately meaningless traditions.

Concepts for Children

Topic: *Jesus Is Born!*

1. On the night that Jesus was born in a town called Bethlehem, there were shepherds in nearby fields guarding their flocks of sheep.
2. An angel suddenly appeared and told them about the birth of the Savior.
3. A vast number of other angels then joined in with praise to God for sending His Son.
4. The shepherds next ran to Bethlehem, where they found Mary, Joseph, and the Christ child.
5. Just as the shepherds were filled with joy over the birth of Jesus, so too we can rejoice and give praise to God.

Lesson Commentary

I. THE MINISTRY OF RESTORATION: ISAIAH 61:1-2

The Spirit of the Sovereign LORD is on me, because the LORD has anointed me to preach good news to the poor. He has sent me to bind up the brokenhearted, to proclaim freedom for the captives and release from darkness for the prisoners, to proclaim the year of the LORD's favor and the day of vengeance of our God, to comfort all who mourn.

The people of Judah who first received Isaiah's message had not yet gone into Babylonian captivity; so they would not have comprehended the full implications of Isaiah's prophecy. Through captivity the people of Judah would later become poor and brokenhearted as prisoners of Babylon. After the fall of Babylon, they would be set free from bondage and would return to their ancestral lands.

The Lord called and commissioned Isaiah to minister to needy people, and the Spirit of almighty God empowered Isaiah for his important task. The prophet would declare the good news of release from captivity. Isaiah's preaching would encourage the poor and bandage the wounds of the brokenhearted. He would tell the captives that God would set them free and declare to the prisoners that the Lord would release them from their exile (Isa. 61:1).

The Year of Jubilee seems to be the background for Isaiah's prophecy. Every 50 years in ancient Israel, property was supposed to be returned to its original owners (Lev. 25:10, 13); and those who sold themselves into slavery to pay off debts were to be freed (vss. 39, 54). Isaiah was to proclaim the year of the Lord's favor, the time when His redemptive blessings would be lavished on His people (Isa. 61:2). As the exiled Jews left Babylon, their land and liberty would be restored to them. As the light of God's freedom shone on them, they also would be delivered from their spiritual and moral bondage.

Isaiah was also to declare the time of punishment of God's enemies. The Lord was not only the Savior of His people but also the judge of the wicked. They would not remain guiltless for their crimes against the Jews. The latter, as they possibly mourned over their sins and over the destruction of their holy city, would find comfort in Isaiah's prophecies.

At the beginning of Jesus' public ministry, He quoted the first part of this passage (up through the first line of Isaiah 61:2; see Luke 4:16-21). Christ did not quote any further because the time of vengeance would not occur until His second coming. During His first coming, the Savior brought Good News to the oppressed and the favor of the Lord to the brokenhearted. Thus, while Isaiah might have served as a partial fulfillment, clearly the Messiah was the prophecy's realization to the fullest extent.

II. THE ANNOUNCEMENT OF THE ANGEL: LUKE 2:8-14

A. The Angel of the Lord: vss. 8-12

And there were shepherds living out in the fields nearby, keeping watch over their flocks at night. An angel of the Lord appeared to them, and the glory of the Lord shone around them, and they were terrified. But the angel said to them, "Do not be afraid. I bring you good news of great joy that will be for all the people. Today in the town of David a Savior has been born to you; he is Christ the Lord. This will be a sign to you: You will find a baby wrapped in cloths and lying in a manger."

The same Messiah about whom Isaiah's prophecies foretold was born in Bethlehem of Judea (Luke 2:1-7). In fact, the Bible reveals that the King of kings entered the world in utterly humble circumstances. For instance, after Mary wrapped her newborn in strips of cloth, she placed Him in a manger, because "there was no room for them in the inn" (vs. 7). In short, Jesus' first crib was a barnyard feeding trough.

The Greek word for "inn" could refer to a private "guest room" (22:11) in a home, or a public place of lodging (10:34). Because Joseph "belonged to the house and line of David" (2:4), he could have had relatives in Bethlehem to stay with. But since the town was crowded for the empire-wide census mandated by Caesar Augustus (vs. 1), a relative's home could be full too.

With Mary's time near, the couple likely looked for a room in a public inn for the delivery, but found it was full as well. The traditional image of an apathetic innkeeper who turned away Joseph and Mary (and Jesus) at the door may or may not be accurate. All the same, we know they had to settle for lodging in a stable (which may have been in a cave adjoining the inn).

At that time of the Savior's birth there were shepherds nearby out in the field, guarding their flocks of sheep by night (vs. 8). Here we learn that angels announced the Messiah's advent, not to princes in opulent palaces, but to caretakers of smelly animals. The Savior would not be the earthly conquering Messiah the nation was hoping for. Also, He would not mobilize the militant Zealots to throw off the Roman yoke. Instead, He came to serve (Mark 10:45) as well as to seek and to save the lost (Luke 19:10).

Moreover, the Gospels reveal that between a humble birth and a debasing (but victorious) death, Jesus lived simply, spoke vividly, and was often in the company of people whom polite society either rejected or ignored. Therefore, it is not surprising that the Redeemer was born in a stable, and lowly shepherds were the first to see the newborn King.

According to Luke 2:9, an angel of the Lord suddenly appeared to shepherds and the Lord's glory radiated around them. Understandably, the men were terrified by the sight. The angel, in turn, directed the shepherds not to be afraid. Instead, they were to listen carefully to the wonderful news the angel was about to proclaim. Such would bring tremendous joy to many people (vs. 10).

The "good news" is that God loves us despite our sinful thoughts, words, and deeds (John 3:16-21; Eph. 2:1-10; 1 John 4:10). Jesus was born to die for our sins, but He would not stay dead (1 Cor. 15:3-4). It is His victory over death that gives us life (vss. 56-57). "Great joy" (Luke 2:10) is experienced when we trust in the Son, who reconciled us to the Father (2 Cor. 5:17-21). We receive eternal life (John 3:36), the Holy Spirit (Eph. 1:13-14), free access to the Lord (Heb. 4:14-16), the assurance that Jesus is always with us (Matt. 28:20), and the guarantee that God will complete the redemptive work He begins in us in Christ (Phil. 1:6). The Gospel is the best news of all, for it celebrates the fact that "the LORD has done great things for us, and we are filled with joy" (Ps. 126:3).

Some have wondered why an angel announced the Messiah's birth to ordinary shepherds, not the powerful rulers or religious leaders of the day. Perhaps it was to stress that it is not the influential or elite who catch God's attention, but those who call for help and place their trust in the Lord.

The angel declared that Israel's Savior, Messiah, and Lord had been born that night in Bethlehem, the famed hometown of King David (Luke 2:11). Christ would make redemption available to all people, including the weak and oppressed—even society's outcasts. Military and political leaders during those times were called "saviors"; but Jesus was unique, being the Anointed One of God. The angel encouraged the shepherds to find the Christ child lying in a manger, wrapped snugly in strips of cloth (vs. 12).

B. The Heavenly Host: vss. 13-14

Suddenly a great company of the heavenly host appeared with the angel, praising God and saying, "Glory to God in the highest, and on earth peace to men on whom his favor rests."

While the angel was talking, many other angels appeared, praising God and proclaiming peace among people with whom God was pleased (Luke 2:13-14). The idea is not so much a general feeling of goodwill toward all people, but rather that God's favor rests on those who experience true peace through faith in the Messiah.

III. THE VISIT OF THE SHEPHERDS: LUKE 2:15-20

A. To Bethlehem: vss. 15-16

When the angels had left them and gone into heaven, the shepherds said to one another, "Let's go to Bethlehem and see this thing that has happened, which the Lord has told us about." So they hurried off and found Mary and Joseph, and the baby, who was lying in the manger.

Sheep need a shepherd. These animals are curious but dumb, and often fail to find their way home. Biblical shepherds, being aware of this, never took their eyes off their wandering flocks. When the animals strayed into a briar patch or fell down a hillside in the rugged terrain of Palestine, the shepherds would search for them and carry them to safety (Luke 15:4).

In the arid climate of Palestine, shepherds had to search constantly for sources of water. They might find a restful stream for the sheep, or they might spot an old well with a quiet pool or trough close by. Often the shepherd carried a small pail to scoop up liquid for thirsty sheep who could not reach the available water any other way.

Since shepherds lived out in the open and were unable to maintain a strict obedience to the law of Moses, they generally were considered unclean. As a result, they were despised by religious legalists and were typically excluded from temple worship. Custom did not allow shepherds to serve as witnesses in legal cases. How ironic that God invited these men to be witnesses of the greatest event of history.

We can imagine the sense of excitement and urgency felt by the shepherds as they agreed to stop what they were doing (important as it was) and hurry to see the newborn Savior (Luke 2:15). It is interesting to note their recollection of what had just taken place. They wanted to verify what the Lord had told them. Although an angel had delivered the message, it was God whose word was made known. The shepherds evidently ran to find the Christ child (vs. 16); and their efforts were not wasted.

B. To Spread the Word: vss. 17-18

When they had seen him, they spread the word concerning what had been told them about this child, and all who heard it were amazed at what the shepherds said to them.

Thankfully, the shepherds mentioned in Luke 2 did not allow the pressures of their daily responsibilities to prevent them from spreading the word about the newborn Messiah. In fact, they were so overjoyed that they told others about their experience (vs. 17). People who listened to the shepherds responded with a mixture of amazement and wonderment (vs. 18).

C. The Response of Mary: vs. 19

But Mary treasured up all these things and pondered them in her heart.

At first Mary, too, must have been astonished by what the shepherds said concerning her firstborn; but Luke 2:19 suggests that Mary did more than just remember what took place. She also treasured the incident and sought to fathom its significance. This remained true even though she did not fully understand all the ramifications of the events that were happening around her.

D. To Praise God: vs. 20

The shepherds returned, glorifying and praising God for all the things they had heard and seen, which were just as they had been told.

Meanwhile, the shepherds returned to the fields, glorifying and praising God for the privilege of what they had heard and seen. Their encounter with the Christ child harmonized with the angelic declaration. The closing remark of Luke 2:20 ("as they had been told") notes a major theme of the third Synoptic Gospel as Luke sought to reassure Theophilus: God does what He says He will do (see 1:1-4).

Discussion Questions

1. What had the Lord anointed the Messiah to do?
2. What had the Lord sent the Messiah to announce?
3. What were the shepherds doing at the time the angel of the Lord appeared to them?

4. How did the shepherds respond to the angelic announcement of the Messiah's birth?

5. How did others respond to the good news being heralded by the shepherds?

Contemporary Application

What good is proclaiming God's message of hope to someone struggling with cancer, or whose parent or spouse has just died, or who has discovered they do not have enough retirement money to get by? As this week's lesson makes clear, there is great value. Consolation and hope are found in the promise of the Messiah's advent.

While we pray and consider sensitive ways of communicating the good news of the Savior's birth, we can have confidence that doing so will be a source of encouragement to others. Presenting the truth of Jesus' coming is a time-tested antidote to despair. When we offer hope and comfort by speaking about the realities of God, we speak the truth. We are offering facts about what the Lord has done, not just guesses and wishes no one has any reason to believe.

The truth of Jesus' advent can seem elusive and unrelated to life when the hurts are overwhelming. At times it is tempting to doubt God's ability to bring restoration and relief. The Lord wants us to reassure those who are grieving that He genuinely is concerned for them and deeply loves them. They need to know that God is always present and will never let them down.

For those experiencing death or desertion of those they love, life can seem empty and dark. Their life is full of bad tidings and gloomy thoughts. Christians are called to bring the Good News to them. In situations such as this, believers become God's messengers of hope and reassurance.

God Gives Strength

DEVOTIONAL READING

Romans 16:17-27

DAILY BIBLE READINGS

Monday December 26
Psalm 119:25-32 Strengthen Me, O God

Tuesday December 27
Romans 16:17-27 God Is Able to Strengthen You

Wednesday December 28
1 Thessalonians 3:1-5 We Sent Timothy to Strengthen You

Thursday December 29
1 Thessalonians 3:6-13 May God Strengthen Your Hearts

Friday December 30
Acts 16:1-5 Paul, Silas, and Timothy Strengthen Churches

Saturday December 31
1 Timothy 1:1-11 Paul Writes to Timothy

Sunday January 1
1 Timothy 1:12-20 Strengthened by Christ

Scripture

Background Scripture: *1 Timothy 1*
Scripture Lesson: *1 Timothy 1:12-20*
Key Verse: *I thank Christ Jesus our Lord, who has given me strength, that he considered me faithful, appointing me to his service.* 1 Timothy 1:12.
Scripture Lesson for Children: *Acts 16:1-5; 1 Timothy 1:12, 14, 17*
Key Verse for Children: *I thank Christ Jesus our Lord, who has given me strength, . . . appointing me to his service.* 1 Timothy 1:12.

Lesson Aim

To underscore the value of trusting God during difficult times of Christian ministry.

Lesson Setting

Time: *About A.D. 62*
Places: *Macedonia and Ephesus*

Lesson Outline

God Gives Strength

  I. God's Grace for Paul: 1 Timothy 1:12-17
    A. *The Apostle's Violent Past: vss. 12-13*
    B. *The Apostle's Amazing Transformation: vss. 14-16*
    C. *The Apostle's Praise to God: vs. 17*
 II. Fighting the Good Fight: 1 Timothy 1:18-20
    A. *Remaining Faithful: vss. 18-19a*
    B. *Taking Note of the Unfaithful: vss. 19b-20*

Introduction for Adults

Topic: *Finding Strength to Serve*

In his *Confessions*, Augustine tells how his mother, Monica, a devoted follower of Christ, faithfully prayed for his repentance, despite his life of immorality and flirting with various heresies. Monica never ceased praying for her son, finding strength in Jesus to persevere. Then one day Augustine turned back to God. Here is what he said of Monica's prayers:

"And You sent Your hand from above, and raised my soul out of that depth of darkness, because my mother, Your faithful one, wept to You for me more bitterly than mothers weep for the bodily deaths of their children. . . . She did not relax her weeping and mourning. She did not cease to pray at every hour and bewail me to You, and her prayers found entry into Your sight."

Introduction for Youth

Topic: *Powered Up for Service*

One evening at church my son and I watched as Myrtle flipped her spiral notebook open and struggled to get her writing into a position where her trifocals could aid her in reading her cursive. The devotion that she read was a retrospective of her life. At the age of 80, she still said life's greatest lesson for her is, "Just trust the Lord."

For an hour my son listened intently as a woman 70 years his senior spoke about heart problems, hospital stays, unfulfilled dreams of becoming an overseas missionary—and, of course, of her loving Lord who always empowered her for Christian service.

If my son had not come with me that night to church, he would not have discovered Myrtle's story. He would not know Myrtle's faith. He would not know that strength to serve is found through faith in the Lord.

Concepts for Children

Topic: *Good Leaders Thank God*

1. During Paul's second missionary trip, he met a young follower of Jesus named Timothy.
2. Paul decided to take Timothy with him.
3. Paul was thankful that God gave him the strength to be faithful in serving Him.
4. Paul gave praise to God for the way in which He poured out His special favor in the apostle's life.
5. We can also thank God for His special favor to us in Christ.

Lesson Commentary

I. GOD'S GRACE FOR PAUL: 1 TIMOTHY 1:12-17

A. The Apostle's Violent Past: vss. 12-13

I thank Christ Jesus our Lord, who has given me strength, that he considered me faithful, appointing me to his service. Even though I was once a blasphemer and a persecutor and a violent man, I was shown mercy because I acted in ignorance and unbelief.

Paul wrote 1 Timothy after he had left his son in the faith in Ephesus to deal with the problems in that church. For some reason, Paul could not stay to handle the situation himself, but left Timothy there as his representative as he journeyed on to Macedonia. Paul probably wrote to Timothy shortly after arriving in Macedonia, to give him further instruction regarding his supervision of the churches in the area of Ephesus.

During Paul's first imprisonment in Rome, Ephesus had become a center of false teaching. Several years earlier Paul had foretold that spiritual frauds would enter the Ephesian church, distort the Gospel, and seek to lead people away from the truth (Acts 20:29-30). Because that prediction had come true, Paul needed Timothy to deal with these false teachers while the apostle was needed elsewhere. Besides dealing with the false teachers, Timothy also needed to give authoritative instructions on church order. In addition, Timothy needed encouragement and written authority to carry out the difficult assignment given to him.

Paul began his First Letter to Timothy by asserting his authority as "an apostle of Christ Jesus by the command of God" (1:1). In response to the false teaching being spread in the city, Paul reestablished his authority as well as the credentials of Timothy, his representative. The description of Timothy as Paul's "true son in the faith" (vs. 2) indicates that the apostle had led Timothy to Christ, most likely during his stay at Lystra on the first missionary trip. By the time Paul returned to Lystra two years later, he was so impressed with Timothy's spiritual progress that he asked Timothy to join the missionary party (see Acts 16:1-3). Timothy soon became one of Paul's must trusted and dependable co-workers in spreading the Gospel.

Getting down to business, Paul renewed his instructions for Timothy to stay in Ephesus to deal with the false teachers in that city's church (1 Tim. 1:3). Apparently the two had arrived in Ephesus together on their travels. Timothy's task was to command "certain men" in Ephesus not to teach strange doctrines that involved "myths and endless genealogies" (vs. 4). Their concentration on these legends promoted unending speculation rather than the work of God.

After identifying the false instructors at Ephesus as self-appointed teachers of the law (vss. 5-7), Paul moved on to show the true purpose of the law (vss. 8-11). From what the apostle says here, we can assume that these teachers were misusing the law to their own ends. Paul declared that the intent of the law was to shine a spotlight on the sinful condition of our heart so that we will run back to Christ to receive His grace and forgiveness. The law, when used properly, did not interfere with the message of salvation. Rather, the law serves as a backdrop that makes the grace of God shine like the sun.

Paul was amazed and grateful that the Lord considered him faithful and appointed him to His service. Not only did the Lord enable the apostle to serve Him, but also He poured out His grace on Paul by forgiving his past. Faithfulness, not Paul's abilities or knowledge, was the apostle's primary qualification for the ministry that resulted from God's grace (vs. 12).

Before his conversion, Paul opposed Jesus' followers. Paul's opposition caused him to use hateful language against Christ as Paul hunted down Jesus' followers to put them in jail. The Greek word Paul used for "violent" (vs. 13) describes an arrogant individual who inflicted pain for the delight of seeing another person suffer; the intent was to bring humiliation as well as injury. Paul used the strongest words possible to describe his malicious spirit before conversion.

B. The Apostle's Amazing Transformation: vss. 14-16

The grace of our Lord was poured out on me abundantly, along with the faith and love that are in Christ Jesus. Here is a trustworthy saying that deserves full acceptance: Christ Jesus came into the world to save sinners—of whom I am the worst. But for that very reason I was shown mercy so that in me, the worst of sinners, Christ Jesus might display his unlimited patience as an example for those who would believe on him and receive eternal life.

Paul was born in Tarsus (now in southwest Turkey) to a family from the tribe of Benjamin (Phil. 3:5). He was named Saul after Israel's first king, who was also from the tribe of Benjamin. At an early age Saul was trained in the tradition of the Pharisees, a Jewish sect strict in observing the laws of Moses.

The fact that Saul was trained under the famous rabbi Gamaliel (Acts 22:3) demonstrates his youthful ability and zeal for the law. That intensity led him to vigorously oppose the early Christians. For instance, when Stephen was stoned, Saul gave his approval to the action (8:1). Shortly thereafter, he took the lead in persecuting believers (9:1-2).

Despite his wicked behavior, Paul had received mercy from the Lord (1 Tim. 1:14). Paul's comment that he had acted ignorantly in unbelief was not intended to excuse his actions or lessen his guilt. Paul had been sincere in believing that he was serving God when he had persecuted the church; but even though Paul had been zealous for God, he had still needed the mercy and grace that were poured out on him. The resulting faith in Paul's life proved that God's work of grace was successful in changing him.

As Paul reflected back on his own life, he verbalized a doctrinal truth that was both trustworthy and deserving of full acceptance. In short, Jesus the Messiah came into the world to provide redemption for sinners. This is the heart of the gospel message. Paul sensed that he was the worst of transgressors (vs. 15). This sentiment should not be regarded as false humility. Paul's violent persecution of Christians convinced him that he was chief of sinners, even though he had strained to keep the letter of the law. Many believers had suffered because of Paul's zeal for Judaism prior to his encounter with Christ on the road to Damascus.

Paul's confession can give us hope as we think of loved ones and friends who seem far from surrendering their lives to the Lord. Because God saved Paul, no one can be regarded as too rebellious to receive His grace. We should not regard anyone as hopeless, but continue to pray for their salvation. Treacherous people who genuinely repent often become unstoppable soldiers in the advancement of God's kingdom.

The grace poured out on Paul's life served as a pattern for all who would trust in Christ and receive eternal life. The early life and subsequent conversion of Paul gave the Messiah the opportunity to demonstrate His utmost patience to provide sinners the opportunity to repent (vs. 16).

C. The Apostle's Praise to God: vs. 17

Now to the King eternal, immortal, invisible, the only God, be honor and glory for ever and ever. Amen.

If Christ could endure the blasphemy of Paul while waiting for him to change, then Jesus can certainly keep His invitation of salvation open to others. Who could attempt to limit the life-changing capacity of God's grace after what He did for Saul of Tarsus? As Paul reflected on this example of God's mercy, he suddenly erupted in praise. God our King is eternal (without beginning or end), immortal (undying), and invisible (unable to be seen by mortals; 1 Tim. 1:17). To this only wise God, we will give honor and praise and glory for all eternity.

II. FIGHTING THE GOOD FIGHT: 1 TIMOTHY 1:18-20

A. Remaining Faithful: vss. 18-19a

Timothy, my son, I give you this instruction in keeping with the prophecies once made about you, so that by following them you may fight the good fight, holding on to faith and a good conscience.

Paul was well aware of the damage false teaching could cause. He thus returned briefly to the subject of Timothy's combat with spiritual frauds. The importance of proclaiming sound doctrine is a theme that occurs throughout the Pastoral Epistles (see 1 Tim. 4:1-2; 6:20-21; 2 Tim. 1:13-14; 4:1-5; Titus 2:1).

Paul's "instruction" (1 Tim. 1:18) refers to the task he described in verses 3-7. Timothy had received a sacred trust to keep the Gospel pure from contamination. In giving this directive to Timothy, Paul was not asking more than Timothy was capable of doing in Christ. In fact, it was in keeping with "prophecies" (vs. 18) made about Timothy. These probably occurred in an assembly of Christians where the Holy Spirit spoke through believers to designate Timothy for his special ministry. This may have been the time referred to in 4:14 when Timothy was ordained in the ministry.

The task of guarding the Gospel required continuous effort in confronting spiritual frauds and teaching what was correct. The military language Paul used depicts a campaign, not just a single conflict. Fighting well in the Lord's battles in fulfill-ment of the prophecies meant Timothy would be involved in a series of conflicts against the opponents of the Gospel and Christ. Because of Satan's efforts, antag-onists to the truth will always exist.

Timothy was to attend to his inner spiritual condition by holding firmly to his Christian faith and keeping his conscience clear (1:19a). Because the false teach-ers had neglected these areas, they had fallen into serious error. Timothy, on the other hand, was to pay close attention to these things as he contended for the faith and sought to teach others the truth.

B. Taking Note of the Unfaithful: vss. 19b-20

Some have rejected these and so have shipwrecked their faith. Among them are Hymenaeus and Alexander, whom I have handed over to Satan to be taught not to blaspheme.

Paul mentioned two men in Ephesus who had made a shipwreck (so to speak) of their faith by failing to preserve their spiritual integrity (1 Tim. 1:19b). Hymenaeus and Alexander were apparently two of the worst offenders in promoting the false teaching Paul described (vs. 20).

Because Alexander was such a common name of that time, it is risky to identify this Alexander with the other Alexanders mentioned in the New Testament. Hymenaeus, however, is probably the man with that name spoken of in 2 Timothy 2:17-18. This person denied the bodily resurrection by claiming it had already hap-pened in a spiritual sense.

The false teachings in Ephesus had serious consequences, making Timothy's task of confrontation all the more important. Paul wrote that he had delivered the char-latans to Satan so that they might be taught not to blaspheme (1 Tim. 1:20). Most scholars agree that the words refer to some type of church discipline, such as removing the offenders from congregational fellowship. The purpose of putting them out into the world, the domain of Satan, was to stop their destructive behav-ior and bring them back to the Lord. Paul used similar words in 1 Corinthians 5:5 and 13 in reference to an immoral believer who was put out of the church fellow-ship because of his inappropriate behavior.

Other commentators, however, see judicial punishment in Paul's words. They believe that he used his apostolic authority to inflict some sort of bodily illness or calamity upon the false teachers in order to curtail the damaging effects of their heretical doctrines.

Discussion Questions

1. How had Paul acted toward the church before his conversion?
2. In what way had God's grace and love overflowed to Paul?
3. What was the basis for Paul considering himself the worst of sinners?
4. What instructions did Paul give to Timothy concerning the false teachers?
5. What bogus doctrine had the religious frauds taught?

Contemporary Application

The call to Christian service does not cease during difficult times; yet in moments of distress, we can lose our bearings and feel as if our resolve to minister has waned. This in turn can cause us to place undue confidence in circumstances, other people, or ourselves.

Misplaced trust in circumstances is imprudent because situations constantly change. When times are good, our reliance on the particulars of life seems wise; however, when times are rough, our decision to rely on circumstances proves to be foolish.

Placing our whole trust in people is also unwise for similar reasons. Our family, friends, and co-workers might be talented, industrious, and creative individuals; yet no one except God is all-knowing, all-powerful, and all-wise. At some point even people we trust the most will let us down.

Relying on ourselves to make it through difficult times is just as foolish as depending on circumstances and other people. There are many aspects of our lives that are simply beyond our control. If we are honest with ourselves, we will humbly admit that ultimately we should put our trust in God. In Him alone will we find strength to serve.

Pray for Everyone

DEVOTIONAL READING

1 Thessalonians 5:16-22

DAILY BIBLE READINGS

Monday January 2
  *Philippians 1:3-11 Paul
  Prays for the Philippians*

Tuesday January 3
  *1 Thessalonians 5:16-22
  Pray without Ceasing*

Wednesday January 4
  *1 Peter 3:8-12 God Hears
  Our Prayers*

Thursday January 5
  *Luke 18:1-8 A Parable
  about Praying*

Friday January 6
  *Matthew 5:43-48 Pray for
  Your Enemies*

Saturday January 7
  *1 Timothy 2:1-7 Pray for
  Everyone*

Sunday January 8
  *James 5:13-18 Prayer Is
  Powerful and Effective*

Scripture

Background Scripture: *1 Timothy 2*
Scripture Lesson: *1 Timothy 2:1-8*
Key Verse: *I urge, then, first of all, that requests, prayers,
intercession and thanksgiving be made for everyone.*
1 Timothy 2:1.
Scripture Lesson for Children: *Acts 25:13-14, 22-23;
26:1, 12-14a, 15-16, 19, 22-23, 27-29; 1 Timothy 2:1*
Key Verse for Children: *I urge . . . that . . . prayers . . .
and thanksgiving be made for everyone.* 1 Timothy 2:1.

Lesson Aim

To encourage the practice of prayer throughout one's
day.

Lesson Setting

Time: *About A.D. 62*
Places: *Macedonia and Ephesus*

Lesson Outline

Pray for Everyone
  I. The Importance of Prayer: 1 Timothy 2:1-4
      A. *The Injunction for Corporate Prayer: vss. 1-2*
      B. *The Evangelistic Intent of God: vss. 3-4*
  II. The Basis of Prayer: 1 Timothy 2:5-8
      A. *Christ the Mediator: vs. 5*
      B. *Christ the Ransom: vs. 6*
      C. *Paul the Herald and Apostle: vs. 7*
      D. *Prayer Free from Acrimony: vs. 8*

Introduction for Adults

Topic: *Everyone Needs Prayer*

A cartoon portrayed a tiny insect peering up at a monster insect. After staring at the monster for a while, the tiny insect said, "And what kind of bug are you?" "I'm a praying mantis," the monster said. "That's absurd!" said the tiny insect. "Bugs don't pray!" With that, the praying mantis grabbed the tiny bug around the throat and squeezed. The bug's eyes bulged, and it screamed, "Lord, help me!" Some people are like that tiny bug. They ignore—even ridicule—prayer until they get squeezed. Then they scream, "Lord, help me!"

What motivates your students to keep praying? What should motivate them? How can you encourage them toward that end?

Introduction for Youth

Topic: *Who Needs Prayer?*

Samuel's daughter had been rebelling against God for quite some time. Lisa had abandoned her family by leaving home, and was living as far from God as she could. But one night, this teenager awoke with the distinct feeling that someone was praying for her.

In fact, a lot of people were praying for Lisa. The entire church family her father pastored was talking to God about her. During their midweek prayer meeting, a member recommended that they should pray for Lisa.

Two days later, Lisa came home. When she learned the details of who had been praying for her, Lisa turned her life over the Lord.

Concepts for Children

Topic: *Good Leaders Pray for Everyone*

1. Paul, a prayerful Christian leader, had been falsely accused and was on trial.
2. Christians use every opportunity to tell others about Jesus' redeeming power.
3. Christians often sacrifice personal safety and well-being in order to proclaim the gospel message.
4. Christian leaders, by the example they set, often teach young Christians to pray.
5. God is pleased when we pray for other people.

Lesson Commentary

I. THE IMPORTANCE OF PRAYER: 1 TIMOTHY 2:1-4

A. The Injunction for Corporate Prayer: vss. 1-2

I urge, then, first of all, that requests, prayers, intercession and thanksgiving be made for everyone— for kings and all those in authority, that we may live peaceful and quiet lives in all godliness and holiness.

The Pastoral Epistles and Philemon are the only biblical letters the apostle Paul wrote to individuals. (All of his other letters were addressed to entire churches.) The letters to Timothy and Titus are called pastoral because they contain instructions to two young leaders about the issues of pastoring and caring for churches. We learn from these ancient sacred texts that believers in leadership need to be spiritually mature and disciplined to withstand the attacks of Satan—attacks that often originate from the people in their own congregations.

Timothy was given charge of the church at Ephesus; Titus was to oversee the churches in Crete. These congregations needed trustworthy leaders who were beyond reproach. False teachers were springing up everywhere, and they needed to be weeded out. Paul's purpose in writing these letters was to arm Timothy and Titus for the spiritual battle of leadership. The apostle wanted to provide them with the authority and tools necessary to teach and protect the flocks God had entrusted to them.

After advising Timothy on how to deal with the false teachers, Paul moved on to give instructions about the significance of prayer in public worship. Most scholars believe the context of 1 Timothy 2 deals with matters of public worship; instructions regarding dress and authority are much better understood in that light. Many of the verses in chapter 2 do not seem to fit settings of private prayer or family devotions.

The "first of all" in verse 1 likely indicates importance rather than sequence of thought. An essential part of public worship is prayer. Public prayer is not something to be neglected or hurried through to get to the other parts of the service. The apostle urged Timothy to make prayer a priority in the assembling of believers.

Paul's instruction here stands in sharp contrast to what takes place in many of our churches today. Fewer churches have regularly scheduled prayer meetings, and those who do find that few attend. In addition, the time allotted to prayer on Sunday mornings continues to shrink. Paul, however, insisted that prayer must be given a central place in public worship as well as in our daily lives.

Paul illustrated the aspects of public entreaties to God by using several different words for prayer. "Requests" shows that God desires us to bring our needs before Him. He wants us to tell Him about what we believe is important for our lives. "Prayers" is the most general word for praying in the New Testament. It includes words addressed to God in a reverent manner. "Intercession" depicts a childlike confidence we can have in addressing God about our needs and those of others. We can be confident as we ask God's blessings for others. "Thanksgiving" refers to expressions of gratitude to God. When we think of all God has done for us, and when we recognize His answers to our needs, requests, prayers, and intercession, we should offer thanks.

At the end of verse 1 the apostle tells us for whom to pray: everybody! Family, relatives, friends, people at work, leaders, and the lost everywhere should be named in our prayers. Such prayer does make a difference. If it were not effective to intercede for the needs and salvation of other people, God would not command us to do it.

Paul singled out one group to represent the scope of such universal praying. He asked that prayers be made for "kings and all those in authority" (vs. 2). The term "kings" referred to the Roman emperor as well as to lesser rulers. The Roman emperor at that time was Nero, who would shortly become a leader in the persecution of believers and the one who would eventually order the execution of the apostle Paul.

National and local politicians are perhaps the most difficult people to remember in our prayers. Perhaps we often disagree with their policies or distrust their motives. But Paul would have us pray for them anyway, especially when we are disturbed by their actions. It was perhaps more difficult for early Christians to pray for a wicked Nero than it is for us to pray for any of our leaders.

The apostle emphasized praying for rulers because their decisions affect our daily lives and the privilege to freely worship. The Greek word Paul used for "godliness" occurs eight times in 1 Timothy, once in 2 Timothy, once in Titus, and nowhere else in Paul's writings. The word describes our attitude and conduct as measured by God's standards and depicts a way of life that shows reverence for God as well as respect for other people. Our ability to live godly and peaceful lives depends on our national leaders. Paul believed that prayer made a significant impact on governmental matters and brought about opportunities to further the Gospel and show reverence for God.

B. The Evangelistic Intent of God: vss. 3-4

This is good, and pleases God our Savior, who wants all men to be saved and to come to a knowledge of the truth.

First Timothy 2:3 gives us the primary motive for praying for all people as well as for our leaders. We should pray for them because it gives God pleasure. The Lord is delighted when we pray for others because He desires for all people to be saved. (This verse does not teach that everyone will be saved, only that God desires for that to happen.) When we pray for the salvation of leaders, some may indeed come to a saving knowledge of the Lord. The Greek word translated "knowledge" refers to a deep and accurate understanding that occurs at salvation and continues to grow afterward (vs. 4).

II. THE BASIS OF PRAYER: 1 TIMOTHY 2:5-8

A. Christ the Mediator: vs. 5

For there is one God and one mediator between God and men, the man Christ Jesus.

Paul discussed the basis of prayer in 1 Timothy 2:5. Because there is only "one God," He is Lord of the entire human race. If there were many gods, then people would not be responsible to any one. But since there is only one true God, it is appropriate to pray for the salvation of everyone, for without Him they have no hope. All of humanity must give an account of their lives to the true and living God.

The declaration of "one God" is the central truth of both the Old and New Testaments. There is only one God and only one way for sinful humanity to approach Him, that is, through the Lord Jesus Christ (see John 14:6).

Christ is the "one mediator" (1 Tim. 2:5) between God and people. A mediator stands between two hostile parties in order to reconcile their differences and bring peace to the relationship. Because Jesus is man and God, He is able to bridge the gap between God's holiness and humanity's sinfulness. Without Christ's mediating work, we would have no hope of establishing peace with God.

The term for "man" in the phrase "the man Christ Jesus" is not the Greek word for male, but a word that represents all of humanity. Paul chose that term to emphasize that in Jesus' role as mediator, He acts on behalf of all people regardless of gender, race, or nationality.

Thus not only is it appropriate to pray for the salvation of others, it is essential that we do so. If people reject Christ, there is no other way for them to receive eternal life (see Acts 4:12). We must not neglect to pray for our lost friends as well as for missionaries who carry the Good News to the lost in foreign lands.

B. Christ the Ransom: vs. 6

Who gave himself as a ransom for all men—the testimony given in its proper time.

Christ's primary act as mediator was giving "himself as a ransom" (1 Tim. 2:6). In the first century A.D., a ransom was the payment given to free a slave. Jesus, acting on our behalf, paid the debt of our sins by dying on the cross. His death frees us from the slavery of sin.

Just as with God's will, Jesus' atonement for the sins of humanity is available for all humankind (vs. 6; compare vs. 4). But again, that does not mean that all people will be saved. John 1:12 says, "To all who received him, to those who believed in his name, he gave the right to become children of God." The good news that Christ gave His life to pay the debt of our sins must be received personally for salvation to occur.

C. Paul the Herald and Apostle: vs. 7

And for this purpose I was appointed a herald and an apostle—I am telling the truth, I am not lying— and a teacher of the true faith to the Gentiles.

Paul's appointment as "a herald and an apostle" (1 Tim. 2:7) was in keeping with the necessity of spreading the Gospel to a lost race. In early times, heralds carried the official messages of a king or someone in authority. Their responsibility was to publicly proclaim that message without including their own opinions. Paul's job was to repeat the message revealed to him, not to teach his own ideas. His assertion that he was telling the truth shows that there were some in Ephesus who challenged Paul's authority as an apostle and his calling as a teacher to the Gentiles.

D. Prayer Free from Acrimony: vs. 8

I want men everywhere to lift up holy hands in prayer, without anger or disputing.

In 1 Timothy 2:8-15, Paul discussed proper order in public worship as it related to men and women. First, he focused on the men's responsibilities as they led in prayer (vs. 8). The instruction for men to pray does not mean that public prayer in a church setting was limited to men or even just to church leaders. In 1 Corinthians 11:5, Paul stated that women could pray in the church if their heads were covered. The desire of Paul for men everywhere to pray also shows that this practice was not limited to the church leaders. He wanted everyone to voice their requests and concerns to God.

While Paul asked that men pray with uplifted hands, his primary concern was not bodily posture but inner holiness. "Anger" (1 Tim. 2:8) deals with personal attitudes of resentment toward others, while "disputing" suggests outward arguments and confrontations. Paul's desire was for men to be at peace with God and others, as far as it depended on them, before they prayed publicly.

So often we focus on what Paul required of women and pass over the obligations he placed on men. While he used more ink writing about the role of women, Paul's desire for men was no less demanding. The apostle did not maintain a double standard. Men who behave abusively and angrily while neglecting their walk with the Lord have no business leading others in prayer. God desires for men to love Him and to show His love to their families, their friends, and to everyone else. Those are the type of men Paul wanted to lead others in prayer.

Discussion Questions

1. What sorts of people did Paul urge believers to pray for?
2. What place does the salvation of the lost have in public prayer requests?
3. For what purpose did Jesus give His life on cross?
4. For what had Paul been chosen to do?
5. How did Paul want believers to pray when they assembled for worship?

Contemporary Application

A key emphasis of this week's lesson is that we should pray in every situation for a host of people. Another key point is that we should turn to God in prayer during every incident of our lives. Those situations are not just major crises that occur once every two or three years, or difficult troubles that come our way every few months, or minor problems that beset us each day. It includes whatever we are doing at the moment. It could be while traveling somewhere, walking around the block, or even chatting with a friend. God is present in each of these situations.

Another key point is that we must be honest and open in our prayers with God. Often when we talk with others, we do not say everything that is on our minds and do not say exactly how our hearts feel. The closer we are to that person, the more we say; but probably we still hold a little of ourselves back for one reason or another. With God, we should not hold anything back.

Finally, we should not only humbly seek God's guidance, but also be sensitive to His leading and then do what He desires. This does not mean, of course, that while we are going somewhere (for example), we should ask Him whether He wants us to turn left or right and expect Him to answer; rather, we should pray to God about how we are reacting and responding to others we encounter along the way.

God Calls Church Leaders

DEVOTIONAL READING

Mark 9:33-37

DAILY BIBLE READINGS

Monday January 9
Deuteronomy 1:9-18 Moses Appoints Israel's Tribal Leaders

Tuesday January 10
Galatians 2:1-10 Paul Is Welcomed as a Leader

Wednesday January 11
1 Thessalonians 5:6-15 Respect Those Who Labor among You

Thursday January 12
Titus 1:5-9 Qualities of a Leader

Friday January 13
Mark 9:33-37 The Greatest Is Servant of All

Saturday January 14
1 Timothy 3:1-7 Qualifications of Overseers

Sunday January 15
1 Timothy 3:8-15 Qualifications of Helpers

Scripture

Background Scripture: *1 Timothy 3*
Scripture Lesson: *1 Timothy 3:2-15*
Key Verse: *They must keep hold of the deep truths of the faith with a clear conscience.* 1 Timothy 3:9.
Scripture Lesson for Children: *Mark 9:30-37; 1 Timothy 3:14-15*
Key Verse for Children: *Jesus . . . said, "If anyone wants to be first, he must be the very last, and the servant of all."* Mark 9:35.

Lesson Aim

To emphasize that a church leader's character is important to the Lord.

Lesson Setting

Time: *About A.D. 62*
Places: *Macedonia and Ephesus*

Lesson Outline

God Calls Church Leaders

  I. Qualifications for Overseers: 1 Timothy 3:2-7
    A. Known for Their Integrity: vss. 2-5
    B. Known for Their Sterling Character: vss. 6-7
  II. Qualifications for Deacons: 1 Timothy 3:8-13
    A. Known for Their Faith and Experience: vss. 8-10
    B. Known for Their Worthy Associations: vss. 11-13
 III. Godly Conduct: 1 Timothy 3:14-15

Introduction for Adults

Topic: *Leading God's People*

From its earliest days the church was an organized body of believers, not a collection of individuals doing as they pleased. Therefore, congregational leadership is critical. Godly, effective leaders are needed because, without them, there could be anarchy in which everyone does what is right in their own eyes.

Clearly, then, congregations need responsible leaders to carry out their missions. Also, churches need qualified leaders to facilitate their spiritual ministries. A well-organized congregation lacking spiritual vitality is just another organization. We must be certain that our churches are not cut off from the life of Christ.

Introduction for Youth

Topic: *Leading by Example*

After one glance at Paul's high standards for Christian leaders, our first response might be that we are not qualified for the task. Of course, it is good to be humble rather than cocky. But the Bible records examples of great leaders—such as Moses and Jeremiah—who felt unqualified for their tasks.

When we feel that way, we open the doors for God to exercise His love, wisdom, and power in our lives. Jesus sent the Holy Spirit to be our teacher and helper. He gives us all the wisdom and strength we need. In fact, Christ's power can be magnified in our weaknesses.

The Holy Spirit gifts the church with leaders. When we open ourselves to the Spirit, He uses us to help others come to saving faith in Christ. This is what it means to lead by example.

Concepts for Children

Topic: *Good Leaders Serve Others*

1. As Jesus traveled with His followers through a region called Galilee, He told them that He would be killed, but that three days later He would rise from the dead.
2. When the group came to a town called Capernaum and settled in a house, Jesus asked His followers what they had been talking about on the road.
3. The group had been arguing about which of them was the greatest.
4. Jesus explained that good Christian leaders are those who serve others.
5. The Lord is pleased when we make every effort to serve others around us.

Lesson Commentary

I. Qualifications for Overseers: 1 Timothy 3:2-7

A. Known for Their Integrity: vss. 2-5

Now the overseer must be above reproach, the husband of but one wife, temperate, self-controlled, respectable, hospitable, able to teach, not given to drunkenness, not violent but gentle, not quarrelsome, not a lover of money. He must manage his own family well and see that his children obey him with proper respect. (If anyone does not know how to manage his own family, how can he take care of God's church?)

In 1 Timothy 3, the apostle Paul moved naturally from his consideration of public worship in chapter 2 to an examination of the qualifications of potential leaders in the church. The offices of overseer and deacon were already in place in the churches at and around Ephesus. Timothy's responsibility was to make sure that the churches selected qualified people for those positions.

Paul referred to the first type of church leader as an "overseer" in 1 Timothy 3, while in another passage he called the same type "elder" (see Titus 1:5-7). Almost all interpreters agree that the words "overseer" and "elder" refer to the same office in the early church. In Acts 20:17-28, Paul used both terms in addressing the same group of Ephesian church leaders. "Overseer" indicates the oversight duties of the office, while "elder" emphasizes personal dignity and maturity. It appears that there were many elders who oversaw the work of a particular church and performed such functions as ruling and teaching (see 1 Tim. 5:17).

Paul applauded the desire of those who aspired to be overseers, implying that ministry opportunities existed for such individuals (3:1). However, Paul did not want the positions to be filled just because there was a need; he desired that competent people be chosen for these leadership roles.

The first qualification is that overseers be "above reproach" (vs. 2). That means their character was to be of such a nature that no one could bring a just cause for blame against them. The next requirement specifies that an overseer be "the husband of but one wife." Some suggest this means that overseers were not to be divorced and remarried, while others see this as a reference to monogamy. (Polygamy was widespread in the first century A.D.) In any case, overseers were to be sexually pure in conduct and thought. If they were married, they were to have no romantic ties with any person but their spouse.

During the time of Paul, the ancient world was in a state of moral chaos. Though the Jews had a high view of marriage, divorce was easy to obtain and all too frequent. And in the pagan world of that time, immorality and polygamy were rampant. In a world deluged with wanton excesses, it was essential for the church to demonstrate the sanctity of marriage through the monogamous, faithful behavior of its leaders.

The qualifications that overseers be "temperate, self-controlled," and "respectable" show that their lives were to demonstrate orderliness. These words emphasize the well-balanced mind of people who are in control of themselves. These people know when to be serious and know the importance of modesty.

The inns of the first century were often places of heavy drinking and fighting. As a result, it was essential that the overseer set an example for the rest of the flock by providing hospitality to strangers. Traveling teachers, believers fleeing persecution, the poor, and widows were some of the people in crisis for whom overseers were to open up their homes.

Because the overseers provided teaching in faith and doctrine to the members of the church, it was imperative that they have some skill in that area. While not all the overseers specialized in teaching, some did take the time to prepare for this valuable ministry. Overseers needed to have some ability in communicating the basic teachings of the faith.

Paul forbade overseers to be "violent" and "quarrelsome" (vs. 3). The words suggest that church leaders were not to be given to acts of physical abuse or be harsh in their dealings with others. Instead, they were to be considerate of the feelings of those to whom they ministered.

It was not uncommon in the first century A.D. for those holding positions of religious authority to strike someone in the face for displaying impiety. For instance, Jesus was unjustly struck in the face for an answer He gave while questioned before the high priest (John 18:22). Also, the high priest Ananias ordered that Paul be struck in the face when he was before the Sanhedrin (Acts 23:2).

That may be why Paul instructed church leaders not to be "violent" (1 Tim. 3:3)—or to not be a "striker," as the King James Version translates it. It is likely that false apostles in Corinth were actually hitting the resident believers in the face (2 Cor. 11:20). Paul would not tolerate such behavior among church leaders.

The apostle also considered it important that an overseer be someone who managed "his own family well" (1 Tim. 3:4). Paul argued that such a record would demonstrate ability to rule well in the church. The reference to children suggests grown children. The apostle was not setting up an acid test that the behavior of small children be used as a guide here, but that the actions of grown children be used as a gauge of the overseer's skill within the home (vs. 5). (Many hold it wrong, however, to see this as a requirement that a pastor be married and have children.)

B. Known for Their Sterling Character: vss. 6-7

He must not be a recent convert, or he may become conceited and fall under the same judgment as the devil. He must also have a good reputation with outsiders, so that he will not fall into disgrace and into the devil's trap.

Because of the danger that pride poses for the Christian leader, Paul insisted those chosen as overseers be mature believers and not new converts. An inflated sense of importance would cause a novice in the faith to fall and incur the same type of judgment imposed on Satan. Most commentators believe this refers to the overseer's loss of position due to pride (1 Tim. 3:6).

Not only were overseers to be respected in the church, but they were also to be looked upon favorably by those outside the church. A congregation that selects overseers with poor reputations for integrity would not only bring reproach upon itself but also leave the leaders open to Satan's attack (vs. 7). The devil seems able to make the most of incidents where Christian leaders fall.

II. Qualifications for Deacons: 1 Timothy 3:8-13

A. Known for Their Faith and Experience: vss. 8-10

Deacons, likewise, are to be men worthy of respect, sincere, not indulging in much wine, and not pursuing dishonest gain. They must keep hold of the deep truths of the faith with a clear conscience. They must first be tested; and then if there is nothing against them, let them serve as deacons.

Apart from the requirements listed in 1 Timothy 3:8-13, we know little about the office of deacon. The basic meaning of the word is "servant" and was used to refer to someone who waited on tables. Even though they did not teach or rule, the deacons performed essential duties in the ministry of a local church. But the fact that they held a lesser office did not mean churches could be careless in selecting them.

The fact that deacons were to be "sincere" (vs. 8) meant they were not to give conflicting statements, depending on the situation. The service of the deacons probably took them to many different homes in the church. It was essential that they not tell conflicting stories, but be consistent in their speech.

Like the overseer, the deacon was also to be careful not to abuse wine. The Greek word for "not given to drunkenness" in verse 3 depicts someone who spent a lot of time drinking. In Paul's day, wine often contained less alcohol than today. The phrase described someone who drank long enough for the effects of the alcohol to become apparent (vs. 8).

While the drinking of wine was prevalent in the culture of the day, church leaders were to exercise care so as not to even begin to come under its intoxicating influence (see Eph. 5:18). Timothy himself had totally abstained from wine and had to be instructed to drink some for his health (see 1 Tim. 5:23).

Neither the overseer nor the deacon were to be motivated by a desire for financial gain (3:3, 8). While Paul would have more to say later about lovers of money (see 6:6-10), here he stressed the need for church leaders to be free from greed. The deacons in particular, as distributors of the goods to the poor, needed to be people who could resist the temptation for "dishonest gain" (3:8) and be trusted with the resources of the church.

Although deacons normally did not teach, Paul insisted that they also be doctrinally sound (vs. 9). "Deep truths" is more literally rendered "mystery." This refers to something that would not have been known if God had not revealed it to us (see 1 Cor. 2:7-10). To possess a "clear conscience" (1 Tim. 3:9) in this regard meant that not only did deacons hold on to the true faith, but it was also reflected in their lives.

While it is essential that our beliefs be free from doctrinal error, it is also imperative that our lives provide an example of what we believe. If we say that Jesus is Lord, we must act as though He is in charge of our lives. We must never forget that non-Christians are watching to see if our lives measure up to what we profess to believe.

It might seem strange that Paul suggested that deacons be tested while nothing about that is said in regard to overseers. Paul meant that deacons' lives should be watched prior to selection to see if they had these listed characteristics (vs. 10). The same thing is implied in the long list of qualifications given for the overseers. When the prospective candidates had proven that they were serious about their faith, they were then to be considered for the offices.

B. Known for Their Worthy Associations: vss. 11-13

In the same way, their wives are to be women worthy of respect, not malicious talkers but temperate and trustworthy in everything. A deacon must be the husband of but one wife and must manage his children and his household well. Those who have served well gain an excellent standing and great assurance in their faith in Christ Jesus.

In 1 Timothy 3:11, Paul addressed the importance of female believers exemplifying integrity. Some think that Paul was referring primarily to the wives of deacons. As support, they note the fact that the requirements for the women appear right in the middle of those for deacons. Those who argue that Paul was giving qualifications for deaconesses point to the grammatical structure of the passage that suggests a new group is under consideration. There may have been women who served in this role in the first-century A.D. church (Rom. 16:1), and perhaps 1 Timothy 3:11 is a reference to the requirements for that position.

In any case, these women were required to show the same strength of character as were the men. This included being dignified, not slanderous, temperate, and faithful in every respect.

The requirements of faithfulness in marriage and well-managed households applied to deacons as well as to overseers (vs. 12). For deacons who served well there was ample reward (vs. 13). They earned respect within the congregation, laid up treasure for themselves in heaven, and enjoyed increased confidence in their faith in Christ. These things did not come just because one held such an office, but because of serving faithfully and using the gifts God had given.

III. GODLY CONDUCT: 1 TIMOTHY 3:14-15

Although I hope to come to you soon, I am writing you these instructions so that, if I am delayed, you will know how people ought to conduct themselves in God's household, which is the church of the living God, the pillar and foundation of the truth.

When Paul left Timothy in Ephesus, he hoped he would be able to return to him soon. Then when Paul realized that circumstances could keep him away longer than anticipated, he wrote 1 Timothy to provide his faithful representative with instructions for the churches under his care. These guidelines gave direction not only in the selection of church officers, but also in the matter of behavior within the church itself (3:14).

The directions were important because Timothy was managing things in "God's household" (vs. 15). This is not a reference to a congregational building, for the church still met in homes scattered throughout the various cities. The reference is to the believers themselves, who make up the church, and emphasizes the family nature of the Body of Christ.

Paul also described the church as "the pillar and foundation of the truth." In ancient times, pillars were used as much for display as they were for support. The statue of a famous person would often be on top of the pillar so that it would stand out from everything around it. As a pillar the church is to proudly display the truth of its faith so that others will be attracted to the saving message of the Gospel; and as the foundation and bulwark of the truth, the church protects the faith entrusted to it from perversion and error.

Discussion Questions

1. What sorts of virtues did Paul say should characterize church leaders?
2. What could happen to novices who are put in positions of church leadership?
3. What does it mean for deacons to be found blameless?
4. What were Paul's plans for visiting Timothy?
5. What did Paul say in 1 Timothy 3:15 about the church?

Contemporary Application

For many people, driving a car poses one of the severest tests to their character. It certainly has nothing to do with how they can operate a car or how they use their driving skills in challenging situations or under difficult circumstances. What it has to do with is maintaining their cool when someone cuts them off or is tailgating them. Some of the most gentle and kind people at any other time can become easily impatient and explosive on the roads.

The character of Christian leaders—from the pastoral staff to volunteer Sunday school teachers—is not just important behind the wheel of car. It is even more crucial when it comes to serving in a church. The Lord not only cares about what we do but also who we are as individuals; and He knows that the two are inseparable.

This week's lesson with its list of spiritual qualifications for overseers and deacons underscores that we cannot escape the issue of Christian character. Ultimately, what is important to God is not what is on the outside but what is in our hearts. Because our character as leaders in the church is important to the Lord, He endeavors to constantly transform us into the image of His Son, Jesus Christ. We can be of good character if we choose; and if we truly love the Lord, we will certainly seek to be like Him.

Guidance for Teaching

Scripture

Background Scripture: *1 Timothy 4*

Scripture Lesson: *1 Timothy 4*

Key Verse: *Watch your life and doctrine closely. Persevere in them, because if you do, you will save both yourself and your hearers.* 1 Timothy 4:16.

Scripture Lesson for Children: *Acts 11:19-26; 1 Timothy 4:7-16*

Key Verse for Children: *Until I [Paul] come, devote yourself to the public reading of Scripture, to preaching and to teaching.* 1 Timothy 4:13.

Lesson Aim

To stress the importance of setting a Christlike example in word and deed.

Lesson Setting

Time: *About A.D. 62*

Places: *Macedonia and Ephesus*

Lesson Outline

Guidance for Teaching

   I. The Lie of False Teaching: 1 Timothy 4:1-5
      A. *Demonic Origins: vss. 1-2*
      B. *Divine Perspective: vss. 3-5*
  II. A Good Minister of Christ: 1 Timothy 4:6-10
      A. *Explain the Truth: vs. 6*
      B. *Aim for Godliness: vss. 7-8*
      C. *Hope in God: vss. 9-10*
 III. A Godly Example: 1 Timothy 4:11-16
      A. *Setting an Example: vss. 11-13*
      B. *Remaining Diligent in Ministry: vss. 14-16*

Introduction for Adults

Topic: *Set an Example*

On May 27, 2003, Cypress Community Christian School (CCCS) in Houston, Texas, held their annual graduation ceremony. In the June 2003 issue of *Update*, the school's official newsletter, Debbie Hodges, secondary principal at CCCS, expressed the appreciation all her colleagues felt toward the parents of the seniors: "Thank you for your endless hours of sacrifice to make CCCS a better place. Thank you for loving your children so much and for setting a Christlike example of servanthood for our students. We could not do our jobs without you. May God bless you."

The is the type of example that the adult members of your class can model before others in your church, regardless of their age. Consider using this week's lesson as an opportunity to encourage them toward that end.

Introduction for Youth

Topic: *Teaching by Example*

Teens reflect the character of individuals they admire but have never met. Adolescents also exemplify the behavior, dress, and habits of family members, friends, peers, and neighbors. Imitating others can be a good thing if those who serve as role models are upright people.

This week's lesson challenges your students not only to consider Jesus as a suitable role model, but also to become a Christlike example for others to follow. The more class members focus their attention on Him and behave in ways that are characteristic of Him, the more they will set a Christlike example in their words and deeds.

Concepts for Children

Topic: *Good Leaders Teach God's Word*

1. The believing Jews, who were treated harshly in Jerusalem and scattered to faraway cities, proclaimed the Gospel wherever they went.
2. Believers must use their God-given gifts to help the church grow spiritually and numerically.
3. A group of church leaders realized that God also wanted Timothy to be a church leader.
4. Timothy serves as a role model for church leaders today because of the wholesome way he spoke and acted.
5. The Lord wants us to tell others about Him through what we say and how we act.

Lesson Commentary

I. THE LIE OF FALSE TEACHING: 1 TIMOTHY 4:1-5

A. Demonic Origins: vss. 1-2

The Spirit clearly says that in later times some will abandon the faith and follow deceiving spirits and things taught by demons. Such teachings come through hypocritical liars, whose consciences have been seared as with a hot iron.

While the church was to be the "pillar and foundation of the truth" (1 Tim. 3:15), the Holy Spirit revealed that some would depart from the true faith and lapse into false doctrine. The Spirit did not express this in symbolic terms or merely suggest it through a dream, but stated it clearly to either Paul or another prophet in the church (4:1). Because of the importance of this matter, it is possible that the Spirit revealed it to more than one apostle or prophet.

"Later times" refers generally to the period between the first and second comings of Christ. The abandoning of the faith spoken of by the Holy Spirit was already taking place in Ephesus. The departure of some from the faith was a characteristic of that time and of all the times that followed, including our own.

Along with predicting the abandonment of the faith by some, the Holy Spirit also exposed the demonic nature of the false teaching that would lead people astray. When people turn away from Christ and the truths of the Gospel, they are falling prey to "deceiving spirits" who lead them progressively further into error. Paul considered Satan to be an enemy constantly at work seeking to pervert the saving message of Christ and mislead people.

Paul referred to the false teachers as "hypocritical liars" (vs. 2). Although they knew better, these leaders had deliberately turned from the faith. They appeared as actors or actresses with masks covering the true nature of their deception. Paul pictured these people as purposely teaching false doctrine in order to deceive others and lead them away from the faith.

The false teachers, however, did not feel any pangs of guilt from their actions, for their consciences had been "seared as with a hot iron." This figure conveys the idea that these teachers had numbed or desensitized consciences. The false teachers had branded their consciences to the point where they no longer sensed any guilt. Even their radical act of distorting the truth left them with no ill feeling from leading others astray.

B. Divine Perspective: vss. 3-5

They forbid people to marry and order them to abstain from certain foods, which God created to be received with thanksgiving by those who believe and who know the truth. For everything God created is good, and nothing is to be rejected if it is received with thanksgiving, because it is consecrated by the word of God and prayer.

These teachers may have sounded quite pious to the unsuspecting follower. After all, they promoted an ascetic lifestyle, forbidding people to marry or to partake of certain foods (1 Tim. 4:3). Probably this was because they had bought into the philosophical idea, current in their time, that matter is evil and only spirit is good. This idea later became part of a heresy called gnosticism, which seriously threatened the church.

Here Paul did not further attack the false teachers' prohibition on marriage, though he certainly did not go along with that prohibition. Rather, he attacked the prohibition against foods. Paul argued that because God created foods, He meant for us to eat them with an attitude of thankfulness. And besides that, everything God created is "good" (vs. 4; see Gen. 1:21, 25, 29-30). Avoiding something God created for us and called "good" cannot make us more spiritual.

For those who do enjoy God's gifts, they must not forget to thank Him for His provisions. A prayer of thanksgiving shows that we recognize God's care for us as well as our dependence on Him. The phrase "consecrated by the word of God and prayer" (1 Tim. 4:5) does not suggest a magic formula but rather a way to set these things apart as God's gifts in keeping with His revealed word. God spoke His word of approval and we speak our word of gratitude.

II. A GOOD MINISTER OF CHRIST: 1 TIMOTHY 4:6-10

A. Explain the Truth: vs. 6

If you point these things out to the brothers, you will be a good minister of Christ Jesus, brought up in the truths of the faith and of the good teaching that you have followed.

Having described the error of the false teachers, Paul told Timothy how to fortify himself and the churches under his care against their devious message. His first responsibility was to "point these things out" (1 Tim. 4:6) to inform believers about the deception of Satan. Timothy was to teach proper doctrine in a calm and articulate manner. This would make him a "good minister of Christ Jesus."

Timothy earned high praise from the apostle because the young man had remained faithful to sound teaching. He had been raised in an atmosphere of faith and adherence to the Scriptures (see 2 Tim. 1:5; 3:15). Now he had earned Paul's commendation for continuing to grow in God's Word while teaching and promoting sound biblical truths.

B. Aim for Godliness: vss. 7-8

Have nothing to do with godless myths and old wives' tales; rather, train yourself to be godly. For physical training is of some value, but godliness has value for all things, holding promise for both the present life and the life to come.

Paul repeated a warning he had given in regard to "godless myths and old wives' tales" (1 Tim. 4:7; compare 1:4). These were the Jewish fables and legends that embellished the Old Testament chronologies and stories. Paul instructed Timothy to avoid them and refuse to be pulled into discussions about them. His focus was to be solely on the sound teachings of the faith.

Instead of concerning himself with Jewish fables, Timothy was to keep on training himself for godliness. He had much more important things to do than listen to pointless stories told by misguided teachers. He was to exercise his spiritual muscles so he could continue to grow strong in his faith.

The reference to training caused Paul to bring up the relative value of physical exercise. The apostle acknowledged that such physical discipline had "some value" (vs. 8). We should not take this as a disparaging remark about bodily exercise; Paul was not seeking to discourage physical fitness. It does have its place. But the gain of physical training, while significant, pales by way of comparison to what godliness can accomplish.

C. Hope in God: vss. 9-10

This is a trustworthy saying that deserves full acceptance (and for this we labor and strive), that we have put our hope in the living God, who is the Savior of all men, and especially of those who believe.

In 1 Timothy 4:9, Paul again highlighted his message with "This is a trustworthy saying that deserves full acceptance." Interpreters of this passage are split on whether this phrase goes with the statement in the previous verse or with the verses after it. In either case, Paul was using athletic metaphors to make his point.

The Greek word translated "labor" (vs. 10) pictures someone who works to the point of exhaustion. "Strive" was used of an athlete who exerted all his energy to win. Together, these terms reveal the strenuous effort that Paul and Timothy put into encouraging godliness among believers while protecting the Gospel against deceitful and futile thinking.

Since their hope was firmly placed in the living God, Paul and Timothy could toil knowing that their efforts would not be in vain. This hope was not just for them but for all who put personal trust in the Savior. The two ministers remained confident that anyone who pursued godliness within a growing relationship with Christ would not be disappointed but would enjoy its benefits forever.

The Lord is the Savior of all people, and in particular those who put their faith in Christ. This statement reflects the fact that Jesus died for all of humanity. While Christ's death was great enough to atone for the sins of the whole world (see 1 John 2:2), that does not mean that everyone will be saved. Other passages make it clear that only those who respond to Jesus' work in faith will be saved (see John 1:12).

III. A GODLY EXAMPLE: 1 TIMOTHY 4:11-16

A. Setting an Example: vss. 11-13

Command and teach these things. Don't let anyone look down on you because you are young, but set an example for the believers in speech, in life, in love, in faith and in purity. Until I come, devote yourself to the public reading of Scripture, to preaching and to teaching.

As Paul's representative to the churches in and around Ephesus, Timothy was to continue to command and teach the need for self-discipline and godliness. Paul made Timothy's role clear: he was to pass on Paul's teaching to the churches under his care (1 Tim. 4:11).

There was, however, a perceived problem. Some regarded Timothy as too young for such a task and had contempt for him. Perhaps the false teachers kept expressing this opinion, hoping to minimize his impact as Paul's representative. The apostle's remarks here were meant not only to bolster Timothy's confidence but also to discourage anyone who might oppose Timothy by attacking him because of his age. No one was to look down on Timothy because of his youth (vs. 12).

While Timothy was much younger than Paul, he was old enough to carry out his responsibilities. The Greek word rendered "young" was used of those who were of military age, which extended to about 40. Timothy was most likely somewhere between 35 and 40 years of age at this time.

One way for Timothy to silence his critics was to continue being an example of the faith he proclaimed. Paul was not saying that Timothy had failed in this area. Rather, as Timothy remained steadfast in all aspects of Christian living, others would recognize his maturity in the faith and respect him for it.

While Paul was away, Timothy was to devote himself to three things. The first item was "the public reading of Scripture" (vs. 13). The early church copied the synagogue practice of reading the Hebrew Scriptures (Old Testament) at every service. Here the apostle encouraged that custom, which by this time also included reading some of the New Testament Scriptures.

In the synagogues, after the Scriptures were read, the people were encouraged to carry out the commands of the reading. That sort of exhortation for others to obey was the "preaching" referred to in verse 13—the second matter Timothy was to devote himself to. "Teaching"—the third detail—consisted of instruction in doctrine and appealed to the minds of the listeners.

B. Remaining Diligent in Ministry: vss. 14-16

Do not neglect your gift, which was given you through a prophetic message when the body of elders laid their hands on you. Be diligent in these matters; give yourself wholly to them, so that everyone may see your progress. Watch your life and doctrine closely. Persevere in them, because if you do, you will save both yourself and your hearers.

Paul's personal instruction to Timothy included a reminder not to "neglect" (1 Tim. 4:14) his spiritual gift. As elsewhere, Paul's words should not be taken as an indication that Timothy had become careless. The apostle's admonition was a reminder that a gift requires attention in order to be effective. Although we are not told the exact nature of the gift, some have suggested that it might have been teaching, the discerning of error, or pastoring.

The scene Paul described in verse 14 may have taken place at the time of Timothy's ordination (see Acts 16:1-3), but we cannot be certain. His gift was identified through a prophetic utterance by someone in attendance. The laying on of hands by the elders symbolized Timothy's reception of the gift as well as his call into the ministry. God was the one who gave him the gift and the ministry in which to use it.

Timothy's spiritual life and ministry were to be his continual concern. Paul commanded him to be "diligent" (1 Tim. 4:15) in these things and to give himself "wholly" to them. These words suggest that Timothy was to undertake his teaching and ministry carefully. As a result of giving himself wholeheartedly to Christ and His work, others would recognize Timothy's progress in the faith.

Like a coach admonishing his star athlete, Paul kept encouraging Timothy to guard his ministry and life and to "persevere in them" (vs. 16). The apostle had given his protégé sound instruction; now it was up to Timothy to remain loyal to the truth in both his life and ministry. As someone called upon to uphold the truth in the face of much false teaching, it was crucial that he guard his own thoughts and feelings. A failure would hurt both Timothy and the cause of Christ in the churches around Ephesus.

The phrase at the end of verse 16, "you will save both yourself and your hearers," should be looked at in light of the context of remaining true to the Gospel. Preachers who do not herald the true Gospel rob their listeners of the opportunity to become believers and call into question the validity of their own faith. Moreover, while we are saved at the time of our conversion to Christ, our salvation is also a process in which we become more and more like Christ (see Phil. 2:12-13). Timothy's faithful devotion to godliness and his ministry would not earn salvation for anyone, but would bring himself and others closer to Christ.

Discussion Questions

1. What was the nature of the false teachers' doctrinal error?
2. How could Timothy demonstrate to others that he was a good servant of Christ?
3. Why was it important for Timothy to train himself for godliness?
4. What sorts of things was Timothy to insist on and teach?
5. How could Timothy be an exemplary role model to others?

Contemporary Application

As followers of Christ, we are to set an example for others in our speech. This means—among other things—being honest and objective, not misleading and exaggerated, in the things we say. It also means being sensitive to how our words might affect others. We can tell people the truth in a mean-spirited way, leaving them feeling misunderstood and resentful, or we can undergird our words with the love of Christ.

We should also be an example of Christ in the things we do. One way is by taking a stand for the truth. If others are maligning or contradicting the Gospel, we should make every effort to defend the faith. If others wrong us, we should not hold a grudge against them; instead, we should readily and unconditionally forgive them. If we see others in need, we should not turn our backs on them; rather, we should do what we can to help.

God Desires Justice and Mercy

DEVOTIONAL READING

Matthew 23:23-28

DAILY BIBLE READINGS

Monday January 23
Psalm 33:1-5 God Loves Righteousness and Justice

Tuesday January 24
Proverbs 28:4-13 Show Justice, Integrity, Righteousness, and Mercy

Wednesday January 25
Matthew 23:23-28 Jesus Demands Justice and Mercy

Thursday January 26
James 2:8-13 Mercy Triumphs over Judgment

Friday January 27
1 Timothy 5:1-8 Show Mercy to All Believers

Saturday January 28
1 Timothy 5:9-16 Show Justice to the Widows

Sunday January 29
1 Timothy 5:17-25 Show Justice to the Elders

Scripture

Background Scripture: *1 Timothy 5*
Scripture Lesson: *1 Timothy 5:1-8, 17-24*
Key Verses: *Do not rebuke an older man harshly, but exhort him as if he were your father. Treat younger men as brothers, older women as mothers, and younger women as sisters, with absolute purity.* 1 Timothy 5:1-2.
Scripture Lesson for Children: *Luke 19:1-10; 1 Timothy 5:25*
Key Verse for Children: *"For the Son of Man came to seek and to save what was lost."* Luke 19:10.

Lesson Aim

To emphasize the value of being humble and respectful of one another.

Lesson Setting

Time: *About A.D. 62*
Places: *Macedonia and Ephesus*

Lesson Outline

God Desires Justice and Mercy

I.   Respect for All: 1 Timothy 5:1-2
II. Honor for Widows: 1 Timothy 5:3-8
    A. *Assistance from Family Members: vss. 3-4*
    B. *Truly Destitute Widows: vss. 5-7*
    C. *Irresponsible Family Members: vs. 8*
III. Double Honor for Elders: 1 Timothy 5:17-24
    A. *Appropriate Compensation: vss. 17-18*
    B. *Due Process: vss. 19-20*
    C. *Appoint Judiciously: vss. 21-22*
    D. *Exercise Discernment: vss. 23-24*

Introduction for Adults

Topic: *Practicing Justice and Mercy*

In *Love Beyond Reason: Moving God's Love from Your Head to Your Heart,* John Ortberg asserts the following: "Envy is wanting what another person has and feeling badly that I don't have it. Envy is disliking God's goodness to someone else and dismissing God's goodness to me. Envy is desire plus resentment. Envy is anti-community."

An envious heart is incapable of showing justice, mercy, and humility, for it is too preoccupied. And its seed of discontentment quickly grows into the weed of resentment. This weed can choke relationships—even among Christians. So how can adult believers eradicate this weed? Extermination begins with developing a right attitude toward God and the blessings He, in His wisdom, bestows. The result is the increased presence of justice and mercy within the Body of Christ.

Introduction for Youth

Topic: *God's Family*

Edith Schaeffer, in her book entitled *What Is a Family?*, relates that the family is an "ever-changing mobile of life, a center for the formation of human relationships, a perpetual relayer of truth, and a museum of memories." She also notes that these days the survival of the family as a living, loving unit is being threatened as never before.

Saved teens can help to create a biblically centered view of God's family by shunning such vices as arrogance and selfishness and embracing such virtues as humility, respect, and mercy. Moreover, they can do their part to enable Edith Schaeffer's vision of the family to become an increasing reality among believers.

Concepts for Children

Topic: *Good Leaders Respect Others*

1. As Jesus made His way through the town of Jericho, He met a man named Zacchaeus who collected taxes for the government of Rome.
2. Zacchaeus took Jesus to his home in great excitement and joy.
3. Some people in the crowds were unhappy that Jesus would have anything to do with a tax collector, whom the people generally disliked.
4. Jesus declared that this was a time of joy because Zacchaeus had come to saving faith.
5. We can also feel happy when others around us put their faith in Jesus for salvation.

Lesson Commentary

I. RESPECT FOR ALL: 1 TIMOTHY 5:1-2

Do not rebuke an older man harshly, but exhort him as if he were your father. Treat younger men as brothers, older women as mothers, and younger women as sisters, with absolute purity.

The diligence with which Timothy was to attend to his personal faith (1 Tim. 4:15) needed to be matched by his care in how he treated people in the churches under his supervision. The attitudes he displayed toward fellow members of the church family would set the tone for effective church ministry. There would be times when members of the church family would need to be dealt with by Timothy. He was to deal with them differently, depending on their gender and age, but he was to treat all of them as members of his own family.

The first example is the case of an older man who had done something wrong. Timothy was not to harshly rebuke such a person. The Greek word translated "rebuke" in 5:1 literally means to "assault with blows"; the sense is that of pounding with words. Rather than rebuking in this way, Timothy was to exhort an older man as his father. The idea behind "exhort" is calling aside to talk with in private. Thus while Timothy was not to ignore an older man's sin, he was to bring up the issue in a respectful, loving way.

Paul briefly mentioned three other types of people. When dealing with younger men, Timothy was to treat them as brothers, that is, to avoid any appearance of self-exaltation because of his position. As for older women, Timothy was to treat them as mothers, showing them respect, just as with older men. In regard to younger women, Timothy was to deal with them as with sisters, in "absolute purity" (vs. 2). Impropriety in that regard could bring reproach upon the church and ruin the ministry of Paul's representative.

Loving exhortation is not for church leaders alone. In Ephesians 4:15, Paul said that believers were to speak "the truth in love." When it comes to admonishing others, we usually fail to say anything at all or fail to confront them respectfully. Paul's solution is that we humbly and gently counsel others with a careful eye on our own lives (see Gal. 6:1).

II. HONOR FOR WIDOWS: 1 TIMOTHY 5:3-8

A. Assistance from Family Members: vss. 3-4

Give proper recognition to those widows who are really in need. But if a widow has children or grandchildren, these should learn first of all to put their religion into practice by caring for their own family and so repaying their parents and grandparents, for this is pleasing to God.

In 1 Timothy 5:3-16, Paul gave many guidelines for churches to follow regarding the treatment of widows. Following the lead of the Jewish synagogue, the early church sought to provide for the needs of widows. One of the first controversies in the church was over the distribution of food to widows (see Acts 6:1).

Although Greek the word for "proper recognition" (1 Tim. 5:3) means to honor or respect, it can also include the idea of financial support. The context strongly suggests that the church was not only honoring widows but also sustaining those widows who had no other livelihood.

While Paul desired to help widows who were really in need, he did not want the church's resources to be wasted on those who had other means of support. If a widow had children or grandchildren who could take care of her, then she was not truly destitute. In that instance, it was the congregation's duty to point out that obligation to her family members. Godly children would welcome the opportunity to please the Lord by paying back their parents for all they had done for them (vs. 4).

B. Truly Destitute Widows: vss. 5-7

The widow who is really in need and left all alone puts her hope in God and continues night and day to pray and to ask God for help. But the widow who lives for pleasure is dead even while she lives. Give the people these instructions, too, so that no one may be open to blame.

The type of widows the apostle Paul had in mind for support were godly women who depended upon the Lord to meet their needs. The congregation's responsibility rested with believing widows who displayed their godliness through faith and continual prayer (1 Tim. 5:5).

The church did not have an obligation, however, to maintain those widows who lived for pleasure rather than for God. Such women were spiritually dead (vs. 6). The implication is that widows who indulged in a wasteful, selfish, or sensual way of life were not to be honored in any sense. The limited resources of the church were not to be used to sustain that type of lifestyle. Timothy was to share these matters (vss. 3-6) with the churches to avoid arguments resulting from poor decisions in supporting widows (vs. 7).

C. Irresponsible Family Members: vs. 8

If anyone does not provide for his relatives, and especially for his immediate family, he has denied the faith and is worse than an unbeliever.

It appears that some in the early church were already taking advantage of the generosity of congregations by letting the church provide for their needy family members. Paul strongly denounced such an attitude by pointing out the necessity of taking care of one's own relatives. Men and women were responsible to provide for their immediate and extended families. To neglect needy members was a practical denial of the faith they claimed to believe (1 Tim. 5:8).

III. Double Honor for Elders: 1 Timothy 5:17-24

A. Appropriate Compensation: vss. 17-18

The elders who direct the affairs of the church well are worthy of double honor, especially those whose work is preaching and teaching. For the Scripture says, "Do not muzzle the ox while it is treading out the grain," and "The worker deserves his wages."

In 1 Timothy 5:9-16, Paul gave various guidelines to help his son in the faith decide which widows the church should put on his list for support. Then, in verse 17, the apostle shifted his emphasis from the support of widows to the support of elders. While some contend that "honor" should be used exclusively in the sense of respect, most commentators believe that the context supports financial reimbursement for church leaders who excelled at preaching and teaching. Those who preached and taught would need to spend considerable time in preparation for those activities. It was only fair that they receive some compensation for their labor.

What did Paul mean by "double honor"? It may imply recognition for both the office and for the effort in performing its duties well. Or it may indicate generosity in their pay or in honor or in both. While this phrase is difficult to understand, Paul was making it clear that church leaders should be held in high regard for their position and for their hard work.

To support his contention of reimbursement for church elders, Paul quoted from Deuteronomy 25:4 as well as from Luke 10:7. Paul also used the Deuteronomy passage in 1 Corinthians 9:9, where he argued for the right of ministers to be financially supported by those who benefit from their ministry. The words of Jesus referring to the worker and wages also strongly indicate that Paul was seeking to build his case for financial support of elders (1 Tim. 5:18).

Deuteronomy 25:4 prohibits keeping an ox from eating as it treads out the grain. As farm animals, oxen were used for plowing and threshing. When threshing, the oxen were often tethered to a post in the middle of the threshing floor. The sheaves of corn were laid on the floor, and the oxen were made to march round and round, pulling a threshing sledge over the grain.

While they were performing this service, the oxen were allowed to feed on as much of the grain as they wished. If a farmer were especially stingy, he could muzzle the oxen so that they would not be able to eat. Usually this was considered unwise, since the animal's increasing frustration level would have a negative effect on its willingness to work.

B. Due Process: vss. 19-20

Do not entertain an accusation against an elder unless it is brought by two or three witnesses. Those who sin are to be rebuked publicly, so that the others may take warning.

Regrettably, there would be times when the elder had to endure the opposite of honor. In these cases, Timothy was not to consider any accusation against an elder unless it could be substantiated by two or three witnesses (1 Tim. 5:19). This Old Testament principle referred to bringing cases to judgment (see Deut. 19:15). But in 1 Timothy 5:19 the witnesses were required to appear before any further action could be contemplated. Moreover, any action taken had to be based on established fact, not gossip or the careless slander of an adversary.

When it was proven that an elder had sinned, that person was to be rebuked before the others so they would think twice before they made the same mistake (vs. 20). The "others" probably refers to the rest of the elders in the church, but some believe that this refers to the whole congregation. If the offense was serious enough to warrant removal from office, then the matter would need to come before everyone in the church.

C. Appoint Judiciously: vss. 21-22

I charge you, in the sight of God and Christ Jesus and the elect angels, to keep these instructions without partiality, and to do nothing out of favoritism. Do not be hasty in the laying on of hands, and do not share in the sins of others. Keep yourself pure.

In dealing with such matters, Timothy or any other church leader would be tempted either to prejudge a matter or show partiality before examining all the facts. Paul solemnly warned Timothy against letting his personal feelings dictate the outcome of an investigation (1 Tim. 5:21). When dealing with such matters, he needed to be mindful of God's presence.

One way to avoid having to discipline elders was to exercise great care in choosing them. Paul's instruction not to be "hasty in the laying on of hands" (vs. 22) refers to ordaining people to the ministry before they had a chance to establish themselves in the faith. Ordination assumes approval of a person for the ministry. Those who ordain unwisely share in the sins of spiritually immature candidates.

D. Exercise Discernment: vss. 23-24

Stop drinking only water, and use a little wine because of your stomach and your frequent illnesses. The sins of some men are obvious, reaching the place of judgment ahead of them; the sins of others trail behind them.

The admonition "Keep yourself pure" in 1 Timothy 5:22 may have moved Paul to reflect on that principle in the life of his spiritual son. Apparently Timothy abstained from wine in seeking to set a good example. Paul, however, let him know that keeping pure did not include jeopardizing his health, and thus encouraged him to drink a little wine for his stomach. Luke, a physician and Paul's traveling companion, may have advised Paul in this matter. Pure drinking water was not readily available in those days; wine would have been safer to drink, especially for someone who was sick (vs. 23).

Paul sought to encourage Timothy, who might have been overly concerned about missing a problem in those he ordained. Some sins would be obvious, while others would be hidden. But even in the cases where the sins were concealed, a careful investigation would bring them to light. If he was patient, the hidden sins would eventually reveal themselves (vs. 24).

The same was true in regard to good works. With some candidates, it would take less time to be able to instantly recognize their qualifications for the ministry. With others, time would again reveal their works in behalf of God's kingdom (vs. 25).

Paul's encouragement to wait before appointing someone to a place of leadership is especially relevant today. Because of the mobility of our society, and because of our need for workers, it is easy to give people responsible positions without taking the time to evaluate their character. As Paul said, it takes a while for a person's sins or good works to come to the surface.

Discussion Questions

1. How do you think Timothy might have related to younger women in a virtuous manner?
2. What responsibility did extended family members have toward destitute widows?
3. How could one discern whether a widow was truly destitute?
4. Why was it important for the church to compensate adequately its hardworking elders?
5. How was the church to deal with renegade elders?

Contemporary Application

It is hard to be humble and respectful when someone has hurt us; yet we are called to forgive. Forgiving is harder than excusing because to forgive we must summon up our courage and hold the other person accountable.

This kind of forgiving means determining to treat the other person as a worthy human being—worthy of our full respect and involvement. To excuse, on the other hand, minimizes the other as being not quite valuable enough to take up our energies. We simply choose to ignore him or her and go on our way. Such displeases God.

Christian leaders are the role models for other believers. First, they must lead by example, as our Lord did. Second, Christian leaders become examples of humility by submitting to Jesus, rather than advocating their own agenda. Third, a godly leader respects every person in the congregation. If that happens, each member in turn will see others as people of value who are appreciated for what they contribute to the church.

Be True to Your Christian Heritage

DEVOTIONAL READING

2 Thessalonians 2:13-17

DAILY BIBLE READINGS

Monday January 30
*Psalm 111 God Gives the
Heritage*

Tuesday January 31
*Jeremiah 17:1-8 We Can
Lose Our Heritage*

Wednesday February 1
*2 Thessalonians 2:13-17
Stand Firm, Hold Fast*

Thursday February 2
*Acts 16:1-5 Timothy's
Mother Was a Believer*

Friday February 3
*2 Timothy 1:1-5 Lois and
Eunice Passed On Faith*

Saturday February 4
*2 Timothy 1:6-10 Be Not
Ashamed of Your Heritage*

Sunday February 5
*2 Timothy 1:11-18 Guard
the Good Treasure Given
You*

Scripture

Background Scripture: *2 Timothy 1*
Scripture Lesson: *2 Timothy 1:3-14*
Key Verse: *I have been reminded of your sincere faith, which
first lived in your grandmother Lois and in your mother
Eunice and, I am persuaded, now lives in you also.*
2 Timothy 1:5.
Scripture Lesson for Children: *2 Timothy 1:2-7; 3:14-17*
Key Verse for Children: *I [Paul] have been reminded of
your sincere faith, which first lived in your grandmother Lois
and in your mother Eunice and . . . now lives in you also.*
2 Timothy 1:5.

Lesson Aim

To stress that the believer's allegiance to Christ must be
wholehearted and unwavering.

Lesson Setting

Time: *About A.D. 67*
Place: *Rome*

Lesson Outline

Be True to Your Christian Heritage

   I. Timothy's Heritage: 2 Timothy 1:3-7
      *A. Paul's Prayers for and Thoughts of Timothy:
         vss. 3-4*
      B. Paul's Exhortation to Timothy: vss. 5-7
  II. Timothy's Courage: 2 Timothy 1:8-14
      A. The Willingness to Suffer for the Gospel: vs. 8
      B. The Centrality of the Gospel of Grace: vss. 9-10
      C. The Suffering of Paul for the Gospel: vss. 11-12
      *D. The Unwavering Commitment of Timothy to
         the Gospel: vss. 13-14*

Introduction for Adults

Topic: *A Heritage of Faith*

Even before George hailed the taxi for the airport, he knew he had lost an opportunity to share the Gospel with his new acquaintances at a national convention. He always found it hard to go to a meeting where he knew almost no one, but he had hoped he would be able to tell someone about the heritage of faith he had in Christ. Yet like so many of us, George had failed once again.

Why is it that believers who want to witness for Christ find it difficult to do so? Fear is a possible reason, as suggested by how often we tense up and breathe faster with our mouths going dry whenever an opportunity to witness comes our way. Mature believers can overcome some of their fear by seeking to maintain a better balance between boldness and graciousness in their witness.

Introduction for Youth

Topic: *Guard the Good Treasure*

"As [this course] examines the development and beliefs of each religion, it is intended to deepen the students' own religious lives by giving a deeper appreciation of God's goodness as we see it at work in the religions in these course." No, this isn't an excerpt from the syllabus of a world religions course offered at a secular university. It is from the syllabus of a Christian high school!

The problem with the previous quote is that it tries to "equalize" Christianity with other religions, as if these can fully share in the goodness of God. In actuality, only Jesus is the way, the truth, and the life (John 14:5-7). And that is why saved teens should be encouraged to guard the good treasure of the Gospel entrusted to their care.

Concepts for Children

Topic: *We Learn from Family*

1. Christian parents and grandparents are a child's first spiritual teachers.
2. Faith is something we cannot keep to ourselves but must share with others.
3. God deserves our praise and thanksgiving for blessing us with families.
4. Families can pass on Christian traditions.
5. As children live out their faith, they become examples to others.

Lesson Commentary

I. TIMOTHY'S HERITAGE: 2 TIMOTHY 1:3-7

A. Paul's Prayers for and Thoughts of Timothy: vss. 3-4

I thank God, whom I serve, as my forefathers did, with a clear conscience, as night and day I constantly remember you in my prayers. Recalling your tears, I long to see you, so that I may be filled with joy.

When Paul wrote his Second Letter to Timothy (perhaps four to seven years after his first letter), circumstances had changed. Some of the challenges facing Timothy as a young leader of the church in Ephesus had worsened. The false teaching that Paul had warned about in 1 Timothy persisted. Some believers continued to be deceived. The church, though it had been founded on solid doctrine and the transforming power of God's grace, had become tainted with deception.

Unlike the challenges faced by other churches with which Paul had worked, such as those in Galatia and Corinth, the threats to the Ephesian church did not come from outside but from within. Some of their own leaders had distorted the truth of the Gospel. It was the very thing Paul had feared might happen when he had admonished the Ephesian elders (see Acts 20:13-38, especially verse 30).

Beyond the changing circumstances in Ephesus, Paul himself faced new challenges—like his imprisonment in a Roman dungeon. Unlike his earlier incarceration, which was a relatively mild "house arrest" experience (see 28:16), Paul now found himself in a dark cell in chains, contending with loneliness and isolation (see 2 Tim. 2:9). Although he didn't give us such details, it is likely he had to endure rats and other unsanitary conditions of primitive prisons.

Despite the apostle's imprisonment, it did not prevent him from including a word of thanksgiving after his greeting recorded in 1:1-2. Paul acknowledged the richness of his spiritual heritage and understood its value for him. Like his godly ancestors, the apostle's conscience was unstained (vs. 3). A clear conscience is essential to unhindered ministry. Even so, Paul admitted that a clear conscience was not a litmus test for innocence (see 1 Cor. 4:4). We must constantly open our hearts to God so that He can lovingly point out sinful motives and attitudes that we are blind to.

Furthermore, Paul prayed for Timothy night and day; this young man was carrying a heavy burden and needed all the support he could get. Timothy's tears at their last parting increased Paul's desire to see his protégé again so that the apostle might be "filled with joy" (2 Tim. 1:4).

B. Paul's Exhortation to Timothy: vss. 5-7

I have been reminded of your sincere faith, which first lived in your grandmother Lois and in your mother Eunice and, I am persuaded, now lives in you also. For this reason I remind you to fan into flame the gift of God, which is in you through the laying on of my hands. For God did not give us a spirit of timidity, but a spirit of power, of love and of self-discipline.

The apostle rejoiced whenever he encountered genuine faith—not the puffed-up self-righteousness of tenured religious leaders, but humble, God-fearing belief. Paul rejoiced to see such faith in Timothy as the apostle had seen in the young man's grandmother and mother (2 Tim. 1:4-5).

Confident of Timothy's faith, Paul hoped to improve Timothy's ministry effectiveness. He admonished the young pastor, "Fan into flame the gift of God" (vs. 6). At Timothy's ordination, in which Paul had played a part, Timothy had received a spiritual gift for ministry. Paul used the metaphor of a flame to describe God's gift. The Lord, who is sovereign and who alone can accomplish His purposes, calls us to work in cooperation with Him. God puts the spark within us, but we must decide whether we will fan the flame or smother it. Paul's word to Timothy was reflective of the apostle's warning to the Thessalonians: "Do not put out the Spirit's fire" (1 Thess. 5:19).

Timothy had been called by God, commissioned for the work, and anointed by God's Spirit. Paul had prayed over him and had seen evidence of the gift of God in Timothy. But Paul was not satisfied with just a good start. He knew that Timothy's commitment to serve had been severely tested by false teachers who challenged his role as leader in the church. The apostle also knew that Timothy would face ongoing adversity if he was to fulfill his work of ministry.

Paul was concerned because he didn't want Timothy to shrink from the challenges of leadership. He wanted Timothy to be fearless, confident of God's power and love. The apostle wanted his young protégé to be disciplined to follow God's call through to the end (2 Tim. 1:7).

II. TIMOTHY'S COURAGE: 2 TIMOTHY 1:8-14

A. The Willingness to Suffer for the Gospel: vs. 8

So do not be ashamed to testify about our Lord, or ashamed of me his prisoner. But join with me in suffering for the gospel, by the power of God.

In light of God's giving a spirit of power instead of a spirit of timidity, Paul called on Timothy to be courageous. It's probable that Paul's current imprisonment was not an isolated occurrence but rather a part of the first widespread persecution of Christians by the Romans, begun by the emperor Nero. If this persecution hadn't already reached Ephesus in Asia Minor, it would. Timothy had to be brave now.

While persecution made Christianity unpopular and put Paul in prison, the apostle urged Timothy not to be ashamed of either the Lord or Paul. It would have been tempting for Timothy to distance himself from Jesus and Paul; nevertheless, that would have been wrong. In fact, Paul called on Timothy to participate in suffering for the Gospel. Paul assured him that God would give him whatever power he needed to endure and learn from hardships. With God's help, Timothy could weather whatever hardships—even opposition—were necessary to spread the Gospel (2 Tim. 1:8).

Timothy had a choice to make. Would he trust God's power to work within him? Or would he shrink from the battle? Like Timothy, we have similar choices to make. God offers us tremendous gifts—salvation, special abilities, spiritual insight and power. The question is, will we use the gifts God has given to boldly answer His call to serve? Will we fan into flame the Spirit within us? Paul's challenge to Timothy speaks to us as well. We may have to face difficulties for the cause of Christ. But we can be confident that God's grace will be sufficient to help us overcome.

B. The Centrality of the Gospel of Grace: vss. 9-10

Who has saved us and called us to a holy life—not because of anything we have done but because of his own purpose and grace. This grace was given us in Christ Jesus before the beginning of time, but it has now been revealed through the appearing of our Savior, Christ Jesus, who has destroyed death and has brought life and immortality to light through the gospel.

Paul reminded Timothy about God's grace, the source of our salvation. Religious efforts and human righteousness cannot save anyone. We are saved by God's grace alone. But the effect of grace doesn't stop with initial salvation. It can also be the source of a holy life. Again, Paul emphasized the futility of works in attaining holiness. Grace is given to us solely as a gift, and its purpose in the life of the believer is to glorify God (2 Tim. 1:9).

This provision was made for us before the foundation of the world, and was revealed, in the fullness of God's time, in the life and work of the Lord Jesus Christ. By destroying the final enemy, death, Jesus made immortality available to every person who would repent of sin and believe (vss. 9-10). Upon this foundation, Paul emphasized the role grace had played in Timothy's spiritual growth. It not only had saved him, but it also had gone on to provide him with the resources for living a holy life.

C. The Suffering of Paul for the Gospel: vss. 11-12

And of this gospel I was appointed a herald and an apostle and a teacher. That is why I am suffering as I am. Yet I am not ashamed, because I know whom I have believed, and am convinced that he is able to guard what I have entrusted to him for that day.

Paul declared himself a herald, an apostle, and a teacher of the Gospel (2 Tim. 1:11). In ancient times the job of a herald was to announce royal decrees and news. A herald would have been something like a modern-day presidential press secretary, but with more pomp and ceremony: Banners and trumpets often introduced the herald's "Hear ye, hear ye!" A herald spoke with royal authority, giving the words of the king to the people.

Paul used the image of a herald for himself because it illustrated the significance of his call as a minister of the Gospel (2 Tim. 1:11). Announcing the good news of the King of kings was an honor and awesome responsibility. Paul's evangelistic activities had landed him in jail. Yet he could proclaim the Gospel—without shame—because of his faith in God.

Paul offered his convictions to Timothy, hoping the latter would take them as his own: (1) "I know whom I have believed"; (2) "[I] am convinced that he is able to guard what I have entrusted to him for that day" (vs. 12). Paul's convictions included a firm belief in Jesus and a confidence that the Lord would preserve everything he had surrendered to Him. The apostle recognized that if God's grace had saved him, it would ultimately bring him through every trial.

D. The Unwavering Commitment of Timothy to the Gospel: vss. 13-14

What you heard from me, keep as the pattern of sound teaching, with faith and love in Christ Jesus. Guard the good deposit that was entrusted to you—guard it with the help of the Holy Spirit who lives in us.

In a time of persecution, Timothy was to renew his commitment to the truths of the faith. There was plenty of pressure to compromise beliefs, but Timothy was to keep on teaching the Gospel as he had heard it from Paul (2 Tim. 1:13). Paul pointed to several keys to help Timothy hold to the pattern of sound teaching. Before we look at what those keys were, let's consider what they were *not*.

First, Paul was not referring to some dogma or creed. Memorizing Bible verses is a valuable discipline, but having a good memory of scriptural truths doesn't ensure that sound teaching will result. Many cult leaders commit great amounts of the Bible to memory, yet they lead people away from the truth and into false teaching. Sound doctrine builds from God's truth, but biblical knowledge alone does not guarantee truthful teaching.

Second, Paul was not referring to religious traditions. While rituals can be beneficial as reminders of spiritual realities, they can also become worn out through overuse. Traditions can evolve over a period of time until the meanings they once held have drained away, leaving them like empty shells. In such cases, pious rituals may even distract people from the core issues of faith.

Third, Paul was not referring to the Jewish law. Earlier, in an attempt to keep himself doctrinally pure, Paul had relied on the law—as well as additional legalisms manufactured by the teachers of the law. At that time Paul had become so preoccupied with trying to live up to an impossible standard that he attacked Christians whom he believed were undermining the standard. His Pharisaical view caused him to miss the grace God was extending to him through Jesus.

Instead of religious legalism, rituals, or creeds, Paul encouraged Timothy to nurture a relationship with Jesus. It was "faith and love in Christ Jesus" that would help Timothy to grip firmly the sound doctrine he had been taught. As valuable as creeds and rituals might be when used correctly, it was faith and love that Timothy needed. Many have admired Jesus for His teachings but failed to surrender their lives to Him or develop a personal relationship with Him.

Faith provides the underpinnings for sound doctrine. Without a simple trust that accepts salvation through Jesus' death and resurrection, there is nothing upon which to build sound teaching. Unless a person experiences forgiveness from sin and the life found in Christ, teaching and studying theology amount to nothing.

Love is the essence of the relationship that believers have with Jesus. Those who agree intellectually that God exists but have not opened their hearts to His love cannot understand sound teaching. Correct words can be found in dusty theology books. But what transforms those words into genuine Christian teaching is the life found in a loving relationship with God. Sound doctrine hinges on the love Jesus has for us and the love we give back to Him.

But faith and love were not the only things Timothy needed to keep his doctrine straight. Paul told Timothy to guard "the good deposit"—the sound teaching of the Gospel—"with the help of the Holy Spirit who lives in us" (vs. 14). Beyond the relationship we have with Jesus—a relationship demonstrated by our faith and love—the help of the Holy Spirit, then, is another key to maintaining sound doctrine.

If we depend only on our natural human understanding to grasp the words on a page of Scripture, we will miss the spiritual truths contained in those words. When God's Word combines with the power of the Holy Spirit, it is supernaturally applied to our hearts.

Discussion Questions

1. What role did Timothy's grandmother and mother serve in his spiritual growth?
2. How could Timothy rekindle the spiritual gift of God within him?
3. To what had Timothy been called as a minister?
4. What was Paul's job in terms of the spread of the Gospel?
5. What sound teaching had Paul conveyed to Timothy?

Contemporary Application

Some today are spiritual captives though they know nothing of metal bars or dark dungeons. They may be physically unrestrained, but their spirits are chained by oppressive fears, painful memories, or guilt. Their lives can be shadowed by emotions such as anger, hatred, or jealousy. Some think they have control over themselves and others, but they do not. They are mirror opposites of Paul.

The reason for such contrasting experiences lies in the fact that spiritual reality is not dependent upon physical circumstances. When God's love touches our lives, we experience a power that transcends the natural. It is truly supernatural. Paul could trust in God's goodness though the evidence around him seemed to suggest that God had forgotten him.

We, like Paul, can learn to look beyond our circumstances and see God's hand upon our lives. Occasionally we may catch a glimpse of His overarching purpose unfolding in the midst of a painful experience; but even when we do not understand why God allows certain events in our lives, our trials need not undermine our trust in Him. In fact, difficulties can be instrumental in raising our sights beyond the evil that surrounds us. Suffering can open us up to spiritual concerns.

Develop Christian Character

DEVOTIONAL READING

1 Peter 2:1-10

DAILY BIBLE READINGS

Monday February 6
Romans 4:13-25 God's Promise Is Realized through Faith

Tuesday February 7
1 Peter 2:1-10 So You May Grow into Salvation

Wednesday February 8
Colossians 1:3-10 Grow in the Knowledge of God

Thursday February 9
2 Timothy 2:1-7 A Good Soldier of Christ Jesus

Friday February 10
2 Timothy 2:8-13 Remember Christ Jesus

Saturday February 11
2 Timothy 2:14-19 Be a Worker Approved by God

Sunday February 12
2 Timothy 2:20-26 Pursue Righteousness, Faith, Love, and Peace

Scripture

Background Scripture: *2 Timothy 2*
Scripture Lesson: *2 Timothy 2:14-26*
Key Verse: *Flee the evil desires of youth, and pursue righteousness, faith, love and peace, along with those who call on the Lord out of a pure heart.* 2 Timothy 2:22.
Scripture Lesson for Children: *Acts 16:9-10; 17:1-4, 10-12; 2 Timothy 2:1-2*
Key Verse for Children: *And the things you have heard me [Paul] say in the presence of many witnesses entrust to reliable men who will also be qualified to teach others.* 2 Timothy 2:2.

Lesson Aim

To underscore the need to diligently labor for Christ.

Lesson Setting

Time: *About A.D. 67*
Place: *Rome*

Lesson Outline

Develop Christian Character

I. Adhering to the Truth: 2 Timothy 2:14-19
  A. *The Uselessness of Quarreling: vs. 14*
  B. *The Value of Handling Scripture Properly: vs. 15*
  C. *The Foolishness of Godless Chatter: vss. 16-18*
  D. *The Church as God's Solid Foundation: vs. 19*

II. Remaining Morally Pure: 2 Timothy 2:20-21
  A. *Noble versus Ignoble Purposes: vs. 20*
  B. *Holy, Useful, and Prepared for Service: vs. 21*

III. Modeling Christlikeness: 2 Timothy 2:22-26
  A. *Shunning Lust and Pursuing Godliness: vs. 22*
  B. *Effectively Leading Antagonists to the Truth: vss. 23-26*

Introduction for Adults

Topic: *Pursue Righteousness*

Back in January many adults made New Year's resolutions, and it's likely that most of these promises have been broken. The reason is that resolutions are difficult to keep. In fact, fewer and fewer people are willing to make resolutions, because they anticipate they'll fail to keep them for even one month.

As you teach this week's lesson, with its emphasis on pursuing righteousness, take time to have your students evaluate their priorities. What resolutions should they make and keep that will help them become more upright in their behavior? What might they do differently to increase their devotion to the Lord? By answering these questions, they'll be better prepared to grow in their walk with Christ.

Introduction for Youth

Topic: *Becoming a Special Utensil*

"I'll do it, and you watch. Then I'll watch and you do it. Finally, I'll let you do it by yourself, with me occasionally checking up on you." This procedure is how young people often learn to do things, from algebra to car repair to juggling. Spiritual growth is no exception.

Believing adolescents crave biblical knowledge and spiritual direction as they learn to walk with Christ. They ask questions about what the Bible teaches, how to avoid temptations, and which decisions are best for them. As their Sunday school instructor, you can encourage them to become a special utensil in the Lord's service, so don't be shy in taking full advantage of this wonderful opportunity!

Concepts for Children

Topic: *We Learn from Teachers*

1. Like Paul, followers of Jesus should take the opportunity, wherever they are, to tell others the Good News.
2. Young Christians can teach others what they have learned about Christ.
3. Paul called Timothy and us to be strong in our faith.
4. Young Christian teachers should not become discouraged by obstacles but put their trust in God.
5. Young Christians should give thanks to God for their teachers.

Lesson Commentary

I. ADHERING TO THE TRUTH: 2 TIMOTHY 2:14-19

A. The Uselessness of Quarreling: vs. 14

Keep reminding them of these things. Warn them before God against quarreling about words; it is of no value, and only ruins those who listen.

In the first portion of 2 Timothy 2, Paul exhorted his son in the faith to remain devoted to Christ despite the prospect of suffering. The apostle used various analogies from everyday life to stress the importance of being a courageous witness (vss. 1-2), a faithful follower (vss. 3-7), and a heavenly citizen (vss. 8-13). In short, God wants His people to be strong in faith and stalwart in character as they labor for Christ in the midst of persecution.

The Lord has not only called us to endure hardship for the cause of Christ but also to diligently spread the saving truth about Him. And in order for us to keep on the right path, we need a good spiritual memory. Without remembering our purpose or our call, we could easily wander off into nonessentials, wasting time and energy on trivial matters.

That's what appears to have happened among some of the believers at Ephesus. They quarreled repeatedly over words—perhaps arguing over minor differences in definitions (2:14). Paul called their conversations "godless chatter" (vs. 16) and urged Timothy to avoid such fruitless discussions.

Paul also told Timothy to remind the members of the church at Ephesus about the basic truths of which he had written. If they were to be the church God intended them to be, they would have to remember their original commitment. Just as Paul had reminded Timothy about Christ's preeminence, so Timothy was to remind the people. Without maintaining that spiritual foundation, they stood in danger of spiritual ruin (vs. 14). Later, when John wrote Revelation, the Ephesian church was again told by the Lord Jesus to return to their first love: "Remember the height from which you have fallen!" (Rev. 2:4-5).

B. The Value of Handling Scripture Properly: vs. 15

Do your best to present yourself to God as one approved, a workman who does not need to be ashamed and who correctly handles the word of truth.

In order better to persuade the people he served, Timothy himself needed to be grounded in the Word of God. Paul used the illustration of a master craftsman—"one approved" (2 Tim. 2:15). A craftsman who can skillfully handle his tools produces useful and valuable products—items he can be proud of. Timothy's "tools" were the Scriptures; the things produced were changed lives, people who bore fruit for God.

C. The Foolishness of Godless Chatter: vss. 16-18

Avoid godless chatter, because those who indulge in it will become more and more ungodly. Their teaching will spread like gangrene. Among them are Hymenaeus and Philetus, who have wandered away from the truth. They say that the resurrection has already taken place, and they destroy the faith of some.

Paul wanted Timothy to see how critical it was to bring people back to center so they could focus on Jesus. If they were allowed to persist in godless chatter, they would become more and more ungodly (2 Tim. 2:16). The teaching from such chatter would eventually become like gangrene, which, though it starts in one place, can spread through the body and lead to death (vs. 17).

Paul offered examples—Hymenaeus and Philetus, false teachers who insisted that the Resurrection had already occurred. Their talk had already destroyed the faith of some (vs. 18). Avoiding fruitless arguments was so important to Paul that he repeated this command in verse 23.

D. The Church as God's Solid Foundation: vs. 19

Nevertheless, God's solid foundation stands firm, sealed with this inscription: "The Lord knows those who are his," and, "Everyone who confesses the name of the Lord must turn away from wickedness."

Even with the danger of false teachers, though, Paul assured Timothy that he could be confident that God's truth was an unshakable foundation. In ancient times inscriptions were often placed on the foundations of large buildings. The words usually indicated the purpose of the building or the person who was honored by its construction. Paul used the metaphor of a foundation to describe the solidarity of God's truth (2 Tim. 2:19).

Furthermore, like a cornerstone with an inscription etched on each side, God's truth has two sides to it. First, God knows those who belong to Him. He understands the condition of people's hearts; He can tell who is false and who is sincere. Second, true followers of Christ will examine their own hearts and repent when necessary. These two statements balance each other: though there may be false followers (known by God) who have infiltrated the church, believers will give evidence of their faith by the way they live.

II. REMAINING MORALLY PURE: 2 TIMOTHY 2:20-21

A. Noble versus Ignoble Purposes: vs. 20

In a large house there are articles not only of gold and silver, but also of wood and clay; some are for noble purposes and some for ignoble.

Paul offered Timothy yet another illustration to reinforce the point he was making. He compared the church to a house containing different kinds of utensils used for different purposes. Some, made of gold or silver, were reserved for special occasions. Others were made of common materials like clay or wood (2 Tim. 2:20). But ordinary pots were not used as part of the holiday table setting. Ordinary pots were used for everyday occasions—some in assignments as undesirable as garbage pails or chamber pots.

B. Holy, Useful, and Prepared for Service: vs. 21

If a man cleanses himself from the latter, he will be an instrument for noble purposes, made holy, useful to the Master and prepared to do any good work.

The church in Ephesus had a problem because certain members were undermining the work of God with their cantankerous ways and false teachings. Timothy would have to learn to distinguish between the special containers and the inferior—those who belonged to the Lord and those who had not turned away from wickedness.

It's the same today. We need discernment so we are not taken in by quarrels over minor issues. In fact, we should evaluate our own behavior: what kind of containers are we? We may attend church or have our names on a membership role. But such things do not in and of themselves make us "useful to the Master" (2 Tim. 2:21). If we want to be used for noble purposes, we must go beyond simply belonging to a church. We must offer ourselves to the Lord to be cleansed from ignoble attitudes and behaviors.

Each person has to decide what kind of container he or she wants to be. If a person's wicked behavior remains unchanged, then he or she is like a garbage pail. If, on the other hand, that person turns away from sin, he or she can be like a piece of fine dinnerware—clean and golden—used for special occasions.

III. MODELING CHRISTLIKENESS: 2 TIMOTHY 2:22-26

A. Shunning Lust and Pursuing Godliness: vs. 22

Flee the evil desires of youth, and pursue righteousness, faith, love and peace, along with those who call on the Lord out of a pure heart.

Paul explained what he had been saying by focusing on Timothy himself. The apostle told Timothy to run away from some kinds of behavior and run toward others. In particular, Paul urged Timothy to "flee the evil desires of youth" (2 Tim. 2:22). Activities or acquaintances that can undermine our faith are nothing to take lightly. When we become too self-confident, we put ourselves in spiritual peril (see 1 Cor. 10:12).

When facing evil desires, Timothy was to turn around and run. On the other hand, we should not run off blindly in any direction. Paul told Timothy to also pursue the characteristics that give evidence of the life of Christ: "righteousness, faith, love and peace" (2 Tim. 2:22).

It's worth noting that three of these four characteristics—things we are to chase after—are listed among the fruit of the Spirit in Galatians: love, peace, and faithfulness (see Gal. 5:22). This suggests that while God's indwelling Spirit will produce godly qualities, we are not to be passive bystanders to the process. Instead, when we give ourselves to God, we are to dedicate ourselves to producing spiritual results in our lives. A spiritual harvest comes to those who have prepared and cultivated their hearts to give Christ room to work. Those who are unwilling to own their sin and pursue righteousness will find that they cannot be cleansed and holy and "useful to the Master" (2 Tim. 2:21).

B. Effectively Leading Antagonists to the Truth: vss. 23-26

Don't have anything to do with foolish and stupid arguments, because you know they produce quarrels. And the Lord's servant must not quarrel; instead, he must be kind to everyone, able to teach, not resentful. Those who oppose him he must gently instruct, in the hope that God will grant them repentance leading them to a knowledge of the truth, and that they will come to their senses and escape from the trap of the devil, who has taken them captive to do his will.

Second Timothy 2:23 points to a stark irony at work in the Ephesian congregation. The church, though it had been founded on solid doctrine and the transformation of God's grace, had become tainted with deception. Unlike the challenges faced by other churches with which Paul had worked, the threats to the Ephesian congregation did not come from outside but from within. Some of their own leaders had distorted the truth of the Gospel. It was the very thing Paul had feared might happen when he had admonished the Ephesian elders (see Acts 20:13-38).

It's no wonder, then, that Paul repeatedly urged Timothy to reject foolish and ignorant controversies. If allowed to fester, such would breed quarrels (2 Tim. 2:23). As the Lord's servant, Timothy was to exchange a combative spirit for a kind and sensitive disposition. He was to focus on becoming as skilled and effective as possible in teaching. Even when dealing with difficult people, he was to remain patient (vs. 24).

When he encountered those who were pugnacious and opposed to the truth, Timothy was still to correct them in a gentle but firm manner. The hope was that God might bring them to repentance and a saving knowledge of the truth (vs. 25). Perhaps the wayward would come to their senses and escape the trap of the devil, who had held them captive to do whatever he wanted (vs. 26).

The temptation to battle with wayward people is often very strong. The compelling desire to "put these people in their place" can make a church leader look just as foolish as the false teachers. The goal of godly instruction is always restoration, never punishment or retribution. With this end in mind, even the most quarrelsome rebels can be won for Christ.

Discussion Questions

1. Why is it important to properly interpret Scripture?
2. What were Hymenaeus and Philetus guilty of doing?
3. What does it mean to be a utensil of gold and silver in the Lord's house?
4. Why should believers shun youthful passions?
5. Why should believers pursue such virtues as righteousness, faith, love, and peace?

Contemporary Application

It has been said that Christianity offers upside-down values. When Jesus works in our lives, we are bound to be different—even opposite—from the people around us. The truth is that if we love God, our values are constantly opposite to those of sinful human nature. Sadly, in the middle of a difficult human situation, we sometimes forget to consider biblical values.

Thankfully, God knows we are frail creatures; but He does expect us to come to Him in faith, asking for strength and wisdom to value what He values and behave toward others as He commands in His Word. He expects us to imitate the unique behavior demonstrated for us by Jesus.

We have learned from our study of 2 Timothy that we cannot avoid experiencing hardship as followers of Christ. Instead of shunning this prospect, we should make the best of it by remaining close to the Lord and single-minded in our devotion to Him. We also should proclaim the Good News, disciple new converts, and shun all associations with evil. When we courageously suffer and diligently labor for Christ, we have the assurance of knowing that God is well pleased and will eternally bless us.

Follow a Good Mentor

Scripture

Background Scripture: *2 Timothy 3—4*

Scripture Lesson: *2 Timothy 3:10—4:8*

Key Verse: *But as for you, continue in what you have learned and have become convinced of, because you know those from whom you learned it.* 2 Timothy 3:14.

Scripture Lesson for Children: *2 Timothy 3:16-17; Psalm 119:1, 9-11, 33-34, 73, 97, 105, 127, 172-174*

Key Verse for Children: *I have hidden your word in my heart that I might not sin against you.* Psalm 119:11.

Lesson Aim

To stress that believers should heed the truth of God's Word.

Lesson Setting

Time: *About A.D. 67*

Place: *Rome*

Lesson Outline

Follow a Good Mentor

    I. The Equipped Believer: 2 Timothy 3:10-17
        A. *Enduring Hardship as an Apostle: vss. 10-11*
        B. *Suffering Persecution: vss. 12-13*
        C. *Remaining Faithful: vss. 14-15*
        D. *Heeding Scripture: vss. 16-17*
   II. The Proclamation of the Word: 2 Timothy 4:1-8
        A. *Faithfully Ministering Scripture: vss. 1-2*
        B. *Taking Note of the Irreverent: vss. 3-4*
        C. *Keeping a Clear Mind: vs. 5*
        D. *Anticipating Eternal Blessings: vss. 6-8*

Introduction for Adults

Topic: *The Marks of a Helpful Mentor*

During their middle years, adults begin to review their lives to see whether what they have done and what they are doing have lasting worth. As adults grow older, they want to know that they aren't just putting in time, but that they're spending their lives on something that has enduring value and will outlive them.

One of the most eternally relevant and lasting activities your students can do is mentor others in the faith. This requires commitment and diligence. It also requires time and patience. Most of all, a deep and abiding faith in Christ is the mark of a helpful mentor.

Introduction for Youth

Topic: *Follow a Good Example*

Why is it important for young people to follow a good example? Consider what Howard Hendricks, the coauthor of *As Iron Sharpens Iron,* has to say. He recalls how several people made a profound influence in his life. The first was a man named Walt. Hendricks wrote the following about him:

"I came from a broken home. My parents were separated before I was born, and neither one paid much attention to my spiritual condition. To put it bluntly, I could have lived, died, and gone to hell without anyone even bothering to care. But Walt cared. He was part of a tiny church in my neighborhood that developed a passion to affect its community for Christ. Had it not been for Walt, I seriously doubt whether I would have ever become a follower of Jesus Christ."

Concepts for Children

Topic: *We Learn from the Bible*

1. Timothy realized the importance of the Bible through his family members, which was later reinforced by Paul.
2. All believers should be continuously taught and trained in upright behavior through God's Word.
3. The psalmist spoke of God's law and commands as treasures to be learned, followed, loved, and lived.
4. The psalmist counsels us today to sing and delight in God's commands and promises.
5. Children need to see the Bible as an important guidebook for them personally.

Lesson Commentary

I. THE EQUIPPED BELIEVER: 2 TIMOTHY 3:10-17

A. Enduring Hardship as an Apostle: vss. 10-11

You, however, know all about my teaching, my way of life, my purpose, faith, patience, love, endurance, persecutions, sufferings—what kinds of things happened to me in Antioch, Iconium and Lystra, the persecutions I endured. Yet the Lord rescued me from all of them.

In 2 Timothy 3, Paul alerted his beloved co-worker and the church at Ephesus about a looming peril. He indicated that distressing times were on the horizon, and that they needed to be prepared in advance for its arrival. The apostle also provided instructions on how to survive in good spiritual condition in the midst of rampant ungodliness (vss. 1-5) and despicable attitudes and actions (vss. 6-9).

Then, in verse 10, Paul reminded Timothy of some of the things the apostle had endured for the cause of Christ. Paul's life of virtue and uprightness stood in sharp contrast to the iniquity and godlessness that were the hallmarks of society. Timothy had followed the apostle's teaching, way of life, purpose, faith, patience, love, and endurance. As is the case in 2:22, these inner characteristics closely parallel the fruit of the Spirit, such as faith, patience, and love (see Gal. 5:22-23). The fourth characteristic—endurance—is a by-product of self-control (see vs. 23).

The younger minister also knew about the persecutions and sufferings Paul had to endure in Antioch, Iconium, and Lystra (2 Tim. 3:11). Acts 13 and 14 recount these episodes, which occurred during Paul's second missionary journey. Despite the apostle's hardships, the Lord rescued His faithful servant from all of them (2 Tim. 3:11).

B. Suffering Persecution: vss. 12-13

In fact, everyone who wants to live a godly life in Christ Jesus will be persecuted, while evil men and impostors will go from bad to worse, deceiving and being deceived.

Some think that the more godly they become, the easier their lives will become. Yet Paul, as righteously as he lived his life, could not avoid hardship and suffering (see Acts 13:50; 14:2, 5, 19). In fact, he believed some of the difficulties he endured stemmed directly from the godly life he sought to live (2 Tim. 3:12).

Christianity is not a religion of escape; it's not a way to avoid trouble, hardship, and difficulty. Paul knew that those who commit themselves to following Christ will, in this world, face opposition. But the apostle had also seen how Jesus helps His followers overcome the troubles that come their way (vs. 11): "In this world you will have trouble," Jesus said. "But take heart! I have overcome the world" (John 16:33).

The apostle revealed that, as the second advent of Christ drew nearer, the downward moral spiral of humankind would intensify. Evil people and charlatans would go from bad to worse. They would continue to deceive others, and in turn would be deceived themselves (2 Tim. 3:13).

C. Remaining Faithful: vss. 14-15

But as for you, continue in what you have learned and have become convinced of, because you know those from whom you learned it, and how from infancy you have known the holy Scriptures, which are able to make you wise for salvation through faith in Christ Jesus.

Timothy was to be wholly different from the frauds Paul had just mentioned. Timothy was to become more Christlike by continuing in what he had learned from Paul and to build on that knowledge (2 Tim. 3:14). From Timothy's childhood he had been taught the holy Scriptures. In these sacred writings he found divine wisdom to receive salvation through faith in Christ (vs. 15). God's Word contained resources Timothy needed to stand up against those who opposed the truth.

D. Heeding Scripture: vss. 16-17

All Scripture is God-breathed and is useful for teaching, rebuking, correcting and training in righteousness, so that the man of God may be thoroughly equipped for every good work.

Paul declared that all Scripture (both individual portions and the composite whole) is inspired by God (2 Tim. 3:16). Thus, the Bible is useful for teaching, reproof (or censure), correction, and training in righteousness. Those who submit themselves to Scripture will be people dedicated to God who are capable, competent, and equipped for whatever good work God desires of them (vs. 17).

We can safely infer from these verses that there is no substitute for Scripture when it comes to combatting false teaching, learning the ways of the Lord, and ministering for Him. We insult God, deceive ourselves, and cheat others when we fail to study the Bible diligently and obey it wholeheartedly. If each of us fills our life to overflowing with God's Word, the spiritual benefits from this act will spill over to a world that needs the knowledge of salvation. There is no superior beacon to guide people to an eternally safe harbor.

II. THE PROCLAMATION OF THE WORD: 2 TIMOTHY 4:1-8

A. Faithfully Ministering Scripture: vss. 1-2

In the presence of God and of Christ Jesus, who will judge the living and the dead, and in view of his appearing and his kingdom, I give you this charge: Preach the Word; be prepared in season and out of season; correct, rebuke and encourage—with great patience and careful instruction.

As Paul drew near the end of his letter to Timothy, he seemed to become more earnest about the admonitions he had been giving. Now he issued a "charge" (2 Tim. 4:1) imposing upon Timothy a solemn responsibility.

Paul had two reasons for strengthening the force of his words. (1) He was well aware of God's coming judgment. The spiritual destiny of many people hung in the balance. Therefore Paul challenged Timothy to effective leadership in the church at Ephesus. (2) Paul considered the fact that Jesus was coming again to fully establish His kingdom. Until that time, all they had known about the Kingdom was its introduction. That's why Timothy's work in the church was more significant than he could imagine—he was helping to build the kingdom of God.

Paul's charge to Timothy included five key elements—aspects that remain important to all who minister in the church. First, Timothy was to "preach the Word" (vs. 2). God wanted him to declare the truth of the Scriptures he had learned from his mother and grandmother while he was growing up (see 1:5; 3:15). Second, Timothy was to be prepared at all times (4:2)—no matter that some occasions might be more convenient to preach than others; no matter that some circumstances might seem unpromising. Regardless of whether it seemed to be the season for a spiritual harvest, Timothy was to be ready to do his part for the Kingdom.

Third through fifth, Timothy was to "correct, rebuke and encourage." He was to provide whatever kind of ministry his listeners might need. Some would need to be shown their sin before they would repent—that's *correcting*. Others would need to be reprimanded for their wrongdoing—that's *rebuking*. Still others who would wither under such a harsh approach would need kind and tender admonishment—that's *encouragement*.

In fulfilling all five parts of his charge, Timothy was to be certain his own attitudes were right. He had to "clean up his own side of the street" before he could help others. He was not to deliver God's message in an arrogant manner. Nor could he allow himself to become frustrated with listeners who were slow to respond. Instead, he was to minister with "great patience and careful instruction."

B. Taking Note of the Irreverent: vss. 3-4

For the time will come when men will not put up with sound doctrine. Instead, to suit their own desires, they will gather around them a great number of teachers to say what their itching ears want to hear. They will turn their ears away from the truth and turn aside to myths.

Paul explained that as the time of Jesus' return drew nearer, people would grow increasingly intolerant of biblically-based teaching; instead, they would follow after their own illicit cravings and search for teachers who would tell whatever their ears were itching to hear (2 Tim. 4:3). Moreover, they would reject the truth for legendary tales (vs. 4).

C. Keeping a Clear Mind: vs. 5

But you, keep your head in all situations, endure hardship, do the work of an evangelist, discharge all the duties of your ministry.

While others would turn to false teaching, Timothy was to maintain his spiritual equilibrium; he was to keep his head "in all situations" (2 Tim. 4:5). He could not permit himself to bend under the influence of shifting views of doctrine. He could not yield to the pressure of strong personalities or those with positions of authority or wealth. Timothy was to remain steady and balanced—an island of integrity surrounded by an ocean of people swayed by popular, though false, teachers.

In addition, Timothy was to "endure hardship." Paul was sending Timothy into battle. Timothy could expect that his authority would be challenged. At times he would feel isolated and abandoned. But knowing this ahead of time, Paul called on Timothy to look to God for the courage and strength (see 2:1) to stay true to his call (see 1:14).

Also, Timothy was to "do the work of an evangelist" (4:5). While Timothy may not have had the spiritual gift of evangelism, he was nevertheless to evangelize. This tells us that though some might be extraordinarily gifted in evangelism (see Eph. 4:11), others who aren't can still work at telling others about God's plan of salvation. Finally, Timothy was to finish his job. He was to "discharge all the duties" of his ministry (2 Tim. 4:5). God doesn't call us to do half our task or to bail out the moment things get tough or opposition mounts. God calls us for a reason. And to do less than that is to leave God's call unanswered.

D. Anticipating Eternal Blessings: vss. 6-8

For I am already being poured out like a drink offering, and the time has come for my departure. I have fought the good fight, I have finished the race, I have kept the faith. Now there is in store for me the crown of righteousness, which the Lord, the righteous Judge, will award to me on that day—and not only to me, but also to all who have longed for his appearing.

Paul seemed to know he was coming to the end of his time on earth. Though he hoped Timothy would be able to come to his side and help him during his imprisonment (see 2 Tim. 4:9), Paul may have felt the words he wrote to Timothy might be the final ones he would pen to anyone.

These last words of Paul seem to be those of a man who was content. He had been faithful to do all that God had given him to do. He had no regrets. He had surrendered his life completely to the Lord, and now he was ready to see the last of his days "poured out like a drink offering" (vs. 6).

Paul was comparing his life to the offerings made by the Old Testament priests (see also Phil. 2:17). They poured wine or oil on a sacrifice just before it was to be burned (Num. 15:1-12). Paul saw this as a picture of something that was irretrievable—once the wine was spilled, it soaked into the sacrifice, the wood, and the ground around the altar. It could not be picked up. It was gone.

Soon Paul would be gone, the last drop of his life having been poured out for the Lord. Because the apostle spoke with such certainty about his impending death, some think Paul had already been sentenced to die. Paul, though convinced that death would soon come, was not looking for sympathy. He almost sounded eager to get things in order so he could make his "departure" (2 Tim. 4:6).

The Greek word literally meant to "unloose." It was as though the apostle was about to be set free from the world with its sin and troubles. Although this is the only place that this word is used in the New Testament, sailors in Paul's time used it to describe the "loosing" of a ship from a dock so it could set sail. It was also used to describe the "breaking up" of an army camp so the soldiers could march away. Paul was ready to break camp and head for his eternal dwelling.

Because he had been obedient to God's call, Paul was confident he would receive his final reward—a crown of righteousness (vs. 8). It was a picture tied to his sports analogy in verse 7: the winning runner and the victorious wrestler were awarded "crowns"—garlands of oak leaves or wreaths of laurel to wear on their heads.

Paul also may have intended an athletic picture in the last part of verse 7 as well: "I have kept the faith" could mean "I have kept the rules" or "I have not fouled out" or "I have stayed on the course." Paul felt strongly about maintaining his commitment so that he would not be disqualified along the way (see 1 Cor. 9:27).

Discussion Questions

1. Why do you think Paul was willing to suffer for the Lord?
2. How can ministers combat false teachers, especially those who try to mislead church members?
3. In what sense is Scripture inspired?
4. What motivates people to reject the truth of God's Word for the lies of Satan?
5. How can the grace of God sustain us in the difficult times we face?

Contemporary Application

Believers have two different audiences they can share God's truth with—the saved and unsaved. The Gospel is the primary truth that believers should proclaim to the lost. Along with the Good News, believers can share other vital truths of the faith.

There is nothing wrong with believers sharing the Gospel with their fellow Christians; but there are other biblical truths they can also share, including information about prayer, discipleship, faithfulness, obedience, wisdom, and grace.

Sharing Christian truth means more than dispensing information. It also includes explaining how God's message can impact people's lives. They need to know how the things taught in the Bible are relevant to them. A thorough knowledge of Scripture is essential. Witnessing without relying on the truths of God's Word is simply sharing opinions. Scripture is the only completely reliable source of divine truth.

Live the Truth, Teach the Truth

DEVOTIONAL READING

Ephesians 4:11-16

DAILY BIBLE READINGS

Monday February 20
*Ephesians 4:11-16 Speak the
Truth in Love*

Tuesday February 21
*2 Peter 1:3-12 Be
Established in the Truth*

Wednesday February 22
*1 John 1:5-10 Walk in the
Light of Truth*

Thursday February 23
*3 John 2-8 Support All
Believers in the Truth*

Friday February 24
*Titus 2:1-5 Teaching Older
Men and Women*

Saturday February 25
*Titus 2:6-10 Teaching
Younger Men and Slaves*

Sunday February 26
*Titus 2:11-15 Teach What
God Expects of Believers*

Scripture

Background Scripture: *Titus 2*
Scripture Lesson: *Titus 2*
Key Verses: *In everything set them an example by doing what
is good. In your teaching show integrity, seriousness and
soundness of speech that cannot be condemned.* Titus 2:7-8a.
Scripture Lesson for Children: *1 Thessalonians 1:1-7;
3:6-9*
Key Verses for Children: *You welcomed the message with . . .
joy and . . . became a model to all the believers.* 1 Thessalonians 1:6-7.

Lesson Aim

To emphasize that biblical truth should lead to godly
conduct among all believers, regardless of their age,
gender, or social status.

Lesson Setting

Time: *About A.D. 63–65*
Places: *Corinth and Crete*

Lesson Outline

Live the Truth, Teach the Truth

   I. The Importance of Godly Living: Titus 2:1-10

      A. For Various Age Groups: vss. 1-6

      B. For Titus: vss. 7-8

      C. For the Enslaved: vss. 9-10

  II. The Basis for Godly Living: Titus 2:11-15

      A. The Grace of God: vss. 11-12

      B. The Work of Christ: vss. 13-14

      C. The Exhortation to Teach: vs. 15

Introduction for Adults

Topic: *Teach Sound Doctrine by Example*

As a Christian leader, Titus was under obligation to command and teach the doctrinal truths Paul had laid before him. Titus was also to instruct the believers on Crete to heed these truths. The congregation needed a godly example to follow as well as sound doctrine to obey. That's why Paul urged his colleague in the faith to be an example of godliness to others.

No better counsel can be given to your students. Their devotion to godliness will make it clear that the doctrine they teach and live by is sound. Others will see that class members take their spiritual lives and ministries seriously. People will be convinced that your students remain true to the Gospel and seek to lead others to Christ.

Introduction for Youth

Topic: *Teaching by Example*

We can all improve in the example we set for others. But such a general statement does not get saved teens any closer to that goal, and the idea of improving every area of their lives might overwhelm them at first.

A more manageable approach is to encourage your students to pick one area of their lives and concentrate on becoming a better Christlike example in this realm. It could be what they say or how they act. Be sure to remind them that their attitudes, actions, and words should reflect the compassion and kindness of Christ even to those who are antagonistic to the Gospel.

Concepts for Children

Topic: *We Learn from Others' Examples*

1. Even in the midst of difficult situations, young Christians can be examples to others.
2. When we invest time, effort, and a caring spirit in teaching other believers, we will be eternally blessed.
3. Christian teachers should regularly praise the progress of children in their walk of faith.
4. Saved children readily imitate their Christian teachers.
5. Children learn much through watching the example of others.

Lesson Commentary

I. THE IMPORTANCE OF GODLY LIVING: TITUS 2:1-10

A. For Various Age Groups: vss. 1-6

You must teach what is in accord with sound doctrine. Teach the older men to be temperate, worthy of respect, self-controlled, and sound in faith, in love and in endurance. Likewise, teach the older women to be reverent in the way they live, not to be slanderers or addicted to much wine, but to teach what is good. Then they can train the younger women to love their husbands and children, to be self-controlled and pure, to be busy at home, to be kind, and to be subject to their husbands, so that no one will malign the word of God. Similarly, encourage the young men to be self-controlled.

Titus, the recipient of this letter, was a Gentile believer who often served as Paul's emissary. When Judaizers infiltrated the church at Antioch, Titus accompanied Paul on his trip to Jerusalem to confer with the other apostles about the matter. The fact that Titus was not required to become circumcised became part of Paul's argument to the Galatians in defense of the Gospel (Gal. 2:1-3).

Titus acted as Paul's liaison to the Corinthian church, where he was well received (2 Cor. 2:12-13; 7:5-7, 13-15). He brought word of the conditions in Corinth to the apostle in Macedonia and returned to Corinth with 2 Corinthians. Titus was also instrumental in seeing to it that the Corinthians followed through on their commitment to contribute to the relief fund for the believers in Jerusalem (8:6-24; 12:18). Paul's choice of Titus for this mission may have been based both upon his Greek heritage and the genuine affection he had for the people of that city (7:15).

At some point during Paul's ministry, he and Titus traveled to Crete. Finding that the church needed to be organized, Paul left Titus behind to complete what was left unfinished (Titus 1:5). Paul's letter was prompted both by the need to appoint suitable leaders in Crete and by the encroachment of false teaching there. The religious frauds rejected the authority of God and strongly opposed the truth of the Gospel. They also encouraged the believers on the island to do the same. Paul wanted Titus to counter this ungodly influence by teaching only what was consistent with sound doctrine (2:1).

Doctrine, however, was not the apostle's only concern. In the clarification that followed, he explained that the things that were in accord with sound doctrine were also matters of character. Clearly, Paul understood belief and behavior to be closely associated.

Thus, with respect to older men, they were to be temperate, dignified, prudent or self-controlled. They were also to be sound in faith, in love, and in perseverance (vs. 2). Older women were to display behavior fitting those who are holy. Instead of being slanderers or slaves to drink, they were to teach what is wholesome and sound (vs. 3).

Godly older women had an opportunity to mentor younger women in the faith. The former should encourage the latter to be virtuous and devoted in love to their families (vs. 4). This required that younger women be sensible (or self-controlled), chaste, fulfilling their duties at home, kind, and submissive to their own husbands. This would prevent God's Word from being discredited (vs. 5).

It's informative to note that in ancient times the family often included more than just the parents and children. Grandparents, other relatives, and servants might also be part of it. Families tended to be large for economic and religious reasons. In an agrarian society family members could help maintain the property, care for livestock, and plant and harvest crops. Children also were seen as blessings from the Lord (Gen. 33:5; Ps. 127:3-5).

Both the husband and the wife shouldered important responsibilities in the home. They were to mutually respect and love each other (1 Pet. 3:1-7). They were to work together as a team to make the home stable and secure (Gen. 2:18; Prov. 31:10-31; 1 Tim. 5:8). Each also had the duty of encouraging their children to love and serve the Lord (Deut. 6:6-7).

The children were taught to honor and obey their parents (Exod. 20:12; Eph. 6:1). Parents, in turn, were expected to show love and respect for their children. The servants of a household were to obey their masters and work diligently for them. The masters likewise were to be humane and fair in the way they treated their servants (Eph. 6:4-9).

In Titus 2:6, Paul turned his attention to "the young men." The apostle declared they were to be prudent and self-controlled. The latter emphasis differed significantly from that taught in ancient Greek Stoic philosophy (which many Cretans were familiar with). The Stoics taught that the wise person should be free from passion, unmoved by grief or joy, and submissive to the laws of nature. They also taught people to recognize their so-called self-sufficiency. These ideas not only eliminated the need for God but also fostered pride in the individual.

Titus was to encourage the believers on Crete to exercise restraint over their emotions, impulses, and desires; yet he was not to give them the impression that their existence was supposed to be cheerless. Titus was to teach them that there was real joy and excitement in serving Christ. They were also to be reminded of their need for redemption and urged to humbly trust in the Savior for it.

B. For Titus: vss. 7-8

In everything set them an example by doing what is good. In your teaching show integrity, seriousness and soundness of speech that cannot be condemned, so that those who oppose you may be ashamed because they have nothing bad to say about us.

Titus was to be an example of good works to the young men in the churches of Crete (Titus 2:7). Every area of his life was to be a pattern of the kind of behavior he was to instill in others. For example, the ministry of Titus was to be free from tainted motives, one of which was the desire to become materially rich. As he reached out to others, he was to be earnest and dignified, not indifferent and crass. By remaining virtuous in what he said and did, Titus would reinforce the truths of the Gospel and give them greater impact.

Titus was to offer doctrinally correct and spiritually uplifting instruction. His teaching was to be so wholesome that no one would be able to justly criticize or censure it. Despite their efforts to discredit the Gospel, the opponents of Titus would be unable to do so and would be ashamed for even trying (vs. 8). Here we see that there is a direct correlation between what we believe and how we act. When we embrace the truth and live by it, we bring glory to God.

C. For the Enslaved: vss. 9-10

Teach slaves to be subject to their masters in everything, to try to please them, not to talk back to them, and not to steal from them, but to show that they can be fully trusted, so that in every way they will make the teaching about God our Savior attractive.

While the gospel message of freedom in Christ drew people from all walks of life, it was especially attractive to slaves. Christian slaves were to heed their masters and do what they wanted in all matters (Titus 2:9). Amazingly, this obligation was not contingent upon the kind of master being served. Slaves owed obedience to masters who mistreated them as well as to those who were good.

Rather than argue with or pilfer from their masters, Christian slaves were to show complete and perfect fidelity. Expressed differently, they were to demonstrate that their faith was genuine and trustworthy as well as wholesome and productive. If they lived in this way, they would showcase the beauty of the teaching about our divine Savior (vs. 10).

II. The Basis for Godly Living: Titus 2:11-15

A. The Grace of God: vss. 11-12

For the grace of God that brings salvation has appeared to all men. It teaches us to say "No" to ungodliness and worldly passions, and to live self-controlled, upright and godly lives in this present age.

By their faithfulness, Christian slaves were living proof of the power of God's grace and its universal scope. The power of the Gospel to save was corroborated by the transformation of their character. The very fact that slaves could be the recipients of grace showed that it was made available to everyone, regardless of class.

In Titus 2:11, Paul emphasized that God's grace had been offered to all humanity. The bestowal of salvation through faith in Christ was not meant to be limited to one group only, but was extended to all people regardless of race or background. Along with the offer of grace came the promise of transformation. In the Greek text, verse 12 is actually a continuation of the sentence begun in the previous verse: "For the grace of God that brings salvation has appeared to all men, teaching us . . ." Consequently, the "it" spoken of in verse 12 is the grace of God.

The experience of God's grace leads to an understanding of the need for self-denial. It was grace that enabled his readers to say no to sin. Negatively, this means that the believer will reject all that is opposed to God, along with "worldly passions"—those desires that are inconsistent with the believer's heavenly calling.

They are worldly in the sense that they reflect the rebellion of the fallen world, which is at odds with its Creator. Renouncing wanton desires is both a continuous process and an ongoing responsibility.

Positively, the experience of God's grace should prompt the believer to live a life that is consistent with the Lord's principles of righteousness. This marked the seventh of eight references to the Greek word for self-control in this letter, most of them occurring in the second chapter (1:8; 2:2, 4, 5, 6, 9, 12, 15).

B. The Work of Christ: vss. 13-14

While we wait for the blessed hope—the glorious appearing of our great God and Savior, Jesus Christ, who gave himself for us to redeem us from all wickedness and to purify for himself a people that are his very own, eager to do what is good.

The traits Paul advocated were to mark Christian living in this present age, a period of time characterized by waiting for the return of Christ (Titus 2:12-13). Although Paul recognized the importance of life in this present age, he expected the believer to be focused on the past and the future as well. A focus on the past enabled the believer to recognize that godliness was possible only because Christ gave Himself for his redemption (vs. 14).

The motive for living such a life was to spring from the expectation that Christ would one day return to claim the believer as His own possession. Believers were to anticipate Christ's visible and glorious return with joyful expectation. Waiting for this blessed hope can, at times, however, seem unbearable.

After all, the world is filled with wickedness that seems to advance unhindered. And yet Christ's return will put an end to all forms of evil. Because they are purified by the blood of Christ, believers are to be a special kind of people, eager to do what is good. By their loving actions, Christians provide a brilliant contrast to the powers of darkness in the world.

C. The Exhortation to Teach: vs. 15

These, then, are the things you should teach. Encourage and rebuke with all authority. Do not let anyone despise you.

Paul closed this section by reminding Titus that he was not to let anyone intimidate him because of the authority he was given. Instead, he was to use the Scriptures to gently correct those who claimed to know Christ but whose lives failed to give evidence of transforming grace (Titus 2:15).

Discussion Questions

1. Why was Titus to teach what was consistent with sound doctrine?
2. How could older women be reverent in their behavior?
3. How could younger men exercise self-control in a morally permissive world?
4. How could the faith of Christian slaves empower them in their bleak existence?
5. Why did Jesus die on the cross for us?

Contemporary Application

There is a strong emphasis in Titus 2:1-15 on adhering to sound doctrine; but wholesome and trustworthy teaching are also a matter of character. The implication is that what we maintain theologically and how we act personally are closely associated. This explains why Paul, in stressing the former, spent so much time talking about the latter.

In particular, the apostle urged us to live disciplined lives as we submit ourselves to the Holy Spirit. We should also carry ourselves with the kind of dignity that is befitting those who are ambassadors for Christ. Such is possible when prudence and balance undergird our judgments.

These virtues are only possible when we maintain a strong faith in Christ, a dynamic love for others, and a commitment to endure the hardships of life with steadfastness and patience. Imagine how stabilizing our spiritual maturity, personal integrity, and genuine compassion can be in the churches where we serve.

Such devotion to the Savior, of course, is not to be confined to religious acts alone, but is to be reflected in our entire manner of life. For instance, we should not falsely accuse others by misrepresenting them through gossip. Moreover, rather than be bored and idle, we should lead productive, wholesome lives. In every area of our existence, when we embrace the truth and live by it, we bring glory to God.

Living in and as God's Creation

God Made Us Special

DEVOTIONAL READING

Genesis 1:26-31

DAILY BIBLE READINGS

Monday February 27
Genesis 1:26-31 God Creates Humankind

Tuesday February 28
Genesis 2:7, 15-25 God Creates Man and Woman

Wednesday March 1
Genesis 9:8-17 God Establishes a Covenant with Noah

Thursday March 2
Psalm 63:1-8 God Is Our Help and Strength

Friday March 3
Psalm 73:21-28 God Is Our Guide and Refuge

Saturday March 4
Hebrews 2:5-10 God Leaves Nothing outside Our Jurisdiction

Sunday March 5
Psalm 8 Created a Little Lower Than God

Scripture

Background Scripture: *Psalm 8*
Scripture Lesson: *Psalm 8*
Key Verses: *What is man that you are mindful of him, the son of man that you care for him? You made him a little lower than the heavenly beings and crowned him with glory and honor.* Psalm 8:4-5.
Scripture Lesson for Children: *Psalm 8*
Key Verse for Children: *O LORD, our Lord, how majestic is your name in all the earth!* Psalm 8:9.

Lesson Aim

To recognize that God, the all-powerful Creator, cares for His most valuable creation—people.

Lesson Setting

Time: *Written sometime during the reign of David (1010–970 B.C.)*
Place: *Israel*

Lesson Outline

God Made Us Special

  I. Praise to the Creator: Psalm 8:1-2
     A. *The Creator's Majestic Name: vs. 1*
     B. *The Creation's Praise: vs. 2*
  II. Reasons for Praise: Psalm 8:3-9
     A. *The Place of Humanity: vss. 3-5*
     B. *The Responsibility of Humanity: vss. 6-8*
     C. *The Creator's Majestic Name: vs. 9*

Introduction for Adults

Topic: *God Made Us Special*

Each generation discovers new wealth in God's creation and just how special humankind is to be overseers of it. These discoveries show how prolific are the mighty acts of God. But each discovery brings new challenges and responsibilities. The more God gives to us as His beloved creatures, the greater our responsibility to exercise wise stewardship according to His commands recorded in Scripture.

Our greatest failure seems to be our lack of gratitude. Simply put, we take God's gifts for granted. Many times we do not even acknowledge His daily provision of our needs. This is sad, for we could not survive very long without the air we breathe, the food we eat, or the water we drink, all of which come from God.

Psalm 8 reminds us that God is supremely praiseworthy. Wherever we look, we find reasons to praise Him. Most of all, when we consider what He has done for us in Christ, we should submit to Him as our Lord. After all, He's the author of life, whether physical or spiritual in nature.

Introduction for Youth

Topic: *We Are Special*

Advertisers pandering to youth outdo themselves to make their products more attractive than their competitors'. For example, when we consider teen fashions, we can see how important it is for adolescents to stand out in a crowd. Yet no matter how impressive our clothes, computers, and cars might be, they are nothing compared to the magnificence of God's creation. We need to be careful, lest we lose sight of God's glory in the welter of things that are supposed to make us happy.

The world has a way of dominating our time, and it tries to shape our desires and values. But as Christians, we are wise to step back and ask why God made us. What does He desire of us? Also, how can we strengthen our faith in Him and not be stunted by the world's values? Meditating on God our Creator, as David did, is a step in the right direction in recognizing the true reason for our being special in His eyes.

Concepts for Children

Topic: *I Am Special*

1. There is no name more wonderful than that of God.
2. God is pleased when we take time to praise Him.
3. Even though God is very great, He still takes time to care for us.
4. God loves us so much that He gives us important things to do.
5. Let us show our love for God by doing what He wants.

Lesson Commentary

I. PRAISE TO THE CREATOR: PSALM 8:1-2

A. The Creator's Majestic Name: vs. 1

O LORD, our Lord, how majestic is your name in all the earth! You have set your glory above the heavens.

Of the 150 psalms, only 34 do not have titles or superscriptions. For the psalms that have them, these titles indicate such things as the author, type of psalm, musical notations, liturgical notations, and historical context in various combinations. The psalms attributed to David contain many references to his life that seem to be taken from 2 Samuel.

We do not know the meanings of many of the words contained in these super-scriptions, especially the worship notations. For example, the superscription for Psalm 8 is "For the director of music. According to *gittith*. A psalm of David." The phrase "for the director of music" suggests that this song is from an early collection of hymns used in temple worship. It's also possible that when the psalm was used in the Hebrew liturgy, the leader of the Levitical choir spoke it before the assembly of worshipers.

The word rendered "*gittith*" (which is also found in the superscriptions of Psalms 81 and 84) may refer somehow to the Philistine city of Gath, making *gittith* a description of a particular Philistine musical setting or singing style. Some manu-scripts have the word translated as "winepress," so commentators have suggested that Psalm 8 was associated in some way with the vintage festival at the Feast of Tabernacles.

Believing scholars are divided as to the reliability of the titles. Some think they were added at a later time, and there is some evidence that these superscriptions did change over time. Others, however, think that they were written as part of the psalms and should be regarded as a part of the sacred text.

The beginning and ending of Psalm 8 suggests that it was a hymn of praise. The interior of the psalm, however, focuses on the Lord's sovereign ordering of the cre-ation. It's for this reason that some classify this hymn as a nature psalm (or psalm of creation).

We don't know the original circumstances leading up to David's writing of this song, but it's not hard to imagine. Many of us can recall times out in the country when we gazed up into the sky on a clear night and saw countless stars extending from one end of the horizon to the other. If such was the case for David, we can only infer how puny he must have felt against the immense expanse of the heavens above which God had set His glory (vs. 1).

Two different Hebrew words are rendered "Lord" in this verse. The first term is *Yahweh,* and underscores the everlasting quality of His self-existence (Exod. 3:14-15). The second term is *Adonai,* and places emphasis on God's supreme and unchallenged authority. It's no wonder that David declared that the name of the all-glorious one was "majestic . . . in all the earth!" (Ps. 8:1). (In Scripture, the name of the Lord was considered a reflection of His character, encompassing all His attributes.)

The Hebrew word translated "majestic" is *addid*, which can also be rendered as "glorious," "powerful," or "delightful." Since the name of the Lord is often equated with His presence in Old Testament thought, verse 1 could also be translated something like, "Yahweh, our Lord, how delightful is your Presence throughout all the earth!"

This psalm ends with the same words it begins with. These words of praise to the name of God form a frame for its central subject—praise from humankind, whom God has made to reflect His majesty. Here we see that people count for something in God's eyes. We are important and valuable to Him—not just because He created us, but also because He sent His Son to redeem us and give us eternal life.

When we visibly give thanks to God for His goodness, we declare to the unsaved that He is our Creator and Sustainer. We bear witness to the truth that every person needs God for present life and future hope. Our words of praise and gratitude to God (such as those recorded in verse 1) might encourage the unsaved to consider the truths of Christ and turn to Him in faith for new life and eternal joy.

B. The Creation's Praise: vs. 2

From the lips of children and infants you have ordained praise because of your enemies, to silence the foe and the avenger.

David recognized that whenever God reveals Himself, whether above the heavens or upon the earth, He is glorious. His praise is chanted on high and echoed from cradle and nursery. This praise is a sufficient answer to God's opponents.

What is sweeter than the songs of children? Our hearts are lifted when we hear them singing the Lord's praises. He is worthy of such adoration, and He sees to it that even helpless "children and infants" (Ps. 8:2) draw the world's attention to Him. The unbelieving world rejects the rule of God, but the forces of darkness cannot silence His praise.

The Savior quoted verse 2 when the Jewish religious authorities complained that some children in the temple courts were singing praise to Jesus as the Son of David. The chief priests and scribes were enraged over what they perceived to be inappropriate conduct and asked the Messiah whether He heard the children's praises (Matt. 21:15-16). The implication is that He was wrong for not stopping them. Jesus, admitting that He did hear the praises, referred His critics to Psalm 8:2 and in this way defended the children against the religious leaders. The boys and girls had spoken more wisely about our Lord than did the chief priests and scribes.

II. REASONS FOR PRAISE: PSALM 8:3-9

A. The Place of Humanity: vss. 3-5

When I consider your heavens, the work of your fingers, the moon and the stars, which you have set in place, what is man that you are mindful of him, the son of man that you care for him? You made him a little lower than the heavenly beings and crowned him with glory and honor.

David gazed into the heavens once again and considered his place in the grand scheme of creation. Did he matter to God? Was he important and valuable compared to the heavenly bodies? David recognized that what he could see in the sky was the work of God's "fingers" (Ps. 8:3). Of course, David knew that God did not have literal fingers, but in lavish poetic style he used a powerful figure of speech to describe God's creative power.

Verse 3 indicates that the heavens belonged to God, for He had made them. We also learn that He set all the solar bodies in exactly the right place for our benefit. Ultimately, it takes faith to acknowledge that even the universe with its infinite distances is the work of God. As Hebrews 11:3 says, "By faith we understand that the universe was formed at God's command, so that what is seen was not made out of what was visible."

The language and context of Psalm 8 indicate that a particular historical event was on David's mind—the creation of Adam and Eve. The passage strongly implies that God still cares for the human race, but the focus of the psalm is on the Creation account and the love God exercised in making the first man and woman.

To respect God's majesty, we must compare ourselves to His greatness. That's what David did when he asked, "What is man that you are mindful of him?" (vs. 4). Here "man" refers to all human beings regardless of gender. David's use of the phrase "son of man" looks upon people as insignificant and transitory. If the entire universe appears microscopic in the sight of the Creator, how much less must be the significance of humanity?

To feel small like this is a healthy way to get back to reality. Of course, God does not want us to become transfixed on our smallness. Rather, He wants us to humbly turn our gaze to Him. David seemed to do this in verse 5 when he noted that God made human beings "a little lower than the heavenly beings." The phrase can be translated "a little lower than God." This would ascribe even more dignity to us than being compared with angels (Heb. 2:7). Also, the phrase translated "a little" (Ps. 8:5) could read "for a little while." This might mean that believers, when glorified in heaven, are somehow "higher" than the angels.

Whichever interpretations are taken, it's clear that God has crowned humankind with "glory and honor." This insight could not be obtained by looking at the sky or by any other part of nature. The writer wrote under the inspiration of the Holy Spirit. David knew that, despite our apparent unimportance in the universe, we humans are in fact highly valued by God.

Our dignity stems from our creation in the image of God (Gen. 1:26-27). Despite Adam's sin, all people bear vestiges of God's image (5:1). Followers of Christ are in the process of having the image of God restored in them (2 Cor. 5:17; Col. 3:10). Therefore, Psalm 8:5 not only applied to Adam and Eve when they were created, but also applies to us. Hebrews 2 also applies it to Christ.

B. The Responsibility of Humanity: vss. 6-8

You made him ruler over the works of your hands; you put everything under his feet: all flocks and herds, and the beasts of the field, the birds of the air, and the fish of the sea, all that swim the paths of the seas.

Psalm 8:6 tells us that the Lord made humanity "ruler over the works" of His hands. The Hebrew term rendered "ruler" conveys the idea of oversight, control, and government with the extent of the authority dependent on the context of where the word is used. In this passage, the psalmist enthusiastically extended the dominion of humans to all of God's creatures upon the earth. Clearly, the writer regarded the rule of people over nature as one of the purposes behind their creation.

It is because humans are the only creatures on earth made in God's image that the Lord put us in charge of the rest of creation (Gen. 1:28-30). And as Psalm 8:6-8 reminds us, we have dominion even over the animal world. This means we have the right to use nature to meet our needs, while at the same time fulfilling our responsibility to take care of nature.

When we candidly take these truths into account, we sense a great opportunity to honor and please God. The Lord has given us everything to bless us and provide for all our needs. We of course need great wisdom in being responsible stewards over God's creation. Ultimately, it is His creation; thus we are not at liberty to despoil it for selfish ends.

Some people claim that humans are no more valuable than any other form of life. But Psalm 8 plainly contradicts that opinion. God has bestowed on us more significance than any other part of the visible creation. Because of our sin, none of us has perfectly achieved the dignity God wanted us to have. That's why the Father sent His Son to put things right and to restore His creation to glory and honor. In fact, as Hebrews 2:6-8 reminds us, Psalm 8:4-6 finds ultimate fulfillment in Christ. It is because of Him that redeemed humanity will be able to fully realize its appointed destiny over the creation.

C. The Creator's Majestic Name: vs. 9

O LORD, our Lord, how majestic is your name in all the earth!

David concluded his psalm with another powerful affirmation of God's glory. The writer's prelude put him in the proper frame of mind to consider God's creation works. And his postlude moved him to exclaim "how majestic" (Ps. 8:9) God's name was "in all the earth." This psalm emphasizes how blessed we are. If we do not take the time to think about God and His work, we will not be moved to praise Him. But when we contemplate the universe that God created, we will want to humbly worship Him.

Discussion Questions

1. In what ways can what comes out of the mouths of "children and infants" (Ps. 8:2) silence the foes of God?

2. When was the last time you felt the starry sky testify to you about God's majesty and power?

3. How does creation indicate that it must have had a master designer?

4. How can some people deny God's existence while studying the details of His creation?

5. Why do you think David ended this psalm the same way he began it?

Contemporary Application

Psalm 8 reminds us that God is worthy of our praise because He both created and sustains us. This truth is also taught in the New Testament. In Matthew 6:25-33, Jesus urged His disciples not to worry about where they would get food to eat, water to drink, or clothes to wear. The Savior indicated that their heavenly Father would graciously provide what they needed, just as He supplied the birds of the air and the lilies that carpeted the fields of Palestine. He would do even more for His people, who were of immeasurably greater value to Him.

As Paul addressed the philosophers of Athens, he declared that God made the world and everything in it and that He gives life and breath to every creature (Acts 17:24-25). The apostle made it clear that this powerful Creator determines the various eras of history and the limits of each nation's territory (vs. 26). Paul also said that this great God gives people the ability to live, move about, and become responsible citizens in their communities (vs. 28).

Finally, James 1:17 reveals that every good thing, every generous action, and every perfect gift comes from the Father who created the lights of heaven. Every aspect of our lives is under God's loving care. This one who is all-powerful, all-wise, and all-knowing deserves nothing less than our highest adoration.

God Created Wonderful Things

DEVOTIONAL READING
Psalm 104:31-35

DAILY BIBLE READINGS
Monday March 6
Psalm 19:1-6 The Firmament Proclaims God's Handiwork

Tuesday March 7
Psalm 66:1-9 Make a Joyful Noise to God

Wednesday March 8
Psalm 136:1-9 God's Steadfast Love Endures Forever

Thursday March 9
Psalm 104:1-13 God, the Great Creator

Friday March 10
Psalm 104:14-23 God's Creation Is Balanced and Orderly

Saturday March 11
Psalm 104:24-30 Manifold Are God's Works

Sunday March 12
Psalm 104:31-35 Rejoice in the Lord

Scripture
Background Scripture: *Psalm 104*
Scripture Lesson: *Psalm 104:1-13*
Key Verse: *Praise the LORD, O my soul. O LORD my God, you are very great; you are clothed with splendor and majesty.* Psalm 104:1.
Scripture Lesson for Children: *Psalm 104:1-2, 14, 19-20, 25-28*
Key Verse for Children: *How many are your works, O Lord! In wisdom you made them all; the earth is full of your creatures.* Psalm 104:24.

Lesson Aim
To learn to appreciate God more through His creation.

Lesson Setting
Time: *Date unknown, though possibly written sometime before the fall of Jerusalem in 586 B.C.*
Place: *Judah*

Lesson Outline
God Created Wonderful Things
I.   The Celestial Realm: Psalm 104:1-4
  A. *God's Greatness, Splendor, and Majesty: vs. 1*
  B. *God's Creation of the Heavens: vss. 2-4*
II. The Earthly Realm: Psalm 104:5-9
  A. *The Earth's Secure Foundations: vs. 5*
  B. *The Earth's Chaotic Waters: vss. 6-9*
III. The Ordered, Habitable World: Psalm 104:10-13
  A. *The Presence of Refreshing Springs: vss. 10-12*
  B. *The Presence of Abundant Rains: vs. 13*

Introduction for Adults

Topic: *God Created Wonderful Things*

In the late 17th century a philosophy emerged called deism, which saw God as a kind of clockmaker who created the universe with a set of unchanging laws, then left it to run by itself until the end of time. This was the period when scientists such as Sir Isaac Newton (1642–1727) were discovering and describing those "laws" of the universe.

Thomas Paine (1737–1809), the great American patriot whose pamphlet *Common Sense* helped inspire the Revolutionary War, also wrote a pamphlet on the deist philosophy called *The Age of Reason.* In it he stated that he did not believe in a God who was still involved in every aspect of His creation.

When we read Psalm 104, however, we obtain a different perspective. We discover that He is very concerned about His creation. If He were not, Jesus Christ would not have gone to Calvary.

Introduction for Youth

Topic: *This Wonderful World!*

Henry Ward Beecher (1813–1887) was an American minister who became famous for his inspirational writings and powerful oratory. In his observations, he saw natural wonders as God's "cathedrals."

Beecher wrote, "Nature is God's tongue. He speaks by summer and by winter. He can manifest himself by the wind, by the storm, by the calm. Whatever is sublime and potent, whatever is sweet and gentle, whatever is fear-inspiring, whatever is soothing, whatever is beautiful to the eye or repugnant to the taste, God may employ. The heavens above, and the procession of the seasons as they month by month walk among the stars, are various manifestations of God."

Concepts for Children

Topic: *God Is an Awesome Creator*

1. God is the Creator of the entire universe.
2. God even created time.
3. God faithfully provides for the needs of all creation.
4. Even people are dependent on God for the things they need.
5. The wonder and vastness of God's creation should move us to praise Him.

Lesson Commentary

I. THE CELESTIAL REALM: PSALM 104:1-4

A. God's Greatness, Splendor, and Majesty: vs. 1

Praise the LORD, O my soul. O LORD my God, you are very great; you are clothed with splendor and majesty.

More and more people these days are embracing a belief called pantheism. This is a theory which teaches that everything is God. He is called the universal Absolute, the Force, and the Power. This belief has led to radical views concerning the environment, animal life, and animal rights. Another popular theological system is panentheism. It teaches that all is *in* God, somewhat as if God were the ocean and we were fish. Supposedly the universe is God's body, but God's awareness or personality is greater than the sum of all the parts of the universe. To say the least, popular views such as these are shallow and insipid.

If we are honest with ourselves, we will admit there is a great source of comfort in the knowledge that God exhibits a personal care and concern for His creation. He is genuinely interested in our everyday activities. That is why we can turn to Him in prayer on a daily basis, especially when circumstances become unusually difficult.

Psalm 104, a portion of which is the focus of this week's lesson, is all about God being the Creator of the universe as well as the one who sustains it. The writer (who remains unidentified) extolled the Lord for His greatness and attributes and for His acts in creation and history. Not surprisingly, experts have categorized this psalm as a hymn of praise.

When studying a psalm, it is helpful to recognize its literary form. This is because the most significant grouping of psalms is by kind, not by author. Each type of psalm has a recognizable form and structure, though individual psalms may vary according to the pattern. When the pattern of a psalm is recognized, outlining the poem, discerning its meaning, and synthesizing its message are greatly enhanced.

In addition to hymns of praise (such as Ps. 8), the Psalter contains individual songs of thanksgiving (Ps. 30), individual laments or petitions (Ps. 6), communal laments or petitions (Ps. 12), royal psalms (Ps. 2), and wisdom psalms (Ps. 37). Admittedly, classifying the psalms is somewhat difficult because a number of them have several different characteristics. For example, some psalms begin with a lament or prayer, but transition to thanksgiving and praise (Ps. 22).

In terms of the broad structure of Psalm 104, it may be divided into the following parts: the prologue, which contains a summons to praise (vs. 1a); the reasons for praise (vss. 1b-30); the conclusion (vss. 31-35a); and the epilogue, which contains another expression of praise to the Lord (vs. 35b).

Commentators have noticed thematic links between this passage and Genesis 1. In the latter portion of Scripture, the manner and order in which God created "the heavens and the earth" (vs. 1) are described. We learn that in the first three days of creation, God formed the earth; then in the second three, He filled what He had formed. At several points during all this creating, God saw that His work was "good" (vss. 4, 10, 12, 18, 21, 25). Then at the end God saw that everything He had made was "very good" (vs. 31).

It's safe to assume that the writer of Psalm 104 was well aware of these truths. But rather than repeat them, he built on the thought of Genesis 1 by taking a more sweeping view of the universe God created. In a figurative sense, the world is God's artistic masterpiece, which the psalmist wants everyone to appreciate fully.

It is fitting, then, that God's people are invited to give praise to the Lord with every aspect of their being (Ps. 104:1). After all, He is their God, the one who created, sustains, and rules over them. Furthermore, His magnificence is unparalleled. Concerning Him alone it can be said that the world is His regal attire. He robes Himself with it (in a manner of speaking) as a showcase of His splendor.

B. God's Creation of the Heavens: vss. 2-4

He wraps himself in light as with a garment; he stretches out the heavens like a tent and lays the beams of his upper chambers on their waters. He makes the clouds his chariot and rides on the wings of the wind. He makes winds his messengers, flames of fire his servants.

After introducing God's people to the Lord's greatness as it is seen in His creation of the universe, the psalmist next directs our attention to the radiance of God as it is manifested in the celestial realm. The writer, continuing the imagery in Psalm 104:1 of the Lord being robed in magnificence, declared in verse 2 that God used "light" as if it were a "garment" to cover Himself. The idea is that the Lord not only brought light—a vital source of life and blessing—into existence but also supremely controls it for His own glory.

The power of God is further seen in His ability to stretch out the starry skies like a tent curtain (vs. 2). He also created and sustains His celestial abode, which verse 3 refers to as "his upper chambers." The "waters" are another way of pointing to lofty rain clouds. The picture is one of the Lord laying out the beams of His heavenly abode in the clouds.

So awesome is the Creator that He makes the "clouds his chariots," and He travels along "the wings of the wind." Some think the wind functions as the wings of chariotlike clouds upon which God rides. Others have suggested that "the wind" personifies a cherub. In this case, the Lord is riding a cherub, and currents of wind propel the glorious creature forward (see 18:10).

In 104:4, we catch a further glimpse of God's supreme power. The winds of a swirling storm are the Lord's "messengers" (or "angels") carrying out His purposes. Likewise, "flames of fire" produced by thunder are God's "servants" to attend to His every bidding (see 148:8). Like earthly monarchs, the Lord has a pavilion, a palace, a chariot, messengers, and courtiers; but all these are of cosmic scale and of celestial nature.

II. THE EARTHLY REALM: PSALM 104:5-9

A. The Earth's Secure Foundations: vs. 5

He set the earth on its foundations; it can never be moved.

The world in which we live is not a static, motionless planet; rather, it is character-ized by tremendous upheaval. Nevertheless, even the land (along with the skies and sea), despite its constant change and variation, remains under God's complete control. From the dawn of creation, the Lord established the continents on their "foundations" (Ps. 104:5); and there is nothing in the entire universe that can cause the land to be upended, for God will not allow it to happen (see 93:1; 96:10). Here we see that He is the Lord of heaven and earth.

B. The Earth's Chaotic Waters: vss. 6-9

You covered it with the deep as with a garment; the waters stood above the mountains. But at your rebuke the waters fled, at the sound of your thunder they took to flight; they flowed over the mountains, they went down into the valleys, to the place you assigned for them. You set a boundary they cannot cross; never again will they cover the earth.

It is true that at one time the watery deep covered the land like a "garment" (Ps. 104:6). According to Genesis 1, it was on the second day of creation that God made the sky by separating surface water from clouds. And it was at this time that the waters of the planet reached above "the mountains" (Ps. 104:6).

Moreover, it wasn't until the third day of creation that God separated dry ground and surface water, making land and seas. At that time the surface waters retreated at the sound of the Lord's rebuke. And when His thunderous voice boomed, the oceans took flight (vs. 7). This was also when God caused the mountains to rise up and the valleys to go down to the place He decreed (vs. 8).

Later in the Genesis account we find a description of the Flood, an incident in which the Lord permitted the earth's surface waters to inundate the entire planet (chaps. 6—8). Then, at the appointed time, God caused the waters to recede grad-ually (8:1-5). The Lord also pledged never again to allow "the waters [to] become a flood to destroy all life" (9:15). As Psalm 104:9 relates, God has set a boundary for the surface waters that cannot be crossed. This in turn prevents them ever again covering the earth.

III. THE ORDERED, HABITABLE WORLD: PSALM 104:10-13

A. The Presence of Refreshing Springs: vss. 10-12

He makes springs pour water into the ravines; it flows between the mountains. They give water to all the beasts of the field; the wild donkeys quench their thirst. The birds of the air nest by the waters; they sing among the branches.

The Lord not only protects every aspect of His creation, but also watches over, pro-vides for, and sustains it. He tends the planet as if it were a gigantic, complex garden.

His desire is for this ecosystem to flourish and thereby bring Him glory. This truth is rooted deeply in the soil of the Genesis 1 Creation account. In particular, it was on the third day that God brought land and seas as well as vegetation into existence. Then on the sixth day, the Lord created animals and humans, both of which live on the land and eat vegetation.

Psalm 104:10-13 complements these truths. For example, verse 10 reveals that God causes the streams, which originate from the springs, to gush forth into the surrounding valleys. The cascading water, in turn, "flows between the mountains." This provides life-giving water for all the animals of the field (vs. 11).

Consequently, the "wild donkeys" are able to "quench their thirst." Also, birds nesting beside the streams partake of the waters and chirp contentedly among the thick foliage of the bushes (vs. 12). The latter, of course, exist because of the presence of the water God has provided.

B. The Presence of Abundant Rains: vs. 13

He waters the mountains from his upper chambers; the earth is satisfied by the fruit of his work.

Even the mountains do not escape the Lord's notice. From the lofty chambers of His heavenly abode, God causes rain to fall from the sky onto the mountains (Ps. 104:13). This enables all sorts of plant and animal life to thrive on the peaks and slopes of the highlands. In fact, as a result of the Lord's deeds, the earth flourishes and is satisfied with unimaginable abundance.

The final phrase of the psalm, "Praise the LORD" (vs. 35), renders the Hebrew word *hallelujah.* It is the first of 23 times that this term is used in the Psalter. Contemplation of the creative and sustaining works of God caused the author to begin and end his hymn with an injunction for his soul to bless the Lord. Perhaps today we need to take time for similar reflection. Meditating on God's many provisions will help our praise!

Discussion Questions

1. Why would the psalmist want to bless the Lord?
2. In what way was the Lord clothed with majesty and splendor?
3. How had God brought glory to Himself in His creation of the world?
4. What do we learn about God from His concern and care for the tiniest of creatures?
5. Why should we take notice of Him who created and sustains all things?

Contemporary Application

God is the source of all blessings, and one need not search far and wide to find them. This is a key emphasis of this week's lesson. From it we can learn to appreciate God more through His creation.

As we give thoughtful consideration to Psalm 104, we discover that the Lord not only created humankind but also provided the necessities to sustain them. In fact, the Bible speaks of the earth as being full of God's riches, all of which are serviceable to the human race for its needs. For instance, the Lord created the great bodies of water, which not only are used for travel but also provide a tremendous source of food. This truth reminds us that there is nothing that God has made in vain.

Ultimately, it is beyond our comprehension as to why God, in His divine wisdom, would do all the mighty works He has performed so that humankind can benefit from and find enjoyment in them. Just as remarkable is the fact that not a day goes by in which the peoples of the world do not benefit from God's blessings in one way or another. Even day and night have their particular blessings.

These truths are not just discernable from human experience. The consistent testimony of Scripture is that, regardless of whether it is water, sunshine, food, oil, minerals, wood, or something else, the earth is a testimony of God's blessings and reflects His love and care. By way of example, Psalm 33:5 declares, "The earth is full of [the Lord's] unfailing love." And we read in Mark 4:28, "All by itself the soil produces grain." May we never tire of showing our appreciation to God for His wonderful creation!

God Created and Knows Us

Scripture

Background Scripture: *Psalm 139*

Scripture Lesson: *Psalm 139:1-3, 7-14, 23-24*

Key Verse: *I praise you because I am fearfully and wonderfully made; your works are wonderful, I know that full well.* Psalm 139:14.

Scripture Lesson for Children: *Psalm 139:1-3, 7-14, 23-24*

Key Verse for Children: *I praise you because I am fearfully and wonderfully made; your works are wonderful, I know that full well.* Psalm 139:14.

Lesson Aim

To rest in the assurance of God's intimate knowledge and active presence in our lives.

Lesson Setting

Time: Written sometime during the reign of David (1010–970 B.C.)

Place: Israel

Lesson Outline

God Created and Knows Us

I. The Lord's Intimate Knowledge of His Servant: Psalm 139:1-3
    A. *The Lord's Personal Awareness: vs. 1*
    B. *The Lord's Active Involvement: vss. 2-3*

II. The Lord's Presence with His Servant: Psalm 104:7-14, 23-24
    A. *The Lord's Inescapable Presence: vss. 7-10*
    B. *The Lord's Penetrating Presence: vss. 11-12*
    C. *The Lord's Marvelous Creation: vss. 13-14*
    D. *The Lord's Continuous Guidance: vss. 23-24*

Introduction for Adults

Topic: *Searched and Known by God*

> At a recent funeral I conducted, one of the surviving children gave me a little booklet of prayers titled, *Adventures in Prayer.* One prayer speaks of God's intimate knowledge of us as well as His loving care for us.
>
> "Lord, I have been so defeated by circumstances. I have felt like an animal trapped in a corner with nowhere to flee. Where are You in all this, Lord? The night is dark. I cannot feel Your presence.
>
> "Help me to know the darkness is really the 'shade of Your hand, outstretched caressingly'; that the 'hemming in' is Your doing. Perhaps there was no other way I would allow You to demonstrate what You can do in my life."

Introduction for Youth

Topic: *God Knows Us like a Book*

> Many teenagers experience strong emotions when they find out someone of the opposite gender likes them. Some of these feelings include amazement and excitement. Perhaps it's a little like that for saved adolescents with respect to their relationship with God.
>
> Even for young people who have little more than a passing knowledge of God's name, He still loves and cares for them. His heart must ache when they do not recognize His care, unseen protection, or concern. Even in the darkest times of their lives He is doing what He knows is best for them. In those overwhelming moments, when it is most difficult to praise Him, still there is cause since He knows them better than they know themselves.

Concepts for Children

Topic: *God Takes Care of Us*

1. God is in control of all things and is present everywhere.
2. God cares for us even before conception.
3. God leads His children through every situation in life.
4. God created our wonderful bodies and knows everything about us.
5. In light of all that God has done for us, let us live to please Him.

Lesson Commentary

I. THE LORD'S INTIMATE KNOWLEDGE OF HIS SERVANT: PSALM 139:1-3

A. The Lord's Personal Awareness: vs. 1

O LORD, you have searched me and you know me.

Believers of all ages have understood that God knows the least detail about them. But deep inside they have also understood that for their own spiritual well-being it was important to open themselves up consciously to God's searching gaze. That's just what David did.

The background of Psalm 139 seems to be a situation of some danger. Perhaps the psalmist exposed his life to God as a way of proving he did not deserve divine punishment through his enemies. But before we get any hint of earthly danger, the psalmist eloquently described God's knowledge of him (vs. 1). The Lord routinely looked deep within David's heart and knew everything about him.

The Bible reveals that God has inherent characteristics or qualities that distinguish Him from His creation. One of His attributes is called *omniscience*, a term that literally refers to "all knowledge." Scripture teaches that God has unlimited awareness, understanding, and insight. In other words, His knowledge and grasp of all things is universal and complete. His comprehension is instantaneous, exhaustive, and absolutely correct. Even though all things are eternally present in God's view, He still recognizes them as successive, finite events in time.

The Lord is aware of every thought people have and every action they perform (1 Chron. 28:9). He can objectively and fairly evaluate the actions of people because He knows everything (1 Sam. 2:3). All wisdom and counsel reside with Him (Job 12:13), and His understanding has no limit (Ps. 147:5). There is nothing in the entire universe that is hidden from God's sight. Everything is exposed by His penetrating gaze (Heb. 4:13).

God's awareness of all things serves two purposes. First, everyone is accountable to the Lord for his or her actions; no one will be able to do evil and get away with it. Second, God's omniscience reminds us that He is intimately aware of our circumstances. He not only sees our plight but also reaches out in love to care for us (Gen. 16:13).

B. The Lord's Active Involvement: vss. 2-3

You know when I sit and when I rise; you perceive my thoughts from afar. You discern my going out and my lying down; you are familiar with all my ways.

As Psalm 139:2-3 reveals, nothing is hidden from God's sight. David acknowledged that the Lord knew when he sat down to rest and when he got up to work. And even though God made His abode in heaven, this did not hinder His ability to perceive David's thoughts and understand his motives.

By mentioning "when I sit and when I rise" (vs. 2) and "my going out and my lying down" (vs. 3), the poet was merely meaning "all my ways." God knew what

David would say before he uttered it. In fact, God did not miss a single one of the psalmist's thoughts. In short, God knew everything the psalmist desired and imagined. Also, regardless of whether David was traveling or pausing from such, the Lord carefully observed everything the poet did.

In verse 3, the poet spoke of God being "familiar" with his daily activities. The word renders a Hebrew term for winnowing grain. Like the sharp-eyed farmer who scrutinizes the harvest and passes judgment on what is to be saved or thrown aside, God examines the human heart. He knows every detail of every life.

We understand enough about our personal thoughts and actions to realize that God is not totally pleased with what He sees. In fact, we may even wonder why God is so patient with our imperfections. Yet rather than casting us aside, God constantly hems us in with His merciful love. The realization that God knows all and still loves each person filled the psalmist with awe (vs. 6).

If God knows our thoughts, some will wonder, then why pray? But prayer is not a news hot line to provide the Almighty with a breaking development taking place on earth. After all, He is fully focused on everything that is taking place and even understands the motives and implications for everyone involved.

There are benefits in praying, even though God knows the situation as well as the words we use in addressing Him. For instance, prayer brings the believer into conscious fellowship with God, gives perspective to issues, and channels strength and peace into the life of the one who is praying. At times, God uses a prayer to change circumstances and make a visible difference in an issue. We are encouraged to pray, believing that God will fulfill His will.

II. THE LORD'S PRESENCE WITH HIS SERVANT: PSALM 104:7-14, 23-24

A. The Lord's Inescapable Presence: vss. 7-10

Where can I go from your Spirit? Where can I flee from your presence? If I go up to the heavens, you are there; if I make my bed in the depths, you are there. If I rise on the wings of the dawn, if I settle on the far side of the sea, even there your hand will guide me, your right hand will hold me fast.

As human beings we are limited by boundaries of time and space. For example, we cannot occupy two places simultaneously. However, God is not subject to such restrictions. He is *omnipresent*, meaning present everywhere at once. Nor is He divided, like minerals that may be scattered over a wide expanse of terrain. At all times, all that is God is totally present everywhere.

David did not arrive at this truth easily. In his imagination he pondered several ways one might try to evade the presence of God (Ps. 139:7). First, the poet thought about ascending to heaven or sprawling out in Sheol, the realm of the dead (vs. 8). Together these places represented the most extreme vertical distances. It's as if David was saying, "If I ascended as high as I could, or descended to the lowest thinkable depth, I could not escape Your reach."

But what about the horizontal extremes? Suppose the poet made the rising sun his chariot and raced to the utmost reach of the western horizon (vs. 9)? Even if

David could somehow settle down on the other side of the Mediterranean Sea (which lies west of Israel), the Lord would still be there to afford support every hour of every day (vs. 10). In contrast to idols, there is no point on any map where God is not fully present to protect and guide His people.

B. The Lord's Penetrating Presence: vss. 11-12

If I say, "Surely the darkness will hide me and the light become night around me," even the darkness will not be dark to you; the night will shine like the day, for darkness is as light to you.

David considered another possibility: hiding (Psalm 139:11-12). Adam and Eve tried to hide from God among the trees of Eden; here David thought about using the night as a screen to hide himself from God. However, he rejected this possibility as well, since God can see in darkness as well as in light.

David had to give up the idea of escaping God. So must we all. And once we have recognized the futility of escape attempts, we can begin to accept happily God's being everywhere, just as we can accept happily God's knowing everything about us.

C. The Lord's Marvelous Creation: vss. 13-14

For you created my inmost being; you knit me together in my mother's womb. I praise you because I am fearfully and wonderfully made; your works are wonderful, I know that full well.

David had reached the point of spiritual maturity at which he had come to accept God's knowledge of him. The poet realized that every day of his life, from the first to the last, was known to God.

In David's day, people knew little about how a human fetus forms in its mother's womb. But David understood that God knows about this because He is the one who causes it to happen. The Lord is in charge of each individual's genetic code and brings together the substances that make up a human being. And since the result is obviously a remarkable creation, David considered the making of a child a sign of God's wisdom (Ps. 139:13-16).

The process that takes place in the "mother's womb" (vs. 13; also called "the secret place," vs. 15, and "the depths of the earth") is like the creation of a work of art. David compared the formation of a human child to the skilled weaving of cloth on a loom. Children are "knit . . . together" (vs. 13) and "woven" (vs. 15) by God inside the womb.

Both the mind and the heart, the intellect and emotions (as well as the will) are the handiwork of God. David exclaimed that the Lord's deeds are awesome; and just as amazing is God's thorough knowledge of every human being from the moment of their conception (vs. 14). We who have seen photographs of fetuses at different stages of growth should be even more amazed than David was.

Next, the psalmist's thoughts turned from the beginning of life to life's entire course. David said that before we were born, God knew everything that would happen on every one of our days as though all of the events were written in a book (vs. 16). As we look ahead, our future may appear cloudy to us, but it is as plain as day to God. Therefore, we can march ahead confidently, knowing that whatever awaits us, God will be with us.

The Lord's thoughts were far beyond David's ability to number—that is, comprehend—them. Nevertheless, God's thoughts were "precious" (vs. 17) to David because they mean that God has the ability and the willingness to care for His children. And even though we may lose consciousness of God when we are asleep, He never loses consciousness of us (vs. 18). At our awakening from sleep (even the sleep of death), we will be with God and He with us. He will never leave us.

D. The Lord's Continuous Guidance: vss. 23-24

Search me, O God, and know my heart; test me and know my anxious thoughts. See if there is any offensive way in me, and lead me in the way everlasting.

Psalm 139:19 marks an abrupt transition. Suddenly the psalmist began talking about wicked people who were God's enemies and his enemies. These men, said David, were "bloodthirsty." Furthermore, they misused God's name, probably by calling down curses on God's faithful servants. They hated God and opposed Him.

Though abrupt, the transition makes sense. The earlier part of the psalm revealed that God's knowledge demonstrates His ability to care for His people and that it makes them love Him. Verses 19-22 reveal the psalmist's confidence that God could deal with his enemies. Those verses also reveal his zeal for God and for God's standards of righteousness.

Though zealous for God, David knew better than to think that he was perfect in God's sight. The poet's "anxious thoughts" (vs. 23) may have been caused by the idea of God's searching him. But he invited God to search him anyway. He believed there was no grossly "offensive way" (vs. 24) in him, as there was in his enemies.

This process of God's searching David's life would bring up some impurities for cleansing. And this cleansing would open the way to greater progress in "the way everlasting" (vs. 24). So the psalmist asked God to test him, cleanse him, and thereby vindicate him.

David's exercise of freely opening his life to God is one each Christian could profitably adopt. Sometimes we try to keep parts of our lives hidden from God. We don't acknowledge before Him some of our most cherished sins. Therefore, we need the courage and the faith to show Him everything about us, realizing that afterward will come the healing and sanctifying work of the Spirit.

Discussion Questions

1. How does God's intimate knowledge of every person prove to be both sobering and reassuring at the same time?
2. What does it really mean that God is present everywhere at all times?
3. Why should we want the Lord to know our every thought?
4. Why is it important for us to lean on God to avoid the way of wickedness?
5. How can we encourage others to follow the everlasting way?

Contemporary Application

According to the Old Testament, God is omnipresent, which means He is present everywhere. The New Testament explains that "everywhere" includes the life of each believer and that He gains particular access through the Holy Spirit. The Spirit is the Christian's constant companion.

Knowing that God is always with us and knows us better than we understand ourselves is a great encouragement. It means that those who trust in Him need never feel lonely, even when human friends have been removed. Nor do Christians need to give in to feelings of inadequacy when called to take a significant risk. God is near to give wisdom and offer courage when one is called to take a step into the unknown.

One way to think about the truth of God's omnipresence is to compare this attribute to radio waves. Although these impulses cannot be seen or felt, they are around us at all times. With these radio waves we are surrounded by a tremendous wealth of information and music to fit every taste; however, access is not automatic. An individual must tune in to receive the benefits. (Admittedly, while an illustration such as this might clarify a character quality of God, such metaphors give only a faint reflection of spiritual realities.)

The God who gives courage to the fearful and promises to be the companion of the lonely is ever-present. By turning to Him in prayer, Christians may draw on His power, especially as they face the challenges of each day.

A Hymn of Praise to the Creator

Scripture

Background Scripture: *Psalm 145*

Scripture Lesson: *Psalm 145:1-13*

Key Verse: *The LORD is gracious and compassionate, slow to anger and rich in love.* Psalm 145:8.

Scripture Lesson for Children: *Psalm 145:1-3, 8-18*

Key Verse for Children: *Every day I will praise you and extol your name for ever and ever.* Psalm 145:2.

Lesson Aim

To emphasize that God is worthy of praise because of His greatness, goodness, and glory.

Lesson Setting

Time: *Written sometime during the reign of David (1010–970 B.C.)*

Place: *Israel*

Lesson Outline

A Hymn of Praise to the Creator

  I. The Adulation of the Lord: Psalm 145:1-3
    A. *The Constant Praise of the Lord: vss. 1-2*
    B. *The Greatness of the Lord: vs. 3*
  II. The Mighty Acts of the Lord: Psalm 145:4-9
    A. *The Lord's Awesome Works: vss. 4-6*
    B. *The Lord's Goodness and Righteousness: vs. 7*
    C. *The Lord's Grace and Compassion: vss. 8-9*
  III. The Kingdom of the Lord: Psalm 145:10-13
    A. *The Glory of the Kingdom: vss. 10-12*
    B. *The Enduring Nature of the Kingdom: vs. 13*

Introduction for Adults

Topic: *Worthy of Praise*

Astute marriage counselors have learned that when couples are having problems, one solution is to help them change their attitude about their relationship. Instead of thinking, "I don't love my spouse anymore," they should act as if they truly did love their spouse, doing all the things someone in love would do. In essence, they are to practice being "in love" with their mate. With time, the actions of love bring back the old feelings of love. By acting as if they really are in love, love grows.

Christians can discover the same thing when it comes to worship. Have the class brainstorm ways they might try acting out their love for God even on bad days when they don't feel like praising Him for anything. Jot their ideas on the chalkboard. As they carry out the actions of worship, they will find God working in their lives, changing their hearts and bringing them closer to Him despite their lackluster feelings. Their lives will be enriched and God will be glorified.

Introduction for Youth

Topic: *Praise God!*

In the Disney movie *Pollyanna*, a young girl is sent to live with her strict Aunt Polly. Soon she learns that the town is a collection of bullied souls who are afraid to stand up to her wealthy and influential aunt. As a result, the entire populace has a chronic case of "sour grapes."

Pollyanna changes that when she starts telling people about her father's "happy thought" system. No matter what the circumstance, one looks for the good that can arise from it. Her idea catches on, and soon the whole town is transformed by one girl's better way of seeing the world.

Saved teens can have a similar impact on their world. This is possible when they reflect on different ways they can praise God. This can be as simple as praying a prayer of thanksgiving every morning or night. It could also be by singing choruses of praise with other believers in a worship service.

Concepts for Children

Topic: *Praise God for His Creations*

1. The Bible directs us to worship the Lord each day.
2. People cannot fully understand the greatness of God.
3. The goodness of God is seen in all His actions.
4. The kingdom of God lasts forever.
5. God's faithfulness to us should increase our faithfulness to Him.

Lesson Commentary

I. The Adulation of the Lord: Psalm 145:1-3

A. The Constant Praise of the Lord: vss. 1-2

I will exalt you, my God the King; I will praise your name for ever and ever. Every day I will praise you and extol your name for ever and ever.

The superscription to Psalm 145 indicates that it was written by David as a hymn of praise. Within this song, the poet extolled his "God the King" (vs. 1) because He is a just and merciful ruler who cares for His people. David's intent was to continually honor the Lord's name, which underscored all that He stood for (vs. 2).

Commentators have noted that this psalm makes use of a poetic technique known as the alphabetic acrostic. In songs of this type, lines or verses or groups of verses begin with the Hebrew letters in their alphabetical order. It's not clear why psalmists used the acrostic. One reason may have been simply because it supplied the poets with a framework upon which to hang their thoughts. A second aim for the acrostic may have been to aid learners in memorizing the psalm. A third possible reason for the acrostic is that it gives the impression of having covered the subject completely—"from A to Z."

The kingship of God spoken of in verse 1 reflects a common theme of the entire Psalter (for example, see 96:10). His sovereign and unending reign as King is not limited to just once race, continent, or hemisphere. God's rule touches every nation, making everyone on earth ultimately accountable to Him. Because there is no other god, the Lord alone is deserving of the worship of all people.

God used Israel as the means of revealing Himself to the world. The Lord's reign over the entire globe means that all people on earth are responsible to Him for their lives and for their worship. Israel was to be God's light, since He was the planet's only hope of salvation.

B. The Greatness of the Lord: vs. 3

Great is the LORD and most worthy of praise; his greatness no one can fathom.

The Bible reveals that the Lord is unique in His self-existence. By way of example, Isaiah 46:9-10 declares that Israel's God stands alone as being divine. And only He can disclose what is going to happen even before it occurs.

Moreover, as Psalm 145:3 reveals, no one can fathom the greatness of the Lord. It is beyond scrutiny. Since God is much greater than anyone can understand, He alone is most worthy of praise. It may be that the more the people of God extol His greatness, the more they will recognize His wonder-working power in their lives.

II. The Mighty Acts of the Lord: Psalm 145:4-9

A. The Lord's Awesome Works: vss. 4-6

One generation will commend your works to another; they will tell of your mighty acts. They will speak of the glorious splendor of your majesty, and I will meditate on your wonderful works. They will tell of the power of your awesome works, and I will proclaim your great deeds.

Psalm 145:4 represents David's summons to the covenant community. They were to declare God's mighty acts from one generation to another. Parents were especially well positioned to announce to their children the Lord's wonderful and powerful deeds.

God's "mighty acts" highlighted His goodness and graciousness to His people. Understandably, the Lord did not want them to forget what He had done for them, so He often reminded them. For instance, God gave them feasts to celebrate so they could have a visual way to remember what He had done for them.

In particular, the feasts of Passover and Unleavened Bread reminded the Hebrews of the time they left Egypt and how the Lord brought them out of that place of bondage. He even protected them from the army of Pharaoh. The Feast of Tabernacles (or Booths) reminded them of their wandering in the wilderness before God brought them to the promised land and enabled them to conquer and settle it. The Lord knew the obedience that would bring spiritual blessing to them depended on how well they remembered what He had done.

As redeemed people such as David recounted God's works of power in their lives, they were to focus on His honor and majestic splendor. They would also ponder His amazing deeds (vs. 5). Moreover, the covenant community would proclaim to others the "awesome works" (vs. 6) of the Lord. Not one of His fearsome acts would go unannounced. In fact, all the nations of the earth were to hear about God's unparalleled greatness.

B. The Lord's Goodness and Righteousness: vs. 7

They will celebrate your abundant goodness and joyfully sing of your righteousness.

David revealed that God not only does great things but also is characterized by greatness. One indication of this is the Lord's "abundant goodness" (Ps. 145:7) or unlimited kindness. A second evidence of God's greatness is His righteousness or justice. No one can match the Lord's display of mercy and power to save. One way the people of God can honor Him for such superlative qualities is by making these a prime focus of their celebration and song.

C. The Lord's Grace and Compassion: vss. 8-9

The LORD is gracious and compassionate, slow to anger and rich in love. The LORD is good to all; he has compassion on all he has made.

The wonderful truths of Psalm 145:8-9 are found elsewhere in the Old Testament. For instance, in Exodus 34:6-7 the Lord declared to Moses that He is compassionate and gracious (see 33:19). In fact, these virtues reflect the very heart of God. He is also slow to anger (see Num. 14:18; Pss. 86:15; 103:8), which means His righteous indignation has a long fuse (as the contemporary saying goes). This in turn gives people the opportunity to repent before divine punishment is inflicted.

Unlike the powerless and lifeless idols worshiped by the unsaved, the God of Israel is "rich in love" (145:8); or, as Exodus 34:6 relates, He abounds in unfailing, covenant love. Likewise, the Lord is faithful and reliable to forgive the iniquity, transgression, and sin of those who abandon their unrighteous ways and turn to Him in faith and obedience (vs. 7).

Moreover, as David declared, the Lord is good to everyone. In fact, He showers His care and compassion on all His creation (Ps. 145:9). Theologians refer to this as God's common grace. The idea is that the Lord extends His undeserved blessings on all humanity and does not discriminate between any particular person or group.

During the first recorded missionary journey, Paul and Barnabas voiced a similar truth to the inhabitants of Lystra. The two declared that God has shown kindness to all humankind by giving them "rain from heaven and crops in their seasons" (Acts 14:17). He even provides people with "plenty of food" as well as inundates their "hearts with joy."

III. THE KINGDOM OF THE LORD: PSALM 145:10-13

A. The Glory of the Kingdom: vss. 10-12

All you have made will praise you, O LORD; your saints will extol you. They will tell of the glory of your kingdom and speak of your might, so that all men may know of your mighty acts and the glorious splendor of your kingdom.

David was confident that all of the Lord's creation—the work of His hands—would praise Him (Ps. 145:10). This was especially true of His saints. This refers to God's loyal followers. They are the ones who looked for opportunities to extol Him in a thunderous chorus of praise. As verse 21 reveals, such was to continue "for ever and ever."

The poet was quite specific regarding what the covenant community would declare. The redeemed were to proclaim the splendor of the divine kingdom. This refers to God's rule and reign over all creation. His saints would also tell the rest of humankind about the Lord's marvelous power (vs. 11). For example, such could be done through celebration and song.

What did David consider to be the overarching goal of such declarations? The intent was that the rest of humankind would acknowledge the "mighty acts" (vs. 12) of the Lord as well as the majesty and glory of His rule. In short, all creation was summoned to recognize the greatness of God.

Verse 12 underscores the importance of all people knowing about the Lord's powerful deeds. This global act of remembrance began with God's people recalling all that He had done for them. He had rescued them from 430 years of slavery in Egypt (Exod. 12:40-41) and performed great signs for Israel (Exod. 14:13-31; Num. 16—17; Josh. 3:7-17). He had protected them from the hostile nations they traveled through (Deut. 23:14), and He had driven out the nations that inhabited their land (Josh. 21:43-45).

In contrast to remembering is forsaking, which begins with forgetting. That's why God placed such a premium on His people (and through them all other people) recalling what He had done (Deut. 4:9-10; 6:12). "To remember" and "to not forget" are like the positive and negative charges on a battery. When the "deeds of the LORD" (Ps. 77:11) are remembered, it positively charges devotion. The command to "forget not all his benefits" (103:2) warns us of the negative consequences when God is forsaken.

B. The Enduring Nature of the Kingdom: vs. 13

Your kingdom is an everlasting kingdom, and your dominion endures through all generations. The LORD is faithful to all his promises and loving toward all he has made.

Human history is strewn with the wreckage of failed empires. Some have dominated the world stage for a season, but eventually all of them fail, being consigned to the ash heap of time. In contrast, the kingdom of God is unending and His dominion "endures through all generations" (Ps. 145:13).

In ancient cultures each nation had its own religion with its own gods. One unique aspect of the Hebrew religion was the belief that its God, the living God, reigns everywhere and without end, and that one day everyone will know it. This vision for the worldwide spread of God's worship appears early and often in the Old Testament. For example, God told Abraham, the founder of the Hebrew race, that "all peoples on earth will be blessed through you" (Gen. 12:3).

Old Testament law provided a way for aliens to enter the covenant community. And prophets kept the vision before the people through such words as these: "I will beckon to the Gentiles, I will lift up my banner to the peoples" (Isa. 49:22). In the Old Testament, God's worldwide worship remained a vision of the future. But when Jesus came, it was time to begin making that vision a reality.

Through the Messiah, the Lord proves just how faithful He is to "all his promises" (Ps. 145:13). In the Redeemer, every pledge finds its ultimate fulfillment. And Jesus' atoning sacrifice at Calvary makes it possible for the Lord to extend His compassion "toward all he has made." This is especially true for believers, who have experienced the fullness of God's grace through faith in Christ.

Discussion Questions

1. What is the spiritual benefit of extolling the Lord?
2. What are some of the mighty acts of God that our generation should declare?
3. In what way has God manifested His compassion over humankind?
4. In what sense is the Lord's kingdom unending?
5. Whom would you like to see become a citizen of God's kingdom?

Contemporary Application

Praise is often stimulated by awe. The more we can explain or rationalize the facts we see around us, the less likely we are to praise God or other people for making something happen. If our response to an event is "That's no big deal," then obviously praise is not likely to follow. However, when we see or hear something that causes us to exclaim, "How did they do that?"—then praise is a natural response. We praise out of wonderment.

This week's lesson seeks to draw us to praise God for that which goes beyond our human explanation. We come to see that He is worthy of praise because of His greatness, goodness, and glory. We learn that He is both Lord and King, whose greatness is beyond discovery.

When we are astounded by the wonder of God's creation, we are more likely to praise Him than when we attempt to explain the world rationally. For example, to realize that a single tongue of a solar flare is more than 40 times the diameter of the earth causes amazement. And even rapidly counting nonstop, it would take us thousands of years to number the stars in just one galaxy. Amazingly, the universe contains untold numbers of galaxies.

When we praise our great and awesome God, we honor Him for the way He graciously takes care of us. We also have an opportunity to express our gratitude to Him for His marvelous deeds and wonderful goodness. Recalling the Lord's compassion on our lives helps us to realize that we are His mortal, dependent creatures who exist to serve and worship Him.

Oppositely, when we neglect to praise God for His goodness and grace, we indicate that we do not appreciate what the Lord has done. We take for granted His abundant provision of food, clothing, and shelter. We trivialize the value of His sovereign care of the world. In our arrogance, we communicate to God that we do not need or want Him and that we can survive and prosper by ourselves.

We know, however, that such an approach to life is to be shunned. Instead, we are called to visibly give thanks to God for His unfailing love and kindness. When we do, we bear witness to the unsaved that every person needs God for present life and future hope. Our words of praise and gratitude to the Lord might even encourage the unsaved to consider the truths of Christ and turn to Him in faith for new life and eternal joy.

When Tragedy Occurs

DEVOTIONAL READING

Psalm 22:1-11

DAILY BIBLE READINGS

Monday March 27
Job 1:1-5 Job, a Blameless and Upright Man

Tuesday March 28
Job 1:6-12 Satan Determines to Strike Job

Wednesday March 29
Job 1:13-22 Job Loses All, but Remains Faithful

Thursday March 30
Job 2:1-10 Job Falls Ill, but Praises God

Friday March 31
Job 3:1-10 Job Curses His Day of Birth

Saturday April 1
Job 3:11-19 Job Wishes for Death

Sunday April 2
Job 3:20-26 Job Questions God's Benevolence

Scripture

Background Scripture: *Job 1—3*
Scripture Lesson: *Job 1:14-15, 18-19, 22; 3:1-3, 11*
Key Verse: *[Job] replied, . . . "Shall we accept good from God, and not trouble?" In all this, Job did not sin in what he said.* Job 2:10.
Scripture Lesson for Children: *Job 1:1-4, 8-11; 2:3-6; 3:1-3*
Key Verse for Children: *[Job] was blameless and upright; he feared God and shunned evil.* Job 1:1.

Lesson Aim

To maintain a strong faith in the midst of adversity.

Lesson Setting

Time: *During the second millennium B.C.*
Place: *The land of Uz, a large territory east of the Jordan River*

Lesson Outline

When Tragedy Occurs

   I. Job's Testing: Job 1:14-15, 18-19, 22
      A. *The Loss of Wealth: vss. 14-15*
      B. *The Loss of Family Members: vss. 18-19*
      C. *The Sterling Attitude of Job: vs. 22*
  II. Job's First Speech: Job 3:1-3, 11
      A. *Job Regretting the Day of His Birth: vss. 1-3*
      B. *Job Wishing He Had Been Stillborn: vs. 11*

Introduction for Adults

Topic: *Living with Tragedy*

According to the *Los Altos Town Crier,* Anabel Pelham expected her Thanksgiving dinner to be uneventful. It was the evening of November 27, 2003, when Anabel "flipped a switch to light her gas fireplace." Instead of a cozy evening, she "got a raging blaze . . . that gutted her Los Altos apartment in a matter of minutes."

At that moment Anabel felt as if her world was collapsing around her. Yet in her time of dire need, all sorts of people reached out to help her, including firefighters, relatives, and neighbors. They assisted her in cleaning up, packing, and moving. Anabel remembers feeling "compassion everywhere she looked."

How can your students live with tragedy? As the previous account suggests, it is through the presence and support of their community of loved ones and acquaintances. For Christians, this especially includes church members. And let us not forget how God can wrap His arms of love around us in moments of devastation and loss.

Introduction for Youth

Topic: *Overcoming Tragedy*

Young people are not immune to the tragedies of life. Perhaps some in your class have experienced the death of a loved one, the breakup of a family, or the withering effects of illness. The physical and emotional toll of such misfortunes can be profound.

In *Overcoming Tragedy,* Carol Carter recommends that people "join others of like faith to give thanks for your blessings, and ask for comfort, faith, and the ability to take this tragedy and turn it into a strengthening opportunity for yourself." This is sound advice for saved teens who have been struck by hardship. Perhaps during the teaching time this week, you can encourage class members to drive the shafts of their faith deep in the bedrock of God's presence, love, and faithfulness.

Concepts for Children

Topic: *Job Trusted God*

1. Job's suffering was not a result of wrongdoing.
2. Job was a man of faith who possessed great integrity.
3. God did not abandon Job in the midst of his suffering.
4. Despite the circumstances in his life, Job made a wise decision to trust God.
5. God will help us through difficult situations.

Lesson Commentary

I. Job's Testing: Job 1:14-15, 18-19, 22

A. The Loss of Wealth: vss. 14-15

A messenger came to Job and said, "The oxen were plowing and the donkeys were grazing nearby, and the Sabeans attacked and carried them off. They put the servants to the sword, and I am the only one who has escaped to tell you!"

In Job 1, we learn something about the family, wealth, and moral and spiritual stature of the main character. We also see that Satan, the enemy of godly people, tried to prove to God that Job was motivated by selfishness, not by a genuine desire to be faithful to God.

Scholars find no answer to questions about who wrote this account, which has fascinated people of faith and no faith down through the centuries. Nevertheless, we do know much about Job. He lived in Uz (vs. 1), possibly southeast of Israel in the territory known as Edom. But some researchers think Uz refers to the country of Uzbekistan in Central Asia. The writer does not date his narrative. However that may be, the setting seems to fit the time of Israel's patriarchs. Perhaps Job was Abraham's contemporary. Job reminds us of the patriarch in his later prosperous years.

Furthermore, the narrative makes no mention of Moses, the law, or any kind of organized religion. Instead, the writer focused on Job's character, family, and wealth. The author gave a very detailed picture of the man. Job was one of those remarkable people described as "blameless and upright." Of course, no one in the Bible is absolutely sinless, except the Lord Jesus Christ. So this account does not mean Job was perfect, but rather that as far as his public standing was concerned, he was free of censure.

Outwardly, Job was a man of integrity, sincerity, and consistency. This was because "he feared God and shunned evil." To fear God means to live in reverential awe and respect of His holiness, majesty, and power. In terms of Job, his moral stature grew in the soil of obedience to and confidence in the one true and living God. There was no separation in his life between his profession of faith and his behavior in all relations of life.

In the prologue of the Book of Job (chaps. 1—2), six short but key scenes set the stage for the main character's debate with his comforters and his ultimate encounter with God, described later. Scene 1 (1:1-5) gives some background information about Job's good character and his family. Scene 2 (vss. 6-12) tells about Satan's first challenge to God, in which the devil gained the Lord's permission to destroy Job's family and possessions. Satan sought to prove that Job would curse his Creator when signs of God's blessing on his life ceased occurring.

Scene 3 (vss. 13-22) records Job's first test and how this virtuous man stood firm and faithful to God even after losing his family and possessions. Scene 4 (2:1-6) divulges Satan's second challenge to God, when the devil gained the Lord's permission to strike Job's body with disease. Scene 5 (vss. 7-10) sets forth Job's second test—the onslaught of painful sores. Finally, scene 6 (vss. 11-13) recounts the arrival of Job's comforters.

Of particular interest is the description of the two councils in heaven (1:6-12; 2:1-6). In looking at these councils, the reader—but not Job—catches a glimpse of the cosmic drama behind the tragic events of Job's life. Both of the councils involved God, His angels, and Satan. The Hebrew word for angels refers to the supernatural beings who were created by the Lord to serve as His messengers and to carry out His bidding. Satan was one of the angels, but after his fall he began to roam the earth seeking to undermine the faith of believers (see 1 Pet. 5:8; Rev. 12:10).

In the first of the two councils, God agreed to the plan suggested by Satan (Job 1:12a). God did, however, limit the damage Satan was allowed to do by saying he could do anything except harm Job himself. It was not God's purpose to single out Job for Satan's attacks. It was His purpose, however, to enable Job to glorify God through his steadfast faith. Having been granted God's permission to do so, Satan left the Lord's presence to begin inflicting his evil against Job (vs. 12b).

Verse 13 begins recording a rapid succession of reports about calamities that fell upon Job's possessions and family. Satan combined both human and natural forces to create these disasters. The Sabeans, who killed Job's servants and stole his oxen and donkeys, were probably from southern Arabia (1:13-15). The fire from the sky that burned up Job's servants and sheep may have been lightning (vs. 16). The Chaldeans, who murdered his servants and led away his camels, most likely were nomads from Mesopotamia (vs. 17).

B. The Loss of Family Members: vss. 18-19

While he was still speaking, yet another messenger came and said, "Your sons and daughters were feasting and drinking wine at the oldest brother's house, when suddenly a mighty wind swept in from the desert and struck the four corners of the house. It collapsed on them and they are dead, and I am the only one who has escaped to tell you!"

The great wind that caused the collapse of the house in which Job's children were feasting was most likely a desert whirlwind, similar to the one out of which God later spoke to Job (Job 1:18-19; compare 38:1; 40:6). Apparently in a matter of minutes, Job learned he had lost his wealth, his servants, and his children.

Our understanding of all that was to come in Job's life must rest on the facts recorded in chapter 1. First, the introduction makes clear that Job's subsequent suffering was not because of his sin or because of any failures in his faith. Later on, of course, he said some rash things when he demanded an explanation from God for his suffering.

Whatever sins he may have committed in attacking God, as it were, those sins followed rather than preceded his suffering. In fact, as 1:8 and 2:3 make clear, it was precisely because of his righteousness and his innocence—and because of God's praise of him—that Job was exposed to his ordeal. So we learn at the outset that the innocent do suffer; and that is a message of prime importance for us.

C. The Sterling Attitude of Job: vs. 22

In all this, Job did not sin by charging God with wrongdoing.

Although Job probably expressed some measure of grief at losing his wealth and servants, it was when he learned that his children had been crushed by a collapsing house that he expressed his greatest measure of sorrow. Tearing one's robe and shaving one's head were common ways of expressing extreme grief in ancient times (Job 1:20a).

When told that all of his 10 children had been killed, Job made no attempt to suppress or mask his anguish. Nor should we attempt to hold back our tears and sorrow when we are faced with losing a dear family member or friend. Rather, openly grieving should be considered part of our natural response in the face of loss. Most Christian counselors agree that the expression of grief is beneficial to our long-term mental, emotional, and spiritual health.

Despite his sorrow, Job fell to the ground in a posture of worship and broke out into a psalm of submission to God's will (vss. 20b-21). In this psalm he acknowledged that, as a mortal man, he could not expect to hold on to earthly blessings indefinitely. In giving Job blessings and in taking them away, God had been within His rights, so Job concluded, "May the name of the LORD be praised" (vs. 21).

Thus instead of cursing God, as Satan had hoped he would do, Job blessed the Lord. He would not accuse God of doing evil to him (vs. 22), and in that way he foiled Satan's attempt at proving that Job only worshiped God for the blessings he might receive from Him.

II. Job's First Speech: Job 3:1-3, 11

A. Job Regretting the Day of His Birth: vss. 1-3

After this, Job opened his mouth and cursed the day of his birth. He said: "May the day of my birth perish, and the night it was said, 'A boy is born!'"

Job 2 records the second heavenly council, in which Satan issued another challenge to God about His servant Job. This second council began with preliminary speeches almost identical to the first. God asked Satan where he had been, and Satan replied that he had been roaming the earth (vss. 1-2). The accuser offered no report of what he had done to Job or of Job's response to his actions. But God showed that He knew what had transpired by reminding the evil one of Job's blamelessness (vs. 3).

Of course, Satan disagreed with God's evaluation of Job's integrity. He cynically countered that Job, like anyone else, was willing to sacrifice his family's skin so as to save his own (vs. 4). Satan argued that if he would be allowed to attack Job's own skin, then Job would give in and curse God (vs. 5). This time God gave Satan permission to attack Job's body, but not without another limitation. Satan could cause any sort of torture he might select, but he could not take Job's life (vs. 6). And so the devil left God's presence and afflicted Job with painful sores (vs. 7). Whatever the nature of the disease, the once majestic landlord ended up on an ash heap, scraping himself with a potsherd because of the interminable itching (vs. 8).

At this point in the account of Job's suffering, his wife came onto the scene. She was apparently the sole family member to have survived all the disasters to fall upon Job. Looking upon her husband in the midst of his suffering, she encouraged him to curse God and die (vs. 9). In Job's way of thinking, it would have been wrong to have accepted God's blessings in the past and then to curse God for the painful troubles He allowed in the present. Thus Job refused his wife's advice and refused as well to give in to temptation. He declared the same trust in God that he had declared after his first test, and proved that God's confidence in him was well placed (vs. 10; compare 1:22).

We read in 2:11-13 that three friends of Job—men named Eliphaz, Bildad, and Zophar—arranged a meeting so that they could offer their support and comfort. But instead of providing consolation (except for the first seven days and nights, in which they remained silent), they would only add to Job's suffering as well as to his mental and spiritual torment. In some ways, with the attendance of these "comforters," Satan continued his attack on Job. In fact, this may have been the evil one's most trying attack of all.

Job's three friends were likely princes and sages in each of their own areas. *Eliphaz's* name was derived from an Arabic word meaning "God is the victor." He was from Teman, an Edomite city south of Canaan that was known to be a center for philosophical discussions. Teman is the only hometown of the three comforters that can be definitely located today.

The name *Bildad* came from a Hebrew phrase meaning "Baal is Lord." Bildad may have been a descendant of Shuah, Abraham's youngest son by his wife Keturah. His tribe of Shuhites probably made their home somewhere east of Canaan, but the precise location of their settlement is unknown (Gen. 25:2, 6). *Zophar* is translated as "little bird." His tribe was from Naamah, perhaps a small town in Arabia.

Perhaps in response to seeing his three friends, Job began to voice his utter despair. While Job cursed the day he was born (Job 3:1), he did not curse God. As Job spoke (vs. 2), he expressed his wish that the day of his birth never existed and that the night in which he was conceived could have been erased from the calendar (vs. 3).

B. Job Wishing He Had Been Stillborn: vs. 11

"Why did I not perish at birth, and die as I came from the womb?"

Job 3:4-10 continues the suffering man's impassioned lament; and then in verse 11 he returned to his bitter refrain concerning why he preferred to have died at birth. If he could travel back in time, Job would have chosen to expire as he came forth from his mother's womb. This was the beginning of his long cry of complaint to God. Job's basic question was "Why, God? Why?" Job suffered not only physically but emotionally as well. He found no peace of mind, no quiet, no rest—only torment (vs. 26).

Discussion Questions

1. How do you think you would have felt if you experienced the sufferings of Job?
2. Why did God allow Job to suffer so greatly?
3. Do you think Job was right to curse the day of his birth?
4. If you were Job, would you have handled his suffering any differently?
5. How can believers maintain their integrity in the midst of hardship?

Contemporary Application

Every day friends of ours struggle with adversity. Their lives change just as dramatically as Job's life did. One day they are secure in material things and in health. The next day they lose their job or suffer a serious illness. Therefore, Job's account is extremely contemporary.

But, unlike Job, many people turn against God when their lives take a sudden turn for the worse. Christians, too, are not immune to thinking dark thoughts about God. Some of this arises from faulty theology. Too many people think God blesses them because they are good. On the other hand, some think God will really hurt them if they don't behave. They try to serve God out of fear.

What we all need is a good dose of strong medicine from the Bible. Expressed differently, we need spiritual vitamins from the lessons of Scripture. Our faith is only as strong as our understanding of God's character and of His love and wisdom demonstrated in Jesus Christ. If we stay close to Jesus, we may not find all the answers to our questions, but we will be safe and sheltered in Him. After all, He is our wisdom, righteousness, holiness, and redemption (1 Cor. 1:30).

When All Seems Hopeless

DEVOTIONAL READING

Job 36:24-33

DAILY BIBLE READINGS

Scripture

Background Scripture: *Job 14; 32:1-8; 34:10-15; 37:14-24*

Scripture Lesson: *Job 14:1-2, 11-17; 32:6, 8; 34:12; 37:14, 22*

Key Verse: *"All the days of my hard service I will wait for my renewal to come."* Job 14:14.

Scripture Lesson for Children: *Job 2:11; 32:1-8; 33:12; 34:12; 37:14, 22*

Key Verse for Children: *"God is greater than man."* Job 33:12.

Lesson Aim

To grow in moral stature with God and others.

Lesson Setting

Time: *During the second millennium B.C.*
Place: *The land of Uz, a large territory east of the Jordan River*

Lesson Outline

When All Seems Hopeless

  I. Job's Reflections on Life and Death: Job 14:1-2, 11-17
     A. *The Brevity of Human Life: vss. 1-2*
     B. *The Finality of Death: vss. 11-12*
     C. *The Longing of Job for Death: vs. 13*
     D. *The Hope of Life after Death: vss. 14-17*
  II. Elihu's Response to Job's Friends: Job 32:6, 8
     A. *The Delay in Elihu's Response: vs. 6*
     B. *The Divine Source of Understanding: vs. 8*
  III. Elihu's Response to Job: Job 34:12; 37:14, 22
     A. *The Uprightness of God: 34:12*
     B. *The Power and Majesty of God: 37:14, 22*

Introduction for Adults
Topic: *When All Seems Hopeless*

Ann was blind from birth. Everything she knew and accomplished in life she owed to her parents' sacrifice and dedication. When her mother fell ill, Ann was distraught. She had never seen her mother. She knew only her voice and touch.

For months Ann sat with her mother in a nursing home, holding her hands and talking to her. But her mother had lost her speech and could not respond. Nevertheless, Ann held on firmly every day, speaking words of comfort and hope.

In times of suffering when all seems hopeless, we hold on to each other and especially to God. Even when God does not seem to reply to our cries, we keep trusting in Him. Faith drives us to prayer and worship every day. In the darkness, we keep pursuing the light by faith. We claim God's promise that nothing can separate us from His love (Rom. 8:31-39).

Introduction for Youth
Topic: *Keep Hope Alive!*

One of the basic therapies for strengthening hand, wrist, and arm muscles is the squeezing of a rubber ball tightly several times a day. At first we feel the tension and pain, but gradually our muscles respond and we are able to function normally. This exercise is prescribed after injuries or surgeries—incidents and events we would prefer to avoid. In cases like these, holding fast to a rubber ball is a discipline that produces results.

God sometimes takes us through tough times to strengthen our spiritual muscles (so to speak). He knows how flabby we get when we neglect our worship and obedience to His good and perfect will. But when He gets our attention, we respond with therapies that give us new love and zeal for Him.

Job's account tells us that it is possible to keep alive our hope in God, even when hard times hit. We surmount our difficulties by Christ's indwelling power and presence.

Concepts for Children
Topic: *Job's Young Wise Friend*

1. Job's three friends (Eliphaz, Bildad, and Zophar) attempted to explain Job's suffering and to comfort him.
2. Then a younger friend named Elihu used God's amazing acts in nature to help Job and his friends get a better understanding of God's power.
3. Elihu explained that God is in control of the universe.
4. Elihu also affirmed that God is greater than humans and does what is good.
5. In trying to deal with suffering, we should acknowledge that God is all-knowing and all-powerful.

Lesson Commentary

I. JOB'S REFLECTIONS ON LIFE AND DEATH: JOB 14:1-2, 11-17

A. The Brevity of Human Life: vss. 1-2

"Man born of woman is of few days and full of trouble. He springs up like a flower and withers away; like a fleeting shadow, he does not endure."

As soon as Job finished his complaint (Job 3), Eliphaz the Temanite replied (4:1). It may have been that Eliphaz wanted to be sympathetic to Job's suffering. But the philosophical questions raised by Job's curses and bleak outlook caused Eliphaz to launch into a retort rather than express an attitude of understanding and compassion. The speech that ensued (chaps. 4—5) set the stage for all else that he and the other comforters would later say. Job responded to Eliphaz's speech by losing his temper. First he verbally attacked his comforters (chap. 6), and then he turned his complaints toward God (chap. 7).

The second of Job's comforters to speak was Bildad (8:1), and he turned out to be as heartless in his advice as had Eliphaz, perhaps even worse. He ignored Job's suffering and attacked Job head-on. Job responded by trying to prove to Bildad that he was not ignorant of God's ways. Job described God's wisdom and power over nature (chap. 9). Job said God is so powerful, in fact, that no one should dare even approach Him. Thus if Job tried to approach God to argue his innocence, he felt certain God would crush him. All he could do was to plead for mercy.

Since Job felt he had no mediator, he decided to argue his own case (chap. 10). He begged God not to find fault in him, especially since God's vision is superior to that of mortals. Job asked why God would want to destroy him after going to all the trouble of creating him. To Job, it almost seemed as if God made him to condemn him—innocent or not. As before, Job said he wished he'd never been born, and asked for a short time of peace before going into the world of the dead.

At the conclusion of Job's speech, Zophar, the third comforter, took the opportunity to have his say (11:1). He went even further than Eliphaz and Bildad in condemning their friend. Job replied to Zophar by commenting on the accusations of his peers (12:1—13:19), and then he spoke directly to God, pleading for His mercy (13:20—14:22). Toward his three friends, Job's attitude was sarcastic. He suggested that when the counselors died, wisdom would die with them. Because they had dealt with his problem only superficially, he proceeded to define it in more depth. He asked why he, a righteous and blameless person, had become a laughingstock when the really evil people were left undisturbed and secure.

All of creation, Job went on to say, was vulnerable to suffering the same injustice. The bottom line was that God sent good or bad things to His creatures regardless of whether they were righteous. This was the real issue, and Job's friends had missed it. Refusing to recant his claim that he was a godly man, Job told his counselors that he would plead his case directly to the Lord, adding, "Though he slay me, yet will I hope in him" (13:15).

On the basis of this hope, Job turned his appeal directly to God to clear him from wrongdoing. "Why do you hide your face and consider me your enemy?" Job cried out to the Lord (vs. 24). As he spoke to God, however, Job became discouraged again and uttered a poem about the futility of human life on earth. Job noted that people, once they are born, endure an existence that is short-lived and filled with trouble (14:1). While life begins full of promise, vigor, and hope, it soon withers like a flower; and like the shadow cast by a passing cloud, a person's life quickly vanishes (vs. 2).

It would be incorrect to conclude that life has no meaning, purpose, or value. For those who have trusted in Christ, quite the opposite is true. They can wholeheartedly pursue their God-given ministries, for they realize that their "labor in the Lord is not in vain" (1 Cor. 15:58).

B. The Finality of Death: vss. 11-12

"As water disappears from the sea or a riverbed becomes parched and dry, so man lies down and does not rise; till the heavens are no more, men will not awake or be roused from their sleep."

Job questioned why God would waste His time judging such a frail and insignificant creature as him (Job 14:3). After all, Job argued, people are unable to attain purity (vs. 4). Also, it is God who determined the length of each person's life, and no one could exceed this divinely preestablished limit (vs. 5). Job pleaded with God to turn away from His angry stare so that His creatures, who were liked hired hands, might complete their assigned tasks in peace (vs. 6).

Job next commented on the hopelessness of death. He noted that even when a tree is cut down, it was able to bud and put forth shoots like a new plant (vss. 7-9). But when people died, they expired and did not rise again (vs. 10). Job reasoned that, as waters disappeared from the sea and a river drained away and dried up (vs. 11), so too all people eventually died and their bodies remained in the grave until the heavens ceased to exist (vs. 12). Job's contention was that, given humankind's grim prospect, why did God bother to judge them?

C. The Longing of Job for Death: vs. 13

"If only you would hide me in the grave and conceal me till your anger has passed! If only you would set me a time and then remember me!"

Job wished that the Lord would conceal him in the grave until His anger had passed (Job 14:13). The Hebrew word translated "grave" is *Sheol* and refers to the realm of the dead. The Israelites, as well as other ancient peoples, believed that the dead occupy a gloomy underworld place: Sheol. They held that in Sheol the dead are mere shadows of themselves, living in darkness, silence, and inactivity.

D. The Hope of Life after Death: vss. 14-17

"If a man dies, will he live again? All the days of my hard service I will wait for my renewal to come. You will call and I will answer you; you will long for the creature your hands have made. Surely then

you will count my steps but not keep track of my sin. My offenses will be sealed up in a bag; you will cover over my sin. "

Job had argued that people die without hope. And yet, in Job 14:13-15, he expressed his desire that there be an afterlife. In particular, Job held out the prospect that God's anger would eventually be appeased and dissipate. Then God would remember the one He had hidden in Sheol and bring about his rescue; in other words, Job longed for the day when he would live again.

From Job's limited perspective he was uncertain about the possibility of an afterlife. Nevertheless, the thought of continued existence after death gave him hope. For believers, the promise of one day being resurrected gives them assurance of eternal life (1 Cor. 15:21-23).

During this period, Job endured unimaginable affliction, which he referred to as "hard service" (Job 14:14). Who could blame him for longing for death? Then he would find relief from his plight and experience renewal. Job envisioned that sometime in the future God would call His servant into His fellowship, and Job would not hesitate to answer the summons. Though Job felt estranged from God, he was eager for the day when the Creator ardently desired His handiwork (vs. 15).

The prospect of eternity in heaven is what undergirded Job, especially as he reflected on the severe way in which it seemed that God dealt with people in this life. Job longed for the possibility that the divine would not watch over him in judgment, but would protect and guide him. Though God might for a season count the missteps of Job, he hoped that one day the Lord would not mark his sins any longer (vs. 16).

In that time of restoration, Job imagined his offenses being "sealed up in a bag" (vs. 17). This is a poetic way of referring to the removal of sin from an individual. Job's other metaphor was of God covering over his sin. The idea is that the Lord would paint over Job's transgressions so that they were forgotten in the next life.

II. ELIHU'S RESPONSE TO JOB'S FRIENDS: JOB 32:6, 8

A. The Delay in Elihu's Response: vs. 6

So Elihu son of Barakel the Buzite said: "I am young in years, and you are old; that is why I was fearful, not daring to tell you what I know."

Job 15—21 presents the second cycle of speeches between Job and his three counselors. These speeches follow the same sequence as the first cycle: speeches by Eliphaz, Bildad, and Zophar, each followed by a response from Job. Chapters 22—31 include the third and final cycle of speeches. Eliphaz and Bildad both spoke, and Job responded by asserting his innocence and integrity.

Perhaps Job thought that the debate with his friends was over. But then a young man named Elihu, who had joined the circle and had remained silent up to this point, decided to speak. His speech is prefaced by a brief narrative (vss. 1-5) in which the author introduced Elihu. He apparently lived in the desert land of Buz, but now he was in the land of Uz to visit Job.

Though there is no mention of Elihu in the first 31 chapters of Job, he had apparently been quietly listening to the speeches of Job and the three friends all along (32:6). The reason Elihu had until this point hesitated to speak out was because Eliphaz, Bildad, and Zophar were all older than he (vs. 4). By waiting to have his turn to speak, he was merely showing respect to his elders as was customary in the ancient Near East, as it still is today in that part of the world.

As all four of the other men fell silent, Elihu grew angry enough to finally speak out. In his remarks he accused Job of overlooking his sin of spiritual pride. Elihu was also angry at Job's three friends. He felt they had failed to refute Job's claims, even though they condemned him for his sinfulness. Moreover, they had given up on their effort to convince Job of his sinfulness. This, too, infuriated Elihu.

B. The Divine Source of Understanding: vs. 8

"But it is the spirit in a man, the breath of the Almighty, that gives him understanding."

Elihu previously believed that a lifetime of experiences gave people wisdom (Job 32:7). But his own experience prompted him to conclude that age alone was no guarantee of prudence and understanding. The Almighty gave sagacity even to younger people such as himself (vss. 8-9).

III. ELIHU'S RESPONSE TO JOB: JOB 34:12; 37:14, 22

A. The Uprightness of God: 34:12

"It is unthinkable that God would do wrong, that the Almighty would pervert justice."

Elihu scolded Job for complaining about the way God was treating him and for asserting his innocence before the divine (Job 34:5). Supposedly Job was guilty of being arrogant, scorning God (vs. 7) and associating with the wicked (vs. 8). Elihu argued that God was characterized by justice and treated people fairly (vss. 10-11). In short, the Almighty did not act wickedly and would never "pervert justice" (vs. 12).

B. The Power and Majesty of God: 37:14, 22

"Listen to this, Job; stop and consider God's wonders. . . . Out of the north he comes in golden splendor; God comes in awesome majesty."

In his next speech (Job 35), Elihu argued that people's behavior—whether wicked or righteous—affects only them, not God. Furthermore, Elihu said that since God does not even necessarily answer the prayers of the oppressed, it was no wonder He did not respond to a rebel like Job. In chapter 36, Elihu again affirmed God's merciful and mighty dealings with people. He exalts, disciplines, or destroys people as they deserve. Based on these observations, Elihu urged Job to turn from evil.

Then Elihu launched into a long description of God's greatness as expressed in His control over nature (chap. 37). Elihu exhorted Job to take time to consider the marvelous works of God (vs. 14), for He alone is glorious in splendor and awesome in majesty (vs. 22). Ironically, Elihu's speeches turned out quite similar to those of the others he had criticized for failing to adequately address Job's situation.

Discussion Questions

1. What value do you think Job put on life during his period of affliction?
2. How do you think Job's relationship with God was affected by Job's suffering?
3. What sort of attitude do you think Elihu displayed in response to Job and his friends?
4. How do you think you would have felt after hearing the words Elihu spoke to Job?
5. How do you think you would have responded to Job during his time of suffering?

Contemporary Application

How easy it is to sit as judge and jury over the predicaments of our friends. Sometimes we hear Christians say about a fellow Christian's plight: "She made her bed. Now she must lie in it." In other words, she got what she deserved. That's what Job's friends told him. How wrong they were!

This does not mean we should fail to warn people about the perils of disobeying God's will and breaking His commands. Sin does bring devastating consequences. But we must not be so presumptuous as to assume we know that sin caused our friend's problems.

The church's public stance toward those in pain was well illustrated when the AIDS epidemic first struck. "This is God's judgment on the alternative lifestyles of those who have the disease!" That was hardly appealing for those dying in the hospitals. Nor did it help those who came down with AIDS because they had been given tainted blood in the hospital.

Of course, God judges sin, but we are not the judges of who deserves what. In reality, every human being deserves God's judgment. When people ask why they are suffering, our job is to direct them to the God of all peace and comfort who has proved His love in the cross of Jesus Christ. When they meet Christ, they may not get all their questions answered, but they can rest in His love and forgiveness.

God Responds with Life

Scripture

Background Scripture: *Job 38:1-4, 16-17; 42:1-6; Mark 16*

Scripture Lesson: *Job 38:1, 4, 16-17; 42:1-2, 5; Mark 16:1-7, 9-14, 20*

Key Verse: *"Don't be alarmed," he said. "You are looking for Jesus the Nazarene, who was crucified. He has risen! He is not here. See the place where they laid him."* Mark 16:6.

Scripture Lesson for Children: *Job 38:1, 4, 16-17; 42:1-2, 5; Mark 16:1-7, 9-14, 20*

Key Verse for Children: *"[Jesus] has risen! He is not here."* Mark 16:6.

Lesson Aim

To trust in the Lord despite present circumstances, especially in light of Jesus' resurrection from the dead.

Lesson Setting

Times: *During the second millennium* B.C.; A.D. *30*
Places: *The land of Uz, a large territory east of the Jordan River; Jerusalem*

Lesson Outline

God Responds with Life

  I. The Lord's Response to Job: Job 38:1, 4, 16-17
     A. The Limited Understanding of Job: vs. 1
     B. The Lord's Sovereignty and Power: vss. 4, 16-17
  II. The Humble Response of Job: Job 42:1-2, 5
     A. Job's Acknowledgement of God's Supremacy: vss. 1-2
     B. Job's Enhanced Awareness of God: vs. 5
  III. The Savior's Resurrection: Mark 16:1-7, 9-14, 20
     A. The Empty Tomb: vss. 1-4
     B. The Declaration of the Angel: vss. 5-7
     C. The Messiah's Postresurrection Appearances: vss. 9-14
     D. The Heralding of the Good News: vs. 20

Introduction for Adults

Topic: *From Death to Life*

The first time a death in the family confronts us, we realize as never before its terrible finality. This is the end. Until then, we think we are immortal. We fail to grasp the fact of our mortality. But, as the apostle Paul revealed, the mortal must be clothed with immortality (1 Cor. 15:53).

The account of Christ's death and resurrection reminds us that "death has been swallowed up in victory" (vs. 54). Jesus experienced death for all of us, so that our sins might be forgiven. He was raised for our justification. His resurrection proves His victory over sin and death.

Death is final only in the sense that it terminates our mortality. It is not the end, but the beginning. Christ's empty tomb guarantees that all who believe shall be saved and enjoy eternal life.

Introduction for Youth

Topic: *New Life*

For many years every Easter a sunrise service has been held in Death Valley National Park in California, one of the hottest spots on earth and the lowest point in the Western Hemisphere. In the winter of 1849, a party of emigrants heading for the California gold fields strayed into this desolate basin and spent two months crossing it. As they were finally climbing the mountains out of the valley, one woman looked back at the forbidding region and named it by saying, "Farewell, Death Valley."

Today, a wooden cross sticking out of sand dunes marks the spot of the sunrise service, which begins when the first light of dawn breaks over the nearby Funeral Mountains. How appropriate it is that a celebration of the Resurrection is held in the so-called "valley of death," for Jesus has conquered death, offering new life to all who believe in Him.

Concepts for Children

Topic: *God Gives New Life*

1. God revealed Himself to Job in a whirlwind and communicated with him.
2. Job learned that God has the power to do things that no human can do.
3. When Job was confronted with the awesome power of God, he was humbled.
4. The resurrection of Jesus from the dead was an awesome display of God's power.
5. God can bring new life to people today when they trust in Jesus for salvation.

Lesson Commentary

I. THE LORD'S RESPONSE TO JOB: JOB 38:1, 4, 16-17

A. The Limited Understanding of Job: vs. 1

Then the LORD answered Job out of the storm. He said:

After waiting for so long in despair and anguish, Job finally received the one gift that must have meant the most to him: God spoke (Job 38:1). God did not, however, give Job an explanation for his suffering. Nor did God list Job's sins, as the counselors possibly would have wanted. God merely exposed Job to the wonders of His power and creation.

God did not appear in a vision, but rather spoke to Job "out of the storm"—perhaps a whirlwind not unlike the one that had killed Job's children (see 1:18-19). No indication is given that Job actually saw the Lord, only that he heard God's voice. The Almighty was evidently angry, but His anger was holy and righteous, as opposed to what had been Elihu's anger. We can imagine how taken aback Job must have been. He probably didn't expect God to speak to him in such a direct manner.

B. The Lord's Sovereignty and Power: vss. 4, 16-17

"Where were you when I laid the earth's foundation? Tell me, if you understand. . . . Have you journeyed to the springs of the sea or walked in the recesses of the deep? Have the gates of death been shown to you? Have you seen the gates of the shadow of death?"

God's first questions to Job dealt with the creation of the earth in terms of constructing a building (Job 38:4-7). Builders in Job's time often based their structures on a foundation of stones. God demanded that Job tell Him where he was when the Lord had laid the earth's foundation (vs. 4). Of course, it was God and God alone who had established the earth at Creation. Job didn't even exist yet.

Verses 8-11 paint a beautiful picture of God's creation and limitation of the oceans. By now Job—the complainer and skeptic—must have begun to understand at least somewhat about the immeasurable might and wisdom as well as sovereignty and power of God.

The Lord's questions to Job continued to flow unrelentingly. The Almighty asked Job about his knowledge of the dawn (vss. 12-15). God then forced Job outside of his small circle of worry and took him to the farthest reaches of the created world. First, God asked Job about journeying (vs. 16). He asked Job whether he had ever traveled to the ocean depths.

Second, the Lord questioned whether Job had ever seen the entrance to the abode of the dead (vs. 17). Third, God asked Job whether he had considered the vast expanses of the earth (vs. 18). Did he really have the answers to the deepest mysteries of the universe? What Job learned from God's questions was how ignorant he was in comparison to the Lord's vast wisdom, as well as how infinitely God controls and understands the world.

II. THE HUMBLE RESPONSE OF JOB: JOB 42:1-2, 5

A. Job's Acknowledgement of God's Supremacy: vss. 1-2

Then Job replied to the LORD: "I know that you can do all things; no plan of yours can be thwarted."

At several points during his suffering, Job had dared to question God's justice by suggesting that the Lord was not running the universe in the way Job thought it should be run. But now, obviously chastened by what God had told him, Job replied humbly and with reverence (Job 40:3).

Job acknowledged before the Lord that he was insignificant (vs. 4), especially when compared to God's overall scheme of Creation. To register his regret for saying too much, Job went on to promise that he would place his hand over his mouth, which would prevent him from saying anything else. Indeed, he had nothing to add to what he had already said (vs. 5). After hearing the voice of God, Job seems to have lost his desire to vindicate himself.

In God's first speech (38:2—39:30), He had exposed Job to His power over the natural universe. In the Lord's second major speech (40:7—41:34), He presented to Job His lordship over the moral universe. In this way God stressed that as the moral Governor, He would ensure that justice prevailed. Accordingly, Job was to rely on and rest in God's omnipotence.

Job replied simply, without trying to indulge in fancy rhetoric, that he understood the message of God's speeches. Job knew God is all-powerful and that nothing can hinder His plans (42:1-2). In God's strong hands all things—even justice for the suffering—will be worked out eventually.

B. Job's Enhanced Awareness of God: vs. 5

"My ears had heard of you but now my eyes have seen you."

Job went on to apologize for his earlier attitude and behavior (Job 42:3-4). Before God's interrogation of him, Job had only known about the Lord indirectly through what he had learned from tradition and from what others had told him. Now through God's questioning, Job experienced the Lord and His nature firsthand. Job learned of God's power and righteousness by being allowed to enter the Lord's presence and listen to His voice. And though he didn't actually see God, Job felt as though he had met the Lord face-to-face (vs. 5).

In light of Job's encounter with the Almighty, it was appropriate for Job to repent of boldly questioning God's wisdom and ability to manage human affairs (vs. 6). In effect, Job was discarding all his previous false notions of God. Job was also placing his assurance in the truth that God was not his enemy but his friend and redeemer. Verses 7-9 state that God scolded Job's friends and ordered them to make a sacrifice to atone for their errant counsel. We then learn in verses 10-17 how God restored Job's prosperity—in fact, giving him more than he had previously possessed.

III. The Savior's Resurrection: Mark 16:1-7, 9-14, 20

A. The Empty Tomb: vss. 1-4

When the Sabbath was over, Mary Magdalene, Mary the mother of James, and Salome bought spices so that they might go to anoint Jesus' body. Very early on the first day of the week, just after sunrise, they were on their way to the tomb and they asked each other, "Who will roll the stone away from the entrance of the tomb?" But when they looked up, they saw that the stone, which was very large, had been rolled away.

At one point in his speeches, Job seemed to wonder whether people could live again after they had died (Job 14:14). The answer, of course, is *yes.* Because the Son has conquered death, all who trust in Him will one day be raised to eternal life. Furthermore, the power and righteousness of the Father about which Job opined are epitomized in the Son's resurrection.

While Mark 15 records Christ's sacrifice, chapter 16 shows God's acceptance of that sacrifice. In fact, the grand confirming act of earthly ministry of Jesus is His resurrection from the dead. Jesus was buried late on Friday afternoon. After sunset on Saturday, when the Sabbath was over, some women purchased aromatic oils for anointing Jesus' body (vs. 2). But by then it was too late for them to do the anointing.

Thus, early the next morning the women headed for the tomb (vs. 2). Their chief concern on this trip was whom they could find to roll away the massive stone blocking the tomb's entrance (vs. 3). But the women worried in vain because the stone had already been rolled aside by an angel (Matt. 28:2; Mark 16:4). The tomb stood open. The risen Lord could have left the tomb without an opening, but the witnesses needed to get in to see that He was gone.

B. The Declaration of the Angel: vss. 5-7

As they entered the tomb, they saw a young man dressed in a white robe sitting on the right side, and they were alarmed. "Don't be alarmed," he said. "You are looking for Jesus the Nazarene, who was crucified. He has risen! He is not here. See the place where they laid him. But go, tell his disciples and Peter, 'He is going ahead of you into Galilee. There you will see him, just as he told you.'"

The young man mentioned in Mark 16:5 was an angel (Matt. 28:5). This heavenly visitor had four facts he wanted the women to know. First, both he and the women were referring to the same man: "Jesus the Nazarene" (Mark 16:6). Second, Jesus "was crucified," and so really had been dead. Third, "He has risen!" and therefore is no longer dead. Fourth, "He is not here" because He had broken the grip of the grave.

The angel specifically wanted Peter to know about Christ's resurrection and that Jesus would be meeting him in Galilee (16:7; compare 14:28). This was a gesture of reassurance and forgiveness extended toward the man who had denied knowing his Lord. Peter probably felt as though he no longer could have a place among the other apostles. From this message he would understand that he was forgiven and accepted again.

C. The Messiah's Postresurrection Appearances: vss. 9-14

When Jesus rose early on the first day of the week, he appeared first to Mary Magdalene, out of whom he had driven seven demons. She went and told those who had been with him and who were mourning and weeping. When they heard that Jesus was alive and that she had seen him, they did not believe it. Afterward Jesus appeared in a different form to two of them while they were walking in the country. These returned and reported it to the rest; but they did not believe them either. Later Jesus appeared to the Eleven as they were eating; he rebuked them for their lack of faith and their stubborn refusal to believe those who had seen him after he had risen.

By comparing early manuscripts, most New Testament scholars have concluded that Mark 16:8 is the last verse of the second Synoptic Gospel that has survived. Perhaps the Gospel originally had another ending that has been lost; or perhaps Mark intended to end abruptly on the note of surprise and amazement that greeted the fact of Jesus' resurrection. After all, the Resurrection not only ends one account but begins another. The history of the Church, which includes us, proceeds directly from the victory over death won by "Jesus Christ, the Son of God" (1:1).

These observations notwithstanding, 16:9-20 represents ancient Christian teaching. For instance, despite the presence of fear and doubt (vs. 8), the good news of Christ's resurrection began to spread (vss. 9-11). Also, as verses 12-13 relate, the Savior made a postresurrection appearance to the two disciples who were walking on the road to a village named Emmaus (see Luke 24:13-35). Furthermore, according to Mark 16:14, Jesus later appeared to the Eleven and censured them for their initial unbelief regarding the report of His resurrection.

D. The Heralding of the Good News: vs. 20

Then the disciples went out and preached everywhere, and the Lord worked with them and confirmed his word by the signs that accompanied it.

Thankfully, Jesus' followers welcomed the truth of His resurrection and proclaimed it with vigor to the world at large (Mark 16:20). In fact, the writing of the second Synoptic Gospel (as well as the rest of the Gospels contained in the New Testament) is a result of this endeavor to proclaim the Good News. Mark's report of the Savior's mission, miracles, teaching, death, and resurrection summarizes the core truths of the Christian faith.

It would be hard to imagine a better introduction to the essence of Christianity than the Gospel of Mark. In writing this book, its author carefully selected and arranged material he had gathered from others. It suited his purposes to ignore all the events of Jesus' life prior to His baptism. But the author described at length many of the later words and works of Jesus. Remarkably, he devoted nearly the entire second half of his Gospel to Christ's last days. Apparently the author believed that Jesus' ministry, especially His death and resurrection on behalf of sinners, was most important for the communication of his message.

Discussion Questions

1. How do you think Job felt as the Lord directly addressed him?
2. Why did the Lord need to remind Job about his place in the created order of things?
3. What lessons do you think Job learned as a result of his encounter with God?
4. What evidence does Mark's Gospel cite for Jesus' resurrection?
5. What difference in your life has Jesus' resurrection made?

Contemporary Application

When God came out of a whirlwind, He gave Job an answer to all his questions: *trust the Lord regardless of the present circumstances.* In the end, all Job's understanding, reason, and doubt had to give way to a complete faith in and worship of his Creator and Savior. This is the same kind of faith that affirms Jesus' resurrection from the dead (Mark 16:6). Because He lives, believers down through the ages have been able to endure the kind of adversity Job encountered.

In addition to teaching about God's nature and humanity's suffering, the Book of Job reinforces the following truths, which the rest of Scripture (including the Gospel of Mark) affirms:

• We simply do not know enough about God and His ways to question His wisdom or justice.
• The theological position "People suffer in proportion to their sins" is a shallow and erroneous doctrine.
• Because God is all-powerful and all-knowing, He can make use of any means and any situations to bring about His purposes.
• God does not abandon those who suffer, but communicates with them as He chooses.
• Regardless of circumstances, people must accept God on His own terms.
• Believers can remain upright even in the midst of physical agony, emotional confusion, and spiritual testing because God is the source of eternal life.

As Christians, we have a significant advantage that Job did not possess. We know Jesus suffered and died for us. We also understand that nothing can separate us from God's love in Christ (Rom. 8:31-39). Therefore, rather than debate the mysteries of God's dealings with Job, we would do well to encourage one another to grow in the grace and knowledge of our risen Savior (2 Pet. 3:18).

Finding Life's Meaning

Scripture

Background Scripture: *Ecclesiastes 1:1-11; John 20:19-23*
Scripture Lesson: *Ecclesiastes 1:1-9; John 20:19-23*
Key Verse: *Jesus came and stood among them and said,
"Peace be with you!"* John 20:19.
Scripture Lesson for Children: *1 Kings 4:29-34;
Ecclesiastes 1:12; 2:2-6, 9-13*
Key Verse for Children: *"So give your servant a discerning
heart . . . to distinguish between right and wrong."*
1 Kings 3:9.

Lesson Aim

To find meaning in the risen Lord even when life otherwise seems futile.

Lesson Setting

Time: *Sometime during the reign of Solomon (about 970–930
B.C.); A.D. 30*
Place: *Jerusalem*

Lesson Outline

Finding Life's Meaning
  I. The Basis for God-centered Living: Ecclesiastes
      1:1-9
      A. *The Emptiness of Self-centered Living: vss. 1-2*
      B. *The Futility of Life Apart from God: vss. 3-9*
  II. The Savior's Appearance to His Disciples: John
      20:19-23
      A. *A Greeting of Peace and Response of Joy: vss. 19-20*
      B. *A Commission to Service: vss. 21-23*

Introduction for Adults

Topic: *Where Is Peace Found?*

People had theorized about the reality of atoms long before their existence could be proven in any scientific way. According to Aristotle's writings, in the fifth century B.C. the Greek philosopher Democritus suggested that apparently solid matter actually consisted of tiny, invisible particles in constant motion. But Aristotle himself was not convinced, and the theory was ignored for centuries.

Over the last 200 years, however, modern science has verified what Democritus suspected. He probably would not have been surprised. He could not see the atoms, nor could he prove their existence; yet he believed—though Aristotle would not.

In this week's lesson, we meet people who saw the resurrected Jesus and believed. Yet Jesus praises those who have enough faith to accept Him as the Son of God, sight unseen. In the midst of doubt and uncertainty, peace can be found in Him.

Introduction for Youth

Topic: *Jesus' Answers to Life Questions*

Our heads nod as we hear the expression "Familiarity breeds contempt." But through overuse its meaning has become dulled. In *God Came Near,* Max Lucado sharpens that meaning for us.

"[Familiarity] won't steal your salvation; he'll just make you forget what it was like to be lost. You'll grow accustomed to prayer and thereby not pray. Worship will become commonplace and study optional. With the passing of time he'll infiltrate your heart with boredom and cover the cross with dust so you'll be 'safely' out of reach of change."

Yes, Jesus invites doubters to view His nail-pierced hands and touch His wounded side so that their questions will be answered and their faith in Him solidified. But He also invites spiritually anesthetized believers to fully appreciate their Savior's sacrifice and thereby rekindle their faith.

Concepts for Children

Topic: *God Makes Us Wise*

1. God gave Solomon wisdom and the ability to make wise decisions.
2. Solomon's wisdom was shared with others and preserved in the form of proverbs and songs.
3. Solomon used creatures from nature to illustrate wise sayings and to help people better understand their world.
4. Solomon sought to obtain happiness and discovered that life has no meaning or fulfillment without God.
5. We find true happiness and lasting joy through faith in the Lord.

Lesson Commentary

I. THE BASIS FOR GOD-CENTERED LIVING: ECCLESIASTES 1:1-9

A. The Emptiness of Self-centered Living: vss. 1-2

The words of the Teacher, son of David, king in Jerusalem: "Meaningless! Meaningless!" says the Teacher. "Utterly meaningless! Everything is meaningless."

Ecclesiastes is a Greek word that is translated "Preacher" or "Teacher" (Eccl. 1:1) or, more specifically, "one who gathers an assembly to address it." Thus the words of the Teacher, recorded in the Book of Ecclesiastes, were to be delivered publicly, perhaps in an outer court of the temple or a palace.

King Solomon, who reigned over Israel for 40 years (about 970–930 B.C.), traditionally has been identified as the author of Ecclesiastes. The strongest evidence for this is that the author—who called himself "Teacher," translated from the Hebrew word *qoheleth*—initially referred to himself as "son of David, king in Jerusalem" (1:1). After a poetic interlude, he made the same reference again—"I, the Teacher, was king over Israel in Jerusalem" (vs. 12).

Admittedly, some scholars question the previous conclusion. Nevertheless, the weight of evidence—such as the book's unity of style, theme, and purpose—indicates that Ecclesiastes had a single author who wrestled with various approaches to life and living. This person is none other than Solomon.

The Teacher apparently intended for his words to be read, not just by those people who were devoted to the Lord, but by a more general, secular audience as well. This would explain why Ecclesiastes is sometimes seen as more worldly than the other books in the Bible. It was meant to step outside of the place of worship and meet common people as they live out their lives.

In verse 2, the Teacher came right to the point. He cried out, "Meaningless! Meaningless!" It is important to note that these words did not necessarily express Solomon's own view of life. Rather, this outcry was how he summed up the lives of those people who decided to eliminate God from their outlook and lifestyle. For the godless, life was meaningless.

Thus, Ecclesiastes begins by arguing how a life without the Lord at its center is chaotic, meaningless, and discontented. In a phrase, life without God is an exercise in futility. Accordingly, the Teacher commended his hearers to a God-centered life by critiquing—sometimes one at a time—various lifestyles and life pursuits in which God was not the basis.

B. The Futility of Life Apart from God: vss. 3-9

What does man gain from all his labor at which he toils under the sun? Generations come and generations go, but the earth remains forever. The sun rises and the sun sets, and hurries back to where it rises. The wind blows to the south and turns to the north; round and round it goes, ever returning on its course. All streams flow into the sea, yet the sea is never full. To the place the streams come from, there they return again. All things are wearisome, more than one can say. The eye never has enough of seeing, nor the ear its fill of hearing. What has been will be again, what has been done will be done again; there is nothing new under the sun.

Solomon taught that life is futile for those who reject God, because they have no hope beyond this earthly existence. All they have is what they work for now, and soon all that will pass away. Ironically, such people typically see life in terms of profit and loss. They strive for earthly profit, often inconsiderate of whom they have to hurt or push aside to get it. But in the end, their decisions—because they have not taken into consideration obedience to God—lead them to total loss. Solomon described this way of life in the form of a rhetorical question: "What does man gain from all his labor at which he toils under the sun?" (Eccl. 1:3). The answer, of course, was nothing.

The Teacher then depicted the cycle of humanity's meaningless toil in terms of human history and nature, touching on the basic elements of the created order. First, he said people come and go, but "the earth remains forever" (vs. 4). This contrast pointed out the relative shortness of a person's life, especially when compared to the apparent permanence of the earth. But just as the cycle of human life continues unabated on its meaningless course, so does the earth.

Second, the Teacher addressed the cycle of the sun. In addition to the ebb and flow of history on the earth, the rising and setting of the sun also followed a seemingly endless cycle (vs. 5). Here Solomon may have implied that the sun actually grew weary of the process of rising and setting every day, perhaps introducing how the day-to-day aspects of life soon grow tiresome. And yet the apparent endless cycle of the sun also reminded his hearers of the briefness of their own lives.

Third, Solomon pointed out how the wind travels north and south, continuously blowing around, "ever returning on its course" (vs. 6). Like the individual lives of human beings, the wind seems to flow everywhere, and yet it never veers off its determined course. The implication for humanity is that we live, and then we die. We have no power to break this cycle.

Fourth, the Teacher described water's cycle of falling to the earth, creating streams, and flowing to the sea, which "is never full" (vs. 7). This cycle repeats itself infinitely. Indeed, the streams flow into the seas and then the water returns to the streams. Like the earth, the sun, and the wind, the water cycle continues unbroken.

Again, it should be noted that the Teacher was not talking about nature from the perspective of a believer. The believer should typically recognize all of nature as testimony to the Creator. But Solomon here was viewing nature through the eyes of those who think there is no God. For such people, there is no loving Creator behind nature, and hence life becomes one long monotonous repetition.

With such a view, "all things are wearisome, more than one can say" (vs. 8). The human mind keeps searching for meaning, but it will never find it in nature alone. As long as a person determinedly denies God, he or she cannot break through the cycle of time and repetition to discover that which is permanent and absolute—God Himself.

Moreover, as long as people hold to such a pagan mind-set, the only conclusion they can draw is that everything that has happened will happen again. In essence, "there is nothing new under the sun" (vs. 9). And if that, indeed, were the case, then nothing we do matters because it has all been done before and has no more meaning now than it did when it was done previously.

II. THE SAVIOR'S APPEARANCE TO HIS DISCIPLES: JOHN 20:19-23

A. A Greeting of Peace and Response of Joy: vss. 19-20

On the evening of that first day of the week, when the disciples were together, with the doors locked for fear of the Jews, Jesus came and stood among them and said, "Peace be with you!" After he said this, he showed them his hands and side. The disciples were overjoyed when they saw the Lord.

When the existence of God is rejected, life seems pointless. And when the Resurrection is denied, life appears hopeless (see 1 Cor. 15:12-19). The Good News is that God exists (Heb. 11:6) and that He raised His Son from the dead, as the account of the empty tomb recorded in John 20 makes clear.

Like the other Gospel writers, John concluded his narrative of the life of Jesus Christ with the Lord's resurrection. Yet John's presentation provides us with unique glimpses into this astonishing event, especially in regard to the reactions of some of the people who were close to Jesus, including Mary of Magdala and Thomas. John's Gospel shows us that Christ's resurrection not only was a decisive affirmation of Jesus as God and Savior, but it also left an enduring impression on the people who loved Him and put their faith in Him.

After Jesus first appeared to Mary of Magdala (vss. 11-17), other people encountered Him on that extraordinary Sunday. Luke recorded Jesus' meeting and discussions with Cleopas and his companion on the road to and at Emmaus and mentioned Jesus' earlier appearance to Peter (see Luke 24:13-35). John, however, skipped these incidents and went to the evening's events of which he was an eyewitness.

Many of Jesus' disciples, which included most of the apostles, had secretly convened to discuss the strange yet marvelous reports that their Lord had risen from the dead. Nevertheless, since they still feared the Jewish officials, they bolted the doors (John 20:19).

As the disciples talked, Jesus suddenly stood among them. John did not explain how Jesus could have entered the house when the doors were locked. On the one hand, Jesus' resurrected body clearly had powers and capabilities it did not reveal as a natural body. On the other hand, John demonstrated shortly afterward that Jesus' body had substance when He showed His pierced hands and side (vs. 20). Incidentally, Luke's account adds that Jesus told His disciples to touch Him to see that He had flesh and bones and was not a spirit or a ghost (see Luke 24:39).

Jesus greeted His friends by exclaiming, "Peace be with you!" (John 20:19). Although this phrase was a common Hebrew greeting, Jesus probably said it to allay their fears at His sudden and unexpected appearance. Luke mentioned that the

Savior's appearance had frightened His followers (see Luke 24:37-38). Once convinced of Jesus' identity and presence, the disciples were overcome with joy (John 20:20). They traveled from the depths of despair to the pinnacle of happiness in a matter of seconds. The presence of Christ can do that in the life of the believer.

B. A Commission to Service: vss. 21-23

Again Jesus said, "Peace be with you! As the Father has sent me, I am sending you." And with that he breathed on them and said, "Receive the Holy Spirit. If you forgive anyone his sins, they are forgiven; if you do not forgive them, they are not forgiven."

Once again Jesus exclaimed, "Peace be with you!" (John 19:21). This time, however, the Redeemer wanted to strengthen the resolve of His disciples to obey His commission and proclaim the message of salvation. In the same way His Father had sent Jesus into the world to fulfill His earthly mission, He was sending His followers into the world to continue His ministry. This commission and the peace of Christ are also given to us as believers today (see Matt. 28:18-20; Mark 16:15; Luke 24:46-49; Acts 1:8).

Jesus not only charged His disciples with a commission to preach the Gospel but also empowered them with the Holy Spirit to do it. John said that Jesus breathed on them, and they received the Holy Spirit. This endowment of the Spirit was made complete 40 days later on Pentecost (John 20:22; see Acts 2:1-4).

Furthermore, Jesus addressed the heart of His commission to His disciples. He spoke about forgiveness (John 20:23). He did not imply that certain Christians, or even the church, possessed the power to determine the salvation of people. What Jesus meant when He talked about forgiving and not forgiving sins was that being pardoned is at the heart of the Gospel message. The disciples were to declare the good news about God's love and forgiveness in Jesus Christ. Those who received it could be declared forgiven by Christ's followers; those who rejected it could be declared unforgiven. These are key truths of the Gospel.

John made it clear why he wrote his account. Admittedly, he could have described many miracles not recorded in his account of Jesus' public ministry that he witnessed. What John did write, however, was sufficient to convince a reader that Jesus is the Messiah and the Son of God, and that by believing in Him he or she might have eternal life (vss. 30-31).

Discussion Questions

1. Is it really true that all of life is futile? Why or why not?
2. What was Solomon's opinion about the cyclical nature of life?
3. Why do people tend to forget, ignore, or discount what has happened in the past?
4. Why do you think Jesus greeted His disciples with a statement of peace?
5. How can you use the postresurrection accounts of Jesus to encourage others to believe?

Contemporary Application

Many of our contemporaries have decided that life is meaningless. They do not arrive at their conclusion as a result of experimentation as King Solomon did. Their lives have been shattered by so many disappointments that they see no purpose in life. They have also deeply imbibed from the purely mechanistic philosophy of life that claims that human beings are just like animals, and that there is no God in heaven who gives purpose to life.

Believers can address meaninglessness from various angles. We can show how a God-centered world view helps us deal with our troubles in positive ways. We can also boldly teach that there is more to life than a cluster of experiences, some good and some bad. Moreover, we can explain how Christ makes the difference.

The basis for this last statement is that Jesus is "the resurrection and the life" (John 11:25). Everyone who has faith in Him will be raised from the dead (vs. 26). In fact, He is the first of a great harvest of believers who will one day be resurrected (1 Cor. 15:20). In the meantime, the Father has given the Spirit as a "deposit guaranteeing our inheritance" (Eph. 1:14) of eternal life.

Because we have incomparable resources in our risen Lord, we can confidently tell His glorious deeds so that others may believe. Therefore, let us confidently spread His light into the lives of people overwhelmed by "fear of death" (Heb. 2:15) so that they might be rescued "from the dominion of darkness" (Col. 1:13) and brought into "the kingdom of the Son."

In God's Time

Scripture

Scripture Lesson: *Ecclesiastes 3:1-8, 14-15*
Key Verse: *There is a time for everything, and a season for
every activity under heaven.* Ecclesiastes 3:1.
Scripture Lesson for Children: *Ecclesiastes 3:1-8*
Key Verse for Children: *There is a time for everything, and
a season for every activity under heaven.* Ecclesiastes 3:1.

Lesson Aim

To find hope in God in the midst of life's good and
bad moments.

Lesson Setting

Time: *Sometime during the reign of Solomon (about
970–930 B.C.)*
Place: *Jerusalem*

Lesson Outline

In God's Time
  I. The Balance and Order of Life: Ecclesiastes 3:1-8
    A. *A Time for Everything: vs. 1*
    B. *Typical Activities of Life: vss. 2-8*
  II. The Sovereignty of God over Life: Ecclesiastes
      3:14-15
    A. *The Permanence of God's Work: vs. 14*
    B. *The Lord's Control of Human Events: vs. 15*

Introduction for Adults

Topic: *Everything Has a Season*

"My family is a wreck and I don't know what to do about it," the elderly widow cried to her pastor. From the woman's emotional state she could only see those things in life that had gone wrong. The widow felt helpless to bring about any changes for the better.

When life seems overwhelming to us, we are prone to depression, fear, worry, and despair. This woman was a firm believer in Christ, but she had been overcome by harmful events. Solomon reminded us that life includes the good and the bad, life and death, peace and war, building and tearing down (to name a few things).

Ultimately, in tough times, we are driven to the roots of our faith. We can pray and ask God to restore us spiritually and refresh us mentally. By means of Scripture reading, prayer, worship, and Christian fellowship we can find hope and peace in life's most difficult seasons.

Introduction for Youth

Topic: *Perfect Timing*

"Get off that treadmill and do some real walking," Joe yelled to his friend in the health club. Treadmills are handy devices for exercise. But to many people life itself seems like a treadmill. It's just like putting one foot down after the other.

The Book of Ecclesiastes reminds us that there are rhythms to life. The only way we can navigate safely through these times and changes—over which we have no control—is to trust in God's perfect control of events. At times this might feel hard for us to do, but it nevertheless can be done.

Thus, when teens feel as if life has become a treadmill for them, they need to refocus the eyes of their faith on the Lord. He can enable them to find joy, satisfaction, and peace in the midst of troubling circumstances. Ultimately, their spiritual and mental health comes from loving and obeying the Lord.

Concepts for Children

Topic: *A Time for Everything*

1. Solomon believed that everything had a God-given proper time.
2. God's ordering of the universe affects the rhythm of life.
3. God's timetable provides a balance for living.
4. Solomon encouraged people not to rebel against God's overall plan, but to find their place in the outworking of His will.
5. We can trust God for the plan He has for our life.

Lesson Commentary

I. THE BALANCE AND ORDER OF LIFE: ECCLESIASTES 3:1-8

A. A Time for Everything: vs. 1

There is a time for everything, and a season for every activity under heaven.

In the first two chapters of Ecclesiastes, Solomon had lamented how life was meaningless when viewed apart from God. The king had also described how life occurred in a vicious cycle, repeating itself again and again. Now in chapter 3 he was ready to take another look at living and dying, this time seeing some semblance of order and meaning because of God's dominion.

Solomon was eminently qualified to expound on this matter, for he enjoyed enormous wealth and power. He also had all the material possessions he wanted. His testimony shreds the modern idea that we can find happiness and success in earthly things.

The Teacher revealed that, when God gives meaning and purpose to life, we do not end up in cynicism and despair. Instead, God gives satisfaction and pleasure in our work, food, homes, and families. The Lord intends us to find our satisfaction ultimately in Him, not in anything the world has to offer. This is the same message we find revealed in the New Testament.

The king discovered that there is "a season for every activity under heaven" (vs. 1). God has ordained a time for practically everything. Our responsibility is to seek the Lord's wisdom so that we may discern what activities go with what seasons.

B. Typical Activities of Life: vss. 2-8

A time to be born and a time to die, a time to plant and a time to uproot, a time to kill and a time to heal, a time to tear down and a time to build, a time to weep and a time to laugh, a time to mourn and a time to dance, a time to scatter stones and a time to gather them, a time to embrace and a time to refrain, a time to search and a time to give up, a time to keep and a time to throw away, a time to tear and a time to mend, a time to be silent and a time to speak, a time to love and a time to hate, a time for war and a time for peace.

Ecclesiastes 3:2-8 lists many of the activities that there are under heaven. We find here 14 pairs of opposites. In Hebrew speech, mentioning opposites together expressed totality (for example, "heaven and earth" stands for all of physical and spiritual reality). Thus these 14 pairs stand for all the activities of life.

"A time to be born and a time to die" (vs. 2a). The Teacher opened his list of the activities of life with the most momentous events of all—birth and death. In Solomon's view, God has a plan for our arrival in time, for the living out of our lives, and for our departure from life. The Teacher had already portrayed how brief a person's life span is. Here he summed up life in its beginning and end. The rest of this poem addresses what comes between birth and death.

"A time to plant and a time to uproot, a time to kill and a time to heal, a time to tear down and a time to build" (vss. 2b-3). These three lines of the poem address creative and destructive activities used for either establishing or undermining. Planting seeds and pulling weeds must be done to reap a harvest. The same is true of life. Some elements must be planted and others uprooted if one's life is to be complete and meaningful.

By saying there is a time to kill, Solomon was not condoning premeditated murder. His point was something more complex than that. Perhaps he was suggesting that we must wrestle for God's wisdom during times when we are confronted with aggression. For instance, when is the right time to resist evil with forcefulness? On the other hand, when is it time to seek compromise and healing?

Of course, there are also times when those who seek to fear and obey God need to tear down negative aspects of their personal lives and times when they need to build up the positive aspects. In that sense, the meaning of "a time to tear down and a time to build" is much like that of "a time to plant and a time to uproot."

"A time to weep and a time to laugh, a time to mourn and a time to dance" (vs. 4). The Teacher covered the range of human emotions—both private and public—in these two lines of the poem. The Hebrew words translated "weep" and "laugh" indicate expressions of an individual's emotions, while the Hebrew words translated "mourn" and "dance" indicate expressions of a group's emotions. In other words, there is a time for an individual to be sad, and a time for that person to be happy. There is also a time for an individual to join with others in lamenting a loss, and a time for that person to join with others in a good time.

"A time to scatter stones and a time to gather them, a time to embrace and a time to refrain" (vs. 5). Various interpretations exist of these two lines of the poem, which focus on friendship and enmity. In ancient times, fields taken by enemies were made unproductive by scattering stones across them. In contrast, stones were gathered from fields as a sign of a people's desire for peace. An opposite interpretation points to the gathering of stones for use in building a wall to keep out invaders. Tearing down those stone walls indicated a people's desire to make peace with their enemies.

According to one interpretation, "a time to embrace" is a call for us to hold someone who is experiencing pain, grief, or reconciliation. And yet at other times, it is best for us to respect a person's privacy by not interfering. A second, more literal interpretation places the Teacher's advice in the context of love and its physical expression between a man and a woman. Thus there is a time to show affection and a time to refrain from showing affection.

"A time to search and a time to give up, a time to keep and a time to throw away, a time to tear and a time to mend" (vss. 6-7a). At least a portion of our lives consists of our concern for accumulating or getting rid of possessions. According to the Teacher, God gives us special times when we must search out for things, friendships, and goals, and hold on to them when we acquire them. But there are other times when He calls us to give these up. The tearing and mending most likely refer to the ancient custom of tearing one's clothes in grief. If so, this line restates verse 4, in

that it shows there is a time to express grief and a time to recover from grief.

"A time to be silent and a time to speak" (vs. 7b). Communication, a key part of our lives as human beings, is like a two-way street. Thus Solomon said there is a time to remain quiet and a time to voice our opinion, a time to listen and a time to remark.

"A time to love and a time to hate" (vs. 8a). Human life can hardly resemble what it is supposed to be without affections. The Teacher realized our lives will be marked with both love and hatred, and he encouraged his hearers to be careful about the times both are exercised. Centuries later, the apostle Paul stressed that Christians should love what is good and hate what is evil (see Rom. 12:9).

"A time for war and a time for peace" (Eccl. 3:8b). As a king, Solomon did not leave out the political endeavors of his hearers. The same emotions that can give rise to love or hatred in two individuals can give rise to war or peace in two communities. Conflicts will always arise. Sometimes wrong is resisted with force; at other times, peace is the goal.

II. THE SOVEREIGNTY OF GOD OVER LIFE: ECCLESIASTES 3:14-15

A. The Permanence of God's Work: vs. 14

I know that everything God does will endure forever; nothing can be added to it and nothing taken from it. God does it so that men will revere him.

Following the poem about God's timing and the seasons of life, Solomon asked, "What does the worker gain from his toil?" (Eccl. 3:9). A modern paraphrase of this question might look like this: "My job seems boring and never-ending. What do I get out of it?"

The Teacher answered his own question by pondering further the nature of the human burden. The first part of the "burden God has laid on men" (vs. 10) is that people are to attempt to determine on a daily basis where we fit into His plan. If we follow the great rhythm of God's timing—described beautifully in the first eight verses—then we will find meaning in the labors of our life. We will discover, as a matter of fact, that His perfect plan is to make "everything beautiful in its time" (vs. 11a).

The second part of the burden God has put upon humanity is that He has "set eternity in the hearts of men; yet they cannot fathom what God has done from beginning to end" (vs. 11b). We spend at least some time contemplating how our lives fit into God's eternal perspective, and this sets us apart from the animals. We do not live only by our instincts. We are different from ferrets and foxes because we attempt to understand—through philosophy, theology, science, and ideology (to name a few disciplines)—the full scope of life. This search only frustrates us, however, because in our finite minds and hearts, we constantly discover anew that the whole picture of life on planet Earth eludes us.

Solomon explained his belief that even though humanity carries such a burden as it toils day in and day out, there is still much in life to enjoy. Apparently one of his greatest yearnings—both for himself and for others—was that people might "be happy and do good while they live" (vs. 12). He said a great source of contentment in life can be found in eating, drinking, and performing satisfying work (vs. 13). How can one find real contentment in the common activities of life? By believing that such daily activity—indeed, all of life itself—is a gift of God.

The Teacher must have recognized that we people can only believe that life is a gift of God when we humbly revere the Lord and place our confidence and faith in Him. We must also acknowledge that that there is a certain finality to whatever God does. His works are perfect in quality and permanent in character. Consequently, people cannot add or remove from what He has done to improve it (vs. 14).

B. The Lord's Control of Human Events: vs. 15

Whatever is has already been, and what will be has been before; and God will call the past to account.

Solomon used a brief poem to take a broader view of history as it affects people. In history we can seek God's will further. In doing so, we begin to discover that history is more than just facts and events repeating themselves without meaning. Things do happen in certain patterns again and again, but with faith in God's sovereignty, we can learn from them in ways that will benefit our behavior today.

We can also be certain that God will "call the past to account" (Eccl. 3:15). This may be both disturbing and comforting. It is disturbing in that it reminds us that if we have not asked God to forgive our own wrongs against others, He will hold them against us. It is comforting in that it means God will not overlook those who have suffered evil at the hands of others, especially believers and innocent people who have been persecuted or slaughtered.

Solomon conveyed similar thoughts in 12:13-14, which also happen to be the closing verses of Ecclesiastes. If we really want to know how to live in a world that at times seems unjust and meaningless, we are compelled to "fear God and keep his commandments" (vs. 13). As a matter of fact, this sums up the totality of our obligation.

The reason to pursue this duty is that, despite the endless cycle of history, despite the evil and greed, despite even death, what we do in life does matter. We know that this statement is true because God cares enough to judge our every thought and action (vs. 14). Thus the foolish, vain, and wicked things we have done will come before God's eyes for judgment. But so also will the kind, good, and gentle acts we have done.

Discussion Questions

1. What do you think the Teacher meant when he said there is a time to plant, and a time to pluck up what is planted (Eccl. 3:2)?
2. In what circumstances might weeping be appropriate? When would merriment be appropriate?

3. When Solomon spoke of seeking and losing (3:6), what do you think he had in mind?

4. Why is it often so difficult to remain at peace with loved ones and friends?

5. What should we do when the circumstances in which we find ourselves do not make sense to us?

Contemporary Application

The author of Ecclesiastes examined the things that human beings live for, including wisdom, pleasure, work, progress, and wealth. And yet no matter what they attempt to attain in life, they all meet the same destiny—they die and are forgotten by others. In that way, the author did not try to hide the futility that people face. Indeed, he emphasized that futility. He taught that all the goals of human beings have limitations—even wisdom. Thus it is useless for them to seek to master their own destiny.

"Meaningless! Meaningless! . . . Utterly meaningless! Everything is meaningless" (Eccl. 1:2) was the author's cry of despair. Indeed, he carried this sentiment throughout the book. The answer to this cry of despair does not become clear until the book's conclusion, in which the writer declared that to discover meaning and wisdom, people must "fear God and keep his commandments" (12:13). Everything in Ecclesiastes must be seen within the framework of these opening and closing statements. The book is a profound, God-breathed treatise that should encourage believers to work diligently toward a God-centered view of life.

This last statement underscores the underlying hope in the book. Even though every human striving will eventually fail, God's purposes will never fail. Through the experience of one who seemed to have tried everything, the author concluded—based upon his faith in the Lord—that God had ordered life according to His own purposes. Therefore, the best thing a person can do is to accept and enjoy life as God has given it.

A Treasure Worth Seeking

Scripture

Background Scripture: *Proverbs 2—3*
Scripture Lesson: *Proverbs 2:1-5; 3:1-6, 13-18*
Key Verse: *Blessed is the man who finds wisdom, the man who gains understanding.* Proverbs 3:13.
Scripture Lesson for Children: *Proverbs 2:1-5; 3:1-6, 13-18*
Key Verse for Children: *Trust in the LORD with all your heart and lean not on your own understanding.* Proverbs 3:5.

Lesson Aim

To learn that God's wisdom is priceless and valuable.

Lesson Setting

Time: *Sometime during the reign of Solomon (about 970–930 B.C.)*
Place: *Jerusalem*

Lesson Outline

A Treasure Worth Seeking

I. Pursuing Wisdom: Proverbs 2:1-5
   A. *Treasuring Godly Instruction: vss. 1-4*
   B. *Growing in Knowledge of God: vs. 5*
II. Heeding Wisdom: Proverbs 3:1-6
   A. *Enjoying a Long and Satisfying Life: vss. 1-2*
   B. *Finding Favor with God and People: vss. 3-4*
   C. *Trusting Wholeheartedly in the Lord: vss. 5-6*
III. Appreciating Wisdom: Proverbs 3:13-18
   A. *Finding Wisdom: vs. 13*
   B. *Affirming Wisdom's Value: vss. 14-15*
   C. *Experiencing Wisdom's Blessings: vss. 16-18*

Introduction for Adults

Topic: *A Treasure Worth Seeking*

"Understanding is the reward of faith. Therefore seek not to understand that you may believe, but believe that you may understand," wrote Augustine.

Of course, some people may argue that understanding must precede faith, that it is a driving force that brings a person to salvation in Christ. Yet, by experience, we also know that after a person becomes a Christian, an expanded spiritual understanding occurs.

Every Christian has the opportunity to gain the kind of understanding about which Augustine wrote. It is comparable to priceless treasure and worth every effort to seek and find. Indeed, through the Holy Spirit, it is "the reward of faith."

Introduction for Youth

Topic: *Wise Up!*

We live in a world where specific knowledge is important, but it's not exclusively important. The ability to discern how the specifics of life balance and blend with each other is the basis of understanding. Knowing how to put this understanding to effective use is the substance of wisdom. The world is craving the kinds of people who have somehow discovered this "magical" ability.

In this week's lesson, your students will learn that the ways of wisdom and understanding are not as "magical" as some would believe. They come from God, who is willing to share them with His people. God's wisdom helps meet all needs common to young people, such as how to stretch our resources to meet our needs; how to establish positive, productive relationships; and how to resolve conflict.

Concepts for Children

Topic: *Obey God*

1. There is value in hearing, accepting, and keeping God's commandments.
2. True wisdom begins in respect for and faith in God.
3. Commitment to God brings long-term guidance for living.
4. Dependence on God provides a sense of stability and peace.
5. We should turn to God for wisdom in our lives.

Lesson Commentary

I. PURSUING WISDOM: PROVERBS 2:1-5

A. Treasuring Godly Instruction: vss. 1-4

My son, if you accept my words and store up my commands within you, turning your ear to wisdom and applying your heart to understanding, and if you call out for insight and cry aloud for understanding, and if you look for it as for silver and search for it as for hidden treasure.

The Book of Proverbs is not the work of one individual during a specific time period. Instead, it is a compilation from several writers who lived during a vast period of time. Most of the proverbs are attributed to one recognizable writer, King Solomon (1:1). According to 1 Kings 4:32, Solomon spoke some 3,000 proverbs and wrote 1,005 songs. It is reasonable to believe that a number of the sayings found in the Book of Proverbs came from Solomon's many wise sayings. Other proverbs are attributed to unfamiliar persons such as Agur and Lemuel (30:1; 31:1). Some proverbs are not attributed to a specific writer.

There are only two reliable reference points for dating the Book of Proverbs. One is the repeated mention of King Solomon, who lived during the tenth century B.C. The other reference point for dating the book is the mention of a collection of Solomon's proverbs compiled by King Hezekiah's committee (25:1). Since Hezekiah lived in the eighth and seventh centuries B.C., we know that at least a portion of Proverbs was compiled during that period as well.

It is helpful to note at the outset that the cultural life of ancient Israel was molded by three groups of leaders: prophets, priests, and wise men. The prophets (such as Isaiah and Ezekiel) taught about obedience, justice, and repentance. The priests performed the ceremonies, rituals, and sacrifices. And the wise men spoke about prudence, practical matters, and successful living.

Though as a group the wise men never had the power of the prophets or the priests, Israel's sages helped mold the development of the nation at the grassroots level. Many of the wise men were elders, such as Job, who would share their discernment at the city gate. These repositories of sound advice often formed academies to teach young people the wisdom that would make them successful in later life. Unlike the wise men of other empires, these sages of Israel emphasized that the basis of all wisdom was the fear of God (see 1:7).

In terms of chapter 2, its theme is how to gain and keep wisdom as an incomparable treasure. In 1:20, wisdom clamors to be heard above the hubbub of society. In chapter 2, the learner must strenuously pursue wisdom according to specific guidelines. Wisdom is to be found in "words" (vs. 1) and "commands," that is, the revelation of God's truth. The search for wisdom is not based on random human speculation and theories. The learner must treasure and explore the teachings of God and seek to penetrate His principles of upright living.

To "accept my words" (vs. 1) means to believe they are valuable and trustworthy, a reliable standard for all personal conduct. This is an act of faith and an acknowledgement that God's ways are best. To "store up my commands" means to learn them and memorize them so they shape one's conduct and moral standards. When decisions must be faced—such as wisdom versus folly—the learner will have a store-house of God's commands upon which to draw.

"Turning your ear to" (2:2) is a beautiful metaphor for obedience to God's commands. People are constantly bombarded by appeals about what to believe and do (1:20-21). The godly person filters out the foolish appeals of sinners and unbelievers. "Applying your heart to" (2:2) focuses on our desires and ambitions. The wise person's main goal in life is to achieve spiritual understanding. This goal is attainable only by strenuous, singleminded effort, including study and prayer. According to verse 3, we are to call out for insight and cry for understanding as if we were sinking in moral quicksand. Traps and enticements to sin are all around us. Our only hope of resistance is to turn to God for help.

The silver and hidden treasure mentioned in verse 4 speak of what society values most. Countless lives have been ruined by the search for this world's treasures, whatever they may be. The point here is that wise, godly people pursue God's wisdom with even greater intensity. If the intensity of spiritual pursuit is not there, we will not find God's way but will be left to wander in spiritual darkness.

B. Growing in Knowledge of God: vs. 5

Then you will understand the fear of the LORD and find the knowledge of God.

If wisdom is pursued as one would seek a hidden treasure, the result will be understanding "the fear of the LORD" (Prov. 2:5). This phrase refers to a wholesome respect for God's character and might. He is holy, just, and all-powerful. He is the Almighty one, rightly deserving our fear—not the normal human fear of danger but the reverence of spiritual awe. The promise to God's children is that their search for wisdom will be rewarded by "the knowledge of God." Finding the Lord in this way is the ultimate outcome of trusting and obeying the Savior (see John 17:3).

II. HEEDING WISDOM: PROVERBS 3:1-6

A. Enjoying a Long and Satisfying Life: vss. 1-2

My son, do not forget my teaching, but keep my commands in your heart, for they will prolong your life many years and bring you prosperity.

In Proverbs 3, Solomon listed a variety of admonitions. Each of these exhortations is followed by a promised reward for those who obey it. Like all the Hebrew teachers of wisdom, the king was careful to emphasize that every action has a natural and logical consequence. Wise actions will be rewarded and foolish actions will be punished.

Solomon began by reminding his student about the importance of keeping these teachings at the forefront of the student's memory. The word the king used for "teaching" (vs. 1) in this instance is the Hebrew term *torah*. This word is also used for the first five books of the Old Testament. Moreover, the same term is used for divine law. In this instance, Solomon used the word to communicate a standard or direction. He wanted his student to use his teachings as a guide to navigate along the path of wisdom.

Solomon emphasized the importance of his student keeping these commands in his heart. This concept carried with it the idea of embracing and actively putting into practice what the student had learned from the teacher. The result would be a long and full life (vs. 2). Generally speaking (though not in every case), the wise live longer than the foolish. In addition to a longer life, the obediently wise person would have a fuller and more meaningful existence. "Prosperity" could mean actual wealth, or in a broader sense, an increased sense of purpose and significance.

B. Finding Favor with God and People: vss. 3-4

Let love and faithfulness never leave you; bind them around your neck, write them on the tablet of your heart. Then you will win favor and a good name in the sight of God and man.

Solomon next encouraged the student to hold on to "love and faithfulness" (Prov. 3:3). The Hebrew terms behind "love" and "faithfulness" consistently showed up in God's covenants with His people. The Hebrew word for "love" here, *hesed*, was often used to describe faithfulness in a relationship. Love and faithfulness add up to integrity.

Solomon wanted his student to wear these precepts like a necklace so that they would always figuratively be in front of the student. These precepts were to be inscribed on the student's heart; in other words, love and faithfulness should be practiced so frequently that they become second nature. The rewards of integrity include the favor of God and a reputation for trustworthiness (vs. 4).

C. Trusting Wholeheartedly in the Lord: vss. 5-6

Trust in the LORD with all your heart and lean not on your own understanding; in all your ways acknowledge him, and he will make your paths straight.

Solomon urged his student to wholly trust God, that is, to acknowledge Him and to seek His counsel when making plans (Prov. 3:5). The king also told his student to avoid putting all of his confidence into his own understanding. This did not mean that the student was to completely set aside his own knowledge and experience. It would be foolish to think that after spending years teaching a student wisdom, Solomon would then tell him to forsake everything he had learned. Instead, the king was reminding his pupil to acknowledge the source of his wisdom and experience—and to humbly admit there was more the Lord could teach him.

The person who trusts God in this manner will be rewarded with a path made straight (vs. 6). The image here is one of the Lord clearing obstacles from the student's way. A person seeing the hilly countryside around Jerusalem would have appreciated this metaphor of a straight path. Though the actual distance between some of the towns around the capital was short, traveling on foot was often arduous. The hills of Israel had to be traveled around or climbed over. In a similar way, the Lord will clear a spiritual path for those who trust in Him.

III. APPRECIATING WISDOM: PROVERBS 3:13-18

A. Finding Wisdom: vs. 13

Blessed is the man who finds wisdom, the man who gains understanding.

In Proverbs 3:11-12, Solomon taught his readers to view affliction prudently. Wisdom regards suffering as a learning experience in which God communicates His love and discipline. Then in verse 13, the king poetically described wisdom's benefits (vs. 13). The Hebrew word rendered "blessed," or happy, is equivalent to the Greek term used in the Beatitudes (see Matt. 5:1-12). According to Solomon, attaining wisdom (and at the same time shunning ignorance) was bliss.

B. Affirming Wisdom's Value: vss. 14-15

For she is more profitable than silver and yields better returns than gold. She is more precious than rubies; nothing you desire can compare with her.

Solomon previously noted that the person who honored the Lord with his or her wealth would experience bulging barns and overflowing vats (Prov. 3:10). The king now revealed that the happiness wisdom brings is worth even more than whatever material wealth one possesses. Whether the item is a highly prized metal (such as silver or gold) or a rare and precious stone (such as a ruby), wisdom from God was far more beneficial and profitable. In fact, none of the earthly things people desire can compare in value with wisdom (vss. 14-15). Jesus expanded upon this concept when He taught that while earthly wealth can be lost, stolen, or suffer decay, heavenly wealth lasts forever (see Matt. 6:19-20).

C. Experiencing Wisdom's Blessings: vss. 16-18

Long life is in her right hand; in her left hand are riches and honor. Her ways are pleasant ways, and all her paths are peace. She is a tree of life to those who embrace her; those who lay hold of her will be blessed.

Though Solomon desired wisdom more than a long life and great wealth, he was not opposed to these things. He was just keeping his priorities in line. The less stressful, more healthy lifestyle that wisdom called for would improve his chances for long, productive years. The king also realized that being a prudent and honest businessperson would allow him greater opportunities to acquire material wealth—money he did not have to feel guilty about.

The fact that Solomon placed long life in wisdom's "right hand" (Prov. 3:16), the place of highest honor, symbolized that a long, full life was to be valued above great wealth. "Peace" (vs. 17) and happiness also came with wisdom. By calling wisdom "a tree of life" (vs. 18), Solomon alluded to the tree mentioned in the Garden of Eden (see Gen. 2—3). Since reentering Eden was now impossible, the student could approach this desired tree by means of wisdom (Prov. 3:16-18).

Discussion Questions

1. Why is it important for young people to treasure up the wisdom of Scripture?
2. Which of Solomon's wisdom statements strike you as being the most important? Why?
3. What does it mean to trust in the Lord with all one's heart?
4. How might God be directing the path of your life right now?
5. What sort of life do believers experience when their existence is centered on God's wisdom?

Contemporary Application

Though many Christians love to quote from Proverbs, it is not an easy book to study. Investigating this portion of Scripture is much like searching through a used-book store. If you are in too much of a hurry, you will walk away empty-handed and frustrated. In contrast, if you take your time and browse carefully, you will discover a variety of treasures that could change your life forever. Though the 500+ wise sayings recorded in this book were written almost 3,000 years ago, they still apply to modern-life situations. And while the cultural details of the proverbs have changed, the truths they express are timeless.

In short, Proverbs is a practical, down-to-earth collection of wise sayings. The proverbs offer sound advice for living a successful life. They also cover such timeless topics as drunkenness, gossip, laziness, stubbornness, friendship, and child-bearing. The book is not particularly about theological ideas, but about practical, personal ethics. The writers did not attempt to prove the existence of God or explain the mysteries of His ways. God's existence and sovereignty are assumed throughout. The proverbs are not much concerned with the age to come and heavenly wonders. Instead, they focus on the here and now on planet earth.

Though the topics covered are varied and complex, their basic approach is straightforward. The fear of God is the beginning of wisdom. To maintain a high moral standard is to demonstrate wisdom. Success is the natural by-product of integrity. Few will choose the path of wisdom. We are prudent when we associate with those who do and become one of them.

Wisdom's Invitation

DEVOTIONAL READING

Proverbs 8:10-21

DAILY BIBLE READINGS

Monday May 8
*Proverbs 8:1-9 Learn
Prudence and Acquire
Intelligence*

Tuesday May 9
*Proverbs 8:10-21 Receive
Advice, Wisdom, Insight,
and Strength*

Wednesday May 10
*Proverbs 8:22-31 Wisdom
Participated in Creation*

Thursday May 11
*Proverbs 8:32-36 Listen to
Wisdom's Instruction*

Friday May 12
*Proverbs 9:1-6 Wisdom
Extends an Invitation*

Saturday May 13
*Proverbs 9:7-12 Wisdom
Multiplies Our Days*

Sunday May 14
*Proverbs 9:13-18 Folly
Extends an Invitation*

Scripture

Background Scripture: *Proverbs 8—9*

Scripture Lesson: *Proverbs 8:1-5, 22-31*

Key Verse: *Does not wisdom call out? Does not understanding raise her voice?* Proverbs 8:1.

Scripture Lesson for Children: *Proverbs 8:1-5, 10-11, 32-35*

Key Verse for Children: *Listen to my instruction and be wise; do not ignore it.* Proverbs 8:33.

Lesson Aim

To understand that accepting God's wisdom is a choice.

Lesson Setting

Time: *Sometime during the reign of Solomon (about 970–930 B.C.)*

Place: *Jerusalem*

Lesson Outline

Wisdom's Invitation

  I. The Summons of Wisdom: Proverbs 8:1-5
     A. *Wisdom's Cry for Attention: vs. 1*
     B. *Wisdom's Strategic Positioning: vss. 2-3*
     C. *Wisdom's Exhortation to All Humankind: vss. 4-5*

 II. The Origin of Wisdom: Proverbs 8:22-26
     A. *Wisdom's Creation: vss. 22-23*
     B. *Wisdom's Exclusive Existence: vss. 24-26*

III. The Antiquity of Wisdom: Proverbs 8:27-31
     A. *Wisdom's Presence at Creation: vss. 27-29*
     B. *Wisdom's Delight in God's Handiwork: vss. 30-31*

Introduction for Adults

Topic: *Wisdom's Invitation*

> In Bible times there was a custom of double invitations. When a great feast or a celebration was planned, the host would send out invitations to all those he wanted to attend. This was so that those invited would know to plan for the appointed time.
>
> When the moment came for the actual feast or celebration, the host would send out a servant to go back to all those who had been invited. The servant would tell them that the time had come and they were now to attend the wonderful event. In fact, failure to come would be considered a serious offense.
>
> Perhaps your students should consider this week's lesson as an opportunity to accept wisdom's invitation to partake of its delightful offerings. They will discover that nothing can compare with the treasures of understanding to be found in the wisdom of God.

Introduction for Youth

Topic: *RSVP to Wisdom*

> What saved teen would not want to be thought of as wise and knowledgeable? Of course, such a person doesn't flaunt the fact that he or she is wise. It's not necessary to bring one's wisdom to anyone else's attention, because wisdom shows itself naturally in a person's lifestyle—in what he or she thinks and says and does.
>
> What about adolescents who realize they aren't as wise as they could be? In a metaphorical sense, God has sent them an invitation marked RSVP (*Répondez s'il vous plaît*)—French for "Please reply." The offer is made through such passages as Proverbs 8. All your students have to do is humbly accept wisdom's generous offer.

Concepts for Children

Topic: *Obey Wise Teachings*

> 1. Knowledge of God's expectations is one of life's most valuable possessions.
> 2. It is important to understand true intelligence and discretion.
> 3. Real happiness is found in following God's instruction.
> 4. To be faithful to God's instruction is to find the fullness of life.
> 5. God is pleased when we commit ourselves to making wise choices in our daily lives.

Lesson Commentary

I. THE SUMMONS OF WISDOM: PROVERBS 8:1-5

A. Wisdom's Cry for Attention: vs. 1

Does not wisdom call out? Does not understanding raise her voice?

In the Book of Proverbs wisdom is repeatedly personified. For instance, in 1:20-33, wisdom announced her value. Later in 3:19-20, wisdom is said to have laid the earth's foundations and set the heavens in place. Then in 8:22-31, wisdom proclaimed to be at God's side assisting in His creative acts. The sages of ancient nations often personified wisdom too. However, in Proverbs, wisdom is not a deity like the idols worshiped in Egypt, Assyria, or Babylon. It is distinct from and subordinate to God. In fact, wisdom is the personification of the attribute of sagacity displayed by the Lord.

By personifying the concept of understanding and discernment, Solomon made wisdom more than a system of information and principles. Also, by referring to wisdom in a personalized way, the king transformed this entity from an "it" into a "she." As a living being (of sorts), "wisdom" became a proper noun and was able to interact with the world around her.

As a "person" (loosely speaking), wisdom was able to rebuke the foolish, praise the discerning, and manifest a wide range of emotions. She stood by God at the creation of the universe and resisted her personified nemesis "folly." As an enduring entity, wisdom was able to go to those who needed her and reach them with a timely message of righteousness and prudence. She did not have to stand idly by and wait for them to seek her out. She had no problem calling attention to herself (8:1).

B. Wisdom's Strategic Positioning: vss. 2-3

On the heights along the way, where the paths meet, she takes her stand; beside the gates leading into the city, at the entrances, she cries aloud.

Solomon portrayed wisdom as a fiery, determined preacher who represented everything that was good about God. She could be found at every intersection and on every hilltop (Prov. 8:2). Interestingly, while wisdom positioned herself in view of all, the wayward woman of chapter 7 lurked at the street corners at night to conceal her presence. This is the difference between prudence and folly.

Moreover, wisdom was present at the gates of every small town and large city where the leadership met to hold court (vs. 3). Anywhere society might gather, she was present to proclaim the truth and seek justice. In fact, her cry was so loud that it could not be missed. No one was beyond the hearing of her voice.

Wisdom cried out in the open plazas because that's where the crowds gathered. Here were the people she desired to teach. Here is where they were especially vulnerable to diverse temptations and thus needed her guidance and warnings in the midst of their daily duties. They were at the parting of the ways that led to either success or destruction. There wisdom cried out loudly so that all could hear and urgently invited them to come—without money and without price—to receive instruction from her.

C. Wisdom's Exhortation to All Humankind: vss. 4-5

"To you, O men, I call out; I raise my voice to all mankind. You who are simple, gain prudence; you who are foolish, gain understanding."

Wisdom was no respecter of persons, and she showed no partiality toward any race or social class. She raised her voice to all humankind (Prov. 8:4). Behind her efforts was her passion to train and correct the immature, the inexperienced, and the naive (vs. 5).

These "simple" ones were not necessarily characterized by evil intentions. Instead, they were often young people who blindly followed selfish and immoral leadership. Many times they would not consider the natural consequences of their actions. Wisdom came and offered to teach them knowledge and improved judgment. She gave them the opportunity to change their imprudent ways before they were beyond her reach. In contrast to the "simple," the "foolish" were people who had hardened themselves in sin. Righteousness was far from their thoughts. Because they lacked moral direction and were bent on wickedness, they hated God's truth (1:22). Wisdom urged to them to gain understanding and spiritual insight (8:5, 9; 14:8).

There is no hope or help for the simple and the foolish unless they turn back from their indifference, apathy, and lawlessness. If they persist in their wrongdoing, they face certain calamity. Their only hope is the promise of salvation in Christ. Repentance from sin and faith in the Son are required. By trusting in the Messiah, they have taken the first steps toward a life of prudence and understanding.

II. THE ORIGIN OF WISDOM: PROVERBS 8:22-26

A. Wisdom's Creation: vss. 22-23

"The LORD brought me forth as the first of his works, before his deeds of old; I was appointed from eternity, from the beginning, before the world began."

In Proverbs 8:12-21, wisdom introduced a family member and partner named prudence. Just as wisdom and prudence have no conflicts of interest, neither do wisdom and God. They both hate evil deeds and corrupt speech. Wisdom gave further personal data, including that she established governments and inspired just laws for the people's good. Those who love wisdom were promised love in return. In addition, she would bestow riches and honor upon them.

Wisdom continued this portion of her personal sketch by flashing back to some of her earliest memories. According to wisdom, she was with God before He created the heavens and the earth (vss. 22-23). Solomon placed these assertions in wisdom's mouth so she could claim the rights and responsibilities of the firstborn. As such, she possessed authority over all the things that were created. Also as the firstborn, wisdom served as the family representative between God and those who followed her. Therefore, no person should act without first consulting her.

The phrase "brought me forth" (vs. 22) has caused a great deal of discussion among Bible scholars. Some think Solomon merely implied that God possessed wisdom as He created. The better option is that wisdom was the first entity God brought into existence and then used as the agent of all creation.

Because of the references to wisdom being the firstborn of creation and the craftsperson at God's side during Creation, some think that Proverbs 8 is a description of the Messiah prior to His incarnation—even though wisdom is personified here as a woman. In Christian history the heretical movement called Arianism picked up on this idea and attempted to use passages such as 8:22-31 to prove that Jesus was a created being. They claimed that Jesus could not be coeternal with the Father if in fact He was a created being, as described in Proverbs 8.

The early church was correct in rejecting Arianism, for Jesus is fully divine and fully human. He who is coequal and coeternal with the Father and the Spirit became a human being (John 1:1-2, 14, 18) in order to redeem the lost (Phil. 2:6-11; Heb. 2:9-18). It is true that Colossians 1:15 describes Jesus as the firstborn of all creation. This does not mean the Savior was the first created entity, but rather that He holds preeminence over all creation.

These clarifications notwithstanding, there is value in seeing a more general connection between the wisdom of Proverbs 8 and the Messiah. For instance, just as the Son is "the exact representation" (Heb. 1:3) of the Father's being or essence, so Proverbs presents wisdom as an attribute of God. Moreover, Paul regarded Jesus as the fulfillment of wisdom (Col. 1:15-20; 2:3), and the apostle affirmed that the Messiah has become our wisdom through His redemptive work on the cross (1 Cor. 1:24, 30).

B. Wisdom's Exclusive Existence: vss. 24-26

"When there were no oceans, I was given birth, when there were no springs abounding with water; before the mountains were settled in place, before the hills, I was given birth, before he made the earth or its fields or any of the dust of the world."

To emphasize the importance of wisdom's preeminent status, Solomon had her echo the Creation account from Genesis 1. The Lord gave birth to wisdom before there were any deep oceans and "springs abounding with water" (Prov. 8:24). Wisdom existed before the mountains and the hills were formed (vs. 25). She even predated the time when God made the earth with its fields and soil (vs. 26).

III. THE ANTIQUITY OF WISDOM: PROVERBS 8:27-31

A. Wisdom's Presence at Creation: vss. 27-29

"I was there when he set the heavens in place, when he marked out the horizon on the face of the deep, when he established the clouds above and fixed securely the fountains of the deep, when he gave the sea its boundary so the waters would not overstep his command, and when he marked out the foundations of the earth."

Wisdom's antiquity is underscored by her presence with God at the dawn of Creation. When the Lord established the heavens, wisdom was already there (Prov. 8:27). She was also present during a host of other creation activity, including the following: when God marked out the horizon on the world's oceans; when He set the clouds above and established the earth's deep foundations (vs. 28); when God established boundaries for the sea so that the waters would not spread beyond their confines; and when He laid foundations to support the planet (vs. 29).

B. Wisdom's Delight in God's Handiwork: vss. 30-31

"Then I was the craftsman at his side. I was filled with delight day after day, rejoicing always in his presence, rejoicing in his whole world and delighting in mankind."

Wisdom was more than an idle spectator while God created the heavens and the earth. She was an active participant. Solomon described wisdom as the Lord's master "craftsman" (Prov. 8:30). The Hebrew term rendered "craftsman" is the same word used to describe Bezalel, who designed and organized the building of the tabernacle (see Exod. 31:1-3). Just as Bezalel used his exceptional abilities as he worked under the leadership of Moses, so wisdom used her extraordinary talents as she assisted God in His Creation.

Wisdom did not recall her work for God as being a tedious process. Instead, she remembered every moment of her work as a joyful experience both for her and the divine (Prov. 8:30). The reason for this joy was not merely pride in wisdom's accomplishments. Her happiness was the natural result of the Lord taking delight in her. The joy wisdom felt being in God's presence carried over to the entire world her hands had helped to create. Indeed, wisdom's love for God's creation, especially humankind, was boundless (vs. 31).

When we ask God for wisdom, we are requesting something that has been around since the foundation of the world. We can trust God's wisdom because of its vast experience and depth of insight. Certainly there is nothing we can face that God's wisdom has not seen countless of times in the lives of others.

Discussion Questions

1. Why do people often fail to take notice of wisdom?
2. Why is it pure folly to ignore the call of wisdom?
3. What part did wisdom have in the creation of the world?
4. How can believers give more emphasis to the importance of wisdom in their lives?
5. What do you think your life would be like if it was completely empty of God's wisdom?

Contemporary Application

Solomon personified wisdom as a zealous evangelist. She did not restrict her preaching only to the Israelites, but sought the needy across the broad spectrum of humankind. Prudence heralded her message to the naive—often young persons—who foolishly followed evil individuals. Wisdom instructed her followers in the way of truth, and her rewards far exceeded the value of material possessions.

Scan your morning newspaper and see how many stories bear out the truth of Proverbs 8. How many of the conflicts reported came about because someone, or a group of people, chose foolishness instead of wisdom? "Those who fail to find me," we can hear wisdom declaring, "harm themselves." In some cases, the harm comes to others as well. Yet, despite this, many people refuse to listen to God. Wisdom in Proverbs begs people to listen. Tragically, some individuals listen only after they have been hurt.

In contrast, we can hear wisdom proclaim, "Whoever finds me finds life." The deepest satisfaction comes from knowing God's Word and obeying His injunctions recorded in it. Our obligation as responsible, prudent Christians is to offer life and to warn of destruction. We must be faithful watchers on the wall, so to speak, crying out with wisdom for people to be careful and to choose God's path of uprightness over the wicked, destructive ways of the world.

The Path of Integrity

DEVOTIONAL READING

Proverbs 10:27-32

DAILY BIBLE READINGS

Monday May 15
*Proverbs 10:27-32 God's
Way Is a Stronghold*

Tuesday May 16
*Proverbs 11:1-5 Wisdom,
Not Pride*

Wednesday May 17
*Proverbs 11:6-10
Righteousness, Not
Treachery*

Thursday May 18
*Proverbs 11:11-15 The
Importance of Guidance and
Counsel*

Friday May 19
*Proverbs 11:16-21 Blameless
Ways, Not Wickedness*

Saturday May 20
*Proverbs 11:22-26
Generosity, Not Stinginess*

Sunday May 21
*Proverbs 11:27-31 Goodness,
Not Evil*

Scripture

Background Scripture: *Proverbs 11*
Scripture Lesson: *Proverbs 11:1-14*
Key Verse: *The integrity of the upright guides them, but the
unfaithful are destroyed by their duplicity.* Proverbs 11:3.
Scripture Lesson for Children: *Proverbs 3:27-31; 11:13,
25; 14:29; 19:22; 20:11*
Key Verse for Children: *Do not withhold good from those
who deserve it.* Proverbs 3:27.

Lesson Aim

To encourage the students to consider the impact of
their attitudes, actions, and words.

Lesson Setting

Time: *Sometime during the reign of Solomon (about
970–930 B.C.)*
Place: *Jerusalem*

Lesson Outline

The Path of Integrity
   I. A Contrast in Attitudes: Proverbs 11:1-3
      A. *Dishonesty versus Honesty: vs. 1*
      B. *Humility versus Arrogance: vs. 2*
      C. *Integrity versus Duplicity: vs. 3*
   II. A Contrast in Actions: Proverbs 11:4-10
      A. *Righteousness versus Wickedness: vss. 4-6*
      B. *Deliverance versus Ruin: vss. 7-8*
      C. *Helpfulness versus Harmfulness: vss. 9-10*
   III. A Contrast in Words: Proverbs 11:11-14
      A. *Constructive versus Destructive Speech: vs. 11*
      B. *Uplifting versus Disparaging Comments: vs. 12*
      C. *Retaining versus Divulging Information: vs. 13*
      D. *Seeking versus Rejecting Counsel: vs. 14*

Introduction for Adults

Topic: *Choosing the Path of Integrity*

Pursuing integrity and righteousness are difficult for adults even more than for young children. If you tell children something is wrong, often they will avoid that activity even when no one is around simply because they may not be insightful enough to consider its moral implications or observe that no one is looking.

Adults, however, have the temptation to consider "situational ethics" and struggle with integrity since they can better assess when no one is looking. As this week's lesson stresses, the integrity of our faith is determined by our attitudes, actions, and words. A living faith nurtures righteousness through a humble spirit and proper motives.

Introduction for Youth

Topic: *The Path of Integrity*

John Hawkins has written a book entitled *Leadership as a Lifestyle: The Path to Personal Integrity and Positive Influence.* In it he notes that leadership is based upon the quality of one's life rather than the power of one's position. He also notes that long-term, effective leadership is built upon character, competence, and commitment that are drawn from one's core beliefs and virtues.

This week's lesson can provide your students with a good starting point for pursuing a lifelong path of integrity. Regardless of whether they aspire to be leaders or followers, they will reap rich eternal dividends from living in a principle-centered way as followers of Christ.

Concepts for Children

Topic: *Do Good to Others*

1. The Bible instructs us in how to treat others with respect.
2. Pride and dishonesty are negative traits to be overcome.
3. Dishonesty and pride can destroy personal virtue.
4. Goals for conduct include doing good and helping others.
5. With God's help, we can become the people He desires.

Lesson Commentary

I. A CONTRAST IN ATTITUDES: PROVERBS 11:1-3

A. Dishonesty versus Honesty: vs. 1

The LORD abhors dishonest scales, but accurate weights are his delight.

Proverbs is part of what Bible scholars have called the "wisdom literature" of Scripture, along with Ecclesiastes and Job. The genre (or literary type) of proverbs was also well-known in the ancient world. In fact, there are a number of parallels between Proverbs 22:17—24:22 and the Egyptian "Instruction of Amenemope," which was written during roughly the same time period. There were probably several "wisdom exchanges" (in a manner of speaking) between Egypt and Solomon's court during Israel's golden years.

Despite being a part of the wisdom literature, Proverbs is unique among the books of the Bible. Unlike other Old Testament books, Proverbs concentrates on the responsibilities of individuals and not of nations as a whole. Admittedly, other biblical books (such as portions of the Psalms, the Sermon on the Mount, and the Letter of James) contain wise sayings, but no other book of the Bible is made up solely of proverbs.

Within the company of Israel's sages the term "proverb" came to stand for any kind of wisdom saying, no matter in what form it was expressed. The forms of proverb-type sayings ranged from extended personifications to short, memorable observations about life.

The Hebrew word for "proverb" carries with it the idea of comparison. Appropriately, many of the proverbs use comparison to teach their truths. A consistent theme in the Book of Proverbs is the comparison between the way of wisdom and the way of foolishness. As the collection of proverbs repeatedly reminds us, wisdom is always the better choice. The benefits of wisdom far outweigh the consequences of foolishness. Persons who follow the way of wisdom tend to succeed, while those who follow the way of foolishness eventually come to ruin.

While the contrasts between the results of wisdom versus those of foolishness are generally accurate, there are always exceptions. There are times when godly, hardworking people do not thrive materially. Likewise, there are times when lazy, deceitful people live with an abundance of material possessions. In reading Proverbs it is best to remember that these sayings teach general rules for life. The wisdom sayings are not comprehensive promises but simply descriptions about the way things usually go.

This disclaimer is not meant to diminish the value or applicability of Proverbs. Indeed, as 1:1-7 stresses, it is worthwhile to lead a life that is prudent. Of course, this ideal life must be constructed on the foundation of a personal acknowledgment of God's power. Failure marks the lives of those who reject this basic but essential premise.

Despite the general theme of wisdom versus foolishness, there is no clear order to the placement of the individual proverbs. For instance, adages about drunkenness can be found side by side with observations about child rearing. In the latter chapters of the book, more proverbs are clustered around specific topics, such as the passage about fools (26:1-12). However, even there the use of topical clusters is not consistent.

Moreover, there is no consistent structure to individual proverbs. Some are longer metaphorical stories. Others are personifications of abstract ideas. Others are short parallel statements that repeat the same idea in slightly different ways or that contrast two opposing concepts or approaches to life. The latter is a kind of literary technique called *parallelism*. In many cases, two (or sometimes three) lines of poetry are, in one way or another, correspondent in meaning. Most of the proverbs in chapter 11 are excellent examples of *contrasting* parallelism. Here we find the second line of a statement supplying a matching but opposite truth as a balance to the first line.

For instance, consider verse 1, in which Solomon contrasted honesty and dishonesty. We first learn that the Lord detests "dishonest scales," or more literally "scales of deception." The king was referring to a common business practice of his day in which vendors in a marketplace would weigh silver on scales against the opposing weight of a stone. By using a heavier stone when measuring the silver, a merchant could make the payment seem less than it was really worth.

Such a practice was an abomination to God, for it represented cheating. In addition, it also undermined the stability of commerce within ancient Israelite society. In contrast, the Lord delighted in "accurate" weights, that is, stones weighed on the scales that gave an honest measurement. More generally, He was pleased with those who adhered to upright business practices.

B. Humility versus Arrogance: vs. 2

When pride comes, then comes disgrace, but with humility comes wisdom.

The Hebrew term rendered "pride" (Prov. 11:2) comes from a verb that means "to boil" or "to seethe." The imagery might be that of the contents in a pot boiling over its edge. Similarly, those who are haughty overstep the boundaries of propriety and bring disgrace upon themselves. The nature of the shame could be the humiliation of being undone by their arrogance. In contrast, the humble are modest in their attitudes, actions, and words. Because of their unassuming ways, they avoid many of the snares encountered by those who are presumptuous; and over the course of a lifetime, the path of humility proves to be the most sensible and reasonable.

C. Integrity versus Duplicity: vs. 3

The integrity of the upright guides them, but the unfaithful are destroyed by their duplicity.

"Integrity" (Prov. 11:3) in the original comes from a primary root that means "to be complete or finished." From an ethical standpoint, there is nothing morally lacking in the lives of the upright. Because they choose to be blameless in all their ways, their integrity brings them true joy and success. In contrast are "the unfaithful." Treachery and deviousness characterize their lives; and their brazen attempts to dupe others eventually bring about their own destruction.

II. A Contrast in Actions: Proverbs 11:4-10

A. Righteousness versus Wickedness: vss. 4-6

Wealth is worthless in the day of wrath, but righteousness delivers from death. The righteousness of the blameless makes a straight way for them, but the wicked are brought down by their own wickedness. The righteousness of the upright delivers them, but the unfaithful are trapped by evil desires.

Scripture teaches that God is the moral governor of the universe and that He holds all people accountable for their actions. According to Hebrews 9:27, after death everyone faces judgment, which will be impartial and fair (Rom. 2:11, 16). But even in this life the Lord considers people responsible for what they do (Job 21:30; Ezek. 7:19; Zeph. 1:18). In that "day of wrath" (Prov. 11:4), namely, the time of divine punishment, material riches will be of no avail. Righteousness, not wealth, will rescue one from impending death.

Expressed differently, living uprightly is a safeguard against mortal danger, primarily because obeying God tends to put the virtuous out of harm's way. As verse 5 indicates, the rectitude of the blameless will smooth their way. In contrast, the wicked choose treacherous, sinful paths that result in their downfall.

This is not to suggest that the godly are shielded from all forms of calamity. Rather, Solomon's point is that living in a good and honest manner is freeing. In fact, in times of adversity the righteous tend to experience peace and protection. Oppositely, the malice of those who are dishonest and treacherous ensnares them, making their escape from their self-inflicted harm virtually impossible (vs. 6).

B. Deliverance versus Ruin: vss. 7-8

When a wicked man dies, his hope perishes; all he expected from his power comes to nothing. The righteous man is rescued from trouble, and it comes on the wicked instead.

Most people, whether upright or wicked, desire to live a long time and be successful. However, those who are evil pursue these goals in a detestable manner. When they die, their expectation of obtaining fortune, power, and fame (among other things) perishes with them. In fact, all they hoped to garner from their feeble power "comes to nothing" (Prov. 11:7). Even the children of the wicked will not prosper from the evil ways of their parents.

In contrast, those who live uprightly have hope for this life and the life to come. In the day of "trouble" (vs. 8), God rescues them. Moreover, the wicked take their place. A prime example of this in the Old Testament would be the Lord's deliverance of Mordecai and allowing Haman to be struck by his own diabolical plans (see Esth. 5:14; 7:10). Of course, the notion of divine justice overtaking the wicked does not preclude the righteous from ever experiencing adversity.

C. Helpfulness versus Harmfulness: vss. 9-10

With his mouth the godless destroys his neighbor, but through knowledge the righteous escape. When the righteous prosper, the city rejoices; when the wicked perish, there are shouts of joy.

Solomon's focus had been on the harm the wicked bring to themselves. In Proverbs 11:9-10, the emphasis shifted to the havoc evil people create in the lives of others. The "godless" (vs. 9) refers to those who are impious and profane. Their speech is characterized by deceptive flattery. The unsuspecting are taken in and undone by what appears to be the kind words (and deeds) of the wicked. The upright, however, have sufficient insight to detect the hypocritical statements of the wicked and escape their devastating effect.

In verse 10, Solomon described the presence of joy at two different fates. When the upright prosper in their endeavors, the inhabitants of a city exult. After all, the virtue of the godly tends to bring about much public good. In contrast, when the wicked perish "shouts of joy" can be heard ringing out from those who were afflicted by their evil ways.

III. A CONTRAST IN WORDS: PROVERBS 11:11-14

A. Constructive versus Destructive Speech: vs. 11

Through the blessing of the upright a city is exalted, but by the mouth of the wicked it is destroyed.

The idea of false flattery, which Solomon broached in Proverbs 11:9, leads naturally to a discussion of the harm and good connected with speech. In verse 11, the king noted that the beneficial words (and deeds) of the upright result in blessing for the rest of a city's population. In fact, a town is built up by the prosperity generated by the righteous. Oppositely, the words of the wicked can destroy the prospects of others. This is partly due to the fact that the counsel of evil people is malicious and deceitful. And it does not take that long for a society to be undone by such slanderous, perverted speech.

B. Uplifting versus Disparaging Comments: vs. 12

A man who lacks judgment derides his neighbor, but a man of understanding holds his tongue.

In ancient times, people regarded themselves as being part of an extended community. And from the biblical perspective, showing hospitality, being considerate, and safeguarding the reputation of one's neighbor were associated with living uprightly. Thus, the godly would shun publicly shaming others. In contrast, the imprudent openly despise and belittle people.

Moreover, an underlying attitude of superiority leads the reckless to discard wisdom and be judgmental toward others. They likewise do not hesitate to show contempt for their fellow human beings. The upright, however, are prudent and discerning. They have the good sense to know that it is foolish to make a public spectacle out of another person's mistake. The godly also realize that those they humiliate now might try to get even with them in the future (Prov. 11:12).

C. Retaining versus Divulging Information: vs. 13

A gossip betrays a confidence, but a trustworthy man keeps a secret.

> The Hebrew term rendered "gossip" (Prov. 11:13) might more literally be translated "going about in slander." The idea is of someone roaming from one person to the next divulging personal secrets, especially with the intent to slander. In short, gossips cannot wait to make injurious remarks about what they perceive to be the faults of others. In contrast, those who are faithful refuse to conceal private information. Instead, the trustworthy can keep a confidence.

D. Seeking versus Rejecting Counsel: vs. 14

For lack of guidance a nation falls, but many advisers make victory sure.

> Imagine a captain failing to steer a ship in the right direction and it is destroyed on the rocks of a nearby shore. Similarly, a nation is shipwrecked (so to speak) in the absence of spiritual and moral guidance. Oppositely, victory in battle and success in commerce result from the abundance of sound advice (Prov. 11:14).

Discussion Questions

1. Why do you think arrogance leads to disgrace?
2. Why are earthly riches of no value in the day of God's judgment?
3. How can believers use speech to promote uprightness?
4. What does it mean to keep a confidence and why is this important?
5. Why is it vital for believers to seek the wise counsel of others?

Contemporary Application

What comes to mind when you consider the word "integrity"? For many it is moral soundness. People of integrity are known for their uprightness and rectitude. They are considered to be trustworthy, fair, and good. These sentiments remain true regardless of whether we are talking about their attitudes, actions, or words.

In terms of attitudes, individuals of integrity are honest rather than dishonest. They are also characterized by humility as opposed to arrogance. With respect to actions, they embrace righteousness and shun wickedness. Moreover, they strive be to helpful, rather than harmful, to others. And in terms of words, their speech is constructive (instead of destructive), uplifting (rather than disparaging), and respectful (as opposed to disrespectful) of others.

Perhaps the path of integrity is most notably seen in the Christlike love described in 1 Corinthians 13. In particular, verses 4-7 reveal that such love is kind and patient. It shuns jealously, arrogance, and rudeness. It also steers clear of being selfish, quick-tempered, and holding grudges. Instead, the love of Christ prompts people of integrity to rejoice in the truth (but not in evil) and to be supportive, loyal, hopeful, and trusting. With such virtues as these God is surely pleased!

Living Out Wisdom

DEVOTIONAL READING

Proverbs 4:10-15

DAILY BIBLE READINGS

Monday May 22
Proverbs 4:1-9 Advice for Children

Tuesday May 23
Proverbs 4:10-15 Keep on the Right Path

Wednesday May 24
Proverbs 10:18-23 Wise People Value Wise Conduct

Thursday May 25
Proverbs 31:1-9 Advice from a Mother

Friday May 26
Proverbs 31:10-15 Portrait of a Capable Wife

Saturday May 27
Proverbs 31:16-23 What an Ideal Wife Is Like

Sunday May 28
Proverbs 31:24-31 A Good Wife and Mother

Scripture

Background Scripture: *Proverbs 31*
Scripture Lesson: *Proverbs 31:8-14, 25-30*
Key Verse: *Charm is deceptive, and beauty is fleeting; but a woman who fears the LORD is to be praised.* Proverbs 31:30.
Scripture Lesson for Children: *Proverbs 4:1-5; 6:20; 31:10, 26-28*
Key Verse for Children: *My son, keep your father's commands and do not forsake your mother's teaching.* Proverbs 6:20.

Lesson Aim

To enjoin students to make godly wisdom a part of their everyday lives.

Lesson Setting

Time: *Between the tenth to sixth centuries B.C.*
Place: *Israel*

Lesson Outline

Living Out Wisdom

  I. Justice for the Needy: Proverbs 31:8-9
 II. A Wife of Noble Character: Proverbs 31:10-14, 25-30
   A. *Distinguished by Incalculable Worth: vs. 10*
   B. *Noted for Virtue and Diligence: vss. 11-14*
   C. *Known for Wisdom and Courage: vss. 25-27*
   D. *Esteemed for a God-centered Life: vss. 28-30*

Introduction for Adults

Topic: *Living Out Wisdom*

Adults often feel caught in the trap of pursuing riches, fame, and influence. This week's lesson reminds us, however, that God's wisdom—personified as a prudent woman—is more valuable than gold, silver, or rubies. And the entire Book of Proverbs teaches that it is the most important thing that the person of integrity seeks. Wise instruction can come from Scripture, parents, or godly friends. However, the ultimate source of wisdom is the Lord Himself, through the Holy Spirit.

Adults who live by the precepts of godly wisdom can exist in peace, even in the midst of conflict and suffering, for they have the priceless hope of Christ's return. Blessings now delayed will be bestowed when Jesus establishes His kingdom and bids His faithful ones to "take your inheritance, the kingdom prepared for you since the creation of the world" (Matt. 25:34).

Introduction for Youth

Topic: *Wise Women*

Proverbs uses the metaphor of the wise woman to emphasize the eternal virtue of being prudent. The *Veggie Tales,* a series retelling Bible stories for children, uses animated vegetables to teach a similar series of spiritual truths.

For example, "Josh and the Great Wall" retells the battle of Jericho. Junior Asparagus is totally frustrated with the murmuring peas, squash, and carrots, who are trying to form their own battle plan. Having learned the value of God's wisdom, he shouts, "Why don't you do it God's way for a change?"

Young people need to know that godly wisdom saves time and energy that otherwise would have to be spent correcting human error. Teens who follow God's rules the first time won't have to clean up a mess later.

Concepts for Children

Topic: *Obey Your Parents*

1. Proverbs affirms the importance of listening to and following the wise advice of parents.
2. Proverbs gives the qualities of a God-fearing wife and mother.
3. Parents have a responsibility for wisely guiding and instructing their children.
4. Children can look to their parents and other authority figures to provide wise instruction.
5. Children should seek parental advice and counsel in the tough decisions they face.

Lesson Commentary

I. JUSTICE FOR THE NEEDY: PROVERBS 31:8-9

"Speak up for those who cannot speak for themselves, for the rights of all who are destitute. Speak up and judge fairly; defend the rights of the poor and needy."

The remainder of the Book of Proverbs was written by an unknown king named Lemuel (31:1). According to Jewish legend, Lemuel was Solomon, which would make Bathsheba the source of the advice he received (see vss. 2-3). Others think Lemuel was probably not an Israelite. In that case, we have no idea what country he was from or the time in which he lived.

In verses 4-7, Lemuel's mother cautioned the king about the dangers of alcoholism. While using alcohol was acceptable for the sick, leaders (such as the king) should never be bound to strong drink. Similar counsel can be found in 20:1. There we learn that the consumption of alcohol can change a thoughtful, peaceful person into a quarreler and a brawler.

In stepping back from this advice we see how important it is to be circumspect in one's actions and attitude, especially toward others. As Paul noted in Philippians 2:4, we should be concerned not only about our own interests, but also about the interests of others. And Micah 6:8 enjoins God's people to promote justice, be merciful, and live humbly before Him.

Similarly, this concern for others can be found in Proverbs 31:8-9. The righteous are urged to speak up as advocates for those who "cannot speak for themselves" (vs. 8). The broader context seems to be a legal proceeding in which the accused are unable to defend themselves in court against the unscrupulous allegations of the wicked. It may be that poverty, ignorance, or oppression prevents the needy from mounting a stalwart legal defense.

Upright leaders will not abandon the helpless and hopeless to the cruelties and inequities of life. By God's grace people of upstanding character will champion the cause of the destitute and homeless and do whatever they can to plead their cause and ensure that their rights are defended (vs. 9).

II. A WIFE OF NOBLE CHARACTER: PROVERBS 31:10-14, 25-30

A. Distinguished by Incalculable Worth: vs. 10

A wife of noble character who can find? She is worth far more than rubies.

In the final portion of Proverbs 31, we find a poem about a wife of noble character. It is a traditional Jewish custom for male participants to recite verses 10-31 to their wives on the evening of the Sabbath. The passage is also recited at the funerals of women.

Bible scholars have noted that the poem is similar to other Old Testament hymns. For instance, like Psalm 119, Proverbs 31:10-31 is written as an acrostic, in which each line begins with a successive letter of the Hebrew alphabet. Also, just as

Psalm 111 offers praise to the Lord for His works, dignity, and strength (among other things), the poem recorded in Proverbs 31 lauds the superlative wife.

In verses 10-31, the wise woman is extolled for her discernment, talents, and energy. It makes sense to regard the virtuous wife as an idealized example of godly women down through the ages. As well, she is a fitting symbol of wisdom, for her personal qualities reflect the desire of all who are upright and prudent, regardless of their gender. Without question, these virtues are the cornerstone of families and societies.

We learn from a careful study of the poem that this particular wife has servants to manage, money to invest, and business deals to negotiate. She is described as being organized, industrious, and successful. She is sturdy enough to withstand hard times and yet tender to the poor. As verse 10 reveals (by way of a rhetorical question), this person is of "noble character" or of high moral worth. Like wisdom, her value exceeds that of rubies (see 3:15; 8:11).

B. Noted for Virtue and Diligence: vss. 11-14

Her husband has full confidence in her and lacks nothing of value. She brings him good, not harm, all the days of her life. She selects wool and flax and works with eager hands. She is like the merchant ships, bringing her food from afar.

An intriguing feature of Proverbs is the personification of numerous wise sayings in the form of a woman who reaches out to the world of humans. This figure spoke with divine authority (1:20-33) and played a role in Creation (chap. 8). The meaning of this exalted female figure in a strongly male-centered society has been the topic of much debate, for female imagery begins (chaps. 1—9) and ends (chap. 31) the book.

Most likely the writers of Proverbs meant "woman wisdom" to be an extension of God's characteristics. Similarly, her direct opposites—"woman folly," "woman stranger," and the adulteress—represent every form of evil opposed by God. In all likelihood, "woman wisdom" was modeled after the real roles of teacher, counselor, and household planner that Israelite women played in their homes and societies.

The wife of noble character certainly fits this description. In fact, as 31:11 reveals, her husband puts his "full confidence in her." His trust is entirely appropriate, resulting in a greatly enriched life for him, her, and their entire family. Such a wife never lets her loved ones down. In fact, the gain they experience from her seems more bountiful than the spoils of war (in a manner of speaking).

The idealized woman contributes what is wholesome and prosperous, in contrast to what is hurtful and harmful (vs. 12). She is the paragon of wisdom, which is characterized by goodness, as opposed to folly, which is known for its evil ways. These sentiments are not theoretical abstractions. As verse 13 reveals, the virtuous wife is hardworking and diligent in her domestic activities and business endeavors, which includes obtaining wool and flax to do her work.

In turn, the wife of noble character pursues her labors with eagerness and enthusiasm. Moreover, she takes pleasure in shouldering her responsibilities. Like a merchant ship, she travels here and there, whether near or far, to acquire whatever food her family needs (vs. 14). She turns out to be an industrious and capable woman who plans ahead to ensure her loved ones are never in want.

Verses 15-24 give further details about the energy and foresight of this amazing woman. She talks to outsiders with skill and prudence as she goes about her daily responsibilities. This frees up her husband to invest his time sitting in the city gates as a civic leader. The virtuous wife is just as concerned for the poor and needy as she is for her own family. Such typifies the inclusive, caring nature of divine wisdom.

C. Known for Wisdom and Courage: vss. 25-27

She is clothed with strength and dignity; she can laugh at the days to come. She speaks with wisdom, and faithful instruction is on her tongue. She watches over the affairs of her household and does not eat the bread of idleness.

Like the finest of garments adorning monarchs, the noble woman is "clothed with strength and dignity" (Prov. 31:25). She is an honorable person in every respect, regardless of whether it concerns ethical integrity, intellectual prowess, or social influence. Underlying all the virtues and talents of this wife is a tough and graceful character.

Though such an idealized wife is a realist when it comes to life, she is not pessimistic about the future. Because she has planned carefully and worked tirelessly on behalf of her family, she can face the days ahead with joy. And regardless of the events to come, she remains cheerful and confident.

When the virtuous woman opens her mouth, she utters words of wisdom. Likewise, kind and loving "instruction is on her tongue" (vs. 26). Her teaching is consistently sensible and thoughtful. All who are graced by it can see her unwavering faithfulness and devotion to the Lord as well as her family.

This is no "ivory tower theologian" (as the saying goes). The wife of noble character is fully engaged in the ongoing matters of life. For instance, she oversees the activities of her large, complex household and is not guilty of being lazy (which is the idea behind trying to obtain food for oneself and others through "idleness"; vs. 27). She remains an innovative, hardworking member of society, even though she might be affluent by the prevailing standards of her day.

D. Esteemed for a God-centered Life: vss. 28-30

Her children arise and call her blessed; her husband also, and he praises her: "Many women do noble things, but you surpass them all." Charm is deceptive, and beauty is fleeting; but a woman who fears the LORD is to be praised.

The virtuous woman enjoys the esteem of her loved ones for her God-centered life. For example, she is so respected that her children stand up in her presence and "call her blessed" (Prov. 11:28). Likewise, her husband offers his praises. In particular, he declares that, while the world is filled with many upstanding and capable women, his wife exceeds them all (vs. 29). In other words, she was the "best of the best" (so to speak) when it came to being wise and upright.

Part of the idealized wife's success was her eternal perspective on life. She was not fooled by the deceptive nature of charm or distracted by the fleeting character of physical beauty (vs. 30). In the words of 1 Peter 3, her attractiveness did not come from "outward adornment" (vs. 3) but from a "gentle and quiet spirit" (vs. 4). In brief, her inner spiritual life was the foundation for all she planned, said, and did.

The culminating virtue of the noble woman was the fear of the Lord (Prov. 31:30). Her reverence for and worship of God was the ultimate reason she deserved to be praised by others. As with all who were wise (see 1:7; 2:5; 9:10), honoring the Lord was the starting point and the high point of the life of the virtuous wife. In fact, this respect for Yahweh is what sets biblical wisdom apart from all its wordly counterparts. Those who truly fear God, like the noble woman of Proverbs 31, have a deep awareness of His sovereignty and power. Accordingly, they revere Him in awe and obey Him unconditionally.

When others recognize spiritual wisdom within us, they will develop a deep respect for us. That is the way to promotion and honor for them. There will be a graciousness about us that cannot be ignored. As a result, a "garland of grace" (4:9) and a "crown of splendor" are promised to those exalting wisdom. In contrast, those who choose to live foolishly and selfishly will be viewed as shameful and unattractive. They will not know the respect and honor they could experience if their lives reflected godliness.

What stops many Christians from desiring wisdom and being willing to search for it? Perhaps it is related to our inability to comprehend fully those rewards associated with upright, virtuous living until we begin to experience them. The poem to the noble wife describes a diligent effort to be prudent and discerning. The spiritual blessings that accrue in this life and the one to follow are indescribable. May we not miss out on them due to ignorance or neglect.

Discussion Questions

1. Why should God's people reach out to those who are less fortunate?
2. In what ways can believers defend the rights of the poor?
3. What is the heart attitude of the capable wife of Proverbs 31?
4. Which qualities of the capable wife do you find most appealing and why?
5. What would life be like if we did not seek to emulate the virtues of the capable wife presented in this chapter?

Contemporary Application

The ode to the noble woman found in Proverbs 31 reminds us of how commendable it is for the Lord's people to possess and exercise wisdom in helpful ways that please and honor Him. When considering this subject, though, it is important to distinguish the difference between prudence and cleverness. Far too often the two are lumped together as though they were the same concept.

Cleverness is usually associated with that which has the appearance of craftiness, slyness, and cunning. In the Book of Esther, Haman is a good example of one who was wily and cagey. He endeavored to manipulate the unjust death of Mordecai on the gallows he had made for the occasion. Thankfully Hanam's scheme failed, and he ended up being hung on his own gallows by the command of King Ahasuerus.

Wisdom, in contrast, has to do with sound judgment, common sense, and understanding that is true and right. Such godly prudence, however, should not be confused with mere knowledge. It is quite possible for one to have an encyclopedic recall of information and not use it in discerning, constructive ways. In fact, the writer of Ecclesiastes recognized that apart from God those who increase in knowledge increase sorrow (1:18).

It has been said that learning will not alter people's natural dispositions or sinful habits. It must be clear that knowledge, or what we might call worldly wisdom, is not something that will necessarily bring about good results. After all, it is possible for someone to use his or her knowledge to produce calamities. Moreover, having knowledge alone does not necessarily mean things will be done properly or people will benefit from it. That's why believers are to seek God's wisdom (see Jas. 1:5).

As God's children, we should embrace the wisdom that He gives to us and use it for His glory. In His wisdom we find happiness and understanding. In fact, the more self is out of the way, the greater will be our service to Him. When we avail ourselves of what God has promised, we are better able to fulfill His divine plan for us. It is a marvelous experience to be part of the working of the Lord's wisdom and to be a recipient of it.

Called to Be a Christian Community

Servants of Unity

DEVOTIONAL READING

1 Corinthians 1:2-9

DAILY BIBLE READINGS

Monday May 29
*Romans 10:9-13 God Is
Lord of All*

Tuesday May 30
*Colossians 1:15-20 We Are
Reconciled in Christ*

Wednesday May 31
*Ephesians 4:1-6 One Body
and One Spirit*

Thursday June 1
*1 Corinthians 1:1-9 Called
Together in Christ*

Friday June 2
*1 Corinthians 1:10-17 Be
United in Christ*

Saturday June 3
*1 Corinthians 1:18-25 We
Proclaim Christ Crucified
to All*

Sunday June 4
*1 Corinthians 1:26-31 God
Brings Us to Christ*

Scripture

Background Scripture: *1 Corinthians 1:10-17*
Scripture Lesson: *1 Corinthians 1:10-17*
Key Verse: *I appeal to you, brothers, in the name of our Lord
Jesus Christ, that all of you agree with one another so that
there may be no divisions among you and that you may be
perfectly united in mind and thought.* 1 Corinthians 1:10.
Scripture Lesson for Children: *Genesis 33:1-11;
1 Corinthians 1:10*
Key Verse for Children: *Be at peace with each other.*
Mark 9:50.

Lesson Aim

To emphasize that focusing on Christ will result in
unity.

Lesson Setting

Time: *A.D. 55*
Place: *Ephesus*

Lesson Outline

Servants of Unity

   I. Divisions in the Church: 1 Corinthians 1:10-12
      A. *The Appeal for Unity: vs. 10*
      B. *The Presence of Factions: vss. 11-12*
  II. Allegiance to Christ: 1 Corinthians 1:13-17
      A. *Christ's United Spiritual Body: vs. 13*
      B. *Christ's Supremacy in All Situations: vss. 14-16*
      C. *Paul's Proclamation of the Gospel: vs. 17*

Introduction for Adults

Topic: *Living in Unity*

Charles Swindoll tells the story he heard about two unmarried sisters who lived together in the same small house. When they had a minor disagreement with each other over a very small issue, they decided not to speak to each other anymore. For years they lived this way, coming and going, eating and sleeping, sewing and reading, but never speaking. Neither was willing to take the first step toward reconciliation or forgiveness.

Sound ridiculous? What about churches where factions sit on opposite sides of the aisle, or part of the congregation meets upstairs while the other part meets in the basement? Or what about one group forming an entirely new church when a congregation disagrees about the color of the church carpet?

Paul had heard about the divisions occurring in the new church he had helped to start in Corinth. So he wrote to them and urged them to set aside their differences and divisions and find unity of mind and heart in Christ. It is a message worth repeating in many divided, and divisive, congregations today.

Introduction for Youth

Topic: *Let's Get Together!*

God has made us all with differing temperaments and differing backgrounds that result in our differing viewpoints. The many denominations and church bodies within Christianity today testify to believers' differing perspectives and convictions about everything from the finer points of theology to differing styles of worship.

So how can we ever hope to get along with each other? It's by remembering that the most essential thing—our unity in Christ—takes precedence over every other thing. In church meetings we need to hear the words "Jesus would want us to . . ." rather than "I think I should . . ." The two statements are not the same.

Concepts for Children

Topic: *Be Peaceful*

1. It was difficult for Esau and Jacob to talk after Jacob stole Esau's birthright.
2. Jacob did not know what to expect when he returned to the land of promise after being away for many years.
3. Once Jacob and Esau met again, they were at peace with one another.
4. The account of Jacob and Esau teaches us the difficulty that arises when one person takes advantage of another person.
5. Paul appealed to the Corinthians and to us today to put away any divisions among ourselves and to become united in our thoughts and actions.

The Lesson Commentary

I. DIVISIONS IN THE CHURCH: 1 CORINTHIANS 1:10-12

A. The Appeal for Unity: vs. 10

I appeal to you, brothers, in the name of our Lord Jesus Christ, that all of you agree with one another so that there may be no divisions among you and that you may be perfectly united in mind and thought.

Paul had established the church at Corinth during his second missionary journey (Acts 18:1-18; A.D. 49–52). Not long after he had left, arguments and divisions arose in the congregation, and some of its members had slipped back into an immoral lifestyle. Paul eventually had to write 1 Corinthians to deal with these problems, clear up any confusion that existed about right and wrong, and answer some questions his readers had about certain issues.

The city of Corinth was located on a narrow isthmus of land in southern Greece about 45 miles from Athens, in the Roman province of Achaia. The lower portion of Greece is connected to the rest of the country by this four-mile-wide isthmus, so all the traffic between the two areas of the country passed by Corinth.

The isthmus was bounded on the east by the Saronic Gulf and on the west by the Gulf of Corinth. Sea captains could literally have their ships rolled across the isthmus on a stone tramway and avoid a 250-mile trip around southern Greece. Consequently, the city prospered as a major trade center, not only for most of Greece but also for much of the Mediterranean area, including North Africa, Italy, and Asia Minor.

Nearby Isthmia hosted the Isthmian games, one of two major athletic events of the day (the other being the Olympic games). This activity created more people-traffic through Corinth and thus increased potential for business and prosperity. Along with material abundance came wickedness and vice, and the presence of such made it difficult for the believers in the city to resist behaving in the same manner as their peers.

Faced with such a challenge, the young church was beginning to experience a variety of dangerous problems. To address these issues, Christian conduct became the central focus of Paul's correspondence to the Corinthians. We can surmise from 16:8 that the apostle wrote this letter from Ephesus during his third missionary journey (A.D. 53–57). Since Paul stayed in Ephesus over two years (Acts 19:8, 10), he likely penned the epistle around A.D. 55.

In 1 Corinthians 1:1-9, the apostle greeted his readers in Corinth, reminded them of his apostleship, and refreshed their memory of their call to be holy. Paul also thanked God for their blessings and assured them that God would keep them strong in the faith. Just as the Corinthian believers could count on God's faithfulness, so we can depend on His being faithful to us regardless of our situation or circumstances.

We can infer from the previous verses that 1 Corinthians is a personal letter. In that day, epistles normally started with an introduction that listed the names of the sender and the recipients. Next came a formal greeting in which thanksgiving was expressed, followed by the body, or purpose for writing. The letter usually concluded with appropriate remarks and a farewell.

Paul's Corinthian letter followed this pattern, though he replaced the typical bland greeting with a salutation combining Christian grace and Hebrew peace. His thanksgiving was also more than a formality. It was a sincere expression of gratitude for the well-being of this congregation. His farewell contained personal greetings and a benediction.

Though the believers at Corinth were abundantly gifted (vs. 7), major shortcomings existed within their ranks. Perhaps the chief issue plaguing the congregation was the people's divisiveness and quarreling (vs. 10). Though Paul had the apostolic authority to give out commands to the Corinthians, he instead appealed to them as fellow believers in Christ. The apostle urged them, as those living under Jesus' lordship, to stop arguing among themselves and cultivate harmony, rather than hostility, in their church. Paul also implored them to be of one mind, whether it involved their thoughts, plans, or actions.

The problem that faced the Corinthians is a common issue today. It is easy for believers to become divided over inconsequential points of doctrine, vague philosophical musings, or even the time of the weekly worship service. Such barriers prevent real unity and fellowship from occurring. As long as such points of tension exist in a congregation, that fellowship will be crippled in its effectiveness to tell those who are not a part of the church about the Savior.

B. The Presence of Factions: vss. 11-12

My brothers, some from Chloe's household have informed me that there are quarrels among you. What I mean is this: One of you says, "I follow Paul"; another, "I follow Apollos"; another, "I follow Cephas"; still another, "I follow Christ."

The congregation Paul established in Corinth included both Jews and Gentiles, higher classes and lower classes, free persons and slaves. Upon the apostle's departure, the philosophical, sexual, and religious temptations of the city took their toll on many of the new Christians, and after a while, began to break down the unity of the church.

The situation in Corinth, however, rather than improving became grave. The apostle learned from members of Chloe's household that quarrels had arisen from among the members of the church (1 Cor. 1:11). Chloe was a Christian woman who lived either in Corinth or in Ephesus, the latter being the place where Paul resided when he wrote his epistle.

Regrettably, the believers began favoring different ministers (vs. 12). Some followed Paul, their spiritual parent, whole others favored Peter. Still others listened only to Apollos, an eloquent preacher who had ministered in Corinth after Paul left (Acts 18:24—19:1). Even today some choose to revere prominent Christian leaders in a way better reserved for Jesus. Rather than being followers of Christ, they have become overly devoted to a magnetic personality. Naturally, when this occurs, as it did in Corinth, disharmony and rivalry arise within the church.

At first glance, Paul may seem to contradict himself when he scolds one group for saying they follow Christ (1 Cor. 1:12) after urging all the groups to be united in the Savior (vs. 10); however, it is possible that this group thought they were superior to the others by claiming to follow Jesus. They may have believed that their pride-filled allegiance to Him made them better than those who claimed to follow the teachings of merely human leaders such as Paul and Apollos.

II. ALLEGIANCE TO CHRIST: 1 CORINTHIANS 1:13-17

A. Christ's United Spiritual Body: vs. 13

Is Christ divided? Was Paul crucified for you? Were you baptized into the name of Paul?

The Corinthian believers had lost sight of the source of their unity. They had become divided over which one of their spiritual teachers they liked most. Because the entire New Testament had not yet been written, they had to depend heavily on the preaching and teaching of people such as Paul, Peter, and Apollos for the gospel message and spiritual insight into the Old Testament. Inevitably, different believers were attracted to certain personalities, leading to arguments and schisms in the church.

In 1 Corinthians 1:13, Paul asked his readers a series of rhetorical questions to get them to think seriously about the implications of their actions. For instance, the congregants were guilty of trying to divide the spiritual body of Christ. The apostle, however, wanted them to realize that while God used different people to proclaim the Gospel, they were all united in their message and focused on pointing people to Christ.

The apostle's main point was that the body of Christ was never intended to be divided into fractured groups. To underscore his point, Paul used himself as an example. It was not the apostle who was crucified on behalf of sinners; rather, Jesus was sacrificed to pay for sins. Likewise, the Corinthians had been baptized into the name of Christ, not Paul. Expressed differently, they had become identified with Jesus and spiritually united with His people. Thus they were to be followers of Christ, not of some infinitely less significant person.

B. Christ's Supremacy in All Situations: vss. 14-16

I am thankful that I did not baptize any of you except Crispus and Gaius, so no one can say that you were baptized into my name. (Yes, I also baptized the household of Stephanas; beyond that, I don't remember if I baptized anyone else.)

As Paul reflected on his ministry at Corinth, he recalled only baptizing two believers there, Crispus and Gaius (1 Cor. 1:14). Crispus had once been a ruler of the Jewish synagogue at Corinth. When he heard Paul proclaim the Gospel, Crispus trusted in Jesus as the Messiah, and so did the household of Crispus (Acts 18:8).

Some think Gaius was the person who hosted Paul when he wrote the letter to the Romans (Rom. 16:23).

Tragically, the recipients of Paul's letter to the Corinthians had taken to identifying with their spiritual mentors rather than Christ. That is why the apostle deemphasized the baptisms he performed while among the Corinthians (1 Cor. 1:15). Paul was not minimizing the importance of baptism, but rather was emphasizing the supremacy of the Savior in all situations.

Upon further reflection, the apostle also remembered baptizing the household of Stephanas (vs. 16). The latter was a member of the church at Corinth. According to 16:15, those in his household were the first converts in Achaia (southern Greece) and among the few whom Paul had baptized; but beyond these believers the apostle did not recall baptizing anyone else.

C. Paul's Proclamation of the Gospel: vs. 17

For Christ did not send me to baptize, but to preach the gospel—not with words of human wisdom, lest the cross of Christ be emptied of its power.

The solution to the Corinthians' problem was to shift their attention away from prominent leaders and back to the Messiah. This did not depreciate the value of those who led them. It just meant that no one could replace Christ and be given more prominence than Him.

Accordingly, Paul realized his place in the church; and that is why he declared his thankfulness for restricting the number of baptisms he had performed in Corinth. Moreover, the apostle did not want this ministry to be a cause of divisions. He also did not want anyone to claim having been baptized in his name, and as a result, promote discord among the Corinthian believers.

Paul sensed that his chief calling was not to baptize people (1 Cor. 1:17). His intent in making such a statement was not to minimize the importance of baptism; rather, he was stating that his main goal was to proclaim the Gospel.

Regarding Paul's preaching, he wrote that his words were not based on clever speech and ingenious salesmanship, but on the redemptive power of Jesus' death at Calvary. Put another way, it was Christ—not eloquent Bible teachers—who alone died to atone for the sins of the lost.

Paul knew that many of the Corinthians were enamored by worldly wisdom. Thus the apostle's words contained an implicit warning. His readers were not to be impressed with empty rhetoric and deceptive arguments and thereby miss the simple message of the cross of Christ.

These statements do not mean Paul was against those who carefully prepared what they said; rather, he was against those who tried to impress others with their knowledge or speaking ability. Thus, the apostle heralded the truth of redemption in plain language so that the cross would not be emptied of its power to save.

Discussion Questions

1. Why did Paul emphasize unity of thought and decision-making among the Corinthians?
2. What was the nature of the divisions that plagued the church at Corinth?
3. Why do you think the recipients of Paul's letter had allowed themselves to give more prominence to magnetic personalities than to the Savior?
4. What effect do you think the presence of schisms among the Corinthians would have had on the proclamation of the Gospel?
5. Why did Paul refrain from using clever speech when he proclaimed the Gospel?

Contemporary Application

I have listened to college students who were studying to be pastors fervently debate the finer points of theology. Then I have seen those same students worship together later in a spirit of unity and love.

I have also been part of a church congregational meeting called to vote on the starting time of the morning worship service. I saw a ballot on which one voter wrote that if his or her preferred time was not selected, he or she would no longer be attending the church! Other such sentiments circulated. A few people even insisted that one of the times on the ballot was more spiritual than the others, because it was more conducive to families with small children. Tempers flared. Relationships became strained. It was ugly.

What is the difference between these two examples? Was there more at stake in one situation than the other? Perhaps. But the real difference lies in the focus and attitudes of the "combatants." The college students recognized that while a group of believers will not always agree on every issue, they can work together harmoniously because of their common faith in the lordship of Christ. From this we see that inconsequential differences should never divide believers.

Servants of Wisdom

DEVOTIONAL READING

Ephesians 1:15-21

DAILY BIBLE READINGS

Monday June 5
*James 1:2-8 Faith and
Wisdom*

Tuesday June 6
*James 3:13-18 Two Kinds of
Wisdom*

Wednesday June 7
*Ephesians 1:15-21 A Spirit
of Wisdom*

Thursday June 8
*Colossians 1:24-29 Warn
and Teach Everyone in
Wisdom*

Friday June 9
*1 Corinthians 2:1-5 Faith
Not Based on Human
Wisdom*

Saturday June 10
*1 Corinthians 2:6-10 We
Speak God's Wisdom*

Sunday June 11
*1 Corinthians 2:11-16
Words Not Taught by
Human Wisdom*

Scripture

Background Scripture: *1 Corinthians 2*
Scripture Lesson: *1 Corinthians 2:1, 6-16*
Key Verse: *This is what we speak, not in words taught us by human wisdom but in words taught by the Spirit, expressing spiritual truths in spiritual words.* 1 Corinthians 2:13.
Scripture Lesson for Children: *Luke 15:1-10;
1 Corinthians 1:9*
Key Verse for Children: *Trust in the LORD with all your heart.* Proverbs 3:5.

Lesson Aim

To stress that the Spirit of God brings discernment to believers.

Lesson Setting

Time: *A.D. 55*
Place: *Ephesus*

Lesson Outline

Servants of Wisdom

   I. Power from God: 1 Corinthians 2:1

  II. Wisdom from the Spirit: 1 Corinthians 2:6-16

      A. *The Wisdom of God Concealed: vss. 6-7*

      B. *The Wisdom of God Revealed: vss. 8-10a*

      C. *The Omniscience of the Spirit: vss. 10b-11*

      D. *The Truths of the Spirit Revealed and Explained:
vss. 12-13*

      E. *The Spiritual Ignorance of the Unsaved: vs. 14*

      F. *The Spiritual Insight of the Saved: vss. 15-16*

Introduction for Adults

Topic: *Finding Wisdom*

"What will this book do for you? . . . Strong, honest, lasting relationships, less anxiety, and a general sense of contentment all should emerge. . . . These techniques will improve your quality of life." Is this an advertisement for the Bible? No. How about for a Christian counseling manual? Guess again.

The previous excerpt was taken from the introduction to *Don't Be a Chump! Negotiating Skills You Need,* by Nick Schaffzin, which promises to give its readers the ability to: turn the tables on more powerful partners; know other people's needs better than they do; and play hardball.

Many seemingly well-intentioned books run contrary to biblical wisdom. In Schaffzin's hardball world, Christians might appear to be Nerf Ball players. After all, our Savior hasn't promised to make us masterful manipulators. He's pledged to make us discerning disciples.

Introduction for Youth

Topic: *The Gift of True Wisdom*

For many teens the wisdom teachings found in Scripture seem vague, distant, and mysterious. This remains so despite their well-intentioned efforts to understand Christian beliefs and habits. Although some can appreciate the sound of the language or the "nice" sentiments, much of it feels as if it were written in a foreign language. They just don't get it.

What's the reason for this confusion? Unless adolescents (as well as anyone else) have the Spirit living in them, much of the Christian life will be incomprehensible to them. God's Spirit makes true wisdom and understanding possible. It is like having a key that can unlock the mystery of faith.

Concepts for Children

Topic: *Trust God*

1. The story of the lost sheep illustrates how God seeks a lasting relationship with people.
2. Jesus taught this parable because of grumbling about the nature of His ministry.
3. God never stops loving us and is always faithful to us.
4. Each person is precious to God, just as the one lost sheep was important to the shepherd and the one lost coin was important to the woman who lost it.
5. When a person abandons sin and trusts in Jesus, it is a cause for rejoicing.

The Lesson Commentary

I. POWER FROM GOD: 1 CORINTHIANS 2:1

When I came to you, brothers, I did not come with eloquence or superior wisdom as I proclaimed to you the testimony about God.

Although Luke said nothing in Acts about Paul's correspondence to the Corinthians, Luke did provide some background information about the founding of the church during Paul's second missionary journey (A.D. 50–52). Paul had come to Macedonia (northern Greece) after a vision he had in Troas (Acts 16:8-10). He established churches in Philippi, Thessalonica, and Berea before heading to Athens. Paul came to Corinth (18:1) after his visit to Athens (17:16-34), an experience that had impressed him with the foolishness of worldly wisdom.

With the support of an influential couple named Priscilla and Aquila (18:2), Paul preached in the synagogue at Corinth until Jewish opposition forced him to focus his ministry on the Gentiles. As a result of the apostle leading a number of people to faith in Christ, a church was established (consisting of both Jews and Gentiles) and soon began to grow (vss. 8-10). Paul's ministry in Corinth lasted a fairly long time (more than 18 months; vss. 11, 18), and he accomplished much while in the city.

In the eyes of unbelievers, the Corinthian Christians were fools. Few if any of them were intellectually impressive, according to the sophisticated society of the day (1 Cor. 1:26). Perhaps that is why they were tempted to incorporate some aspects of Greek philosophy into their belief systems. To do so would give them a more respected status within their society. Paul affirmed that most of his readers were lowly, powerless people; but the apostle reminded them that God had revealed to them wisdom in the person of His Son (vss. 27-31).

The believers at Corinth had discovered this wisdom through Paul's preaching. Like them, the apostle had found significance in Christ. Paul explained that when he had first ministered in Corinth, he had not attempted to persuade the people in a way that would call attention to himself; rather, he had spoken simply and straightforwardly as he declared the truths of God (2:1).

If superior eloquence and wisdom were not responsible for Paul's success in Corinth, then how could it be explained? It was not due to physical and emotional wellness, for the apostle arrived in the city in a run-down, discouraged state (vs. 3). Ultimately, the conversions in Corinth could be traced to the Holy Spirit working powerfully through Paul as he proclaimed the crucifixion (and resurrection) of Christ (vss. 2, 4). Thus, what had occurred was a work of God, not being based on human wisdom (vs. 5).

Throughout 1 Corinthians 2, we find a contrast between divine wisdom and human wisdom. The former is the ability to evaluate a range of options and to follow the best course of action. One's decision is based on biblical knowledge and understanding (Prov. 2:6). In contrast, human wisdom uses philosophy and reasoning to fathom the mysteries of existence and the universe.

Whereas people with mere human wisdom may brag about how much they know, those with divine wisdom humble themselves before the Lord in reverence and worship (1:7; 11:2). The worldly wise flaunt authority and live for themselves, while the divinely wise heed the laws of the land and obey God (17:24; Jas. 3:13-18).

II. WISDOM FROM THE SPIRIT: 1 CORINTHIANS 2:6-16

A. The Wisdom of God Concealed: vss. 6-7

We do, however, speak a message of wisdom among the mature, but not the wisdom of this age or of the rulers of this age, who are coming to nothing. No, we speak of God's secret wisdom, a wisdom that has been hidden and that God destined for our glory before time began.

Paul had previously argued that the success of the Gospel cannot be attributed to the skill of its messengers, nor is it reliant upon what the world calls "wisdom." Now the apostle shifted his emphasis and showed that the Good News is based on wisdom after all—a higher wisdom, the wisdom of God. Moreover, Paul contrasted the wisdom of God with the wisdom of the world. Thus when the apostle had been critical of wisdom earlier in his letter, he had been referring to human wisdom and not God's wisdom.

Paul spoke God's wisdom among those who were "mature" (1 Cor. 2:6) Christians. They were the ones who had believed his message. This wisdom belongs neither to this world nor to this world's rulers, who in any case have only temporary power. The wisdom of God, in fact, is seen in the cross of Christ, the meaning of which was and still is hidden from the world but has been made known to believers in the Messiah.

The apostle declared that he and his associates heralded "God's secret wisdom" (vs. 7). The idea is that previously the Gospel had been unknown and obscure, for people had not fully understood it. Moreover, before the world began, God decreed His redemptive plan and program for our eternal benefit and glory. Now that Christ had been raised from the dead, the Holy Spirit empowered ministers such as Paul to explain what Jesus had done.

B. The Wisdom of God Revealed: vss. 8-10a

None of the rulers of this age understood it, for if they had, they would not have crucified the Lord of glory. However, as it is written: "No eye has seen, no ear has heard, no mind has conceived what God has prepared for those who love him"— but God has revealed it to us by his Spirit.

The central truth of Paul's preaching was that God had determined to save sinners and bring many into His glory through the crucifixion of Jesus. For a time, though, God had kept this truth a mystery. Indeed, if the rulers of this age—such as the chief priests, Pilate, and Herod Antipas—had understood the divine plan of salvation, they would not have crucified Christ. Paul's reference to Him as "the Lord of glory" (1 Cor. 2:8) underscores His status as the divine Messiah.

The apostle was possibly thinking about Isaiah 64:4 and 65:17 when he said no one had seen or heard of such a marvelous plan of salvation. Indeed, no one had conceived of the good things God had prepared for those who love Him (1 Cor. 2:9). Paul noted that what was once a mystery became revealed to believers through God's Spirit (vs. 10a).

C. The Omniscience of the Spirit: vss. 10b-11

The Spirit searches all things, even the deep things of God. For who among men knows the thoughts of a man except the man's spirit within him? In the same way no one knows the thoughts of God except the Spirit of God.

Only the Holy Spirit understands the wisdom of God and can convey that wisdom to us. Thankfully, it is not secret knowledge reserved only for a select and privileged few; instead, God freely discloses His former mysteries to all believers in Christ through His Spirit.

Paul explained that the Spirit searches all things, including the deep things of God (1 Cor. 2:10). The apostle did not mean that the Spirit literally searches to discover divine truth. After all, the Spirit is Himself divine and He already knows all things; instead, Paul was saying that the Holy Spirit *comprehends* God's essence, His attributes, and His redemptive plans for those who trust Christ as Savior and Lord.

Paul used an analogy to illustrate the Holy Spirit's knowledge of God (vs. 11). No one can give an accurate reading of what goes on inside a person—all the emotions, thoughts, and desires—except that person's own spirit. Likewise, no one can understand what is taking place within the mind of God except the Spirit of God. The Spirit knows God intimately, as no human can; and it is only the Spirit who leads believers into a truly personal knowledge of God.

D. The Truths of the Spirit Revealed and Explained: vss. 12-13

We have not received the spirit of the world but the Spirit who is from God, that we may understand what God has freely given us. This is what we speak, not in words taught us by human wisdom but in words taught by the Spirit, expressing spiritual truths in spiritual words.

Paul related that God has given His Spirit, not the world's spirit, to believers. The Holy Spirit in turn teaches us the wonderful things God has freely bestowed on us. Salvation in the Messiah is one of the Lord's supreme gifts, and it is made available to all who receive it by faith. This was an important truth that Paul was making to the Corinthians. The wisdom that he shared with them was from the Spirit of God (1 Cor. 2:12).

Conversely, what the apostle had taught the Corinthians was not based on human wisdom. This is evident by the statement "expressing spiritual truths in spiritual words" (vs. 13). This obscure phrase has been understood in various ways; for example, it could signify comparing one spiritual reality with another spiritual reality, interpreting spiritual truths to those who are spiritual, or explaining spiritual concepts in spiritual language.

Regardless of which option is preferred, Paul's main point is clear. The Spirit is the source of divine truth. Additionally, the spiritual truths mature believers receive from Him they pass on. This in turn enables spiritual growth to occur within individuals and within the church.

E. The Spiritual Ignorance of the Unsaved: vs. 14

The man without the Spirit does not accept the things that come from the Spirit of God, for they are foolishness to him, and he cannot understand them, because they are spiritually discerned.

The "man without the Spirit" (1 Cor. 2:14) refers to unbelievers. The main difference between them and Christians is who or what directs their lives. Unbelievers are steered by their own fallen inclinations.

Because non-Christians depend solely on wisdom derived from the world, they refuse to receive or accept the gifts of God's Spirit. In fact, what the Spirit graciously offers (especially, salvation in Christ) seems foolish to unbelievers. Furthermore, they do not fully appreciate what Christ offers because such can only be spiritually examined, discerned, and appropriated through the Spirit. As long as unbelievers reject the assistance of the Spirit, they remain spiritually blind.

F. The Spiritual Insight of the Saved: vss. 15-16

The spiritual man makes judgments about all things, but he himself is not subject to any man's judgment: "For who has known the mind of the Lord that he may instruct him?" But we have the mind of Christ.

In contrast to people who rely on worldly wisdom, Christians are dominated by the Holy Spirit's presence within them. The Spirit instructs, enlightens, regulates, and guides believers. Therefore, people who are controlled by the Holy Spirit are able to evaluate the worth of all things through the discernment He gives.

Moreover, Christians are not subject to the scrutiny and condemnation of unbelievers. After all, the latter have no insight into the things of the Spirit, especially what it means to trust in Christ for salvation and live by faith in Him (1 Cor. 2:15). Some claim that, as Christians, they are beyond the counsel or discipline of other believers; but the fact that Paul was writing to the Corinthian believers to reprove them undercuts this idea.

To substantiate his claim that unbelievers are not qualified to judge believers regarding spiritual matters, Paul referred to a rhetorical question written by the prophet Isaiah (vs. 16). Paul may have also quoted Isaiah 40:13 to illustrate his earlier point that the mystery of God's salvation had been revealed through the cross of Christ.

All those who believe that Jesus' crucifixion (and resurrection) has brought them salvation can comprehend spiritual truths in a manner similar to the way Christ Himself understands them; and because the Holy Spirit has made these truths known to believers, they genuinely have the "mind of Christ" (1 Cor. 2:16). In addition, with the Spirit's help, believers remain in tune with the Lord's thoughts and will.

Discussion Questions

1. In what sense is God's wisdom directed to mature believers?
2. In what way is God's wisdom a mystery?
3. If brilliant unbelievers are unable to fathom divine wisdom, how are Christians able to do so?
4. Why do the unsaved refuse to accept the things freely offered by the Spirit?
5. What does it mean for believers to have the mind of Christ?

Contemporary Application

It is tragically commonplace these days for a gifted speaker with questionable motives and dubious biblical views to win a following and gradually substitute his or her own authority for that of Scripture. That is how most religious cults gain a toehold in society. Christians need to evaluate the teaching we hear, making certain that it is grounded in God's Word and honors Christ.

It is not enough just to disregard bad teachers, but we should also listen to good teachers. From the latter we learn how to be faithful to God, how to be more like Christ, and how to serve Him. Good teachers will help us comprehend these things of God.

Growth toward maturity also requires us to set aside time for individual Bible reading. When we look into Scripture for ourselves, the Holy Spirit makes us aware of God's purposes and plans. As the Spirit illuminates Scripture, we receive guidance about making an important decision or find strength to take a step that seems difficult. At other times the Spirit gives us fresh insight into a character quality of God or we are jarred into dealing with some issue that is hindering our spiritual growth.

None of these things occur because we are especially shrewd or astute. They come to us through the help of the Holy Spirit, who understands the deep things of God and reveals His ways to those who seek them.

Servants Together

DEVOTIONAL READING

Matthew 13:3-9

DAILY BIBLE READINGS

Monday June 12
Matthew 13:3-9 Spreading God's Word

Tuesday June 13
Matthew 13:24-30 Growing Together

Wednesday June 14
Hebrews 5:7-14 The Need for Teachers

Thursday June 15
Ephesians 3:14-21 Strengthened with Power through the Spirit

Friday June 16
1 Corinthians 3:1-9 Servants Through Whom You Believe

Saturday June 17
1 Corinthians 3:10-15 Building on the Foundation of Christ

Sunday June 18
1 Corinthians 3:16-23 Do Not Boast about Human Leaders

Scripture

Background Scripture: *1 Corinthians 3:1-15*
Scripture Lesson: *1 Corinthians 3:1-15*
Key Verse: *For we are God's fellow workers; you are God's field, God's building.* 1 Corinthians 3:9.
Scripture Lesson for Children: *Matthew 7:24-27; 1 Corinthians 3:10-11*
Key Verse for Children: *Do not merely listen to the word, and so deceive yourselves. Do what it says.* James 1:22.

Lesson Aim

To underscore the importance of cooperation in ministry.

Lesson Setting

Time: A.D. 55
Place: *Ephesus*

Lesson Outline

Servants Together

  I. Spiritual Immaturity in the Church: 1 Corinthians 3:1-4
    A. *Infants in the Christian Life: vs. 1*
    B. *Spiritual Milk, Not Solid Food: vs. 2*
    C. *Worldly Living: vss. 3-4*
  II. Partnership in Ministry: 1 Corinthians 3:5-15
    A. *God Working through Believers: vss. 5-6*
    B. *Joint Ministry and Individual Rewards: vss. 7-9*
    C. *Christ as the Foundation of the Church: vss. 10-11*
    D. *Accountability at Christ's Return: vss. 12-15*

Introduction for Adults

Topic: *Building Together*

In his book *The Making of a Leader,* Chua Wee Hian uses a chart to contrast the nature of secular and servant authority. We might call the difference between self-led and Spirit-controlled leadership.

Secular authority prizes (among other things) giving orders, seeking personal advancement, and receiving the service of others. In contrast, servant authority values loving obedience, seeking what's best for others, and desiring to serve others.

Which of these approaches would your students say can move their church toward Christian unity and peace? Obviously, it is leadership based on the servant-authority model. Within our homes and churches, this approach will enable the viewpoints of others to be heard, and the Holy Spirit to have the best opportunity to guide decision making.

Introduction for Youth

Topic: *Faithful Teamwork*

There may be more than 500 different brands of churches in the United States alone. Some are large, multinational denominations serving millions, while others are single churches with fewer than 30 members.

To those outside the church, the sheer variety of Christian "flavors" is an indication that we are a hopelessly fractured bunch who can't agree on what we believe. But despite our different styles and tastes, all of us who have accepted Christ and strive to follow Him share a common goal. We all want to faithfully work together as a team to do God's will. This is a worthwhile aspiration to pass on to your students.

Concepts for Children

Topic: *Obey God's Word*

1. Jesus used the idea of rock and sand to illustrate the need for us to have a proper foundation for living.
2. A good foundation gives stability in difficult times.
3. Each person must build with care on that foundation.
4. Following Christ is like building a house on a solid rock foundation.
5. Jesus wants us to our build lives on the strong foundation of Him and His Word.

The Lesson Commentary

I. SPIRITUAL IMMATURITY IN THE CHURCH: 1 CORINTHIANS 3:1-4

A. Infants in the Christian Life: vs. 1

Brothers, I could not address you as spiritual but as worldly—mere infants in Christ.

Paul had drawn a sharp contrast between persons with the Spirit and those without Him. The apostle desired to write to the Corinthians as people fully controlled by the Spirit. Sadly, however, he could not. Though he addressed his readers as members of his spiritual family, he also wrote with disappointment that their outlook remained worldly.

To make his point, Paul used two contrasting terms rendered "spiritual" and "worldly" (1 Cor. 3:1). When applied to believers, the former referred to those who allowed the Holy Spirit to control their lives. Oppositely, to be worldly means one's life is dominated by the flesh. The apostle was not implying that the human body is evil; instead, he meant that ever since the Fall, human nature is corrupt or sinful.

The focus, then, is the metaphysical realm in which morality and ethics are a concern. Those who operate in harmony with their sinful human nature allow the value system of the world to influence them. Christians are to resist living in this way, for the evil world system reflects the mindset of Satan (Eph. 2:1-3), not that of God (Jas. 4:4; 1 John 2:15-17).

Paul also referred to his readers as being "infants in Christ" (1 Cor. 3:1). By this time the Corinthians should have made considerable progress in their maturity as Christians. Tragically, though, they were like spiritual babes. Each congregant was mostly concerned with himself or herself, rather than one another as well as the Lord Jesus.

In 1 Corinthians, Paul identified three groups of people. The "man without the Spirit" (2:14) is a non-Christian who does not possess the indwelling of the Third Person of the Trinity. These individuals can neither comprehend nor accept the Gospel; and because they see it as foolish, they refuse to apply it to their lives in any way.

Those who are "spiritual" (vs. 15) possess the Holy Spirit and yield themselves to Him; in other words, they are Christians. Because these believers are under the Spirit's control, they are mature, discerning, and Christlike. They are unconditional in their love for others and are willing to put the interests of others above their own.

The "worldly" (3:1) person is a spiritually immature Christian. Although these believers possess the indwelling Holy Spirit, they have not yet yielded themselves to Him in a way that is evident by their behavior. In fact, they exhibit worldly prejudices and viewpoints that are characteristic of non-Christians.

B. Spiritual Milk, Not Solid Food: vs. 2

I gave you milk, not solid food, for you were not yet ready for it. Indeed, you are still not ready.

Paul told his readers that when he first arrived in Corinth to minister to them, he had preached and taught them only the most basic principles of salvation. He did this because they were young in the faith and were not mature enough to comprehend deeper, more profound truths (1 Cor. 3:2).

Paul compared his teaching at that time to feeding infants milk, rather than solid food (such as meat). Because milk is easier for newborns to digest, it is the most appropriate sustenance for them to take in. Over time, however, the digestive system of children physically matures to the point where milk is not the only form of nutrition they consume.

The same is also true spiritually. At some point it is normal for Christians to be mature enough to take in more substantive truths of the faith. In fact, it would be abnormal if all they could handle were the elementary principles found in Scripture (see Heb. 5:11-14).

C. Worldly Living: vss. 3-4

You are still worldly. For since there is jealousy and quarreling among you, are you not worldly? Are you not acting like mere men? For when one says, "I follow Paul," and another, "I follow Apollos," are you not mere men?

It was Paul's desire that the believers in Corinth would have matured in their faith and walk in Christ. If they had grown spiritually, Paul and other church leaders would have taught them more complex spiritual truths. Sadly, however, that had not happened. Even worse, they had remained worldly in their behavior.

Paul backed up this assertion by noting that the Corinthians were plagued by jealously, dissensions, and schisms (1 Cor. 3:3). Their actions indicated that they remained under the influence of their sinful human nature and behaved like ordinary people, that is, those without the Spirit's influence. The apostle particularly noted how his readers bickered over which church leader they would follow (vs. 4). They acted no better than their unsaved peers when they asserted their allegiance to ministers such as Paul or Apollos and thereby fractured the spiritual body of Christ.

II. PARTNERSHIP IN MINISTRY: 1 CORINTHIANS 3:5-15

A. God Working through Believers: vss. 5-6

What, after all, is Apollos? And what is Paul? Only servants, through whom you came to believe—as the Lord has assigned to each his task. I planted the seed, Apollos watered it, but God made it grow.

Paul had no problem with the Corinthians encouraging and supporting their spiritual leaders. What he did have a problem with was their nearly idolizing these leaders. An unhealthy devotion to a particular leader was to be avoided. As part of his explanation, the apostle tried to help the Corinthians realize who people like Apollos and himself were. In short, they were nothing more than God's servants helping people to trust in Christ as their Savior. Each servant performed the task the Lord had assigned him or her to do (1 Cor. 3:5).

Using gardening imagery to convey his meaning, Paul wrote that God had appointed him to plant seeds—in essence, to establish new churches. In contrast, Apollos had been called to water the planted seeds—in essence, to help existing churches grow and mature. Paul and Apollos were fellow workers striving for the same goal; and yet beyond the work of either man was the work of God Himself, who was solely responsible for enabling the church to grow (vs. 6).

B. Joint Ministry and Individual Rewards: vss. 7-9

So neither he who plants nor he who waters is anything, but only God, who makes things grow. The man who plants and the man who waters have one purpose, and each will be rewarded according to his own labor. For we are God's fellow workers; you are God's field, God's building.

In 1 Corinthians 3:7-9 Paul elaborated on what he had told the Corinthians. Although he referred principally to those engaged in full-time Christian ministries, the apostle also conveyed four points about the work of all Christians. First, believers cannot produce any spiritual results on our own (vs. 7). We who plant and water are God's servants, attendants to that which the Lord produces and grows.

Second, though Christians may have various functions in the work of the church, we all have only one ultimate purpose (vs. 8). Thus we have to be unified in our goal and willing to work together to accomplish the divine aim. Third, each believer will be rewarded according to his or her faithfulness in fulfilling a God-given task. Thus, while Christians are to be unified in our endeavor, we are individually responsible to God and will be judged on an individual basis. Fourth, as servants belonging to God, Christians are fellow workers operating together in His church (vs. 9).

At the end of verse 9, Paul switched from using gardening imagery to using construction imagery as he compared the Corinthians to a building belonging to God. Regardless of whether the metaphor is that of a cultivated field or a freestanding structure, the truth is the same. God reigns sovereign over the church and its ministers.

C. Christ as the Foundation of the Church: vss. 10-11

By the grace God has given me, I laid a foundation as an expert builder, and someone else is building on it. But each one should be careful how he builds. For no one can lay any foundation other than the one already laid, which is Jesus Christ.

Paul next compared himself to an expert builder who, because God had graciously given him the ability to do so, had laid the structure's foundation. The apostle accomplished this through the proclamation of the Gospel. Others, such as Apollos, were like laborers who had built the structure on its foundation. This was achieved by teaching the people how to become more spiritually mature (1 Cor. 3:10).

Paul realized that the Lord will one day scrutinize all that His servants have done. That is why the apostle threw in a note of caution. Ministers need to be careful how they perform their tasks. Paul added to the warning by writing that there is not to be any foundation other than Jesus Christ (vs. 11). No worldly belief system is an acceptable basis for a church. Only the gospel of Christ is a firm enough foundation to support the kind of church God wants.

D. Accountability at Christ's Return: vss. 12-15

If any man builds on this foundation using gold, silver, costly stones, wood, hay or straw, his work will be shown for what it is, because the Day will bring it to light. It will be revealed with fire, and the fire will test the quality of each man's work. If what he has built survives, he will receive his reward. If it is burned up, he will suffer loss; he himself will be saved, but only as one escaping through the flames.

After issuing the Corinthians a warning, Paul turned his attention to the types of material ministers might use to build upon the church's foundation. Those who proclaim the Gospel and behave in a way consistent with its teaching are like laborers who select the most valuable materials (such as precious metals and costly stones) for constructing the building. Those who compromise the Gospel and behave in ungodly and careless ways are like laborers who use the most worthless materials (such as wood, hay, and straw) to construct the building (1 Cor. 3:12).

The apostle wrote that a time of evaluation is coming in which the quality of each believer's work will be judged (vs. 13). This evaluation will take place at Jesus' return. Paul's constant motivation was to be pleasing to the Lord in that day (2 Cor. 5:9-10) and receive His commendation (1 Cor. 4:5). Furthermore, each believer's works will be tested by the fire of God's justice. Those buildings that are constructed with imperishable materials will remain standing, while those buildings that are constructed with perishable materials will be reduced to ashes.

Ministers who do their work faithfully by building the church with quality materials will stand the test of the Lord's penetrating scrutiny and accordingly be rewarded (vs. 14). He will save those who do their work less faithfully (assuming, of course, they are true believers)—but just barely (vs. 15). The implication is that they miss out on some rewards.

Paul said the less faithful ministers will "suffer loss." Bible scholars differ on what the nature of this "loss" is. Some claim it is the regret the ministers will experience when, at the judgment, they will not have any works to present to Christ. Others say that the loss is the ministers' missing out on the reward of those who have diligently labored for the kingdom of God.

Discussion Questions

1. How had the Corinthians displayed spiritual immaturity?
2. What role did Paul see for himself as a servant in the spiritual body of Christ? What role did the apostle see for Apollos?
3. In what sense were ministers such as Paul and Apollos fellow workers?
4. Why was it important for ministers to build on no other foundation than Jesus Christ?
5. When will the Christian service of individual believers be scrutinized and by whom?

Contemporary Application

The Corinthians' quarreling revealed deep-seated selfishness, pride, and envy. Because their actions were no different from those of sinful persons, Paul said they should put such behavior to an end. As long as strife and division beleaguered the church, it would remain not only worldly but also for the most part ineffective.

As we Christians examine Paul's instruction to the Corinthians, it would be good for us to think about our own level of spiritual maturity. Our behavior is evidence of how much we have grown spiritually. The Holy Spirit will assist us if we long to express compassion and understanding to other believers, and He will shower us with His grace by enabling us to become more unified with them.

One of the best ways to help us grow in Christian maturity is to accept and fulfill responsibilities available to us in the church or with regard to some other Christian activity. For instance, we can continue to serve faithfully as Sunday school teachers. This demands that we not only study God's Word more seriously during our preparations than we otherwise would on our own, but also that we use the spiritual knowledge we have learned from our walk with the Lord.

Having ministry opportunities challenges us to use the spiritual gifts God has given us. It throws us into situations that strengthen our character; and it provides us with insights we cannot gain if we sit back and remain inactive Christians.

Admittedly, not all Christians are involved in laying the foundation or building a church as ministers; yet, as the previous paragraphs suggest, all of us can serve God in our own ways. Let us be sure that we devote ourselves to doing those things that have eternal significance. By proclaiming the truth of the Gospel and living in the power of the Holy Spirit, both our work and we ourselves will meet with the Lord's approval. In turn, we will reap His eternal reward.

Servants in Ministry

DEVOTIONAL READING

Matthew 23:8-12

DAILY BIBLE READINGS

Monday June 19
1 Peter 4:1-11 Good Stewards of God's Grace

Tuesday June 20
John 13:2-9 Jesus Washes Peter's Feet

Wednesday June 21
John 13:12-17 Serve One Another

Thursday June 22
Mark 10:41-45 Become a Servant

Friday June 23
1 Corinthians 4:1-7 Stewards of God's Mysteries

Saturday June 24
1 Corinthians 4:8-13 We Are Fools for Christ

Sunday June 25
1 Corinthians 4:14-21 A Fatherly Admonition on Responsibility

Scripture

Background Scripture: *1 Corinthians 4:1-13*
Scripture Lesson: *1 Corinthians 4:1-13*
Key Verse: *So then, men ought to regard us as servants of Christ and as those entrusted with the secret things of God.* 1 Corinthians 4:1.
Scripture Lesson for Children: *Matthew 25:14-23, 28-29; 1 Corinthians 4:1-2*
Key Verse for Children: *It is required that those who have been given a trust must prove faithful.* 1 Corinthians 4:2.

Lesson Aim

To emphasize that Christian servanthood is humble, not glamorous.

Lesson Setting

Time: *A.D. 55*
Place: *Ephesus*

Lesson Outline

Servants in Ministry

   I.   Stewards of God's Mysteries: 1 Corinthians 4:1-5
       A. *Christ's Servants and Teachers: vs. 1*
       B. *Accountable to the Lord: vss. 2-5*
  II. Despised for Christ's Sake: 1 Corinthians 4:6-13
       A. *Operating according to Scripture: vs. 6*
       B. *Shunning Arrogance: vs. 7*
       C. *Being Honored versus Being Disgraced: vss. 8-9*
       D. *Remaining Christlike despite Maltreatment: vss. 10-13*

Introduction for Adults

Topic: *Serving Responsibly*

Michael H. Hart is the author of *The 100: A Ranking of the Most Influential Persons in History*. He not only provides a list of influential figures from world history, but also reasons for the way he ranked various luminaries. Moreover, the author includes brief biographies of each of the individuals.

Number three on the list is Jesus Christ, behind Muhammad and Isaac Newton (respectively). And the apostle Paul appears sixth on the list, coming after Buddha and Confucius (in that order). Undoubtedly, most Christians would place the Savior at the top of the list, with Paul much farther up in the rankings.

Behind the Messiah, Paul should be a role model for Christians, especially how he responded to mistreatment. By looking at the apostle's life and teachings, we can learn to be patient and conciliatory toward those who mistreat us. In fact, following Paul's example is the subject of this week's lesson.

Introduction for Youth

Topic: *Leaders: Servants and Stewards*

Thomas à Kempis, author of the classic devotional *The Imitation of Christ*, reminds us that "Jesus has many lovers of the heavenly kingdom, but few bearers of his cross. He has many desirous of consolation, but few of tribulation. . . . All desire to rejoice with him, few are willing to endure anything for him, or with him. Many follow Jesus to the breaking of the bread, but few to the drinking of the cup."

Paul knew that the only service that really mattered was service that God had called him to and that he did in a way that was pleasing to the Lord. Only genuinely humble and obedient service matters to God.

Concepts for Children

Topic: *Be Responsible*

1. The story Jesus told illustrates that equal opportunities do not come to everyone.
2. We also learn that the result of our actions and responses is not necessarily just or fair.
3. We sometimes make decisions out of fear rather than out of responsibility or principle.
4. Jesus' story emphasizes that we must take good care of what we have been given.
5. When we do a good job of caring for a few things, God trusts us to care for many things.

The Lesson Commentary

I. STEWARDS OF GOD'S MYSTERIES: 1 CORINTHIANS 4:1-5

A. Christ's Servants and Teachers: vs. 1

So then, men ought to regard us as servants of Christ and as those entrusted with the secret things of God.

What Paul wrote in 1 Corinthians seems to be determined by the kinds of problems that had surfaced in Corinth. In fact, many scholars have suggested that the letter is roughly organized on the basis of a distinction between matters that had been reported to Paul (chaps. 1—6) and problems that the Corinthians had raised in a letter to him (chaps. 7—16).

Behind the great diversity of issues in this epistle lie some deep and recurring problems in the Corinthian church. Challenges to Paul's authority, pride in personal spirituality, and especially a lack of love were fundamental issues that the apostle needed to address. In the course of responding to differing problems in the church, Paul set forth his teachings on such key doctrines as God's sovereignty, the nature of the church, sanctification, and the bodily resurrection.

In chapter 4, Paul returned to the issue of the Corinthians favoring different ministers, but with a new slant. He wanted to point out that all servants of Christ were equal because they all faced the same hardships and adversities in proclaiming the Gospel. The apostle had detected that an undercurrent of opposition to him had developed among the Corinthians. Thus he went on the defensive, explaining why the church should not turn against its founder. He implied that the problem could be resolved by the people considering their ministers as servants of Christ and stewards of God's mysteries. The idea would be that one did not criticize someone else's slave or steward, and neither should the Corinthians have criticized Paul.

"Entrusted" (vs. 1) renders the Greek word *oikonomous*, from which we get our word *economy*. The Greek term refers to those given the oversight of their master's household. These slaves managed buildings, fields, finances, food, other servants, and sometimes even children of the owner. In a spiritual sense, believers are stewards whom Jesus has entrusted with the gospel message.

In using the phrase "the secret things of God," Paul referred to the divine truth that Christ, through His death on the cross, has secured salvation. This truth, previously unrevealed, has now been disclosed. In this present era, the Lord uses His servants to make known His once-hidden truths and explain them to all people.

B. Accountable to the Lord: vss. 2-5

Now it is required that those who have been given a trust must prove faithful. I care very little if I am judged by you or by any human court; indeed, I do not even judge myself. My conscience is clear, but that does not make me innocent. It is the Lord who judges me. Therefore judge nothing before the appointed time; wait till the Lord comes. He will bring to light what is hidden in darkness and will expose the motives of men's hearts. At that time each will receive his praise from God.

Paul conceded that, as servants, he and other ministers have a responsibility to prove themselves worthy of the trust placed in them. They were not to pursue their own agendas, but were to faithfully do the bidding of the Savior (1 Cor. 4:2). Nevertheless, Paul disputed the idea that, in the case of Christ's servants, other human beings have the right to judge their faithfulness. The apostle, therefore, was not concerned if a human tribunal, such as the Corinthian church or a human court, judged him, for their judgment would not ultimately matter.

Paul did not even judge himself (vs. 3). After all, servants are not their own masters, with the right of examining their ministries. If the apostle did judge himself, however, he would acquit himself, for his conscience (his inner sense of right and wrong) was clear; but then a clear conscience is not proof of innocence, for a person's conscience is not the ultimate seat of judgment (vs. 4).

If the Corinthian church, human courts, and Paul's conscience were not suitable judges of his faithfulness to his calling, then who was his judge? The apostle declared that it was the Lord. Only the master has the right to judge the servant. The Lord's judgment of Paul and other people will take place after Christ's return. Thus the apostle urged his readers to refrain from passing judgment and to wait until Jesus' evaluation comes (vs. 5).

When Christ judges believers, all the acts, thoughts, and motives that have been hidden deep in our hearts and minds will be revealed. That sort of illumination and revelation is something people could never do. We never know all the facts about others, which is another good reason to refrain from judging.

In relation to believers, the issue at the judgment seat of Christ will not be our spiritual status (a determination of whether we are saved or lost), but rather the bestowal of rewards (see 2 Cor. 5:10). At that time the Savior will bring our deepest secrets to light and disclose our inner motives (1 Cor. 4:5). Christ's bestowal of rewards will be conducted in a fair and impartial manner. It is then that each person will receive recognition from the Lord. True believers need not fear future judgment, for we will stand acquitted through our faith in Christ (Rom. 8:1). That will, however, be the time when our rewards for eternity are determined, based on how faithfully we have fulfilled our calling.

With respect to the Corinthians, Paul was not trying to show how they were wrong about him; rather, he demonstrated that they did not have the right to judge him at all. He was God's servant, and only God could judge him.

II. DESPISED FOR CHRIST'S SAKE: 1 CORINTHIANS 4:6-13

A. Operating according to Scripture: vs. 6

Now, brothers, I have applied these things to myself and Apollos for your benefit, so that you may learn from us the meaning of the saying, "Do not go beyond what is written." Then you will not take pride in one man over against another.

To this point in 1 Corinthians, Paul had already figuratively applied his comments about gardeners, builders, and stewards to himself and Apollos. Now the apostle stated that he had the Corinthians' benefit in mind when he used himself and Apollos as examples. He wanted his readers to learn a lesson from it all. In the latter part of 4:6, Paul told the Corinthians not to exceed what was written in Scripture. Here we see the apostle directing his readers back to the Hebrew sacred writings for guidance. They were not to go beyond the teaching of God's Word in their treatment of their spiritual leaders. Paul wanted the Corinthians to view their leaders from a biblical perspective.

The Corinthians had become puffed up in being a follower of one minister over against another. If Paul's readers were to recover a biblical perspective, they would not be so arrogant. The apostle discerned that pride was at the root of the division of the Corinthian church. Humility would lead to greater unity and harmony.

B. Shunning Arrogance: vs. 7

For who makes you different from anyone else? What do you have that you did not receive? And if you did receive it, why do you boast as though you did not?

In addition to priding themselves in being followers of a particular spiritual leader, the Corinthians apparently were also priding themselves in their own talents and attainments. Paul thus admonished them with a series of rhetorical questions (1 Cor. 4:7). Here we see that they had no reason to be inflated with pride. After all, nothing distinguished them as being superior to anyone else. All that they enjoyed as Christians had been graciously given to them by God. This being the case, they could not take credit for their attainments. Paul said they were wrong to boast as if they acquired these things on their own.

C. Being Honored versus Being Disgraced: vss. 8-9

Already you have all you want! Already you have become rich! You have become kings—and that without us! How I wish that you really had become kings so that we might be kings with you! For it seems to me that God has put us apostles on display at the end of the procession, like men condemned to die in the arena. We have been made a spectacle to the whole universe, to angels as well as to men.

Making use of irony, Paul showed the Corinthians how foolish, immature, and shortsighted was their arrogance. The believers in Corinth thought they already possessed all that they wanted. They behaved as if they were rich. They became haughty, as if they were reigning as kings and had attained their position without anyone's help. The apostle wanted his readers to know that humility and thankfulness, not arrogance and presumptuousness, should follow one's conversion to Christ (1 Cor. 4:8).

The Corinthians had been blessed with a variety of spiritual gifts; but they, having received the Holy Spirit, were behaving as though they had already reached their spiritual destination. Despite the fact that Jesus had not yet returned and that they still had much spiritual maturing to experience, the Christians at Corinth were acting as if the Savior had already established His final kingdom, and they were kings reigning with Him!

As Paul thought about it, he wished his readers really were kings, for then he could share in their blessings. As it was, he and the other apostles had a very hard life. Paul probably used the term "apostles" (vs. 9) here in a broad sense, referring not only to the original 12 disciples of Jesus, but also to others who, like Paul, were prominently heralding the Gospel.

To illustrate what he meant, Paul drew an analogy from gladiatorial contests of the day. Typically a procession would march into the arena where various events occurred. Paul said the apostles were on display at the end of the convoy where the condemned walked.

Before great crowds in local arenas, seasoned fighters would combat each other to the death. In other events, the Romans would carry out public executions involving condemned prisoners. Officers would usher them into the arena, where they were tortured and then subjected to the attacks of ravenous beasts. The last ones brought in for slaughter were the grand finale. Bloodthirsty crowds would heckle and cheer as they watched the spectacle unfold.

Another possibility is that verse 9 alludes to the triumphal parade of a victorious Roman general. In ancient times, the Roman Senate would honor a conquering general with a victory march through the city. The chief magistrates walked at the head of the procession, followed by members of the Roman Senate, musicians playing trumpets, booty seized from the enemy, a white ox to be sacrificed, the main captives in chains, various military officers, the conquering general riding in a four-horse-drawn chariot, and finally his troops. Along the way incense was burned.

In either option, Paul's main point is clear. The persecution of the apostles was on display for the whole world, so that all beings—both human and angelic—could see them die for their faith. Thus, while the Corinthians were trying to reign like kings, their spiritual leaders were being marched toward their deaths.

D. Remaining Christlike despite Maltreatment: vss. 10-13

We are fools for Christ, but you are so wise in Christ! We are weak, but you are strong! You are honored, we are dishonored! To this very hour we go hungry and thirsty, we are in rags, we are brutally treated, we are homeless. We work hard with our own hands. When we are cursed, we bless; when we are persecuted, we endure it; when we are slandered, we answer kindly. Up to this moment we have become the scum of the earth, the refuse of the world.

Hoping to dispel the Corinthians' arrogance, Paul launched into a series of contrasts between their pride and the apostles' humility. Whereas the Corinthians regarded themselves wise Christians, the apostles had become fools for Jesus' sake. Whereas the Corinthians regarded themselves spiritually powerful, the apostles served the Lord in weakness. Whereas the Corinthians felt they had gained a status superior to others, the apostles were shamed and treated like common criminals (1 Cor. 4:10).

Paul did not want the Corinthians to be blind to the humiliation and indignity that he and the other apostles endured. Speaking from experience, Paul recited how he and his missionary colleagues had continued to proclaim the Gospel while going hungry and thirsty. They were inadequately clothed, badly treated, and homeless (vs. 11). In order not to be a financial burden to any of the people to whom they preached the Gospel, they earned their own living with physical labor (vs. 12).

Despite all the afflictions, Paul said the apostles did not repay harsh treatment with cruelty; rather, they prayed for God to be gracious to those who verbally abused them. They patiently endured persecution; and they responded pleasantly when lies were told about them (vs. 13). Paul indicated that their gracious responses had done nothing to change their circumstances. In fact, Paul and his colleagues continued to be treated like the world's dirt and scum.

Discussion Questions

1. What responsibilities belong to stewards of the Gospel?
2. Why does idolizing different Christian leaders rather than worshiping the Savior cause division and strife among believers?
3. How would you describe the attitude of the Corinthians toward Paul?
4. What did Paul mean by the phrase "We are fools for Christ" (1 Cor. 4:10)?
5. Why do you think Paul responded to hardship and opposition as he did?

Contemporary Application

Although North American Christians do not suffer flogging and stoning as a result of our faith, we should not be surprised if others occasionally treat us badly for any number of reasons. Because of sin, such is inevitable in this world. Those who are not for Christ are against Him; thus as we live for the Lord, unbelievers will oppose us. Even our fellow Christians will occasionally let us down and do something that hurts us.

Whatever mistreatment we experience, Paul is an excellent example for us to follow. When he was cursed, he blessed others; when he was persecuted he patiently endured it; and when he was slandered, he humbly appealed for his antagonists to desist.

If you are passed over for a promotion because of your boss's anti-Christian bias, your first reaction is likely to be outrage; but after cooling off, you could approach your boss humbly to discuss his or her attitude and decision. Then you can wait patiently for another opportunity for promotion.

If your friend betrays a confidence about a private family matter, you are going to feel anger and disappointment; but you can reconcile yourself to endure the disgrace. Also, you can talk with the other person about the betrayal of confidence and about how to restore your friendship.

It is not always easy to be patient and conciliatory, but when we are, we then are following the biblical pattern for Christ's followers who have been mistreated. Moreover, we will be following in the way shown by Paul, who suffered much more than any of us are likely to.

Called to Relationships

Scripture

Background Scripture: *1 Corinthians 7:1-20, 23-40*
Scripture Lesson: *1 Corinthians 7:2-15*
Key Verse: *I wish that all men were as I am. But each man has his own gift from God; one has this gift, another has that.* 1 Corinthians 7:7.
Scripture Lesson for Children: *Matthew 6:25-33; 1 Corinthians 7:32*
Key Verse for Children: *I would like you to be free from concern.* 1 Corinthians 7:32.

Lesson Aim

To stress that believers are called to high standards in marriage and in a single life.

Lesson Setting

Time: *A.D. 55*
Place: *Ephesus*

Lesson Outline

Called to Relationships

I. Advice for Husbands and Wives: 1 Corinthians 7:2-7
    A. *The Sensibility of Marriage: vs. 2*
    B. *The Priority of Sexual Intimacy in Marriage: vss. 3-6*
    C. *The Gift of Marriage and the Gift of Singleness: vs. 7*

II. Advice on Singleness and Divorce: 1 Corinthians 7:8-11
    A. *Being Married Rather Than Burning with Lust: vss. 8-9*
    B. *Preserving the Marriage Relationship: vss. 10-11*

III. Advice for Believers' Marriages: 1 Corinthians 7:12-15
    A. *The Sanctifying Nature of Marriage: vss. 12-14*
    B. *The Divine Summons to Live in Peace: vs. 15*

Introduction for Adults

Topic: *Living in Relationships*

Liz (not her real name) came to our Bible study with great joy. A single mother with a 10-month-old baby, she looked forward to getting together weekly with other ladies to study God's Word. It was not an easy life for her, but she believed it was God's best for her at that time.

You see, Liz is a Christian who had become pregnant as the result of a one-night stand with a non-Christian man she barely knew. Although she could have married him, she believed that two wrongs would not make a right. Liz also believed that if God wanted her to have a husband and her son to have a father, the Lord would provide a Christian man who would not only love her but also her child. In the meantime, she planned to keep herself chaste and to thank God for the blessing of her son. Liz could not change the past—but she could allow God to change her as a result of what happened in the past.

Three years later, God provided Liz with a Christian husband and father. In a day when immorality continues to consume people's lives, we should do all we can to promote the joys and privileges of love that is honoring to God, namely, the love that is shared in marriage.

Introduction for Youth

Topic: *One Special Person*

George Crenshaw, a retiree, was enjoying his duty as a camp counselor at a church retreat near Mount Rainier, Washington. After two weeks, the high school boys he was leading had come to trust and respect him. In fact, on their last night at the camp, while they were gathered around a campfire, the boys felt confident enough to share some of their most private feelings and ask for the advice of George.

At some point the conversation turned to physical intimacy. The boys couldn't believe their ears when they heard George say, "Well, not everybody who is single is having sex. I mean, I haven't." The boys couldn't believe their ears. "It's true," George told them. "I've been a bachelor all my life. I believe the Bible when it tells me that our bodies are the temple of the Spirit. God wants me to be holy. And I've committed myself to honoring that call in my life."

Christians owe it to God to maintain high standards in their married or single lives. What they are called to do may seem foolish to others, but the reward will be lives that please the one who made us.

Concepts for Children

Topic: *God Teaches Us to Trust*

1. God takes care of all of creation—plants, animals, and all of nature.
2. God also provides for our basic needs.
3. God even wants us to be free from anxiety.
4. The reason is that worrying brings only unhappy results.
5. In light of these truths, let us seek to please God in all we do.

The Lesson Commentary

I. ADVICE FOR HUSBANDS AND WIVES: 1 CORINTHIANS 7:2-7

A. The Sensibility of Marriage: vs. 2

But since there is so much immorality, each man should have his own wife, and each woman her own husband.

It is helpful when reading 1 Corinthians 7 to understand how the Greeks of the first century A.D. viewed male-female relationships. Prostitution was an accepted part of Greek life. Marriage and monogamy were encouraged because they helped keep society orderly, but marriages could be dissolved easily. Consequently, divorce was widespread. The paramount interest of Greek males was the pursuit of pleasure, which they often found in sports and sexual relationships.

Worshiping the Greek gods and goddesses did little to promote moral living, since the pagan deities were believed to have affairs with humans in their own pursuit of pleasure. While some Greek philosophers encouraged moral living and self-control, that was not the norm in Greek society, where the view prevailed that the best way to get rid of bodily desires was to fully satisfy them.

The congregation at Corinth seemed to be in opposition to their culture, so they wrote to Paul for advice. The first topic the apostle addressed concerned marriage. Because of Paul's comments in the opening verses of chapter 7, some mistakenly believe he had a low view of this sacred institution. For example, in verse 1 he asserted that it is good for a man not to touch, or have intimate relations with, a woman. Then the apostle seems to encourage marriage only as a means to avoid immorality.

Paul's comments need to be taken in context. Later in the chapter, the apostle refers to an impending crisis in Corinth as his reason for discouraging marriage at that time (vs. 26). While we do not know for sure, some have suggested that this refers to persecution against the church in Corinth. Also, in Ephesians 5:21-33 and the instructions for church leaders in 1 Timothy 3, Paul spoke favorably about marriage.

With respect to 1 Corinthians 7:1, Paul may have been citing a slogan his readers used to justify their actions. In this case, they were promoting celibacy, perhaps because they believed they were already so spiritual that they could and should live without physical intimacy.

As was previously noted, depravity and prostitution were rampant in Corinth. Paul, being a realist, stated that no one should attempt a way of life (such as celibacy) for which he or she was ill-suited. Ultimately, it was better to marry than burn with passion in a society full of immoral temptations (vs. 2). In this case, Paul was simply advocating the advantage of marriage in such a culture.

B. The Priority of Sexual Intimacy in Marriage: vss. 3-6

The husband should fulfill his marital duty to his wife, and likewise the wife to her husband. The wife's body does not belong to her alone but also to her husband. In the same way, the husband's body does not belong to him alone but also to his wife. Do not deprive each other except by mutual consent and for a time, so that you may devote yourselves to prayer. Then come together again so that Satan will not tempt you because of your lack of self-control. I say this as a concession, not as a command.

Within the context of marriage, couples should have normal physical relations. This means the husband should give to his wife what is hers by right as a married woman. Similarly, the wife should give to her husband what is his by right as a married man (1 Cor. 7:3).

Paul gave two reasons why it would be wrong for either married partner to deprive the other of physical intimacy for extended periods of time. First, a spouse could not claim his or her body as exclusively belonging to him or her; in a manner of speaking, that body also belonged to the mate (vs. 4). Second, a long-term denial of physical intimacy could foster a lack of self-control in which Satan might tempt a spouse to commit adultery (vs. 5).

Accordingly, Paul told the Corinthians to stop withholding physical intimacy from their spouses. The only exception would be when a couple mutually agreed to devote themselves to prayer (and perhaps the practice of other related spiritual disciplines such as fasting); but this arrangement was supposed to be only for a specified period of time.

The apostle qualified his advice to the Corinthians by writing that this particular teaching was a concession, not a command (vs. 6); in other words, Paul was not *instructing* the married believers to abstain from physical intimacy temporarily for the sake of prayer, but rather *allowing* it.

C. The Gift of Marriage and the Gift of Singleness: vs. 7

I wish that all men were as I am. But each man has his own gift from God; one has this gift, another has that.

Making a concession for temporary celibacy was as far as Paul would go in endorsing the apparent desire of some Corinthians to cease physical intimacy in marriage; nevertheless, Paul saw some advantages in complete celibacy, such as he himself— a single man—practiced. Thus in one sense, the apostle would have liked for everyone to be single as he was; but he recognized that God gave some people the gift to be married, and He gave other people the gift to remain unmarried (1 Cor. 7:7).

Bible scholars are divided on the question of whether Paul was ever married, and the facts are such that a final conclusion may never be reached. From the apostle's remarks in verse 7, most agree that at the time he wrote 1 Corinthians, he was indeed single.

Those, however, who think Paul was once married cite his connection to the Sanhedrin before his conversion. Because of the apostle's strong ties with this religious council, some say he was once a member of it. Voting members of the Sanhedrin were required to be married and the father of children.

Those who think Paul never married are unconvinced that his association with the Sanhedrin implies that he was a member of that council; and even if the apostle was a member, the marriage requirement for the Sanhedrin has been disputed.

Some scholars believe this prerequisite was not instituted until after Paul's involvement with this council.

II. ADVICE ON SINGLENESS AND DIVORCE: 1 CORINTHIANS 7:8-11

A. Being Married Rather Than Burning with Lust: vss. 8-9

Now to the unmarried and the widows I say: It is good for them to stay unmarried, as I am. But if they cannot control themselves, they should marry, for it is better to marry than to burn with passion.

Paul next gave advice to three groups: the unmarried and the widowed (1 Cor. 7:8-9), Christian couples (vss. 10-11), and Christians married to unbelievers (vss. 12-16). With respect to the first group, Paul told the unmarried and the widows it was better for them to remain single as he himself was (vs. 8).

Presumably, being unmarried helped enable Paul to devote himself wholly to the Lord's work. Thus perhaps the apostle wanted his readers to have the opportunity for a similar dedication; but Paul quickly added that if the unmarried and the widows of Corinth could not exercise self-control, they should marry. After all, uniting in marriage was far better than to be inflamed with unfulfilled passions that one then tried to satisfy in ungodly ways (vs. 9).

B. Preserving the Marriage Relationship: vss. 10-11

To the married I give this command (not I, but the Lord): A wife must not separate from her husband. But if she does, she must remain unmarried or else be reconciled to her husband. And a husband must not divorce his wife.

Paul next directed his comments to Christian couples. He clarified that what he said was more than his own advice; it was a command from Jesus Himself. The apostle may have had in mind a saying of Jesus such as is found in Matthew 5:31-32. Paul stated that a spouse was not to divorce his or her mate (1 Cor. 7:10-11). Most likely, the apostle was addressing couples in which both partners were Christians. Allowing for the fact that at least one woman in the church had already separated from her husband, Paul said such a woman had two options. She could remain unmarried or be reconciled to her husband (see Matt. 19:9).

III. ADVICE FOR BELIEVERS' MARRIAGES: 1 CORINTHIANS 7:12-15

A. The Sanctifying Nature of Marriage: vss. 12-14

To the rest I say this (I, not the Lord): If any brother has a wife who is not a believer and she is willing to live with him, he must not divorce her. And if a woman has a husband who is not a believer and he is willing to live with her, she must not divorce him. For the unbelieving husband has been sanctified through his wife, and the unbelieving wife has been sanctified through her believing husband. Otherwise your children would be unclean, but as it is, they are holy.

There remained some issues that Jesus had not addressed during His earthly ministry. The instruction that Paul next gave was one of those issues. What the apostle wrote, however, had the Lord's full sanction and authority. This is because the Holy Spirit was guiding Paul's words, enabling him to offer God's wisdom on the subject (see 1 Cor. 14:37).

The apostle's focus was on real situations of mixed marriages in Corinth, namely, between believers and unbelievers. Paul said that if an unbelieving partner was willing to live with the believer, the Christian was not to divorce the unsaved spouse (7:12-13). It is helpful to note that the apostle was talking here about couples who were already married when one of them became a Christian. Paul was strongly against believers marrying unbelievers (see 1 Cor. 7:39; 2 Cor. 6:14-18).

Paul had good reason for his instruction to remain in a mixed marriage. He said the unbelieving partner was sanctified, or set apart to God, through the converted partner (1 Cor. 7:14). In such a marriage, the unbeliever would witness the godly influence that the Christian spouse brought to the relationship.

Paul also said the children from mixed marriages were not spiritually separated from God but rather holy. In such a marriage, children would receive a godly influence from at least one parent, which was more than children of two unbelieving parents would receive.

B. The Divine Summons to Live in Peace: vs. 15

But if the unbeliever leaves, let him do so. A believing man or woman is not bound in such circumstances; God has called us to live in peace.

Paul had talked about mixed marriages in which the unbelieving partner was willing to stay with the believing partner; but what should Christians do if the unsaved spouse abandons the saved spouse? The apostle said that if the unbelieving partner leaves the believer, the Christian is to let him or her go.

In such a situation, the Christian is "not bound" (1 Cor. 7:15). Some interpreters say this means the believer was under no obligation to try to preserve the marriage compact. Other people interpret this to mean that the believer was free to remarry. Still others maintain that while divorce is allowable, remarriage is not, for Paul's injunction in verse 11 still applies here.

The apostle reminded his readers that God has summoned His people to live in peace (vs. 15). Again, the meaning of the apostle's statement is disputed. Some say Paul meant the believing spouse was to do the peaceful thing by staying in the marriage, if the unbeliever wanted the relationship to continue, so that salvation might come to the unbeliever. Others say Paul meant the believer was not to cause a disturbance by trying to preserve a marriage the unbeliever did not want.

Paul tempered his teaching about mixed marriages by encouraging Christians to try to hold their marital unions together. The apostle certainly did not want believers to feel at liberty to heedlessly end their marriages just because their spouses were unbelievers. Thus he reminded them of the hope that God would use them to bring their unbelieving spouses to Christ (vs. 16).

Discussion Questions

1. What obligations do husbands and wives have to each other?
2. What guidelines did Paul give couples about abstaining from physical intimacy?
3. What was Paul's advice to those who were single or widows?
4. What were Paul's instructions to a believer married to an unbelieving spouse?
5. What did Paul mean that children within a mixed marriage are sanctified by the believing spouse?

Contemporary Application

Like the Corinthians, we live in a society where scriptural standards of commitment, responsibility, and moral behavior are rarely practiced. The world says, "Do whatever feels good." Almost anything goes. Truth and ethics seem irrelevant.

God's Word says a resounding "No!" to this relative morality. Christians are called to the highest moral standards of commitment and responsibility. Our bodies are God's temples, dedicated to His service (1 Cor. 6:19-20). We must glorify God in our marriage or in our relationships as a single person.

Those who follow God's standards in marriage develop trust in a relationship. When the trust is broken, the marriage is in trouble. The single person honors God by obedient abstinence. Disaster occurs when casual, physically intimate encounters replace God's will.

Society may think that these standards are strict and strange; however, like a fence around a field, God provides protection and freedom within limits for single and married persons alike. Moreover, God's rules for the family protect both parents and children.

Those married to unbelievers receive encouragement that their faithful witness may win members of their family. God cares for the single person, who learns to trust the Lord and to be used in His service. God also provides healing when His standards are broken. When we confess our sins and receive Christ's forgiveness, we can begin to rebuild broken relationships (1 John 1:9).

Because God's rules are clear, His redeemed children know what He expects. As we follow the Lord, either as married or single persons, we grow spiritually by learning commitment, responsibility, and trust, to God and to others. Then we can show God's standards to a very confused world.

Called to Help the Weak

Scripture

Background Scripture: *1 Corinthians 8:1-13*
Scripture Lesson: *1 Corinthians 8:1-13*
Key Verses: *Food does not bring us near to God; we are no
worse if we do not eat, and no better if we do. Be careful, how-
ever, that the exercise of your freedom does not become a stum-
bling block to the weak.* 1 Corinthians 8:8-9.
Scripture Lesson for Children: *Mark 12:28-34;
1 Corinthians 8:1*
Key Verse for Children: *"Love your neighbor as yourself."*
Mark 12:31.

Lesson Aim

To note that believers can choose to limit their freedom out of concern for others.

Lesson Setting

Time: A.D. *55*
Place: *Ephesus*

Lesson Outline

Called to Help the Weak

I.   Food Sacrificed to Idols: 1 Corinthians 8:1-8
 A. *Love versus Knowledge: vss. 1-3*
 B. *One God, Creator, and Lord: vss. 4-6*
 C. *Consumption of Food versus Spirituality: vss. 7-8*
II. Freedom Exercised Judiciously: 1 Corinthians 8:9-13
 A. *Causing the Weak to Stumble: vs. 9*
 B. *Undermining the Faith of the Weak: vss. 10-11*
 C. *Voluntarily Limiting Personal Freedom: vss. 12-13*

Introduction for Adults

Topic: *To Eat or Not to Eat*

It is ironic that many Christian adults will declare that they are servants of Jesus Christ. And yet, when they are challenged to exhibit a servant attitude toward their fellow believers, they insist on their perceived rights.

George Barna conducted a survey of adults who claimed to be "born-again" believers. Interestingly, 41 percent of these said they agree with the following statement: "When it comes right down to it, your first responsibility is to yourself."

Although the majority of adults in Sunday school classes disagree with that attitude, a considerable number hold this view—some of whom may be in your class. Be aware that they may feel uneasy about Paul's exhortation that Christians give up their rights for the sake of others.

Introduction for Youth

Topic: *A Matter of Taste?*

Paul taught the Corinthians that being lovingly responsible to other believers was more important than showing off their spiritual knowledge. They were not to eat meat or do anything else that would cause a weaker Christian to stumble.

For some modern social practices, the Bible gives no specific instruction, only guiding principles. Some struggling or immature believers, however, may be tempted by these questionable areas. In Christian love, we should choose to limit our freedom and avoid anything that we know would harm another believer.

Concepts for Children

Topic: *God Teaches Us to Love*

1. The first commandment directs us to love God with all our heart, soul, mind, and strength, and others as ourselves.
2. Loving God and others is more important than tithes, offerings, and other sacrifices.
3. Living by the first commandment requires a compassionate heart, understanding what is expected of us, and acting accordingly.
4. Some of the religious leaders understood Jesus' mission and accepted His teachings.
5. Knowledge makes us proud of ourselves, while love makes us helpful to others.

The Lesson Commentary

I. FOOD SACRIFICED TO IDOLS: 1 CORINTHIANS 8:1-8

A. Love versus Knowledge: vss. 1-3

Now about food sacrificed to idols: We know that we all possess knowledge. Knowledge puffs up, but love builds up. The man who thinks he knows something does not yet know as he ought to know. But the man who loves God is known by God.

Because of the many temples and shrines in Corinth, it is no wonder that Paul's readers had questions regarding meat sacrificed to idols. Sharing meals together in some place associated with idols was an accepted and popular practice. These gatherings were a large part of the social etiquette of the day and to avoid them essentially cut one off from friends and neighbors. Also, meat that had been offered to idols was served there.

After a sacrifice, portions of the meat remained for the one making the offering. If the sacrifice was public, the leftover meat might be sold to the markets for resale. Thus even when Christians bought meat in a shop, they could not tell whether it had been offered to an idol. If believers were invited to a friend's house for a meal, they would not know whether the meat was left over from the host's own sacrifice.

Believers thus had three questions: (1) Should they eat meat offered to a false god in a heathen feast? (2) Should they buy and eat meat offered to an idol? and (3) When invited to the home of a friend, should they eat meat that had been offered to idols?

Before answering any questions, Paul set some parameters for his instruction. Perhaps quoting a Corinthian slogan, the apostle said, "We all possess knowledge" (1 Cor. 8:1). Probably his readers believed that because they had the knowledge, they likewise had freedom to do such things as eat meat sacrificed to idols.

Paul agreed that the Corinthians had a wealth of information about life; nonetheless, he believed that the basis for determining one's behavior primarily should be love, not knowledge. The apostle contrasted the two by noting that while knowledge can make one filled with arrogance, love spiritually edifies the body of Christ. By loving each other and understanding each other's point of view, believers would help to build each other up in the faith.

After emphasizing the importance of love, Paul deemphasized the importance of supposed knowledge. He noted that a person's claim to be in the know is in fact proof that the person does not have a proper sort of knowledge (vs. 2). Ironically, understanding begins when we recognize that we are not as knowledgeable as we would like to be.

The apostle implied that the right kind of knowledge is defined in terms of being in a relationship with God, not acquiring and retaining data—even religious information (vs. 3). When people go beyond knowing about God to knowing and loving Him intimately, they show that they are known and loved by Him as well.

B. One God, Creator, and Lord: vss. 4-6

So then, about eating food sacrificed to idols: We know that an idol is nothing at all in the world and that there is no God but one. For even if there are so-called gods, whether in heaven or on earth (as indeed there are many "gods" and many "lords"), yet for us there is but one God, the Father, from whom all things came and for whom we live; and there is but one Lord, Jesus Christ, through whom all things came and through whom we live.

Idolatry permeated Corinthian society, and pagan mythology provided people with a way of looking at the world. For instance, business and entertainment often took place with the supposed blessings of the gods. Paul pointed out that the idols were nothing more than humanlymade objects and that they represent no real existence or power; however, the apostle later stated in 1 Corinthians 10:20 that demons were behind the people's idolatry. In essence, demons encouraged people to set up idols—though the idols themselves were lifeless—to distract people from worshiping the one true God.

Some have suggested that the statements "an idol is nothing" (8:4) and "there is no God but one" were actually slogans the Corinthians used. If so, Paul wanted to spotlight how his readers had misused the truths behind these sayings. For example, while pagan deities did not really exist, nevertheless many people *believed* that they existed. People worshiped all sorts of "gods" (vs. 5) and "lords," some of which they venerated as objects they could see and some of which they believed to exist in heaven (see Deut. 10:17; Ps. 136:2-3).

Christians, however, knew the truth that there is only one God and one Lord (1 Cor. 8:6; see Deut. 6:4; Isa. 45:5). Paul further described God as the Father, who was the source of all creation, and the Lord as Jesus Christ, through whom all creation came into existence. In addition, the apostle noted that the believer lives for God alone and gets his or her power to live for the Father from the Son.

C. Consumption of Food versus Spirituality: vss. 7-8

But not everyone knows this. Some people are still so accustomed to idols that when they eat such food they think of it as having been sacrificed to an idol, and since their conscience is weak, it is defiled. But food does not bring us near to God; we are no worse if we do not eat, and no better if we do.

Although many former idol worshipers had become Christians, Paul said that not all of them understood—at least on an emotional level—that the idols had no real existence (1 Cor. 8:7). To these believers, eating meat that had been offered to idols was equivalent to idolatry. Thus by consuming such food they defiled their moral consciences. In short, they saw themselves as sinning.

Some have suggested that part or all of verse 8 records another slogan used by the Corinthians. As before, Paul agreed that there was nothing inherently wrong with eating meat that had been offered to idols. He also affirmed that food neither deepens nor diminishes our relationship with God.

The impact of food, however, on a person's spirituality was not the main issue being addressed by the apostle. Paul's concern was for the effect that one believer's action (namely, consuming idol-sacrificed meat) would have on the faith of other Christians who were troubled in their conscience by the act.

II. FREEDOM EXERCISED JUDICIOUSLY: 1 CORINTHIANS 8:9-13

A. Causing the Weak to Stumble: vs. 9

Be careful, however, that the exercise of your freedom does not become a stumbling block to the weak.

Paul warned the Corinthians about allowing the exercise of their liberty to cause other believers whose moral awareness lacked maturity to stumble in their Christian walk (1 Cor. 8:9). Two different words in the Greek language are translated as "stumbling block" in the New Testament. The weaker word, used in this verse, pictures someone tripping over a stone and falling. The sense is of bumping into an object, such as the behavior of the stronger believers, and stumbling.

The other word pictures a trap that is baited for an unsuspecting animal. Paul used it in 1:23 to describe Israel's failure to recognize her Savior; however, the Cross was not the trap, but the preconceived ideas of the Jews regarding the person and work of the Messiah.

B. Undermining the Faith of the Weak: vss. 10-11

For if anyone with a weak conscience sees you who have this knowledge eating in an idol's temple, won't he be emboldened to eat what has been sacrificed to idols? So this weak brother, for whom Christ died, is destroyed by your knowledge.

Paul asked his readers to suppose that a believer with a weak conscience sees another believer, who understands that an idol has no real power, eating meat at a temple (1 Cor. 8:10). The believer with a weak conscience would be encouraged to partake and thus to do what his or her conscience had forbidden. By recklessly disregarding the weakness of fellow believers, stronger Christians could damage the faith of others, individuals for whom the Savior died (vs. 11).

Archaeological evidence exists that some first century A.D. temples had banqueting rooms where feasts were held periodically, serving surplus meat from the shrine offerings. Meat was rare and expensive, so often the only place it would be available to most people was at a pagan temple. While these feasts could be held just for the wealthy citizens in town, sometimes the entire city was invited. At Corinth, two banqueting rooms have been unearthed beneath the Asclepion, the temple dedicated to Asclepios, the Greek god of healing.

C. Voluntarily Limiting Personal Freedom: vss. 12-13

When you sin against your brothers in this way and wound their weak conscience, you sin against Christ. Therefore, if what I eat causes my brother to fall into sin, I will never eat meat again, so that I will not cause him to fall.

Paul said that the careless actions of some Corinthians was tantamount to sinning against fellow Christians as well as wounding their weak conscience; and because they were members of the spiritual body of Christ, the insensitive believers had also sinned against their Savior (1 Cor. 8:12). Such a situation was deplorable to Paul. He thus declared that if the eating of certain foods led to the spiritual undermining of another believer's faith, the apostle would never consume idol-sacrificed meat. It was Paul's intent not to cause a weaker Christian to spiritually fall (vs. 13). As we learn from 1 Corinthians 9, this was just one way in which the apostle was willing to adjust his lifestyle for the sake of others.

It should be noted that Paul did not invoke the decree in which the Jerusalem council advised Christians, particularly Gentile believers, to abstain from meat offered to idols (Acts 15:29). Since the decree was specifically addressed to other churches (those in Antioch, Syria, and Cilicia), perhaps the Corinthians would not have regarded it as authoritative for them. Whatever Paul's reason for not imposing this decree on his readers, he must have felt it would be more effective to motivate them on the basis of love rather than on regulation.

Discussion Questions

1. Why is love for God much better than mere knowledge about God?
2. What difficulties might the Corinthians have faced as monotheists in a polytheistic culture?
3. In what sense do Christians either have a weak conscience or a strong conscience?
4. How did the actions of the Christians with a strong conscience negatively affect the believers with a weak conscience?
5. How is endangering the faith of a Christian with a weak conscience a sin against the Savior?

Contemporary Application

This week's Scripture passage teaches that love, not knowledge, is the most important aspect of Christian relationships. Exercising our freedom in Christ matters less than strengthening the faith of a spiritually weak believer. Consider the example of Jesus. According to Philippians 2:7, He laid aside His kingly privileges as God to become a human being. When we limit our freedom for the sake of others, we are showing a similar kind of love.

It is not a matter of who is right and who is wrong on a certain issue, for Christians may have differing convictions; instead, Paul was calling us to look out for those with less spiritual maturity who may be harmed in some way by our actions. Such consideration for other believers often involves personal restraint.

The Holy Spirit can help us to be sensitive to questionable things. He can also enable us to remember that younger believers are walking behind us (in a manner of speaking), and we should be careful of the footprints that we leave; but limiting Christian freedom also involves giving time to doing positive things. For instance, when we limit watching our favorite television program and instead have refreshments with a Christian friend who is struggling, we are using our freedom responsibly.

Called to Win the Race

Scripture

Background Scripture: *1 Corinthians 9:24—10:13*
Scripture Lesson: *1 Corinthians 9:24—10:13*
Key Verse: *Do you not know that in a race all the runners run, but only one gets the prize? Run in such a way as to get the prize.* 1 Corinthians 9:24.
Scripture Lesson for Children: *Daniel 1:8-15; 1 Corinthians 10:11-13*
Key Verse for Children: *God did not give us a spirit of timidity, but a spirit of power, of love and of self-discipline.* 2 Timothy 1:7.

Lesson Aim

To recognize that living for Jesus requires unwavering commitment, self-control, and humility.

Lesson Setting

Time: *A.D. 55*
Place: *Ephesus*

Lesson Outline

Called to Win the Race

 I. Maintaining Unwavering Commitment: 1 Corinthians 9:24-27
 A. *An Illustration from Athletic Competition: vss. 24-25*
 B. *Self-Discipline for the Cause of Christ: vss. 26-27*
 II. Warnings from Israel's History: 1 Corinthians 10:1-13
 A. *Divine Blessings and Divine Judgment: vss. 1-5*
 B. *Admonitions against Several Vices: vss. 6-10*
 C. *Smugness and Spiritual Stability: vss. 11-13*

Introduction for Adults

Topic: *Called to Win*

What does it take to be a winning athlete? Regardless of the sport, experienced coaches seem to have a common list of characteristics they mention. These traits include being teachable, possessing an intense desire to improve and succeed, being willing to practice and make sacrifices, and having the ability to think in the heat of the moment.

If we were to cull through Scripture, we might come up with a list of our own for how to be successful in our walk with Christ. Undoubtedly, the various traits just mentioned would help. But beyond them would be the desire to abide in Christ, operate in the power of the Spirit, remain true to the Gospel, and be concerned for the needs of others. Additional virtues that make us "winners" in God's eyes include humility, sensitivity, kindness, compassion, and patience. What would your students add to this list?

Introduction for Youth

Topic: *Called to Be a Winner*

The apostle Paul may have been among those who observed the Isthmian Games held at Corinth in A.D. 51. He was at least familiar with some of the events and the training regimen undertaken by those who participated in such games. The Stoic philosopher Epictetus, who lived around A.D. 55 to 135, also described the kind of rigorous training to which these competitors submitted:

"Would you be a victor in the Olympic Games? So in good truth would I, for it is a glorious thing; but pray consider what must go before, and what may follow, and so proceed to the attempt. You must then live by rule, eat what will be disagreeable, refrain from delicacies; you must oblige yourself to constant exercises at the appointed hour in heat and cold; you must abstain from wine and cold liquors; in a word, you must be as submissive to all the directions of your master as to those of a physician."

In athletics discipline and perseverance are important to be a winner. Similarly, growing Christians are like runners in a race determined to win.

Concepts for Children

Topic: *God Teaches Us Courage*

1. While God's people were in a place called Babylon, enemies of their faith were trying to wipe out their traditions.
2. Daniel and three other trainees were godly Jews who did not want to eat and drink anything considered unclean by their people.
3. Like Daniel, if believers trust and obey God, He will be with them in every situation.
4. Both Daniel and Paul are examples of what happens when God's people follow Him completely.
5. God is faithful and just and will help us to overcome all obstacles in living for Him.

The Lesson Commentary

I. MAINTAINING UNWAVERING COMMITMENT: 1 CORINTHIANS 9:24-27

A. An Illustration from Athletic Competition: vss. 24-25

Do you not know that in a race all the runners run, but only one gets the prize? Run in such a way as to get the prize. Everyone who competes in the games goes into strict training. They do it to get a crown that will not last; but we do it to get a crown that will last forever.

In 1 Corinthians 9:24, Paul likened self-denial for the sake of the Gospel to runners training for a race. He pointed out that though there are a number of competitors in an event, only the victor received the prize. Paul urged the Corinthians to live the Christian life with such dedication and fortitude that they would obtain a great eternal reward.

Some think the Isthmian games formed the backdrop of Paul's remarks. This event was one of four great national festivals of ancient Greece. The games were held once every two years in the spring. They took place on the southern part of the Isthmus of Corinth in honor of Poseidon, the Greek god of the sea. The events of the games included footraces, boxing, wrestling, musical contests, gymnastics, and horsemanship. A herald declared the rules of the contest and the name and country of each competitor. The name, country, and father of each winner were also announced. Palm branches or a wreath made from dry parsley, wild celery, or pine was the reward champion athletes received for winning an event at the games.

The apostle's readers knew how strenuous and demanding participating in the Isthmian games could be. In order to compete, an athlete had to undergo specialized training. He had to exercise self-control and self-discipline so that he would be mentally and physically prepared to beat his opponents. Paul noted that the victorious athlete was rewarded with a wreath that over time would deteriorate. In contrast, the believers' reward would be a crown that would last for all eternity (vs. 25).

B. Self-Discipline for the Cause of Christ: vss. 26-27

Therefore I do not run like a man running aimlessly; I do not fight like a man beating the air. No, I beat my body and make it my slave so that after I have preached to others, I myself will not be disqualified for the prize.

Again citing himself as an example, Paul encouraged his readers to maintain an unwavering commitment to the Gospel. He said he could not afford to be like an aimless runner or careless boxer (1 Cor. 9:26); rather, he disciplined his body so that it would become useful to him in his supreme goal of proclaiming the Gospel (vs. 27).

In ancient athletic contests, participants who violated the rules would be barred from competition. Metaphorically speaking, Paul did not want to transgress the truth of the Gospel and be disqualified; instead, he sought to pass the test of God's assessment and receive His approval. Expressed differently, the apostle wanted to retain the privilege of receiving an eternal reward for a lifetime of faithful Christian service.

II. WARNINGS FROM ISRAEL'S HISTORY: 1 CORINTHIANS 10:1-13

A. Divine Blessings and Divine Judgment: vss. 1-5

For I do not want you to be ignorant of the fact, brothers, that our forefathers were all under the cloud and that they all passed through the sea. They were all baptized into Moses in the cloud and in the sea. They all ate the same spiritual food and drank the same spiritual drink; for they drank from the spiritual rock that accompanied them, and that rock was Christ. Nevertheless, God was not pleased with most of them; their bodies were scattered over the desert.

Previously in his letter Paul had warned the Corinthians not to engage in idolatry. Specifically, he had discussed eating food sacrificed to idols (1 Cor. 8). In chapter 10, Paul used illustrations from Israel's exodus from Egypt and wandering in the Sinai wilderness to show what befalls people who reject God by succumbing to idolatry.

The generation of Israelites whom Moses led out of Egypt had unparalleled opportunities to witness the majesty of God and grow strong in faith. In an extraordinary act of deliverance, the Lord led them all through the Red Sea. Every day they received divine guidance from the cloud that went before them (vs. 1). The cloud indicated that the Hebrews were under the leadership and guidance of the Lord (Exod. 13:17—14:31).

Through those events that generation became identified with Moses. Being in a sense "baptized into Moses" (1 Cor. 10:2), the Israelites were under the submission of this aged leader in a way similar to the manner in which believers are submitted to Christ through baptism. Furthermore, God miraculously fed the Israelites every day with manna (Exod. 16; 1 Cor. 10:3). On more than one occasion He caused water to gush from rocky formations to satisfy the multitude and their livestock (Exod. 17:1-7; Num. 20:1-13).

The people understood that they were eating and drinking out of God's merciful and loving hand. The manna and gushing rock represented the grace that would appear fully and personally in Christ, the Rock (1 Cor. 10:4). Put another way, our crucified and risen Savior was the one who provided deliverance for the Israelites.

Regrettably, though, this privileged generation did not live up to its heritage. Most of these Hebrews died in the wilderness because they rebelled against God, provoking His displeasure and judgment against them (vs. 5). Possibly some Corinthian believers assumed they could get away with certain sins, like idolatry (see vs. 14), because they had been baptized and were participating in the Lord's Supper (see vss. 16-17). That would explain why Paul wrote as he did, describing long-ago events in terms of the two Christian ordinances.

The apostle was warning his readers that baptism and communion would not automatically protect them from God's judgment, just as God's miracles at the Red Sea and in the Sinai wilderness did not shield the Israelites from destruction (see vss. 21-22). If the Corinthians were astute, they would flee idolatry (vs. 14). It was not enough to know that idolatry was wrong. Paul's readers had to intentionally run away from it. The apostle was urging not only weak Christians to abandon this sin but also believers with strong consciences whose actions might cause weak Christians to spiritually stumble.

B. Admonitions against Several Vices: vss. 6-10

Now these things occurred as examples to keep us from setting our hearts on evil things as they did. Do not be idolaters, as some of them were; as it is written: "The people sat down to eat and drink and got up to indulge in pagan revelry." We should not commit sexual immorality, as some of them did—and in one day twenty-three thousand of them died. We should not test the Lord, as some of them did—and were killed by snakes. And do not grumble, as some of them did—and were killed by the destroying angel.

So that the Corinthians did not misunderstand his point, Paul told them that the events from Israel's history were examples from which they could learn key lessons. The tragedy that overtook an entire generation of Israelites could serve as a warning to the Corinthians. God was strengthening their faith and their labors; nevertheless, they were to be careful to remain focused on the Lord and not get involved in wickedness (1 Cor. 10:6).

Paul next directed the Corinthians' attention to notorious incidents from Israel's history to serve as a backdrop for his instruction. First, in verse 7, Paul warned his readers not to be idolaters like the Israelites, who worshiped a golden calf while Moses was on Mount Sinai. According to Exodus 32:6, the Israelites feasted and reveled after engaging in idolatrous worship; and verse 35 reveals that the people were struck with a plague because of their idolatry.

Second, Paul warned his readers not to engage in sexual immorality as some of the Hebrews had done. When the apostle mentioned 23,000 who were killed in one day (1 Cor. 10:8), he probably was referring to the Israelites whom God punished for their idolatrous worship of Baal of Peor and their fornication with Moabite women (Num. 25). Both the Hebrew and Greek texts of verse 9 indicate 24,000 were killed. The larger figure could indicate the total number who perished over a longer period of time.

Third, Paul warned the Corinthians not to put Christ to the test as the Hebrews had tested God (1 Cor. 10:9). In referring to a time when the Lord sent venomous snakes among the Israelites, Paul was evidently thinking about the punishment of those who had complained because they had to eat manna (Num. 21:4-9).

Fourth, Paul warned his readers not to complain as some of the Hebrews had done on various occasions (1 Cor. 10:10). One incident took place at Kadesh Barnea (Num. 14:1-4). It was sparked by an unfavorable account that a group of Israelites had made after returning from spying out the land of Canaan (13:1-24). Except for Joshua and Caleb, who had dissented from the report, all the other men were wiped out by a plague (14:36-38). In another episode, the whole Israelite community grumbled against Moses and Aaron because of how they had dealt with a threat to their authority (Num. 16:41-50; see vss. 1-40). God sent a plague, and before Aaron could stop it, many had died.

According to Paul, the consequence of the people's grumbling and rebellion was death in the desert at the hands of the "destroying angel" (1 Cor. 10:10); but the term "destroyer" (which appears in other English translations of this verse) does not appear in either of the previous incidents mentioned, though it is applied to the angel of death who carried out the final plague against the Egyptians (Exod. 12:23). In the Bible the angels are seen as performing various functions on earth, primarily as messengers between God and humans.

Some scholars think the destroying messenger was a fallen angel, but there is no indication in the biblical text that God's executioner was demonic. In fact, an angel of the Lord struck Herod Agrippa dead (Acts 12:23). Though angels are to minister to those who will inherit salvation (Heb. 1:14), they are certainly to be feared by those who refuse to submit to God's will.

C. Smugness and Spiritual Stability: vss. 11-13

These things happened to them as examples and were written down as warnings for us, on whom the fulfillment of the ages has come. So, if you think you are standing firm, be careful that you don't fall! No temptation has seized you except what is common to man. And God is faithful; he will not let you be tempted beyond what you can bear. But when you are tempted, he will also provide a way out so that you can stand up under it.

The judgments on the ancient Hebrews for their sins, as recorded in the Old Testament, function as examples (1 Cor. 10:11). Paul spoke of these incidents as warnings for those on whom the end of the ages has come. The apostle was not talking about those living at the time of Jesus' second coming, but about people living since the earthly lifetime of the Savior. His life, death, and resurrection in one sense inaugurated the final era of history.

As a way of summing up the warnings reflected in the examples from the history of the Israelites, Paul cautioned his readers against spiritual smugness (vs. 12). Those who thought they had God contained and under their control—so that they did not need to worry about yielding to temptation—ought to take a fresh look at the Exodus generation of Hebrews. The Lord blessed them, but they still fell because of sin.

We are all born with a corrupt moral nature inclined to do evil. We also do not have the ability to change ourselves. Only God can transform us and give us the strength to resist evil. Thus, despite the power of evil to tempt us to sin, that enticement is not irresistible.

The Lord in His faithfulness will provide a coping strategy for every tempted believer who relies on Him rather than on his or her own wisdom and strength. Furthermore, God does not permit enticements that are too great for the believer to resist, nor does He allow anyone to be trapped by temptation with no righteous choice available (vs. 13). Down through the centuries, these truths have given hope for beleaguered Christians.

Discussion Questions

1. What does it mean to run the race of the Christian life with a view toward winning?
2. How can believers avoid being disqualified in their service for Christ?
3. Why did God strike down the Israelites in the wilderness?
4. Why should believers shun indulging in sexual immorality?
5. How can the Lord enable believers to overcome temptation?

Contemporary Application

We all know believers who would never commit adultery, theft, or murder, and yet their tempers are abominable or their tongues wag at both ends. They think their lives are holy and righteous, but observers would disagree. Satan takes advantage of their self-satisfaction, while the Lord grieves over them.

Paul often warned believers to be aware of temptations around them. In fact, Christians might be even more vulnerable to temptation when they feel spiritually strong. For example, some believers might feel that because they are mature in Christ, they will not be enticed to lust when they view something inappropriate.

Another type of ignorance of temptation to sin is when people mix false ideas with biblical teaching without recognizing the seriousness of their error. For instance, a Christian husband might bully his wife and children, then try to justify it by appealing to scriptural teaching about submission and authority.

The previous remarks underscore that we not only need to be more aware of the temptations we face, but even more importantly we need to seek God's help in overcoming them. Mere knowledge of how we are being enticed to sin will only make the temptation more desirable and us less resistant.

God's help can come to us in many ways. For example, we may be tempted to hate someone who has mistreated us. One way God might help us overcome this enticement is by getting us to read His Word about Jesus' loving attitude toward His enemies. Alternatively, we may be tempted to behave immorally. One way the Lord might help us overcome this enticement is by getting us involved in Christian work so that we are too busy to be tempted.

Reliance on God surfaces many ways of resisting enticements; however, the promise of 1 Corinthians 10:13 does not mean that conquering temptations will be easy. Breaking patterns of enticement to sin developed over long periods of time may require the intervention of pastors and counselors over another period of time; but God promises it can be done.

Called to the Common Good

DEVOTIONAL READING

1 Corinthians 12:27-31

DAILY BIBLE READINGS

Monday July 17
*1 Corinthians 14:6-12
Strive to Excel in Spiritual
Gifts*

Tuesday July 18
*1 Timothy 6:13-19 Be Rich
in Good Works*

Wednesday July 19
*1 Corinthians 12:1-6
Varieties of Gifts*

Thursday July 20
*1 Corinthians 12:7-11 All
Gifts Activated by the Spirit*

Friday July 21
*1 Corinthians 12:12-20 The
Body Consists of Many
Members*

Saturday July 22
*1 Corinthians 12:21-26 If
One Member Suffers, All
Suffer*

Sunday July 23
*1 Corinthians 12:27-31
Strive for the Greater Gifts*

Scripture

Background Scripture: *1 Corinthians 12:1-13*
Scripture Lesson: *1 Corinthians 12:1-13*
Key Verse: *To each one the manifestation of the Spirit is
given for the common good.* 1 Corinthians 12:7.
Scripture Lesson for Children: *1 Corinthians 12:4-20, 26*
Key Verse for Children: *Each man has his own gift from
God.* 1 Corinthians 7:7.

Lesson Aim

To stress that God works through each believer's spiritual gifts.

Lesson Setting

Time: A.D. *55*
Place: *Ephesus*

Lesson Outline

Called to the Common Good

I. The Source of Spiritual Gifts: 1 Corinthians 12:1-6
   A. *The Spirit and What Believers Say: vss. 1-3*
   B. *The Sovereignty of God and Spiritual Gifts: vss. 4-6*

II. The Diversity of Gifts and the Unity of the Spirit:
   1 Corinthians 12:7-11
   A. *Spiritual Gifts for the Common Good: vs. 7*
   B. *Varieties of Spiritual Gifts: vss. 8-10*
   C. *Gifts and the Spirit's Control: vs. 11*

III. The Unity and Uniqueness of Believers:
   1 Corinthians 12:12-13
   A. *The Human Body: vs. 12*
   B. *The Spiritual Body of Christ: vs. 13*

Introduction for Adults

Topic: *All for One*

Michael Jordan is often considered the best basketball player ever. Yet when he first joined the NBA's Chicago Bulls out of the University of North Carolina, the Bulls failed to have a winning season for years. Jordan told the management that to win championships, the Bulls would have to build a strong and solid team. He could not win championships on his own. Only when the management listened to Jordan's advice and brought in other multitalented players like Scottie Pippen and Horace Grant did the Bulls begin winning back-to-back championships.

God, too, is interested in building a strong and solid team called the Church. To do so, God grants a perfect mix of talents, skills, and gifts. Yes, some players on His team may have more talents than others, but only when the players work together—as a team—or as Paul called it, a body—are championships won!

Introduction for Youth

Topic: *Called to Share Your Gifts*

As a young woman, Senia Taipale knew that God had given her a gift for comforting others. She felt called to ministry, but she did not believe that God wanted her to be a pastor. Others questioned whether she understood God's calling at all. But, in time, God made clear His plans for her gifts. Today, Senia oversees the chaplaincy program at a large Midwestern hospital. It seems a perfect fit.

"When people are in the hospital, they're worried, stressed," Senia points out. "Patients don't usually have folks who can take the time to come in and just listen to them. A hospital chaplain's job is to get to the patients and listen to their stories. I try simply to be a listener and a companion on the patient's spiritual journey." For that, Senia is uniquely gifted.

Concepts for Children

Topic: *God Teaches Us How to Use Gifts*

1. Gifts of the Holy Spirit are seen in different ways in different people.
2. Believers are empowered by the Spirit in order to strengthen their fellow Christians.
3. Although the spiritual gifts believers have may differ, God's people remain united through their faith in Christ.
4. Peace among believers exists because each of them is equally important.
5. All gifts are needed to help everyone in the church grow spiritually.

The Lesson Commentary

I. THE SOURCE OF SPIRITUAL GIFTS: 1 CORINTHIANS 12:1-6

A. The Spirit and What Believers Say: vss. 1-3

Now about spiritual gifts, brothers, I do not want you to be ignorant. You know that when you were pagans, somehow or other you were influenced and led astray to mute idols. Therefore I tell you that no one who is speaking by the Spirit of God says, "Jesus be cursed," and no one can say, "Jesus is Lord," except by the Holy Spirit.

The believers at Corinth did not have a proper understanding of spiritual gifts (1 Cor. 12:1). Thus Paul began his teaching by reminding his readers about how they had once lived as unbelievers. By some means they had been enticed and led astray into idol worship, which was prevalent in their city, even though none of the idols could speak a word (vs. 2).

In contrast to the idols, the Spirit of God is not mute. The Third Person of the Trinity speaks through followers of Christ, never moving them to curse (that is, defame or demean) Jesus but rather prompting them to confess Him as Lord (vs. 3), which in turn implies His full divinity. Of course, anyone can mouth the words "Jesus be accursed" or "Jesus is Lord"; but no one who curses the Lord ever has the Spirit's prompting to do so. Similarly, no one ever proclaims the Lord—and really means it—without the Spirit's prompting.

There is disagreement regarding the purpose of Paul's remarks in verses 1-3. The backdrop was the Corinthians' overemphasis on the gift of speaking in tongues to the exclusion of all other gifts. The apostle's point may be that having an inspired utterance is, in itself, not what is most important; instead, the *content* of that utterance is of primary concern.

B. The Sovereignty of God and Spiritual Gifts: vss. 4-6

There are different kinds of gifts, but the same Spirit. There are different kinds of service, but the same Lord. There are different kinds of working, but the same God works all of them in all men.

The Greek word rendered "gifts" (1 Cor. 12:4) is *charismata*. The singular form of this word is *charisma*. Both terms relate to the word *charis*, which means "favor" or "grace." While *charisma* denotes a personal endowment of grace, *charismata* refers to a concrete expression of grace. The main idea is that the Spirit bestows His gifts of grace on Christians to accomplish God's will.

Paul listed three categories of spiritual gifts through which the Holy Spirit manifests Himself in the church. There are "different kinds of gifts," "different kinds of service" (vs. 5), and "different kinds of working" (vs. 6). Despite the diversities and differences, all spiritual gifts have the same source—the triune Godhead: the Spirit (vs. 4), the Lord Jesus (vs. 5), and God the Father (vs. 6; see 2 Cor. 13:14; Eph. 4:3-6).

II. THE DIVERSITY OF GIFTS AND THE UNITY OF THE SPIRIT: 1 CORINTHIANS 12:7-11

A. Spiritual Gifts for the Common Good: vs. 7

Now to each one the manifestation of the Spirit is given for the common good.

God does not bestow special abilities to people for their own individual profit; instead, regardless of the gift, the ministry in which it is used, or the result of such service, the intent is the benefit of the entire Christian community. Spiritual gifts, then, are not superior human abilities, but God-given abilities that minister God's love in the church. The Spirit moving through human hands and hearts enables the presence of Christ to be demonstrated through various gifts (1 Cor. 12:7).

Central to Paul's teaching on spiritual gifts is the principle that whatever is done in any assembly of believers, the chief aim should be the glorification of God and the edification of fellow believers, not self-promotion or self-glorification. Later, Paul explained that this can only be accomplished through the agency of Christian love (chap. 13).

B. Varieties of Spiritual Gifts: vss. 8-10

To one there is given through the Spirit the message of wisdom, to another the message of knowledge by means of the same Spirit, to another faith by the same Spirit, to another gifts of healing by that one Spirit, to another miraculous powers, to another prophecy, to another distinguishing between spirits, to another speaking in different kinds of tongues, and to still another the interpretation of tongues.

In 1 Corinthians 12:8-10, Paul enumerated nine spiritual gifts. The list is representative, not exhaustive, of the special abilities the Spirit bestows on believers for the common good of all believers. Some of the same gifts, as well as others, are listed in Romans 12:6-8, 1 Corinthians 12:28-31, Ephesians 4:11, and 1 Peter 4:10-11; nonetheless, how many spiritual gifts there are remains unclear.

The "message of wisdom" (1 Cor. 12:8) apparently involves a special insight and ability to communicate doctrinal truth. The "message of knowledge" is related to the practical application of spiritual truth to life, or it may involve divinely given insight. The exercise of both of these gifts is evident in Paul's letter to the Corinthian church.

The gift of "faith" (vs. 9) does not refer to saving belief, but to an extraordinary ability to trust in God (see 13:2). Those who possess the "healing" (12:9) gift have the ability to restore health to the sick and the infirm through supernatural means. The manifestation of "miraculous powers" (vs.10) indicates giftedness to perform signs and wonders. It is demonstrated in a variety of ways, including the ability to cast out demons (see Acts 19:11-12).

The gift of "prophecy" (1 Cor. 12:10) may enable a believer to proclaim revelations from God, including predictions of future events. The "distinguishing between spirits" is the ability to tell which messages and acts come from God and which come from demons. To some present-day believers, this special ability may be confusing.

In Paul's time, the local church would occasionally receive a word of prophecy from someone who had that gift. Agabus would be an example of such a spokesperson for God. Agabus foretold that a great famine would engulf the Roman world (Acts 11:27-28) and that Paul would be taken in chains to Jerusalem (21:10-11).

In the early church, there were also false prophets who claimed to receive revelations from God. Examples of these would be pagan ecstatics in Asia Minor and Jewish mystics. These non-Christian messages were to be tested by those in the church who had the special ability of distinguishing between pronouncements that were and were not of divine origin (see 1 Thess. 5:20-21).

The church still receives false prophecies from those such as cult leaders. These frauds imply that God talks to them in a special way, so the gift of distinguishing spirits remains important. First John 4:1-3 implies that all Christians, to a certain extent, have an obligation to test the spirits. This is done by comparing a presumed message from God with the truth of Scripture. If the two do not match up, then the declaration coming from the alleged prophet is false, possibly even demonic.

Speaking in different kinds of "tongues" (1 Cor. 12:10) is perhaps the most controversial of the spiritual gifts identified in Scripture. Two different views have been put forth as to what Paul meant. One group says this special ability is an example of "glossolalia," from two Greek words meaning "tongue" and "speech." According to this view, the gift is the utterance of unintelligible sounds that do not conform to normal means of communication. Thus tongues in this sense are not languages by which human beings converse with one another.

A second group maintains that giving utterance in tongues means speaking in languages that are known to others but of which the presenter is not a native speaker. Expressed differently, if one has this gift, he or she can speak in a foreign language without having learned it. For example, at Pentecost, when the apostles proclaimed the Gospel in Jerusalem, visitors from many different parts of the world understood the message in their own native language (Acts 2:8, 11). No interpretation was necessary.

The context of Paul's remarks in 1 Corinthians 12 includes his discussion in chapter 14. In verse 2, the apostle noted that those with the gift of tongues did not speak to people but to God; in fact, others are not able to understand the mysteries being uttered by means of the Spirit. Since these tongues are not readily understood languages, they require those with the gift of interpreting tongues (12:10) to clarify what is being spoken (14:27-28).

Believers often disagree about which gifts, if any, are still given by God's Spirit to Christians today. Some argue that all of the gifts Paul described are still bestowed on the church because its needs are still the same and because there is evidence of these gifts operating in believers today. Others maintain that one or more of the gifts ended with the early church, while most of the gifts still exist. For example, one group holds that the gift of apostleship died out with the original Twelve, but the remaining gifts are still in operation. Another group thinks all of the so-called miraculous gifts—such as tongues, healings, and prophecies—were only given to the early church and not to the church today.

C. Gifts and the Spirit's Control: vs. 11

All these are the work of one and the same Spirit, and he gives them to each one, just as he determines.

Despite the controversy surrounding the issue of spiritual gifts, it is important to remember that all of these special abilities are given as the Holy Spirit sees fit (1 Cor. 12:11). He remains sovereign in the allocation and activation of the gifts to each believer. Thus, they are not meant to be sought after as marks of superiority; also, believers should not look down on some gifts as being inferior.

III. THE UNITY AND UNIQUENESS OF BELIEVERS: 1 CORINTHIANS 12:12-13

A. The Human Body: vs. 12

The body is a unit, though it is made up of many parts; and though all its parts are many, they form one body. So it is with Christ.

Having listed several of the spiritual gifts, Paul went on to emphasize that each special ability is essential to the ongoing operation and vitality of the faith community. To make his point, the apostle drew an analogy between the church and a human body. A human body has many different parts, and yet it is a single entity. It is a unity made up of a diversity. The same is true with the church (1 Cor. 12:12).

B. The Spiritual Body of Christ: vs. 13

For we were all baptized by one Spirit into one body—whether Jews or Greeks, slave or free—and we were all given the one Spirit to drink.

Like a human body, the church is a diversity of believers existing in concord. What brings together diverse people in the church is the common experience of having the Spirit. Paul described it as being "baptized" (1 Cor. 12:13) by "one Spirit" and being made to drink of "one Spirit."

Baptism signifies the union that exists between the Messiah and every believer. It represents the death of the old nature in us and our rising as new creatures in Christ. Because we are all baptized into one body by the same Spirit, and because we all take in (or fully appropriate) the Spirit, we are all members of the same family of God.

In the Roman world ethnic and social distinctions were clearly drawn. From the earliest period of the empire, wealthy citizens of noble birth were regarded as possessing greater value than those of the lower classes of society. Also, such groupings as Jews and Greeks or slaves and free set up barriers between people; but the Spirit tore down those barriers within the church, making all Christians part of the same faith community. The result is that believers exist as unique, spiritually gifted individuals who are united in the Body of Christ.

The Spirit remains the tie that binds Christians together. As Jesus' followers, let us recognize our unity in the Spirit. We should treat other believers not as members of a separate body but as different parts of our own body; and we should not let ethnic and social distinctions divide us.

Discussion Questions

1. Why did Paul not want his readers to be uninformed regarding the nature and purpose of spiritual gifts?
2. What role does each of the member of the Godhead have in the distribution and usage of the spiritual gifts?
3. How are the gifts of the Holy Spirit different from superior human abilities?
4. Why did Paul insist that all the spiritual gifts were from the same source?
5. Why is the human body a good example of both diversity and unity?

Contemporary Application

Pastor Matthew was fatigued, frustrated, and burned out. He had pastored the little country church with less than a hundred members for six years—ever since his first week out of seminary. Wanting to do a good job in the eyes of God as well as the eyes of the congregation, he had initially set himself to his task at full throttle.

Within six months the pastor was preaching three times a week, leading an adult Bible study and three small groups, counseling five or six people a week, visiting the hospitalized and sick, and calling on prospective members. He also performed a host of administrative duties—such as printing and copying the weekly bulletin and newsletter, arranging bulletin boards, mailing out correspondence, meeting with the church's various committees, and leading a much-needed building campaign.

Pastor Matthew decided to bare his soul over lunch to an older, neighboring minister. After listening intently and patiently to Pastor Matthew's troubles, his friend asked him, "What have you done to encourage your church members to use their spiritual gifts?"

As Pastor Matthew pondered his answer, he realized that he had assumed numerous tasks that had once been carried out by his members. It was as if every time a role came open in the church, he took it on without asking other gifted members to shoulder the task themselves. Rather than fulfill his pastoral role of equipping the saints, he had assumed too many duties himself.

God never intended the church to be a "one-man show." He provides numerous spiritual gifts throughout every congregation so that individual members of the church operate together as the Body of Christ (1 Cor. 12:27).

Called to Love

DEVOTIONAL READING

John 3:16-21

DAILY BIBLE READINGS

Monday July 24
*John 3:16-21 God So Loved
the World*

Tuesday July 25
*Romans 8:31-39 God's Love
in Christ Jesus*

Wednesday July 26
*John 13:31-35 Love One
Another*

Thursday July 27
*Romans 13:8-14 Loving
One Another Fulfills the
Law*

Friday July 28
1 John 3:11-18 Let Us Love

Saturday July 29
*1 Corinthians 13:1-7 Love
Defined*

Sunday July 30
*1 Corinthians 13:8-13 The
Greatest Gift Is Love*

Scripture

Background Scripture: *1 Corinthians 13*

Scripture Lesson: *1 Corinthians 13*

Key Verse: *And now these three remain: faith, hope and love.
But the greatest of these is love.* 1 Corinthians 13:13.

Scripture Lesson for Children: *1 Corinthians 13:4-13;
John 3:16*

Key Verse for Children: *Love never fails. 1 Corinthians 13:8.*

Lesson Aim

To appreciate the role that Christlike love serves within
the church.

Lesson Setting

Time: A.D. *55*

Place: *Ephesus*

Lesson Outline

Called to Love

   I. The Importance of Love: 1 Corinthians 13:1-3

      A. *Several Noteworthy Gifts: vss. 1-2*

      B. *Two Impressive Actions: vs. 3*

  II. The Nature of Love: 1 Corinthians 13:4-7

      A. *What Love Is and Is Not: vss. 4-6*

      B. *Love's Persevering Quality: vs. 7*

 III. The Permanence of Love: 1 Corinthians 13:8-13

      A. *The Temporary Nature of Spiritual Gifts: vss. 8-10*

      B. *The Promise of More Fully Knowing the Lord:
vss. 11-12*

      C. *The Greatness of Love: vs. 13*

Introduction for Adults

Topic: *Love Comes First*

Anthony Campolo tells the story of a 13-year-old hydrocephalic girl living in a Haitian missionary hospital. The girl, brain-damaged and deformed, rocked nervously on her bed, day after day, year after year. The Haitian nurses, though very busy with more hopeful cases, lovingly tended this girl, feeding her, changing her diapers, and tending to her safety needs.

One day the girl accidentally rocked herself off her bed and onto the cement floor, seriously injuring herself. The nurses could have dismissed the fall as being "God's will" and cut down on her care. Instead, they chose to increase her care and to spend long hours in prayer for her.

Loving the unlovely is a Christian's mandate and challenge. Will we love those we find physically and mentally repulsive? Will we care about and care for society's "hopeless"?

Introduction for Youth

Topic: *Called to Love*

Pastor Jeff Wallace shared the following: "With my daughter Gracie's hand in mine, we walked out of the convention hall where we had heard a gifted preacher convey afresh the love and grace and mercy of the Lord. I had noticed Gracie's rapt attention as the preacher spoke. I, too, was greatly moved and impressed by his message.

"I thus wasn't surprised when Gracie looked up at me and asked, 'Daddy, did you think that was a good preacher?' 'Oh, yes, sweetheart, he is a great preacher,' I responded. 'Do you think he's a better preacher than you are?' 'Oh, yes, sweetheart, he's a much better preacher than I am.' 'Not really, Daddy,' she concluded. 'The only preacher better than you is Jesus!'

"Of course, my confidence in my preaching ability was little affected by my daughter's opinion. But my heart was overjoyed by her expression of pure love and devotion. Love does that. It always affects. It always brings joy. It always builds up."

Concepts for Children

Topic: *God Teaches Us How to Love*

1. The most powerful gift is worthless unless it is powered and tempered by love.
2. Love is an active, dynamic, healing response to life situations.
3. Love is the most important aspect of Christian character because it is motivated by God's love for us.
4. God's love endures when even faith is brief and hope fades.
5. It is impossible to love unconditionally without the abiding presence of the Holy Spirit.

The Lesson Commentary

I. THE IMPORTANCE OF LOVE: 1 CORINTHIANS 13:1-3

A. Several Noteworthy Gifts: vss. 1-2

If I speak in the tongues of men and of angels, but have not love, I am only a resounding gong or a clanging cymbal. If I have the gift of prophecy and can fathom all mysteries and all knowledge, and if I have a faith that can move mountains, but have not love, I am nothing.

First Corinthians 13 has been called a "hymn to love." It is sublime in tone and powerful in content. In a sense this chapter carries on the discussion of spiritual gifts that Paul had begun in the previous chapter; but primarily chapter 13 is Paul's description of Christian love. We learn that love is not a spiritual gift; rather, it is the way in which all spiritual gifts should be used.

Greek, the language of the New Testament, has four significant words for love: *eros, storge, philia,* and *agape*. The word *eros* is used primarily for physical love between the genders; but because of its debasement in pagan society, it does not occur in the New Testament. The word *storge* has special reference to love between parents and children, but could be used for the love between a ruler and his people or of a nation for its god.

The most common term for love in Greek is *philia*. This is the word of affectionate regard. It is used of love between friends, husbands and wives, parents and children (for example, Matt. 10:37; John 11:3, 36; 20:2). The term *agape* is the most common word for love in the New Testament. It is perhaps the characteristic term of Christianity. This is the love that speaks of unconditional esteem which God has for His children, and the high esteem and regard they should have for Him and their fellow human beings, especially other believers.

Paul began his discussion by naming off certain representative gifts and actions, the first of which is speaking in "tongues of men and of angels" (1 Cor. 13:1). There are a number of views regarding what Paul meant. One possibility is that these were actual languages or dialects being spoken by people and angels. A second possibility is that the tongues were unintelligible words of ecstasy spoken by the person or angel in praise to God. A third possibility is that Paul was speaking in exaggerated terms to include every conceivable form of speech.

The apostle posed a hypothetical situation in which he could speak those kinds of tongues. As impressive as this may be, apart from love, Paul's speech would have been like the sound made by a noisy gong or a clanging cymbal—musical instruments used in pagan rituals. Put another way, his utterances would be just noise having little meaning. The absence of love would rob the gift of its value.

Paul next referred to three other spiritual gifts: prophecy, knowledge, and faith (vs. 2). Again the apostle spoke hypothetically, describing a situation in which he had these gifts in abundance. He might be able to deliver messages from God, have insight into all sorts of spiritual mysteries and truths of the divine, and have such a strong belief that he could dislodge mountains from their foundations.

From a human standpoint, these gifts would be impressive; but if while Paul had these special abilities he was without love, then from the standpoint of God, the apostle would be an absolute zero. The absence of love would rob the gifted one of his value.

B. Two Impressive Actions: vs. 3

If I give all I possess to the poor and surrender my body to the flames, but have not love, I gain nothing.

Paul finally referred to two impressive actions that he might perform. The first of these would be giving all his possessions to the poor (1 Cor. 13:3). Throughout the Bible we see the importance of helping those who lack what they need materially.

The second action involves the apostle surrendering his body to be burned at the stake. This presumably refers to martyrdom by means of the flames. Other early manuscripts have "If I . . . surrender my body that I may boast." In this case, Paul may have been referring to serving others without regard to one's welfare and to boasting in the Lord in a wholesome manner about the sacrificial act.

Regardless of whether burning or boasting is to be paired with helping the poor, the apostle's point in verse 3 remains the same. He taught that if he did these actions and yet was devoid of love, he would not gain anything through what he had given up. The absence of love would rob service of its value.

II. THE NATURE OF LOVE: 1 CORINTHIANS 13:4-7

A. What Love Is and Is Not: vss. 4-6

Love is patient, love is kind. It does not envy, it does not boast, it is not proud. It is not rude, it is not self-seeking, it is not easily angered, it keeps no record of wrongs. Love does not delight in evil but rejoices with the truth.

Using both positive and negative terms, Paul described for the Corinthians what he meant by love. The apostle had previously spoken hypothetically about himself, but now he personified love for his readers. Probably the apostle chose his words carefully to implicitly condemn errors committed by his readers.

First, Paul noted that Christlike love is known for its patience and kindness. One of these terms is passive, while the other is active. As believers, we are to have a long fuse to our temper. We must not retaliate when wronged; rather, we are to remain steadfast in spirit, consistently responding to others in a gracious and considerate manner (1 Cor. 13:4).

Next, Paul described in a series of terms what love is not and does not do. Instead of envying people, love is thankful for God's blessing in their lives. Rather than arrogantly parading itself about, love is humble. Christian charity is never rude or shameless. It does not seek its own interests or demand to gets its own way, but is concerned with the welfare of others (vs. 5).

Love is not easily provoked to rage or irritated. Likewise, it is not resentful.

Expressed differently, love does not keep track of the wrongs that others have inflicted. In addition, love never finds pleasure in the misdeeds and evil schemes of others. This last quality is paired with another. Love does not praise iniquity and injustice, but exalts in the truth of God (vs. 6). Similarly, love is overjoyed when others promote what is right in God's eyes.

B. Love's Persevering Quality: vs. 7

It always protects, always trusts, always hopes, always perseveres.

Paul noted four things that love does in fullness (1 Cor. 13:7). It bears all things, meaning it has the ability to face trials and patiently accept them. Love believes all things, meaning it searches for what is finest in people and accepts as true the very best that they have to offer. Love hopes all things, meaning it maintains confidence in God's ability to turn evil circumstances into good. Finally, love endures all things, meaning it remains faithful to God to the end of all ordeals.

III. THE PERMANENCE OF LOVE: 1 CORINTHIANS 13:8-13

A. The Temporary Nature of Spiritual Gifts: vss. 8-10

Love never fails. But where there are prophecies, they will cease; where there are tongues, they will be stilled; where there is knowledge, it will pass away. For we know in part and we prophesy in part, but when perfection comes, the imperfect disappears.

Paul noted that love will never fail or come to an end; in other words, Christian charity will last forever (1 Cor. 13:8). His readers had become overly enamored with their Spirit-given abilities. They did not realize that love should have been infinitely more important to them than whatever gift they might have had. Their priorities would be straight when they made the love of Christ a foremost concern in their lives.

Paul next stressed that one day even the most spectacular of spiritual gifts will cease to be needed. For example, God will render prophecy inoperative, cause miraculous tongues to fall silent, and end the need for the gift of knowledge. Here the apostle was contrasting two periods—an earlier one in which the spiritual gifts are needed and a later one when they are not needed; yet Bible interpreters differ over the time scheme Paul had in mind.

One view is that the first period extended between Pentecost (when the church was established) and the end of the apostolic period (when the church supposedly reached spiritual maturity). With the completion of the New Testament canon, the second period has already begun. Another view is that the first period is the time between Christ's first and second comings, with the second period following after the Messiah's return to earth.

Paul used several examples to illustrate the difference between the two periods. First, the distinction is like the difference between the partial and the complete, or between the imperfect and the perfect (vss. 9-10). The gifts of knowledge and prophecy, for example, put believers in touch with God only imperfectly; but in the later period, Christians will be in full and perfect contact with Him.

B. The Promise of More Fully Knowing the Lord: vss. 11-12

When I was a child, I talked like a child, I thought like a child, I reasoned like a child. When I became a man, I put childish ways behind me. Now we see but a poor reflection as in a mirror; then we shall see face to face. Now I know in part; then I shall know fully, even as I am fully known.

Paul next illustrated his meaning by drawing an analogy involving childhood and adulthood. The apostle said that when he was a child, he talked, thought, and reasoned as a child; but now that Paul had become an adult, he had set aside childish ways (1 Cor. 13:11).

Childhood is like the first period, and childish ways are like spiritual gifts. Just as childish ways are appropriate for a child, so spiritual gifts are appropriate for people in the first period; but then (to follow the analogy further) adulthood is like the second period. It is a time in which we will put away our spiritual gifts, for they will not be appropriate any longer.

For his next illustration, Paul used an analogy involving a mirror (vs. 12). In that day, mirrors were made out of polished metal and provided a poor, distorted image of what they were reflecting. The glimpse of the Lord that we get as He is reflected in our spiritual gifts is like looking in such an imperfect mirror. In the second period, however, our vision of the Lord will not be mediated by our spiritual gifts, for we will see Him face-to-face.

Bible scholars have disputed Paul's exact meaning here. Was the apostle saying that vision using a mirror is *blurry* or *reflected?* Put another way, does the exercise of our spiritual gifts provide us with a *poor* sense of who God is, or do they give us an *indirect* sense? In either option, the contrast between our vision of the Lord (involving spiritual gifts) in the first period and our vision of Him (not involving spiritual gifts) in the later period still stands.

The apostle switched from the language of sight to that of knowledge when he noted that he, like all believers in the first period, knew God only partially; but Paul looked forward to a time when he would know God fully. Of course, the apostle was not suggesting that human beings will ever have knowledge equaling that of God. Moreover, the Lord is not limited, as people are, by conditions of the first period. He already knows all people fully, completely, and perfectly.

C. The Greatness of Love: vs. 13

And now these three remain: faith, hope and love. But the greatest of these is love.

First Corinthians 13:13 contains Paul's summation of his teaching about love. He said that Christian charity is for now *and* for eternity. The apostle likewise mentioned that faith and hope abide together with love, though the latter was the greatest of the trio. These three characteristics, in a sense, sum up the Christian life.

"Faith" denotes trust in the Savior and commitment to His teachings. "Hope" refers to an unshakable confidence that the promises of the Father will ultimately be fulfilled by the Son. Thanks to Paul we have already learned what "love" denotes.

Some interpreters have suggested that the apostle meant that faith and hope, like love, are eternal, since they can be considered manifestations of love. Paul, however, perhaps more likely included faith and hope in verse 13 to remind his readers that love is for now, just as are faith and hope.

When the apostle went on to say that love is the greatest virtue, he probably meant that Christian charity eclipses faith and hope because it lasts forever; but the latter two virtues, like the spiritual gifts, are for this age only. Faith is not necessary in eternity because then we will be in the very presence of God. Likewise, hope is not necessary in eternity because then our expectations will have been fulfilled.

Discussion Questions

1. Why are the gifts of prophecy, knowledge, and faith pointless in the absence of love?
2. How is it possible for Christians to be patient and kind when others are rude to them?
3. What enables a believer characterized by love to bear, believe, hope, and endure all things?
4. What was Paul's main purpose in stressing that spiritual gifts are temporary but love is permanent?
5. In what sense will love last forever?

Contemporary Application

To love the way God does involves making a conscious decision. The Lord Himself is the best example of this. As Romans 5:8-10 teaches, God chose to reach out to us in love even when we were His enemies. Despite our sin, God decided to bring peace and wholeness to our relationship with Him.

There will be times when we do not feel like loving other people. It is in those moments that we need to look to God for supernatural help. He is ready and willing to give us the strength to love in a Christlike fashion; but first we must submit ourselves to God's will.

In addition, when God enables us to love despite our desire not to, nonbelievers will see the power of Christ's love working through and in us. In a morally corrupt society in which people yearn for a power greater than what they have, so as to give them meaning and value, the love of Christ in us will draw them to Him. Here, then, is another reason to choose to love—to surrender our will to Jesus' will and thus be a beacon to others.

If we are to be more loving, we must also examine our attitudes and actions. We need to consider how we love others in our ministries and relationships. Furthermore, we should look for ways in which we can be more loving.

Giving Forgiveness

DEVOTIONAL READING

Matthew 18:21-35

DAILY BIBLE READINGS

Monday July 31
*Matthew 6:9-15 Forgive
Others Their Trespasses*

Tuesday August 1
*Matthew 18:21-35 Jesus
Teaches about Forgiveness*

Wednesday August 2
*Mark 11:20-25 Forgive, So
God May Forgive You*

Thursday August 3
*Colossians 3:12-17 You Also
Must Forgive*

Friday August 4
*2 Corinthians 2:5-11
Forgive and Console Your
Offender*

Saturday August 5
*2 Corinthians 7:2-7 Paul's
Pride in the Corinthians*

Sunday August 6
*2 Corinthians 7:8-16 Paul's
Joy at the Corinthians'
Repentance*

Scripture

Background Scripture: *2 Corinthians 2:5-11; 7:2-15*
Scripture Lesson: *2 Corinthians 2:5-11; 7:2-15*
Key Verse: *Godly sorrow brings repentance that leads to salvation and leaves no regret, but worldly sorrow brings death.*
2 Corinthians 7:10.
Scripture Lesson for Children: *Matthew 7:7-12;
2 Corinthians 1:10-11*
Key Verse for Children: *"For everyone who asks receives; he
who seeks finds; and to him who knocks, the door will be
opened."* Matthew 7:8.

Lesson Aim

To understand that forgiveness brings repentant sinners back into meaningful fellowship.

Lesson Setting

Time: *A.D. 56*
Place: *Macedonia*

Lesson Outline

Giving Forgiveness
I. Forgiveness for the Offender: 2 Corinthians 2:5-11
    A. *A Desire to Forgive: vss. 5-6*
    B. *A Need for Comfort: vss. 7-11*
II. Concern for the Church: 2 Corinthians 7:2-15
    A. *Paul's Appeal for Love: vss. 2-4*
    B. *Paul's Ardent Interest in the Church: vss. 5-7*
    C. *Paul's Joy over the Corinthians' Repentance:
       vss. 8-13a*
    D. *Confirmation of Confidence: vss. 13b-15*

Introduction for Adults

Topic: *Forgiving and Reconciling*

In *Tramp for the Lord,* Corrie ten Boom tells of a decision she made in her 80s to forgive individuals who had wronged her. For years, she had kept letters as evidence of their wrongdoing. A friend pointed out her need to correct the situation. Heeding the advice, Corrie finally whispered, "Lord Jesus, who takes all my sins away, forgive me for preserving all these years the evidence against others! Give me grace to burn [these letters] as sweet-smelling sacrifice to Your glory." As she burned the letters, a full sense of forgiveness came.

Meaningful fellowship can occur only after a person seeking forgiveness receives it. Like Corrie ten Boom, we cannot withhold from other Christians the forgiveness God has so freely give us.

Introduction for Youth

Topic: *Restoring Relationships through Forgiveness*

"To refuse forgiveness is to fall into Satan's trap," asserts John MacArthur in *The Freedom and Power of Forgiveness.* "Unforgiveness has all the opposite effects of forgiveness: it hinders humility, mercy, joy, love, obedience, and fellowship—and therefore it is as destructive of individual character as it is of harmony in the church."

Forgiving someone who has strayed from the Lord but is now repentant can be difficult for younger members of the church to do. Yet such compassion not only can bring this person back into the Lord's flock, but can also help him or her become a productive follower of Christ once again.

Concepts for Children

Topic: *God Answers Prayers*

1. Prayer is a privilege that comes with great benefits.
2. Praying for others can bring unexpected blessings for both the person praying and the others for whom one is praying.
3. God can be trusted to answer our prayers.
4. God's answers to prayers are good.
5. God is pleased when we spend time each day in prayer.

The Lesson Commentary

I. FORGIVENESS FOR THE OFFENDER: 2 CORINTHIANS 2:5-11

A. A Desire to Forgive: vss. 5-6

If anyone has caused grief, he has not so much grieved me as he has grieved all of you, to some extent— not to put it too severely. The punishment inflicted on him by the majority is sufficient for him.

Paul most likely penned 2 Corinthians in the fall of A.D. 56 while in Macedonia (the northern section of Greece). His chief purpose was to refute the accusations of false teachers against him. Having gained the ear of the church at Corinth, these charlatans apparently asserted that Paul was untrustworthy and double-minded, and that he ministered solely for the purpose of self-elevation.

The apostle's motivation, however, in defending himself in this letter did not arise from self-interest or pride, but from his desire to protect the church at Corinth. Because Paul's integrity was so closely linked to the message of the Gospel, a successful effort to discredit him would have inevitably led to an undermining of the faith he and his missionary team preached in the city.

Paul had planned to visit the church at Corinth soon after sending his first letter to them (1 Cor. 4:19). Later, however, he changed his plans and decided to stop at Corinth on the way to Macedonia and then again on his return trip from that region. From Corinth he hoped to go on to Jerusalem and deliver the gift that the Gentile churches had been collecting for the suffering believers in Palestine (1 Cor. 16:1-4; 2 Cor. 1:15-16).

Paul's plans, however, changed when he faced dangerous opposition in Asia Minor and after he learned that there were still serious problems in Corinth that required direct intervention (2 Cor. 1:8-10; 13:2). Paul therefore made an emergency visit that he later described as painful (2:1). After this difficult second visit to Corinth, Paul wrote another letter to the church, which he penned out of much distress and anguish (vs. 4).

Some scholars think Paul was referring to 1 Corinthians; but most are convinced the apostle was speaking of a letter that has since been lost. First Corinthians does not seem to reflect the emotional state described in 2 Corinthians 2:4, nor does it seem like the kind of letter that would spark the regret described in 7:8.

One unnamed person at Corinth had been the cause of some serious offense in the church. Traditionally, this individual has been identified with the man who married his stepmother after his father's death (see 1 Cor. 5:1-5). More likely, though, the individual was someone else—such as a ringleader of the anti-Pauline faction at Corinth—who either publicly offended the apostle or one of his representatives.

Whatever the man's offense, the believers in Corinth had taken Paul's advice to enact corporate discipline. The apostle wrote that the offender had caused more sorrow for the church than for him (2 Cor. 2:5). Though a majority of the congregation had chosen to heed his advice, at least a few did not agree (vs. 6).

B. A Need for Comfort: vss. 7-11

Now instead, you ought to forgive and comfort him, so that he will not be overwhelmed by excessive sorrow. I urge you, therefore, to reaffirm your love for him. The reason I wrote you was to see if you would stand the test and be obedient in everything. If you forgive anyone, I also forgive him. And what I have forgiven—if there was anything to forgive—I have forgiven in the sight of Christ for your sake, in order that Satan might not outwit us. For we are not unaware of his schemes.

Paul said the man's correction had been enough. No doubt because of the offender's repentance, Paul urged the church to forgive and comfort him. The apostle said he did not want to see the man become overwhelmed with excessive grief to the point of despair (2 Cor. 2:7). Paul further encouraged his readers to demonstrate their love toward the repentant individual (vs. 8). This reaffirming love was not a contradiction of the apostle's instructions in the sorrowful letter. Indeed, it was fully in line with his purpose of making the person realize the seriousness of his sin, then repent and rejoin the Christian fellowship.

Paul had written his instructions about disciplining the man to test the Corinthians' obedience (vs. 9). Surely he was pleased to see them pass the test. Such cooperation reassured Paul that his readers would also obey his instructions to forgive the individual and bring him back into their midst. Paul even offered to add his own forgiveness to that of the church (vs. 10). Christ was the apostle's witness in this matter and the basis for his authority in forgiving the offender. Paul also had the welfare of the Corinthian congregation in mind. The apostle knew that Satan might gain an advantage over the church if the matter was prolonged (vs. 11).

Perhaps if the sinner was left sorrowing without comfort, the devil might tempt him to leave the church; or perhaps if the disciplining process was prolonged, a division might be created in the fellowship. In any case, Paul was aware that Satan is always scheming to harm Christ's followers, and the apostle did not want to leave the devil any opening.

II. CONCERN FOR THE CHURCH: 2 CORINTHIANS 7:2-15

A. Paul's Appeal for Love: vss. 2-4

Make room for us in your hearts. We have wronged no one, we have corrupted no one, we have exploited no one. I do not say this to condemn you; I have said before that you have such a place in our hearts that we would live or die with you. I have great confidence in you; I take great pride in you. I am greatly encouraged; in all our troubles my joy knows no bounds.

After Paul's digression in which he urged believers not to be yoked with unbelievers (see 2 Cor. 6:14—7:1), he restated his request for the love of the Christians at Corinth. His entreaty for them to open up their hearts to him (7:2), picks up the thought he had left off in 6:13. Though the apostle's heart was full of love for his readers, he sensed that something was restraining their feelings for him (see 6:12). Apparently he thought the attacks against him in Corinth were the cause of the believers' constraint; so once again he emphasized that his motives were pure and that the attacks on him were slanderous. He denied having wronged anyone, undermined their faith, or exploited them.

Paul did not want the Corinthians to think that he was putting the blame on them for the charges the false teachers brought against him. The apostle was seeking to clear himself of any wrongdoing in their eyes, not accuse them of wrongdoing. Thus he reassured his readers that his love for them remained strong. It could not be destroyed by the changing situations in this life or even by death (7:3).

Despite the hesitancy of Paul's readers toward him, he remained confident of them (vs. 4). Although the apostle realized that the situation in the church would never be ideal, Titus's report had reassured him that they were progressing in the Christian faith (see vs. 7). Indeed, Paul took pride in the Corinthians for all their good qualities. He was filled with joy despite the afflictions he continued to endure (vs. 4).

B. Paul's Ardent Interest in the Church: vss. 5-7

For when we came into Macedonia, this body of ours had no rest, but we were harassed at every turn—conflicts on the outside, fears within. But God, who comforts the downcast, comforted us by the coming of Titus, and not only by his coming but also by the comfort you had given him. He told us about your longing for me, your deep sorrow, your ardent concern for me, so that my joy was greater than ever.

The apostle picked up the train of thought he had left off in 2 Corinthians 2:13, in which he described how eager he was to receive news from Titus about the church at Corinth. While Paul had continued his ministry at Ephesus, he had sent Titus to Corinth and had made arrangements to meet him sometime later. Titus was to bring him news of how the Corinthian church was faring, especially about how they had responded to his letter.

Paul traveled to Troas hoping to find Titus there; but failing in that, the apostle left the city, looking to meet up with Titus in Macedonia. Paul's concern increased as his search intensified for his Christian coworker. In fact, during this time Paul experienced weariness and pain; and as he waited in Macedonia, he felt afflicted in every way (7:5). On the outside, Paul endured opposition upon his arrival in Macedonia. These attacks by adversaries from outside the church increased the apostle's tension as he waited for Titus. Paul was also troubled by inner fears over the church at Corinth. In particular, he was apprehensive about the reception Titus received.

Paul's reunion with Titus completely changed the apostle's outlook. He was greatly encouraged by seeing again his friend (vs. 6). Earlier in this letter, Paul had praised God for comforting him in distressing situations (see 1:4). In this case, God used Titus to encourage His downcast servant.

Paul's joy did not result, however, simply from seeing Titus. The apostle was greatly encouraged by the positive report he received about his readers. In fact, Titus himself was comforted by what had happened during his visit and was able to give an uplifting account. The Corinthians were zealous to repent over the things they had done and condoned, uphold Paul's endeavors, and obey his instructions (7:7).

C. Paul's Joy over the Corinthians' Repentance: vss. 8-13a

Even if I caused you sorrow by my letter, I do not regret it. Though I did regret it—I see that my letter hurt you, but only for a little while—yet now I am happy, not because you were made sorry, but because your sorrow led you to repentance. For you became sorrowful as God intended and so were not harmed in any way by us. Godly sorrow brings repentance that leads to salvation and leaves no regret, but worldly sorrow brings death. See what this godly sorrow has produced in you: what earnestness, what eagerness to clear yourselves, what indignation, what alarm, what longing, what concern, what readiness to see justice done. At every point you have proved yourselves to be innocent in this matter. So even though I wrote to you, it was not on account of the one who did the wrong or of the injured party, but rather that before God you could see for yourselves how devoted to us you are. By all this we are encouraged.

Part of Titus's favorable report concerned the response of the Corinthians to Paul's letter (see 2 Cor. 2:3-4). Perhaps Titus took this document with him upon his visit to Corinth. Now reunited with Paul, Titus told the apostle that the letter had caused considerable pain among its readers. Paul admitted that at first he regretted having caused such grief; but since the faith of the Corinthians had been enhanced, he was convinced of the letter's effectiveness (7:8).

In fact, Paul said he rejoiced over the sorrow of his readers because it had led to their repentance (vs. 9). He carefully pointed out that it was not their distress but the result of it that had brought him joy. While the apostle found no satisfaction in their pain, he was glad to see the changes resulting from the difficult process.

Paul was aware of the harm that could have occurred if the sorrow of his readers produced bitterness rather than repentance; but because their grief had led to what God intended, the apostle felt relieved. In contrast to godly sorrow (which leads to repentance and salvation), worldly grief leads to death (vs. 10). The former signifies a change of heart, whereas the latter is agitated and depressed over getting caught in sin.

In the case of the Corinthians, they took Paul's letter with utmost seriousness. Their concern over the offense that had been committed in their midst moved them to eagerly and earnestly clear themselves of guilt by association. They had felt indignation at the one who had sinned as well as with themselves for not taking care of the matter earlier. With a proper fear of God, they exercised church discipline and showed that as a whole, they were innocent in the matter (vs. 11).

Admittedly, when Paul wrote the stern epistle, he had the offender and the offended in mind; yet these concerns were eclipsed by the apostle's desire for the Corinthians to demonstrate before God their allegiance to Paul and respect for his apostolic authority (vs. 12). He rejoiced that his readers now understood how much they really cared for Paul as the one who had brought them the Gospel (vs. 13).

D. Confirmation of Confidence: vss. 13b-15

In addition to our own encouragement, we were especially delighted to see how happy Titus was, because his spirit has been refreshed by all of you. I had boasted to him about you, and you have not embarrassed me. But just as everything we said to you was true, so our boasting about you to Titus has proved to be true as well. And his affection for you is all the greater when he remembers that you were all obedient, receiving him with fear and trembling.

Besides the response of the Corinthians to his letter, Paul also rejoiced over the joy Titus exuded when he arrived in Macedonia (2 Cor. 7:13). Perhaps when he departed for his mission at Corinth, he had serious doubts about how he would be received; but now his mind was put at rest. He rejoiced all the more in what God had accomplished. Before Titus left for Corinth, Paul had spoken to him with pride regarding the believers in the city. The apostle's subsequent meeting with Titus confirmed the confidence Paul had expressed. He was not disgraced in this matter, for his words had been proven true (vs. 14).

The Corinthians received Titus with respect and deep concern. This is evident by their eagerness to meet all their obligations to Paul's representative (vs. 15). They had apparently displayed extreme thoroughness in following the apostle's instructions. He in turn reiterated his gladness in being able to have complete confidence in the Corinthianshlkgdv.

Discussion Questions

1. Why did Paul feel it was necessary to write a stern letter to the Corinthians?
2. What role did Titus serve in resolving the issue?
3. Why was Paul filled with unease as he waited for the arrival of Titus?
4. What brought Paul relief?
5. In retrospect how did Paul feel about writing a stern letter to the Corinthians?

Contemporary Application

Relying on our own strength, most of us are incapable of forgiving those who have wronged us or our loved ones; instead, our natural instinct is to seek some way of avenging the pain we have suffered. Some of us even enjoy dwelling on the many ways we can get back at them, or thinking how God or the penal system can punish them.

Jesus, however, has called us not to succumb to hate and anger; and He has provided us with the power to sincerely and actively forgive our antagonists. Certainly we can do no less for Him, since He has forgiven us for putting Him on the cross and betraying Him so many times. The burden of revenge belongs to God alone.

Our Savior, of course, is not asking us to dismiss sin as though it were a harmless act of innocence; nor should a church make light of the sinful behavior of its members. Open sin should never be brushed aside. It should always be dealt with properly, with firmness and compassion.

Even so, Christians in general, and church fellowships in particular, should be ready to forgive believers who repent. The desire to forgive reflects what Jesus would do. Forgiveness was not only needed in Corinth. All believers since then have also been in the other position, when they needed to be forgiven. As Jesus said, we should do for others what we would want them to do for us (Matt. 7:12).

Giving Generously

Scripture

Background Scripture: *2 Corinthians 8:1-15*
Scripture Lesson: *2 Corinthians 8:1-15*
Key Verse: *For you know the grace of our Lord Jesus Christ, that though he was rich, yet for your sakes he became poor, so that you through his poverty might become rich.*
2 Corinthians 8:9.
Scripture Lesson for Children: *Matthew 28:1-10, 16-20; 2 Corinthians 4:5*
Key Verse for Children: *For we do not preach ourselves, but Jesus Christ as Lord.* 2 Corinthians 4:5.

Lesson Aim

To recognize how generous giving demonstrates the working of God's grace in believers' lives.

Lesson Setting

Time: A.D. *56*
Place: *Macedonia*

Lesson Outline

Giving Generously
  I.   Generosity More Than Expected:
       2 Corinthians 8:1-7
       A. *The Generosity of the Macedonian Churches: vss. 1-2*
       B. *The Intensity of the Macedonians' Commitment: vss. 3-5*
       C. *The Importance of the Corinthians' Commitment: vss. 6-7*
  II. Finish the Work of Generosity: 2 Corinthians 8:8-12
       A. *The Grace of the Savior: vss. 8-9*
       B. *The Fulfillment of the Promise to Give: vss. 10-12*
  III. Generosity Makes for Equality: 2 Corinthians 8:13-15
       A. *The Desire for Equality: vs. 13*
       B. *The Meeting of the Needs of Others: vss. 14-15*

Introduction for Adults

Topic: *Giving Generously*

In his book *A Dance with Deception,* Charles Colson states that most of the money given to secular charities comes from religious believers. The more religious a person is, the more likely he or she is to be generous. People who attend church frequently are three to four times more generous in their giving than are people who attend church infrequently or not at all. Even more interesting is that poor Christians give a larger percentage of their income than do wealthier Christians.

One missions agency reported that by the year 2007, 25 percent of all American career missionaries will be called home from their fields of service due to a lack of financial support. That is frightening! As the older generation grows smaller, and their financial support with them, the younger generation needs to step up to the plate of financial responsibility.

This week's lesson challenges us to give to the Lord's work. In short, hold everything you own with an open hand.

Introduction for Youth

Topic: *Giving Graciously*

A recent report from Nehemiah Ministries suggested that in churches of 350 members or fewer, 50 percent of the members give nothing in the offering. As the church membership increases to 500 and larger, those who give nothing increases to 75 percent!

J. Vernon McGee, in *Thru the Bible,* tells of a wealthy friend who gave great amounts to the Lord's work. How did he stay so wealthy when he gave so much away? "Well," the man answered, "the Lord shovels it in and I shovel it out, and God has the bigger shovel."

While saved teens can't assume that God will make them rich, they can learn from the experience of giving generously that, as they give to God, He gives to them. They simply can't outgive the Lord!

Concepts for Children

Topic: *Good News about Jesus*

1. The gospel message is that Jesus lived, died, rose again, and lives forever.
2. The Good News is for people from all nations.
3. Jesus' resurrection proved His power over life and death and gives all believers hope for everlasting life.
4. Despite Jesus' return to heaven, He remains spiritually present with His followers to help them carry on His work.
5. Just as Mary Magdalene told Jesus' followers about His resurrection, so too we can tell others that Jesus is alive from the dead.

The Lesson Commentary

I. GENEROSITY MORE THAN EXPECTED: 2 CORINTHIANS 8:1-7

A. The Generosity of the Macedonian Churches: vss. 1-2

And now, brothers, we want you to know about the grace that God has given the Macedonian churches. Out of the most severe trial, their overflowing joy and their extreme poverty welled up in rich generosity.

In 1 Corinthians 16:1-4, Paul instructed his readers to put aside some money every week for the needy believers in Jerusalem. With this systematic manner of giving, the church members could gather a sizable sum without putting an undue burden on themselves. Paul had placed great importance on this collection throughout his missionary journey and had been promoting it for several years.

Recent accusations, however, against the apostle, along with the painful visit and the resulting letter, may have distracted the Corinthians, taking their attention away from the project they had once embraced with enthusiasm (see 2 Cor. 9:2); but now that Paul sensed his readers had experienced a change of heart, he felt confident enough to once again bring up this matter.

Before issuing a plea for the Corinthians to give, Paul told them about the sacrificial response of the Macedonian churches, hoping that would motivate his readers (8:1). The apostle referred to the Macedonians' generous giving as a grace granted to them by the Lord, thus emphasizing God's role in the matter; in other words, their generosity did not stem from their human nature, but from God's work in them.

The financial liberality of the churches in Macedonia came in the midst of persecution and extreme poverty (vs. 2). A few years earlier, Paul himself experienced opposition to the Gospel when he was in Philippi, Thessalonica, and Berea (see Acts 16:16-24; 17:5-9, 13-14). That antagonism continued long after these churches were established and may have contributed to their financial desperation; but despite being afflicted and poor, these believers responded with gladness to help meet the needs of the Christians in Jerusalem—people they did not even personally know.

B. The Intensity of the Macedonians' Commitment: vss. 3-5

For I testify that they gave as much as they were able, and even beyond their ability. Entirely on their own, they urgently pleaded with us for the privilege of sharing in this service to the saints. And they did not do as we expected, but they gave themselves first to the Lord and then to us in keeping with God's will.

The contributions of the Macedonians surpassed all expectations, especially when compared to their ability (2 Cor. 8:3). They were giving sacrificially, far beyond what they could afford; and they were doing so willingly. Indeed, Paul was probably more concerned about their attitude in giving than about the amount they actually gave.

The apostle noted that the Macedonians begged him to accept their offering. This suggests Paul was reluctant at first to accept their gift; but because of their earnest desire to participate in this ministry to the Jerusalem believers, he eventually accepted the offering (vs. 4).

The Macedonians kept their priorities straight by first giving themselves to God and His service. Their donation of money then followed. Because they had dedicated their whole being to the Lord's service, they were ready to give what few possessions they had in harmony with God's will (vs. 5).

Some have suggested that an earlier sharing of goods and possessions contributed to the poverty of the Jerusalem Christians (see Acts 4:32-37). Others say it resulted from their efforts to help the poor among the many who came to Christ in the early days of the church (see 6:1-6). Furthermore, 11:28-29 speaks of a far-reaching famine about A.D. 43. The aftermath may still have been felt years later.

Moreover, because of Jewish fervor and exclusivism, it is easy to imagine the persecution believers in Jerusalem may have experienced. Those who owned businesses could have seen a dramatic drop in sales as other Jews stopped buying their goods. Others perhaps felt the isolation of futile attempts to find work for themselves. In any event, the needs of the large body of believers in Jerusalem had become great and needed attention.

C. The Importance of the Corinthians' Commitment: vss. 6-7

So we urged Titus, since he had earlier made a beginning, to bring also to completion this act of grace on your part. But just as you excel in everything—in faith, in speech, in knowledge, in complete earnestness and in your love for us—see that you also excel in this grace of giving.

The response of the Macedonians encouraged Paul to take the steps necessary to complete the collection among the Corinthian believers. The apostle urged Titus, who had been involved from the beginning with the collection at Corinth, to supervise the renewed effort (2 Cor. 8:6). Again Paul referred to the Christian giving as a grace, that is, an act of charity that the Lord had enabled the Corinthians to perform (see vs. 1).

As an incentive for giving, Paul reminded his readers of their rich spiritual resources. Since they already excelled in many Christian graces and in the gifts of the Spirit, the apostle encouraged them to excel in the grace of giving as well (vs. 7). Because God's grace was already evident in their lives, it was only natural to expect that His grace would carry over into their acts of generosity.

II. FINISH THE WORK OF GENEROSITY: 2 CORINTHIANS 8:8-12

A. The Grace of the Savior: vss. 8-9

I am not commanding you, but I want to test the sincerity of your love by comparing it with the earnestness of others. For you know the grace of our Lord Jesus Christ, that though he was rich, yet for your sakes he became poor, so that you through his poverty might become rich.

Paul realized that when charity is coerced, it is insincere at best. Thus the apostle did not command his readers to be generous; nonetheless, he mentioned that he was testing the genuineness of the Corinthians' love by how they responded to his advice

(2 Cor. 8:8). He reminded them of the Macedonians' attitude toward giving, inducing them to express their love with the same eagerness as their fellow Christians had done.

The supreme example of sacrificial giving, however, was that of Christ. Before the Son came to earth as a man, He was with and equal to the other members of the Godhead. Jesus' incarnation was like going from unimaginable wealth to extreme poverty; yet He made this sacrifice willingly as a demonstration of His love. Also, by doing so, He enabled us to become rich as we share in the salvation that will ultimately lead us to the glories of spending eternity with Him (vs. 9).

B. The Fulfillment of the Promise to Give: vss. 10-12

And here is my advice about what is best for you in this matter: Last year you were the first not only to give but also to have the desire to do so. Now finish the work, so that your eager willingness to do it may be matched by your completion of it, according to your means. For if the willingness is there, the gift is acceptable according to what one has, not according to what he does not have.

Paul now explained the reasons why he thought the church should complete its collection as soon as possible. His readers had begun their donation the year before the apostle wrote 2 Corinthians. In fact, they were the first to get behind the cause and promote the idea of contributing to the needs of the Jerusalem believers. The Corinthians were also the first to begin making contributions (8:10).

Sometimes it takes a lot more determination and effort to finish the projects we begin than to initiate them. This may have been true for the Corinthians, whom Paul implied needed to complete their effort for the sake of their reputation if for nothing else. Thus the apostle reminded them of their initial eagerness to participate in the offering. Then he told them that it was now the time for them to rekindle their interest in that work and to keep their promises (vs. 11).

Of greatest importance to Paul, and to the Lord as well, was not the amount the Corinthians donated, but their enthusiasm and willingness. The apostle said that their gifts would be acceptable according to what they possessed, not according to what they did not possess (vs. 12). The standard was the resources (along with the attitude) of the donor, not a set amount.

III. GENEROSITY MAKES FOR EQUALITY: 2 CORINTHIANS 8:13-15

A. The Desire for Equality: vs. 13

Our desire is not that others might be relieved while you are hard pressed, but that there might be equality.

Because of the possibility of being misinterpreted in his push to collect money for the church in Jerusalem, Paul took great pains in precisely describing his intentions and desires in this matter. He did not want the offering to plunge the Corinthians into poverty while the believers in Judea became rich. Expressed differently, the relief effort was not meant to cause financial hardship to the church in Corinth while enriching the congregation in Jerusalem (2 Cor. 8:13).

In short, the purpose was not to exchange financial burdens, but rather to share equally in them. The believers in Corinth were enjoying a degree of financial prosperity denied to those in Judea. Paul suggested that they give to their sister church so that both congregations could share in God's blessings upon them.

B. The Meeting of the Needs of Others: vss. 14-15

At the present time your plenty will supply what they need, so that in turn their plenty will supply what you need. Then there will be equality, as it is written: "He who gathered much did not have too much, and he who gathered little did not have too little."

Paul explained the idea of equality further in 2 Corinthians 8:14, suggesting that someday the roles might be reversed. At the present time his readers were enjoying an abundance while the believers in Jerusalem were experiencing a lack of money and goods. It was possible, however, that in the future the roles would be reversed, with the church in Jerusalem contributing out of its abundance to pressing needs in Corinth.

Some take this repayment to be spiritual in nature, suggesting that the return from the Jerusalem church would consist of spiritual blessings. Later, in 9:13-14, Paul did speak of the spiritual benefits that would come from Judea as a result of the giving; but in chapter 8, the reference is probably material in nature, as the context emphasizes equality in regard to what each possessed.

To illustrate his concept of equality, Paul referred to how God supplied the Israelites with manna while they were wandering in the wilderness (Exod. 16:18). There were those who gathered more and there were those who gathered less, yet the needs of all were supernaturally met with neither surplus nor lack (2 Cor. 8:15).

Paul was not an idealist promoting a radical political agenda; but he was calling for an attitude of mutual respect among believers, who shared in the same salvation as equal heirs of eternal life. Here we see that helping the poor and needy was an important part of the ministry of the early church (for example, Gal. 2:10; Eph. 4:28; Jas. 1:27). It was something to be done out of love and concern, not under compulsion.

Discussion Questions

1. In what way had the believers living in Macedonia displayed overflowing generosity?
2. How did Paul use the example of the Christians in Macedonia to rekindle enthusiasm among the Corinthians?
3. What is the ultimate basis for Christian giving?
4. Who within the church could benefit from the generous giving of their fellow believers?
5. How is the Lord honored when believers are gracious in their giving?

Contemporary Application

There is no better example of sacrifice and self-giving than that of the Messiah. No one else has ever given up so much to suffer so much on behalf of others; yet it was precisely because He impoverished Himself by entering our sinful sphere (earth) that we can become spiritually rich by receiving eternal life.

Most of us are not wealthy, but however much we give, the principle is the same: the more generously and cheerfully we give to God's work, the more blessings He gives us. That does not mean that if we give the Lord five dollars He gives us back 10 dollars, but that He eternally blesses us more as we give more.

Jesus told the Twelve that even though they had given up everything to spread the Gospel, they would be rewarded a hundred times over in this world and receive eternal life (Mark 10:29-31). We know that neither the Twelve nor Paul became materially wealthy heralding the Good News; however, as Paul told the Philippians, God had amply met all of the apostle's needs according to His abundant provision in Christ and in the process had richly blessed the Philippians for their generosity (Phil. 4:17-19). He wants to do the same for us, too.

Giving Is a Witness

DEVOTIONAL READING

Psalm 37:16-24

DAILY BIBLE READINGS

Monday August 14
James 1:12-17 Every Giving Act Is from Above

Tuesday August 15
Luke 6:32-38 Give and You Shall Receive

Wednesday August 16
Matthew 6:1-6 Do Your Giving Quietly

Thursday August 17
Romans 15:25-29 Pleased to Share Their Resources

Friday August 18
2 Corinthians 9:1-5 Arrangements for the Jerusalem Collection

Saturday August 19
2 Corinthians 9:6-10 A Cheerful Giver

Sunday August 20
2 Corinthians 9:11-15 Generosity Glorifies God

Scripture

Background Scripture: *2 Corinthians 9:1-15*
Scripture Lesson: *2 Corinthians 9:3-15*
Key Verse: *God is able to make all grace abound to you, so that in all things at all times, having all that you need, you will abound in every good work.* 2 Corinthians 9:8.
Scripture Lesson for Children: *Matthew 6:19-21; 2 Corinthians 9:1-8*
Key Verse for Children: *God loves a cheerful giver.* 2 Corinthians 9:7

Lesson Aim

To emphasize that generous giving reaps generous blessing.

Lesson Setting

Time: *A.D. 56*
Place: *Macedonia*

Lesson Outline

Giving Is a Witness

I. The Mandate for Generous Giving: 2 Corinthians 9:3-5
   A. *Sending a Delegation of Believers: vs. 3*
   B. *Ensuring the Promised Gift Is Ready: vss. 4-5*

II. The Marks of Generous Giving: 2 Corinthians 9:6-11
   A. *Stinginess versus Generosity: vs. 6*
   B. *Cheerful Giving: vs. 7*
   C. *Grace from God to Be Generous: vss. 8-11*

III. The Motive for Generous Giving: 2 Corinthians 9:12-15
   A. *Praise and Thanks to God: vss. 12-13*
   B. *Prayers to God for Others: vss. 14-15*

Introduction for Adults

Topic: *Reasons for Giving*

Kent Boone, a pastor in West Virginia, has frequently told his congregation that tithing and generous giving to the church will not be hardships for them, no matter how tight their finances may be: "I believe that God will bless your giving and reward you in ways you cannot begin to imagine." He has even—controversially—offered to refund anyone's annual tithe if they weren't convinced that God had responded to their giving with generous blessings of His own. Pastor Kent has never been taken up on his offer.

He is quick to emphasize, however, that God cannot be played like the stock market or a slot machine. It isn't a matter of giving $10 and getting $15 back. God's blessings—and His complete understanding of what we truly need—transcend finances. But one truth is clear. God gives to us in the same manner in which we ourselves give. Now that is a great reason to give generously!

Introduction for Youth

Topic: *Giving: A Witness to God's Generosity*

Steve Kroft, the minister of a large interdenominational church in the Midwest, says, "I read once where someone remarked, 'If there are going to be any books in heaven, they'll be the books we have loaned out or given away.' Now, if you look at my bulging bookcases, you might think I haven't taken that to heart, but I have. That quote made me realize that so many of the things I try to hold on to and protect in this world have no real value. They only gain eternal value when I let go of them. My whole attitude toward giving has changed as a result."

Pastor Steve discovered that giving is a witness to God's generosity and that He blesses such generosity in eternally tangible ways. In fact, that generosity reaches far beyond the nearest bookshelf.

Similarly, saved teens (as well as all believers) are called to give generously to the Body of Christ. After all, every good thing they have God has given to them. Thus, they should give back to Him both freely and cheerfully.

Concepts for Children

Topic: *Giving with Joy*

1. During Jesus' time, a penniless widow was dependent on the generosity of others to survive.
2. God is more concerned with our attitude toward giving than the amount of the gift.
3. If we trust in God and do not rely on our own understanding (see Prov. 3:5), God will make provision for our needs.
4. God will also spiritually bless us to the same extent with which we are willing to share our possessions with others.
5. God wants us to live selfless lives, placing the needs of others before our own.

The Lesson Commentary

I. THE MANDATE FOR GENEROUS GIVING: 2 CORINTHIANS 9:3-5

A. Sending a Delegation of Believers: vs. 3

But I am sending the brothers in order that our boasting about you in this matter should not prove hollow, but that you may be ready, as I said you would be.

Paul was so confident in his expectations of how the Corinthians would receive the delegation headed by Titus that the apostle did not feel it was necessary for him to spell out what the response of his readers should be to the visitors (2 Cor. 9:1). Paul trusted that the Corinthians knew what to do in such situations, and he was sure that they would follow through in displaying Christian love to his representatives.

The apostle knew about the eagerness of his readers to help other believers. This readiness had been demonstrated in their initial response toward contributing money to meet the needs of the saints in Jerusalem (vs. 2). In fact, it was the Corinthians' original enthusiasm for the offering that had stirred the Macedonians to action. Paul credited his readers for their willingness to give and took it as a sign of God's work in their lives. As before, his confidence regarding the Lord's work led the apostle to boast about the Corinthians.

While there was no need for Paul to go on commending his readers for their love, he did sense a need to urge them to finish the task they had embraced. That was his reason behind sending Titus and some others (vs. 3). The latter were chosen by the Macedonian churches and are unnamed (see 8:16-24).

Titus was the obvious choice for Paul to send to Corinth, because he had often served as the apostle's emissary and was a Greek himself. Titus seems to have been one of Paul's converts (see Titus 1:4). The apostle viewed him as a kindred spirit who shared the same concerns (2 Cor. 8:16). Paul described Titus as a partner and fellow worker (vs. 23). He joined the apostle early in his ministry and continued to assist him up until his death (see 2 Tim. 4:10).

The delegation would complete all the arrangements for the collection so that Paul could deal with other matters when he arrived (2 Cor. 9:3). The apostle was eager to ensure that his boasting about the Corinthians did not turn out to be in vain. He had not said anything untrue about them, but unless they made rapid progress, his words would appear unfounded. The apostle had put his own honor at stake as a result of his confidence in the believers at Corinth.

B. Ensuring the Promised Gift Is Ready: vss. 4-5

For if any Macedonians come with me and find you unprepared, we—not to say anything about you—would be ashamed of having been so confident. So I thought it necessary to urge the brothers to visit you in advance and finish the arrangements for the generous gift you had promised. Then it will be ready as a generous gift, not as one grudgingly given.

Because Paul would be bringing representatives from the Macedonian churches with him on his upcoming trip to Corinth, he was especially eager for his readers to finish their collection before the delegation arrived. Otherwise, the apostle as well as the Corinthians would be humiliated by the confidence he had placed in them. Thus Paul urged the believers at Corinth to do all that was possible to keep from embarrassing him or themselves (2 Cor. 9:4).

The apostle, however, did more than simply urge his readers to complete the collection. To forestall being put to shame, he explained again that he was sending Titus and some other representatives to help the Corinthians conclude their offering before the apostle arrived with the Macedonians.

Twice in verse 5 Paul used the term "generous," which is translated from the Greek word *eulogia*, meaning "fine speaking" or "praise." By using this term, the apostle may have implied more than one meaning in urging his readers to make a bountiful gift. He may also have been suggesting that their gift arose from their thanksgiving to God and that the gift be one worthy of praise—a first-class contribution. In any case, he told the Corinthians that their donation should originate from a willing spirit and not be given grudgingly.

II. THE MARKS OF GENEROUS GIVING: 2 CORINTHIANS 9:6-11

A. Stinginess versus Generosity: vs. 6

Remember this: Whoever sows sparingly will also reap sparingly, and whoever sows generously will also reap generously.

In Paul's day, farmers carried seed in a container in one hand and scattered it with the other. At harvest time, reapers used a sickle to cut the stalks of grain, which were bundled into sheaves. The farmer who planted only a few seeds could not expect to reap a big harvest. The way to receive a bountiful crop was to sow a lot of seeds. Paul implied that just as a planted seed is not lost, so the money given to believers in Judea would likewise not be lost, but would bring a return for the Corinthians (2 Cor. 9:6; see Prov. 11:24-26; 22:8-9; Luke 6:38).

B. Cheerful Giving: vs. 7

Each man should give what he has decided in his heart to give, not reluctantly or under compulsion, for God loves a cheerful giver.

Paul did not want his readers to feel obligated to contribute to the fund for the Jerusalem church. He insisted that they were free to make their own decision. He apparently desired each person to decide on an amount, and then to give according to that resolve. Giving accompanied by reluctance or the pressure to do so—and resulting in bitterness at having to part with the money—is not giving at all. In such cases the person would probably be better off not contributing.

Godly giving, Paul said, is done by the "cheerful giver" (2 Cor. 9:7), who is thankful that he or she can serve the Lord and help others. This type of giver enjoys God's special approval. This verse sums up the heart of Christian generosity.

While the Lord encourages and eternally blesses generous giving, He desires for us to donate thoughtfully and freely. He is not impressed with those who give for selfish reasons and then feel sad or resentful over their loss of money; but believers who contribute cheerfully and sacrificially will discover God's blessing in a wide variety of ways.

C. Grace from God to Be Generous: vss. 8-11

And God is able to make all grace abound to you, so that in all things at all times, having all that you need, you will abound in every good work. As it is written: "He has scattered abroad his gifts to the poor; his righteousness endures forever." Now he who supplies seed to the sower and bread for food will also supply and increase your store of seed and will enlarge the harvest of your righteousness. You will be made rich in every way so that you can be generous on every occasion, and through us your generosity will result in thanksgiving to God.

Paul told the Corinthians that if they responded to the need in Jerusalem in a generous and sacrificial manner, they would discover God's grace in abundance (2 Cor. 9:8). That grace would more than make up for any spiritual or material lack in their lives, and would also enable them to perform more godly deeds for others.

In fact, Paul said his readers would be like the person mentioned in Psalm 112:9, whose generous gifts to the poor were described as "righteousness [that] endures forever" (2 Cor. 9:9). God's rewards for sacrificial giving will far exceed anything we can imagine. To emphasize the Lord's ability to bless His people, Paul pointed out that it is God who gives seed to the sower in the first place (vs. 10; see Isa. 55:10; Hos. 10:12). Likewise, only God can enable the believer to perform works of righteousness, such as sacrificial giving.

The Lord provides more seed to the one who is willing to faithfully sow and increase this harvest of righteousness accordingly. Thus to the one who generously gives, God will make a way for him or her to actually give even more (2 Cor. 9:11); and in each incident of sacrificial giving, even the recipients of such donations will be drawn closer to God as they express thanks to Him.

Perhaps the most controversial aspect of these verses centers on the nature of what Paul promised believers in return for their generosity. Some insist that it is God's intention to make Christians prosperous in this life. Others, however, maintain equally as strongly that Paul was promising only spiritual blessings.

The real answer may lie somewhere between these two positions. God certainly gives gifts of a spiritual nature, such as grace (vs. 8) and righteousness (vs. 10); but He also enables believers to overflow in every good work (vs. 8) and be munificent in every circumstance (vs. 11). Thus if we receive wealth in return for our giving, it is not so that we can live the high life but so that we can give more.

III. The Motive for Generous Giving: 2 Corinthians 9:12-15

A. Praise and Thanks to God: vss. 12-13

This service that you perform is not only supplying the needs of God's people but is also overflowing in many expressions of thanks to God. Because of the service by which you have proved yourselves, men will praise God for the obedience that accompanies your confession of the gospel of Christ, and for your generosity in sharing with them and with everyone else.

Paul emphasized that the Corinthians' generosity would serve another purpose in addition to providing for needy believers. Their contribution would also glorify God by encouraging others to worship Him (2 Cor. 9:12). For the apostle, that aspect of giving was just as important as helping the needy. True Christian giving draws attention to the Lord as the provider of all things.

Paul observed that not only would the recipients thank God for the gift, but they would also praise Him for what the donation signified: the proof of the Lord's work in the lives of the Corinthians (vs. 13). With all the problems dealt with by the church at Corinth, some might have begun to question the sincerity of their faith; but a gift from them to the Jerusalem saints would cause believers everywhere to glorify God for both the Corinthians' obedience and their sacrificial generosity.

B. Prayers to God for Others: vss. 14-15

And in their prayers for you their hearts will go out to you, because of the surpassing grace God has given you. Thanks be to God for his indescribable gift!

As the Jerusalem Christians praised God for the gift they received, they would also sense their oneness in the Savior with the believers in Corinth and be drawn to them in Christian love. Paul's readers would be included in the prayers of the saints in Jerusalem, who would consistently intercede for their new friends. This intercession alone would be a significant return for the extraordinary grace of God evident in the Corinthians' gift (2 Cor. 9:14).

Paul once again turned his readers' minds toward Christ. The apostle thanked the Father for the "indescribable gift" (vs. 15) of His Son (see John 3:16). At the same time, Paul reminded the Corinthians that no matter how sacrificial their gift to the poor believers in Jerusalem would be, Jesus' offering far exceeded it. The Messiah had provided the ultimate example of sacrificial giving when He laid down His life for the redemption of sinners.

Was Paul successful in his efforts to organize the collection in Corinth for the Jerusalem church? The Letter to the Romans, which Paul wrote in Corinth several months after 2 Corinthians, indicates the apostle did achieve his objective. In Romans 15:26, he told his readers that the churches in Macedonia and Achaia (including Corinth) gave to the fund for the poor Christians in Jerusalem.

Discussion Questions

1. Why was Paul sending others in advance to Corinth?
2. What warning did Paul give to the Corinthians regarding giving?
3. What practical guidelines for giving did Paul outline?
4. How would God respond to the Corinthians' giving?
5. What did Paul say were the motives for generous giving?

Contemporary Application

The agricultural metaphor recorded in 2 Corinthians 9:6 provides the first of three principles that Paul wanted his readers to remember as they prepared their donations for the needy Judean saints: *Give, and you will receive.* Some have used this idea to reduce Christianity to a get-rich-quick scheme. That is wrong, of course, but the basic truth in this verse holds. As we cultivate a lifestyle of openhandedness, our own needs will be met.

The second principle is this: *Giving should be voluntary and joyous.* Paul wanted each of the Corinthians to decide what amount to give, and then to donate it gladly. The apostle promised that God loves a cheerful giver (vs. 7). We get our word *hilarious* from the Greek term rendered "cheerful." Giving should be an enjoyable act, not a grudging or guilt-induced one.

Third, *God's grace abounds in "all things"* (vs. 8). Paul was not just talking about money. In every aspect of our lives, we depend on God's grace. He will not necessarily choose to bless us as much as He blesses others; but He is certainly capable of blessing us beyond our imaginations, not so that we can live in luxury, but so that we can support good causes.

Ultimately, God deserves all praise and thanksgiving for the mutual generosity of believers, and they should be concerned that He gets it. By giving to others, Christians can be the cause of such expressions being sent heavenward.

The Giving of Sufficient Grace

Scripture

Background Scripture: *2 Corinthians 12:1-10*
Scripture Lesson: *2 Corinthians 12:1-10*
Key Verse: *"My grace is sufficient for you, for my power is made perfect in weakness."* 2 Corinthians 12:9.
Scripture Lesson for Children: *2 Corinthians 12:19; 2 Timothy 2:15-16, 19-22*
Key Verse for Children: *Pursue righteousness, faith, love and peace.* 2 Timothy 2:22.

Lesson Aim

To learn that believers never lack God's grace to endure any hardship they encounter.

Lesson Setting

Time: A.D. *56*
Place: *Macedonia*

Lesson Outline

The Giving of Sufficient Grace

  I. Paul's Vision of Heavenly Glory: 2 Corinthians 12:1-6
    A. *Revelations from the Lord: vs. 1*
    B. *An Indescribable Experience: vss. 2-4*
    C. *A Desire to Refrain from Boasting: vss. 5-6*
  II. Paul's Thorn in the Flesh: 2 Corinthians 12:7-10
    A. *An Affliction from God: vs. 7*
    B. *An Assurance of God's Grace: vss. 8-9*
    C. *Strength despite Weakness: vs. 10*

Introduction for Adults

Topic: Leaning on Grace

In the 1880s, Anthony Johnson Showalter had learned from two dear friends that their spouses had died. This prompted him to write the tune and words to the refrain of the familiar hymn "Leaning on the Everlasting Arms." Showalter then asked Elisha Albright Hoffman to write the rest of the lyrics.

The song is about leaning on the grace of God, especially in times of hardship. The first stanza is as follows: "What a fellowship, what a joy divine, leaning on the everlasting arms. What a blessedness, what a peace is mine, leaning on the everlasting arms." Why not have your students either sing or reflect on the spiritual truths expressed in these words?

Introduction for Youth

Topic: God's Strength in Tough Times

Saved teens are not immune to overwhelming circumstances. When the hard knocks of life strike, what thoughts can help them to handle the crisis? The words of Dale and Juanita Ryan, which appear in their devotional book entitled *God's Help in Tough Times,* are worth sharing:

"Scripture offers us courage and hope in times of our greatest fear and despair. Scripture tells us that God is with us in our darkest moments. We can walk through the valley of the shadow of death because God walks with us. He protects us. He leads us through the valleys."

Concepts for Children

Topic: Work with a Cheerful Heart

1. Christians can please God by always striving for excellence.
2. Every Christian should know the Scripture and live a disciplined life.
3. The believer continuously seeks godliness, faith, love, and harmony with other believers.
4. Everything a believer does should be to support, inform, encourage, and lift up others.
5. Believers should not engage in silly, idle talk that may cause others to lose sight of God and what God desires of them.

The Lesson Commentary

I. Paul's Vision of Heavenly Glory: 2 Corinthians 12:1-6

A. Revelations from the Lord: vs. 1

I must go on boasting. Although there is nothing to be gained, I will go on to visions and revelations from the Lord.

Although Paul carefully limited his boasting to the things the Lord had done through his ministry, he still felt he had to speak proudly about his work. The presence of false apostles at Corinth made it necessary for him to defend his ministry. While Paul never specifically identified the imposters, a portrait of them can be pieced together from 2 Corinthians. The spiritual frauds came from outside Corinth and needed letters of recommendation (3:1). Many Bible scholars believe they were from Judea.

Paul complained about the pretenders invading his sphere of ministry (10:13-16). They preached a false gospel—one that may have deemphasized Christ's role in the salvation of believers (11:4). The deceivers apparently declared themselves to have spiritual authority that was superior to Paul's (vs. 5) and claimed to be apostles of Christ (vs. 13).

The false teachers may have been seeking to earn a living from those to whom they preached and taught their bogus doctrine (vss. 7-9). The frauds were, in actuality, ministers of Satan, while masquerading as apostles of the Lord (vss. 14-15). The imposters may have been Judaizers, placing more emphasis on their Hebrew heritage than on the grace of the Messiah (vs. 22). They were also guilty of putting the Corinthians in bondage (vs. 20).

It was Paul's intent to counter the self-commendations of the deceivers; and yet in the process, the apostle ended up boasting about his weaknesses (vs. 30). He noted that God had worked through his limitations and difficulties from the beginning of his ministry. Moreover, the Lord had always sustained Paul (vss. 31-33). Despite the apostle's reluctance to continue boasting, there remained one more area where he felt it was necessary to counter the claims of his opponents in Corinth. If his rivals could boast about their visions and revelations, so could he (12:1).

Although the vision Paul bragged about was beyond anything the false apostles (or anyone else) could imagine, he noted that it was counterbalanced by a thorn in the flesh (vs. 7) to keep him from becoming conceited. Thus Paul's weaknesses kept him humble and reliant on God despite any visions he was privileged to undergo.

B. An Indescribable Experience: vss. 2-4

I know a man in Christ who fourteen years ago was caught up to the third heaven. Whether it was in the body or out of the body I do not know—God knows. And I know that this man—whether in the body or apart from the body I do not know, but God knows—was caught up to paradise. He heard inexpressible things, things that man is not permitted to tell.

Paul's reluctance to talk about his vision is evident by his reference to himself in the third person, as though he were speaking about someone else. This vision occurred 14 years earlier (about A.D. 41), after his conversion but before his first missionary journey. It is possible that he had this experience around the time he spent ministering in Antioch (see Acts 11:25-26).

In the vision Paul was caught up to "the third heaven" (2 Cor. 12:2) or "paradise" (vs. 4). Contemporary Jewish writings subdivided the heavens into three or more layers. It is unclear how much of this thinking Paul accepted, though his wording here suggests he embraced the Jewish belief in the plurality of the heavens.

If we assume that the first heaven is the sky and the second heaven the more distant stars and planets, the third heaven refers to the place where God dwells. Paradise is the abode of blessedness for the righteous dead. For believers, it also signifies dwelling in fellowship with the exalted Redeemer in unending glory.

Though Paul was clear about what he saw, he was unclear about whether he remained in his body or drifted out of it during this experience. The apostle wrote that only God knew for sure what really happened to him (vs. 3). The fact that he was suddenly caught up into paradise may account for his uncertainty regarding his state during this time.

Paul apparently entered the throne room of God when he received a revelation from the Lord. The apostle saw things so sacred and mysterious that he could not express them and heard words that he was not permitted to repeat (vs. 4). This experience was probably given to Paul to fortify him for all the persecution he was to endure in the coming years. Surely this vision served as a constant reminder to him of the glory awaiting him after all his days of affliction on earth (see Acts 9:15-16; Rom. 8:17).

C. A Desire to Refrain from Boasting: vss. 5-6

I will boast about a man like that, but I will not boast about myself, except about my weaknesses. Even if I should choose to boast, I would not be a fool, because I would be speaking the truth. But I refrain, so no one will think more of me than is warranted by what I do or say.

Paul did not want his readers to form their opinion of him solely on the basis of his vision. That God had granted him a peek into glory did not add to the apostle's personal status or importance. His boasting was still in what God could accomplish despite his weakness, not in this spectacular revelation (2 Cor. 12:5).

Paul would not be a fool for speaking the truth about his experience; and though his vision was real, he did not want anyone's estimate of him to be based on something that could not be verified. Perhaps he was also warning the Corinthians against gullibly accepting the frauds' claims to have had visions. In any case, Paul held himself back from boasting any more about his experience, wanting his readers instead to remember something they could see for themselves—how God had worked through the apostle's weakness (vs. 6).

II. PAUL'S THORN IN THE FLESH: 2 CORINTHIANS 12:7-10

A. An Affliction from God: vs. 7

To keep me from becoming conceited because of these surpassingly great revelations, there was given me a thorn in my flesh, a messenger of Satan, to torment me.

Because of the extraordinary character of the revelations he had experienced, Paul could have been tempted to think more highly about himself than he ought; but such an enticement was prevented as God allowed the apostle to be tormented by a "thorn in the flesh" (2 Cor. 12:7) to keep him humble. The phrase could indicate something mental or physical as well as huge or tiny in nature. After implying that his affliction had come from God, Paul also called it a "messenger of Satan."

The obscurity of the apostle's language makes any identification of his vexation impossible; but that has not kept interpreters from pulling in information from biblical and extrabiblical sources in order to venture a guess. Some have suggested that Paul's affliction may have been Jewish persecution that hindered his work and proved to be an embarrassment in his effort to reach the Gentiles.

Another theory states that the apostle's problem could have been impure thoughts or some other type of temptation. Most ideas, however, relate Paul's thorn in the flesh to some sort of physical ailment. One popular view holds that severe nearsightedness was the problem. Others propose that it might have been epilepsy, a speech impediment, or a recurring illness, such as malaria.

How could this affliction (regardless of its nature) be both of God and of Satan at the same time? One possibility is that the devil actually harassed Paul, while the Lord permitted as well as set limits on the extent of the tormenting He would allow. Ultimately, the apostle's vexation was a case in which God in His grace brought good out of evil.

B. An Assurance of God's Grace: vss. 8-9

Three times I pleaded with the Lord to take it away from me. But he said to me, "My grace is sufficient for you, for my power is made perfect in weakness." Therefore I will boast all the more gladly about my weaknesses, so that Christ's power may rest on me.

Paul implored the Lord Jesus three times to remove this affliction (2 Cor. 12:8). Although the apostle's request was legitimate, he did not receive the answer from the Savior that he wanted; rather, in the midst of Paul's excruciating suffering, the Lord Jesus revealed a profound truth.

The Redeemer declared that His grace was sufficient for the apostle, for His power was made perfect in weakness (vs. 9). Put differently, the fullness of the Almighty's strength is most evident in the frailty and limitations of human weakness. This one statement, which many consider to be the pinnacle of 2 Corinthians, sums up Paul's approach to ministry.

Although the Lord Jesus refused to remove Paul's affliction, He promised him that he would never lack the gracious favor to endure the weakness brought about by this or any other hardship. Thus, instead of being able to avoid tribulation in his life, the apostle would be given strength to triumph over it. This in turn became the focus of his boasting in the Lord.

C. Strength despite Weakness: vs. 10

That is why, for Christ's sake, I delight in weaknesses, in insults, in hardships, in persecutions, in difficulties. For when I am weak, then I am strong.

Paul made general reference to his afflictions, which included infirmities, verbal and physical abuses, dire circumstances, persecutions, and calamities. All of these things he endured for the sake of Christ because the Savior was glorified in Paul being weak. Thus he was quite content with his infirmities so that he could be filled with the power of the Lord (2 Cor. 12:10).

Paul went on to tell his readers that they were responsible for coercing him into making this foolish speech (vs. 11). The believers at Corinth probably knew as much about Paul's character, ministry, and devotion to the Lord as any other church of that time. Yet instead of coming to his defense against his accusers, the Corinthians had readily accepted the claims of these false teachers. Since the church at Corinth had remained silent, Paul was forced to defend himself by boasting—something he certainly preferred not to do.

As he had done earlier (see 11:5), Paul claimed to be in no way inferior to the "super-apostles." While some have taken this to refer to the original disciples of Jesus, it is more likely that Paul was talking about the false apostles in Corinth. His ironic tone—both in 11:5 and 12:11—indicates that Paul was mocking the Corinthians for accepting the claims of those who made superior statements about themselves. The church at Corinth should have immediately realized that the false apostles' teaching was heretical.

Though Paul defended his rights as an apostle, he also referred to himself as "nothing" (12:11). By doing so, he may have been citing one of his rivals' charges against him. On the other hand, he may have been pointing out that his apostolic calling and empowerment was from God, not something he had devised for himself. While he himself was nothing, God's grace to him was everything.

Discussion Questions

1. What was the nature of the visions and revelations of the Lord that Paul experienced?
2. Why was Paul so reluctant to boast about his extraordinary experience?
3. What did God do to prevent Paul from becoming arrogant over his being caught up into paradise?
4. Why did the Lord not remove Paul's thorn in the flesh?
5. How is it possible for the Lord's strength to be made perfect in our weakness?

Contemporary Application

One of the dominant themes of 2 Corinthians is God's perfecting of His power in human infirmities. Paul referred to his weaknesses many times to demonstrate the working of God's might in his life. The greater his frailty, the greater the Lord's show of strength in him; also, the more Paul suffered, the more God sustained and used him for His glory.

It is amazing that in the midst of all Paul's hardships he did not become resentful. In fact, the apostle welcomed them, for they provided the opportunity to display Christ's strength in his life. Paul was content to perform a ministry that included all kinds of infirmities as long as he was assured that Jesus Himself worked through Paul's sufferings to confirm his apostleship.

God's power also works through us despite our infirmities. He can turn even the most impossible situations into victories and use our greatest weaknesses and failures to promote His kingdom in the world. As we give everything over to God, including all the credit for our accomplishments, we will begin to see Him do marvelous things through our lives.

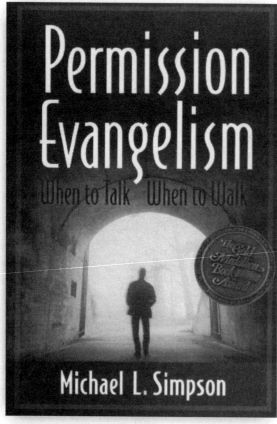

The Word at Work Around the World

What would you do if you wanted to share God's love with children on the streets of your city? That's the dilemma David C. Cook faced in 1870's Chicago. His answer was to create literature that would capture children's hearts.

Out of those humble beginnings grew a worldwide ministry that has used literature to proclaim God's love and disciple generation after generation. Cook Communications Ministries is committed to personal discipleship—to helping people of all ages learn God's Word, embrace His salvation, walk in His ways, and minister in His name.

Faith Kidz, RiverOak, Honor, Life Journey, Victor, NextGen . . . every time you purchase a book produced by Cook Communications Ministries, you not only meet a vital personal need in your life or in the life of someone you love, but you're also a part of ministering to José in Colombia, Humberto in Chile, Gousa in India, or Lidiane in Brazil. You help make it possible for a pastor in China, a child in Peru, or a mother in West Africa to enjoy a life-changing book. And because you helped, children and adults around the world are learning God's Word and walking in His ways.

Thank you for your partnership in helping to disciple the world. May God bless you with the power of His Word in your life.

For more information about our international ministries, visit www.ccmi.org.